VOLUME FORTY THREE

# ADVANCES IN
# CHILD DEVELOPMENT
# AND BEHAVIOR

## Contributors to This Volume

Luca L. Bonatti

E. Bonawitz

Sophie Bridgers

Daphna Buchsbaum

Nicolo Cesana-Arlotti

Colin R. Dawson

Stephanie Denison

S. Denison

Baxter S. Eaves

Gyorgy Gergely

LouAnn Gerken

Alison Gopnik

T.L. Griffiths

Pierre Jacob

Natasha Z. Kirkham

Tamar Kushnir

Jeff Loucks

James Negen

Marjorie Rhodes

Barbara W. Sarnecka

Laura Schulz

Elizabeth Seiver

David M. Sobel

Jessica A. Sommerville

Erno Téglas

Michaela B. Upshaw

Fei Xu

VOLUME FORTY THREE

# RATIONAL CONSTRUCTIVISM IN COGNITIVE DEVELOPMENT

Volume Editors

**FEI XU**
*Professor, Department of Psychology,*
*3423 Tolman Hall, University of California,*
*Berkeley, CA 94720-1650*

**TAMAR KUSHNIR**
*Assistant Professor, Department of Human Development,*
*Cornell University, M Van Rensselaer Hall,*
*Room G62B, Ithaca, NY 14853-4401*

Serial Editor

**JANETTE B. BENSON**
*Department of Psychology,*
*University of Denver,*
*Denver, Colorado, USA*

AMSTERDAM • BOSTON • HEIDELBERG • LONDON
NEW YORK • OXFORD • PARIS • SAN DIEGO
SAN FRANCISCO • SINGAPORE • SYDNEY • TOKYO

Academic Press is an imprint of Elsevier

ELSEVIER

Academic Press is an imprint of Elsevier
225 Wyman Street, Waltham, MA 02451, USA
525 B Street, Suite 1900, San Diego, CA 92101-4495, USA
Radarweg 29, PO Box 211, 1000 AE Amsterdam, The Netherlands
The Boulevard, Langford Lane, Kidlington, Oxford, OX51GB, UK
32, Jamestown Road, London NW1 7BY, UK

First edition 2012

**Library of Congress Cataloging-in-Publication Data**
A catalogue record for this book is available from the Library of Congress

**British Library Cataloguing in Publication Data**
A catalog record for this book is available from the British Library

ISBN: 978-0-12-397919-3
ISSN: 0065-2407 (Series)

For information on all Academic Press publications
visit our website at store.elsevier.com

Printed in the United States of America
12 13 14   10 9 8 7 6 5 4 3 2 1

# CONTENTS

# CONTRIBUTORS

**Luca L. Bonatti**
ICREA, Universitat Pompeu Fabra, Barcelona, España

**E. Bonawitz**
Department of Psychology, University of California at Berkeley, Berkeley, California, USA

**Sophie Bridgers**
Institute of Human Development, Department of Psychology, University of California at Berkeley, Tolman Hall, Berkeley, CA 94720, USA

**Daphna Buchsbaum**
Institute of Human Development, Department of Psychology, University of California at Berkeley, Tolman Hall, Berkeley, CA 94720, USA

**Nicolò Cesana-Arlotti**
ICREA, Universitat Pompeu Fabra, Barcelona, España

**Colin R. Dawson**
School of information: Science, Technology, and Arts 1040 E. 4th Street University of Arizona, Tucson, AZ 85721-0077, USA

**Stephanie Denison**
Department of Psychology, University of California, Berkeley, Berkeley, CA, 94720, USA

**S. Denison**
Department of Psychology, University of California at Berkeley, Berkeley, California, USA

**Baxter S. Eaves Jr.**
Department of Psychological and Brain Sciences 317 Life Sciences Building, University of Louisville, Louisville, Ky 40292, USA

**György Gergely**
Department of Cognitive Science, Cognitive Development Center, Central European University, 1015 Budapest, Hattyú u. 14, Hungary

**LouAnn Gerken**
Department of Psychology 1503 E University Blvd. University of Arizona, Tucson, AZ 85721-0068, USA

**Alison Gopnik**
Institute of Human Development, Department of Psychology, University of California at Berkeley, Tolman Hall, Berkeley, CA 94720, USA

**T. L. Griffiths**
Department of Psychology, University of California at Berkeley, Berkeley, California, USA

**Pierre Jacob**
Institut Jean Nicod, UMR 8129, CNRS/ENS/EHESS, ecole Normale Supérieure, 29, rue d'Ulm, 75005 Paris, France

**Natasha Z. Kirkham**
Centre for Brain and Cognitive Development, Birkbeck College, University of London, London, England, UK

**Tamar Kushnir**
Department of Human Development, Cornell University, Ithaca, NY 14853

**Jeff Loucks**
Department of Psychology & Center for Child and Family Well-being, University of Washington, Campus Box 351525, Seattle, WA 98195

**James Negen**
Department of Cognitive Sciences, University of California, Irvine, CA 92697-5100

**Marjorie Rhodes**
Department of Psychology, New York University, New York, NY 10003

**Barbara W. Sarnecka**
Department of Cognitive Sciences, University of California, Irvine, CA 92697-5100

**Laura Schulz**
Department of Brain and Cognitive Sciences, Massachusetts Institute of Technology, Boston, Massachusetts

**Elizabeth Seiver**
Institute of Human Development, Department of Psychology, University of California at Berkeley, Tolman Hall, Berkeley, CA 94720, USA

**Patrick Shafto**
Department of Psychological and Brain Sciences 317 Life Sciences Building, University of Louisville, Louisville, Ky 40292, USA

**David M. Sobel**
Department of Cognitive, Linguistic, and Psychological Sciences, Brown University, Providence, Rhode Island, USA

**Jessica A. Sommerville**
Department of Psychology & Center for Child and Family Well-being, University of Washington, Campus Box 351525, Seattle, WA 98195

**Erno Téglás**
Cognitive Development Centre, Central European University, H-1015 Budapest, Hungary

**Michaela B. Upshaw**
Department of Psychology & Center for Child and Family Well-being, University of Washington, Campus Box 351525, Seattle, WA 98195

**Fei Xu**
Department of Psychology, University of California, Berkeley, Berkeley, CA, 94720, USA

# PREFACE

## Fei Xu[1] and Tamar Kushnir[2]

[1]University of California, Berkeley
[2]Cornell University

## What Is Rational Constructivism?

The main goal of this volume is to compile a set of papers synthesizing new research from the last few years, under the umbrella term "a rational constructivist approach" to the study of cognitive development. The papers come in three flavors: syntheses of a body of empirical work and its theoretical underpinnings, explications of how computational models (especially Bayesian models) may help us understand cognitive development, and philosophical reflections on the research enterprise.

Much of this work was motivated by the idea that we need an approach to cognitive development that is neither extreme empiricism nor extreme nativism. Nativist theories have primarily focused on specifying innate concepts and core knowledge systems, and how abstract, symbolic representations underpin not only our mature conceptual system but also that of infants and young children (Chomsky, 1988; Fodor, 1975; Pinker, 1994; Spelke, 1994), whereas empiricist theories have focused on specifying associative learning mechanisms and the graded nature of our learning and representations (Elman et al., 1996; Karmiloff-Smith, 1992; Smith, 2001). The inadequacy of both extreme nativist and extreme empiricist views has led researchers to try to find a substantive middle ground (e.g. Johnson, 2010; Newcombe, 2010).

The new perspective on cognitive development represented in this volume has been dubbed "rational constructivism" (e.g. Xu, 2007; Xu, Dewar, & Perfors, 2009; Xu & Griffiths, 2011), as it blends elements of a constructivist account of development with the account of learning as rational statistical inference that underlies probabilistic models of cognition (Chater & Oaksford, 2008; Griffiths, Chater, Kemp, Perfors, & Tenenbaum, 2010; Tenenbaum, Kemp, Griffiths, & Goodman 2011). Although the work is still quite new and opinions differ, here are some tenets that we think unite the rational constructivist approach.

• Human learning is best described as a form of rational Bayesian inference: the learner starts with some prior probability distribution over a set of hypotheses, and computes the posterior probabilities of these hypotheses given the strength of the evidence as given by Bayes rule. This is a computational level characterization; that is, it describes the inferential process without making a priori commitments to how that process is instantiated at the algorithmic level (Marr, 1982).

- Hypotheses can be represented as probability distributions. Inferences are probabilistic and graded, so hypotheses are not simply ruled in or out. Instead, learners may be more or less confident about the various hypotheses.

- Learners represent the world not just by forming associations and correlations, but by constructing abstract, causal, generative models.

- Learners acquire new concepts and biases in the course of development; the newly acquired knowledge becomes part of the prior and thus constrains subsequent learning.

- Domain-general learning mechanisms may give rise to domain-specific knowledge.

- Representations may differ in their strengths; some support predictions, actions, and explanations, while others may not.

- Learners are actively engaged in the learning process, from infancy to adulthood.

## How Is the Rational Constructivist View Different from Other Views

We are in the early days of developing a new theory, and our thinking is still evolving. In terms of how to characterize human knowledge, rational constructivism fully endorses the view that human knowledge is best characterized by symbols and rules (see e.g. Fodor & Pylyshyn, 1988; Marcus, 2001; Pinker & Prince, 1988) and human learning is best captured by inferential mechanisms, not just associative learning mechanisms. At the same time, rational constructivism endorses the view that early learning is statistical: the inferences and representations may be graded and partial, much like what has been instantiated in neural networks (e.g. Elman et al., 1996; Colunga & Smith, 2005; Karmiloff-Smith, 1992).

This view also departs from the traditional Piagetian view of development (Piaget, 1954), in at least two ways—development does not progress through stages, driven by qualitative changes in the child's logical capacities, and development does not start with sensorimotor primitives and a lack of differentiation between the child and the world (see Carey, 2009, for discussion). Instead, the construction of new concepts and new learning biases are driven by a rational inferential learning process. It remains to be seen how these inferential learning mechanisms account for the rapidly developing domain knowledge in infants and how we might want to rethink the issue of characterizing the initial state.

## Some Answers, More Questions

The chapters in this book investigate the nature, power, and limits of these early inductive learning mechanisms. They are a testament to the remarkable progress that has been made, as well as to the number of unanswered questions that remain. These questions are posed, and answers and speculations are offered by many contributors:

1) How sophisticated are infants and young children's probabilistic inference mechanisms? What are the limits? This question is the main focus of Chapters 1, 2, and 4, all of which provide evidence for early rational inferential (as opposed to associative) learning.
2) Bayesian models provide good analyses of many aspects of cognitive development at the computational level, but what are the algorithms and how are they implemented in the neural hardware? Chapter 6 offers a Bayesian account of the general learning processes; Chapters 8 and 11 present Bayesian models on social learning and number.
3) If infants are engaged in hypothesis testing, where do the hypotheses come from? How do they construct the hypothesis space? Chapters 3 and 13 take up these issues from different perspectives.
4) In many cases, children exhibit what seems to be quite irrational behavior, and they make systematic errors in reasoning, at least from the adult perspective. Can some of the differences between children's reasoning and adults' be viewed through the lens of rational constructivist learning? Chapters 7, 8, 9 provide examples of how it might be possible to answer this question in three different conceptual domains.
5) Social learning in infants and children has received much attention in recent years. Chapters 5, 11, and 12 address issues in this domain: is social learning rational? How can a rational constructivist framework help explain social learning?

6) Lastly, with limited amounts of evidence, infants and young children can revise their beliefs and acquire new concepts. But much learning in childhood takes place on a much larger time-scale, and the conceptual change that results from such learning is much more profound. It is an open question whether the same underlying process can explain these long-term changes and developments. Chapter 10 discusses these issues.

## REFERENCES

Carey, S. (2009). *The origins of concepts*. Oxford University Press.
Chater, N., & Oaksford, M. (Eds.). (2008). *The probabilistic mind: prospects for Bayesian cognitive science*. Oxford: Oxford University Press.
Chomsky, N. (1988). *Language and the problem of knowledge*. Cambridge, MA: MIT Press.
Colunga, E., & Smith, L. B. (2005). From the lexicon to expectations about kinds: the role of associative learning. *Psychological Review, 112*, 347–382.
Elman, J., Bates, E., Johnson, M., Karmiloff-Smith, A., Parisi, D., & Plunkett, K. (1996). *Rethinking innateness: A connectionist perspective on development*. Cambridge, MA: MIT Press.
Fodor, J. (1975). *The language of thought*. Cambridge, MA: Harvard University Press.
Fodor, J., & Pylyshyn, Z. (1988). Connectionism and cognitive architecture. *Cognition, 28*, 3–71.
Griffiths, T. L., Chater, N., Kemp, C., Perfors, A., & Tenenbaum, J. B. (2010). Probabilistic models of cognition: exploring representations and inductive biases. *Trends in Cognitive Sciences, 14*, 357–364.
Johnson, S. (2010). *Neoconstructivism*. New York: Oxford University Press.
Karmiloff-Smith, A. (1992). *Beyond modularity*. Cambridge, MA: MIT Press.
Marcus, G. (2001). *The algebraic mind*. Cambridge, MA: MIT Press.
Marr, D. (1982). *Vision*. Cambridge, MA: MIT Press.
Newcombe, N. (2010). What is neoconstructivism? In S. Johnson (Ed.), *Neoconstructivism* New York: Oxford University Press.
Pinker, S. (1994). *The language instinct*. William Morrow.
Pinker, S., & Prince, A. (1988). On language and connectionism: analysis of a parallel distributed processing model of language acquisition. *Cognition, 28*, 73–193.
Smith, L. B. (2001). How domain-general processes may create domain-specific biases. In M. Bowerman, & S. Levinson (Eds.), *Language acquisition and conceptual development*. Cambridge University Press.
Spelke, E. S. (1994). Initial knowledge: six suggestions. *Cognition, 50*, 431–445.
Tenenbaum, J. B., Kemp, C., Griffiths, T. L., & Goodman, N. D. (2011). How to grow a mind: statistics, structure, and abstraction. *Science, 331*, 1279–1285.
Xu, F. (2007). Rational statistical inference and cognitive development. In Carruthers, P, Laurence, S., & Stich, S. (Eds.). (2007). *The innate mind: Foundations and the future*, Vol. 3 (pp. 199–215). Oxford University Press.
Xu, F., Dewar, K., & Perfors, A. (2009). Induction, overhypotheses, and the shape bias: some arguments and evidence for rational constructivism. In B. M. Hood, & L. Santos (Eds.), *The origins of object knowledge* (pp. 263–284). Oxford University Press.
Xu, F., & Griffiths, T. (2011). Probabilistic models of cognitive development: towards a rational constructivist approach to the study of learning and development. *Cognition, 120*, 299–301.

# CHAPTER ONE

# The Probable and the Possible at 12 Months: Intuitive Reasoning about the Uncertain Future

## Nicolò Cesana-Arlotti*, Erno Téglás**, and Luca L. Bonatti*, [1]

*ICREA, Universitat Pompeu Fabra, Barcelona, España
**Cognitive Development Centre, Central European University, H-1015 Budapest, Hungary
[1]Address correspondence to: Luca L. Bonatti, ICREA, Universitat Pompeu Fabra, C. Roc Boronat, 138, Edifici Tanger, 55.110, 08018 Barcelona, España. Email: lucabonatti@mac.com

## Contents

## Abstract

How do infants predict the next future event, when such a prediction requires estimating the event's probability? The literature suggests that adult humans often fail this
task because their probability estimates are affected by heuristics and biases or because
they can reason about the frequency of classes of events but not about the probability
of single events. Recent evidence suggests instead that already at 12 months infants
have an intuitive notion of probability that applies to single, never experienced events
and that they may use it to predict what will happen next. We present a theory
according to which infants' intuitive grasp of the probability of future events derives
from their representation of logically consistent future possibilities. We compare it and
other theories against the currently available data. Although the evidence does not
speak uniquely in favor of one theory, the results presented and the theories currently
being developed to account for them suggest that infants have surprisingly

*Advances in Child Development and Behavior*, Volume 43
ISSN 0065-2407,
http://dx.doi.org/10.1016/B978-0-12-397919-3.00001-0

sophisticated reasoning abilities. These conclusions are incompatible with most current theories of adult logical and probabilistic reasoning.

*The facts in logical space are the world*

**L. Wittgenstein, Tractatus, 1.13**

# 1. INTRODUCTION

Often we have no idea what will happen next. We do it more often than we think. One sign of proof is our survival, which requires us to anticipate future events. True, we are not the only living beings on earth, and so survival is not particularly indicative of any distinctive ability at predicting the future. However, humans do more than just survive: they radically modify their environment. Take a look at your surroundings and estimate how much of your environment is comprised of man-made things. Almost every single object in our natural environment—by now, cities, houses, offices, and not forests and prairies—and almost every single action we make drips with human inventiveness. This incredible richness is proof of the continuous, neurotic pressure to plan and invent new things, to think ahead at what happens if I do this and that, and to make and realize plans: an ability that we can trace back to the beginning of the human species (Amati & Shallice, 2007). We take all these for granted. Our question here is: if this ability is based, among other things, upon the ability to think about the future, how do we and when can we represent future states of affairs?

We should not expect to find a single answer to these questions. Certainly, as David Hume famously argued (Hume, 2000), often even when we think of simple physical events, experience is our guide to predict the future. I have seen the sun rising in the past, and on the basis of this repeated experience, I predict that the sun will rise tomorrow. Many organisms, besides humans, can learn from the regularities around them (Hauser, Newport, & Aslin, 2001; Toro & Trobalón, 2005). However, equally often we jump into the future with only a scant experience of the past. We can do it in different, nonexclusive ways. We may anticipate novel future outcomes because we possess hardwired systems that, in limited domains, generate future states of affairs. Or we may freely combine already acquired knowledge and information from different domains, although we have never experienced that particular combination. We may also anticipate the future in the absence of experience because we think that the next future event logically follows from what we know: if I know that if John meets Mary he will be happy, and I know that he will meet Mary tomorrow, I need no experience to anticipate that tomorrow he will be happy. And, given that (barring logical consequences) the future is the realm of uncertainty, we may predict future events because we have a sense of what is likely to follow. This paper mostly concerns these two notions—logic and probability—and their interrelations. We want to first present a theory about their relations. We will then present some relevant data about the origin of these abilities. Finally, we will sketch some future directions of our research.

## 2. CAN HUMANS REASON ABOUT THE PROBABLE AND THE POSSIBLE?

That humans can reason logically, or probabilistically, cannot be taken for granted. In fact, the bulk of the literature on adult human reasoning has been taken to support the opposite conclusion: the existence of logical and probabilistic abilities has been severely challenged. For logical reasoning, since Wason's famous work on the selection task (Wason, 1968), studies showing logical mistakes have flourished (e.g. Evans, 1989). At best, logical reasoning has been relegated to a secondary ability of minor importance. Thus, the widely held dual process account (e.g. Evans, 2003, 2008; Stanovich & West, 2000; Sloman, 1996) claims that two distinct cognitive systems underline reasoning: an evolutionary primitive (set of) system(s), providing preanalytic answers to problems (sometimes called System 1), and a more recent system by which humans can achieve abstract thinking (System 2). System 1, which we share with other animals, is considered to be at the origin of most problem solving. It is a fast, nonverbal, emotionally driven, associative, and intuitive source of responses to situations. It generates answers that are driven by biases, heuristics, or pragmatic factors and may thus lead humans to make many errors, when such nonlogical strategies are inappropriate. By contrast, System 2 is described as a uniquely human, verbal, explicit, serial, "rational" form of reasoning. Its advantage is to permit abstract reasoning and hypothetical thinking, but its disadvantages are many. It is slow, weak, easily overwhelmed by even minimally complex problems and extremely variable among individuals. This theory, as Evans wrote, "quite literally proposes the presence of two minds in one brain" (Evans, 2003, p. 5).

If such a theory is correct, there is no point in writing this paper. Not only are animals nonlinguistic beings but so are infants. Hence, by definition, under this theory, they would only possess one of the two minds: the intuitive, associative, and irrational mind. Fortunately, we believe that there are empirical data and principled arguments to show that this is not the case. For the moment, we only want to note that clearly the theory, which is based entirely on experiments with adults, has not considered its developmental implications. If System 2 is the explicit, logical, linguistic, and weak rational reasoning system, how would it ever enter within an infant mind which only contains System 1? The very same problems raised by Fodor against Piaget many years ago (Piaget, Chomsky, & Piattelli-Palmarini, 1980) would entirely apply to this theory, with equally devastating consequences.

To a first approximation, knowing how to deal with probabilities is even more fundamental than the ability to reason about logic in order to anticipate future events (but see later). But even in this domain, a long series of studies championed by Tversky and Kahneman seems to suggest that humans are very poor probabilistic reasoners (e.g. Tversky & Kahneman, 1974, 1981). When participants have to judge the likelihood of single future events, their responses are driven not by rational evaluations of what is likely to be the case but by heuristics and biases that may lead to serious mistakes. Even apparent alternatives to the "Heuristics and Biases" theory, such as the frequentist approach (Cosmides & Tooby, 1996; Gigerenzer & Hoffrage, 1995), share one point in common with it. They also consider human abilities at handling logic and probability as severely constrained. For Cosmides, humans can reason logically only in limited contexts of social exchange (Cosmides, 1989) but do not possess the ability to reason generally with logical rules because evolution could not have favored the selection of such a general-purpose reasoning mechanism.

These issues are inextricably linked with more general questions, spanning from the nature of the mind to the foundations of probability. Let us briefly see why. One of the main divides in the foundations of probabilities concerns the status of attributions of probabilities to single events. On the one hand, it looks very natural to say that I have a certain degree of belief that a future event will occur. That is, intuitively we seem to think that there is nothing wrong in saying that I am afraid that tomorrow it will rain. Translated in terms of beliefs, this statement corresponds to a belief, with certain strength, that tomorrow it will rain. In its turn, translated in terms of probabilities, this belief may be interpreted as a certain internal state in which we attribute a degree of probability to the future event "Tomorrow it will rain." Thus, beliefs could be thought of as subjective degrees of probabilities about single future events.[1] However, according to frequentists, the reality of the world is that tomorrow it will either rain or not rain: there is no sense in which tomorrow "it will 60% rain." Thus, so the argument goes, from a realistic standpoint, single-case probabilities are meaningless. If one wants to make sense of probabilities, the only way to do it is to treat probabilities as frequencies: the subjective, Bayesian understanding of probabilities is irredeemably subjective and, as such, should have no place in science. It should be clear now how far a question about single-case prediction leads us into very controversial areas, obliging us to take a standpoint on many vexed philosophical issues.

We can see the frequentist view as the psychological adaptation of the frequentist point of view in probability. According to this theory, because ontologically probabilities are frequencies, psychologically they can be understood only as collections of experienced events. Cosmides and Tooby are quite explicit about this. Our sense organs, so they argue, can only discern what can be observed and "the 'probability' of a single event is intrinsically unobservable." Thus, again, evolution could not have selected a mechanism computing single-case probabilities. What, instead, we can observe are "encountered frequencies of actual events" (Cosmides & Tooby, 1996, p. 15). Hence, frequency detection mechanisms, tracking collections of experienced events, could survive selective pressure but not systems predicting the probability of single future events. We do not want to comment on this evolutionary argument, which we believe to be seriously flawed. We only want to notice that, taking this perspective to its extreme consequences, we should conclude that our intuitions about the future are entirely dependent on our experience of the past.

This brief review offers a bleak picture of human reasoning abilities. The ability to draw logical inferences, to estimate the probability of the next future event, and to base our predictions on such estimates are landmarks of rational cognition. The fact that humans fail in both domains certainly does not allow us to be optimistic about the rationality of mankind. Yet, recent discoveries suggest that the bleak picture is only a partial reconstruction of the real richness of human cognition, and not because humans possess a weak System 2 that sometimes gets it right but because logical and probabilistic

---

[1] For the purpose of this discussion, it is not important to take a stand as to whether a Bayesian view of beliefs is a good account of beliefs. Our point here is only that there are ways to naturally read degrees of beliefs as probabilities assigned to propositions, quite independently of the computations of frequencies with which a certain proposition turns out to be true.

abilities are much deeper inside the fiber of the human mind. First, a wide set of modeling and experimental studies shows that adults spontaneously make predictions that are well captured by Bayesian models (e.g. Griffiths, Kemp, & Tenenbaum, 2008; Griffiths & Tenenbaum, 2006; Tenenbaum, Griffiths, & Kemp, 2006). Now, in a Bayesian approach, being rational is being able to predict the next future event from a priori hypotheses about what will happen and from the ability to revise them based on what really happened. Such predictions cannot be formulated without the adequate logical and probabilistic inferential mechanisms—the very same ones that the heuristics and biases and the dual process theories assume humans do not possess.

Second, recent studies on biased reasoning show that participants process correct normative information (logical or probabilistic) even in tasks in which they are influenced by heuristics or in which they are under cognitive load. For example, De Neys and Schaeken (2007) showed that the amount of pragmatic interpretations of the meaning of utterances reduces in favor of their logical interpretations under cognitive load. Likewise, in conditions in which beliefs conflicted with reasoning structure, memory access to words that were associated with beliefs was impaired, suggesting that at a fairly low level reasoning inhibits the retrieval of nonlogical beliefs (De Neys & Franssens, 2009). These data suggest that logical abilities do not reside only in the more effortful, abstract, and frail component of the cognitive system but are as intuitive and immediate as System 1 according to the dual process theory.

Third, previous and recent data, which the works mentioned above nicely complement, show that adults implicitly draw elementary logical inferences when thinking about everyday situations (Braine, O'Brien, Noveck, Samuels, Lea, Fisch et al., 1995; Lea & Mulligan, 2002; Lea, O'Brien, Fisch, & Noveck, 1990), even when they are unaware of doing so (Reverberi, Pischedda, Burigo, & Cherubini, 2012). Indeed, recent neuropsychological data show that specific patterns of neural activities can predict participants' sensitivity for the elementary logical structure of stories and formal problems, but no neural pattern predicts the tendency to rely on (at least some) heuristics (Reverberi, Bonatti, et al., 2012; Reverberi, Shallice, D'Agostini, Skrap, & Bonatti, 2009). This result suggests that, if anything, logical processes in adults occupy a more central role than heuristics.

The point we want to make is that from our current understanding of reasoning a picture emerges that is much richer than the one advertised by most literature on adult reasoning. It suggests that theories that consider logical and probabilistic reasoning processes of secondary importance in our mental life, such as the dual process theory, cut the pie in the wrong way (De Neys, 2012).

The dual process theory describes human reasoning as characterized by the opposition between intuitive, fast, and immediate heuristics and a slow, verbal, and frail logical reasoning. There is no such opposition. Instead, already at the level of intuition—as it were, deep down in the machine—humans seem to possess basic logical and probabilistic inferential devices. If so, then it is quite possible that the same machinery is already available at early, prelinguistic stages of knowledge representation, as a foundation of the way humans think, organize their plans, and use their knowledge to predict future states of the world. We now want to inspect this possibility and offer a theory about what this machinery could provide to the overall efficiency of our cognitive processes.

## 3. INFANTS' REASONING ABILITIES: DOMAIN-SPECIFIC MECHANISMS, GENERAL SYSTEMS OF INFERENCES, AND FUTURE PREDICTIONS

The last three decades of research have revealed the existence of several domain-specific reasoning mechanisms that may guide infants in predicting future situations in limited domains. Notably, we know that infants understand basic physical principles (Baillargeon, Spelke, & Wasserman, 1985; Spelke, Breinlinger, Macomber, & Jacobson, 1992). They interpret agents' behaviors as goal-oriented (Woodward, 1998, 1999) optimal solutions toward the realization of their intentions (Gergely & Csibra, 2003; Gergely, Nádasdy, Csibra, & Bíró, 1995). They possess dissociable systems for precisely representing small arrays of individual objects and imprecisely representing large quantities (e.g. Feigenson, 2005; Feigenson & Carey, 2005; Feigenson, Dehaene, & Spelke, 2004; Xu & Spelke, 2000).[2]

All the abilities we mentioned above have sometimes been described as independent modules, or core domains, not necessarily interconnected.

---

[2] While such abilities might be used proactively to predict the continuation of an event, we have surprisingly little evidence that infants do indeed use such domain-specific knowledge to proactively predict future events. The violation of expectation method, upon which most of our knowledge about infants' domain-specific abilities rests, allows us to conclude that infant are surprised at a given (unexpected) outcome but not that they predicted the opposite, expected, outcome. At least in the case of agency, we do know that infants do not need to experience the end state of an action in order to attribute a goal to the actor and infer a future goal state (Southgate & Csibra, 2009), but this evidence is much less widespread than what one would need to prove that domain-s-pecific systems are actively predicting future states of affairs. However, for the purpose of this discussion, we will not distinguish surprise at an unexpected outcome and prediction of the expected outcome, although they are possibly distinct.

Indeed, according to some authors, it is the emergence of language that allows humans to glue together originally separated, possibly noncommunicating, information processors into a unitary cognitive architecture (e.g. Carruthers, 2002; Mithen, 1996; Spelke, 2003). One consequence of this thesis is that prelinguistic infants may not naturally integrate information coming from different domain-specific mechanisms to reason about the future optimally.

Yet infant cognition is not a simple collection of independent modules. Infants also possess domain-general cognitive abilities. Of particular importance is the ability to extract absolute and relative frequencies of different kinds of events, such as speech events, or visual stimuli (Fiser & Aslin, 2002; Saffran, Aslin, & Newport, 1996). This ability may help explain how infants solve several learning problems in various domains. However, frequency computations can guide future predictions only through past experiences and hence are mute to the problem of whether infants can reason about the future in the absence of past experience. Abilities that are more difficult to explain on the basis of simple past experience have been discovered by Xu and Garcia (2008) and Téglás, Girotto, Gonzalez, and Bonatti (2007). Although these studies have important differences that we will discuss below, both show that infants intuitively make inferences about probabilities that do not require frequency detection mechanisms and cannot be simply explained on the basis of previous experience.

Xu and Garcia (2008) showed that infants seem to have an intuitive grasp of the relation between samples and populations. Given a sample, infants can infer the distribution of the population from which it had been drawn. Conversely, given a full population, they expect a sample drawn by it to reflect the distribution of the population. They are willing to infer the statistical relations between samples and population only when samples are randomly drawn (Xu & Denison, 2009), reinforcing the view that infants have a basic grasp of random processes—precisely what, according to traditional studies in the heuristics and biases tradition (Gilovich, Vallone, & Tversky, 1985; Kahneman & Tversky, 1972; Tversky & Kahneman, 1993), adults often fail to display. While certainly the kinds of situations tested by Tversky and Kahneman are more complex, the contrast is intriguing. Xu and her colleagues also showed that infants are able to integrate information from different sources in their inferences. At 11 months, they can use information about other people's intention in order to infer that a sampling process is random (Xu & Denison, 2009), and at 20 months, they also consider a violation in the randomness of a drawing as evidence for the preferences of agents (Kushnir, Xu, & Wellman, 2010). These findings point at the fact that infants' reasoning is more structured than what a passive, purely data-driven mechanism would predict. General-purpose mechanisms transcending individual core domains seem to be available early in development, enabling infants to rationally exploit the relevant source of information when reasoning about future states of affair.

While these results witness how rational infants can be in drawing inferences in conditions of uncertainty, they do not clarify another fundamental issue to understand whether infants can predict future events: can they estimate the likelihood of single future events in the absence of experience? This is what, according to frequentist theorists, humans cannot do. Téglás et al. (2007) explored this issue and argued that 12-month olds can do exactly that. Téglás and colleagues showed infants a simple situation in which three yellow objects and one blue object bounced inside a container with an opening on its lower side, as in a lottery machine (Fig. 1.2, left). Objects could be grouped into classes identified by the shape and color of the objects. After a period in which the objects bounced inside the container, an occluder covered its contents, so that the movements of the objects could not be seen. Then, before the end of the occlusion period, one of the objects exited the container. Finally, the occluder faded out and infants could look at the final scene. In the absence of any other information, a sense of probability would lead one to expect that one object of the most represented class would exit the container. Indeed, infants looked longer at the improbable outcome, in which the single object exited the container, signaling their surprise at an improbable single outcome.

Crucially, in this experiment, infants could predict the next single future event without having ever experienced it. In order to explain how infants could do that, it is not sufficient to postulate that infants have simple frequency detection mechanisms that track distributions of traits in samples and populations. Even in a frequentist view, infants could grasp such relations, and yet be unable to make single-case predictions about inexperienced outcomes. Something more is needed: an intuition of the probability of the next future event, that is, exactly the kind of intuition that, according to both the frequentist and the heuristics and biases views of human reasoning, adults do not possess.

## 4. A THEORY OF PROBABILISTIC REASONING: FROM LOGICAL REPRESENTATIONS TO SINGLE-CASE PROBABILITIES

We have argued that evidence exists that infants have an intuitive understanding of probabilities that is much more developed than most current theories of adult reasoning would incline one to think. However, we have made no mention of infants' logical abilities. The reason is simple: there is no information on this topic. What we want to do now is to speculate on how a theory of logical abilities could also explain infants' probabilistic reasoning. We first explicate the theory, and then we will discuss some of its consequences.

Let us ask the following question: How would a mechanism estimating the likelihood of single future events in the absence of experience look like? Here is a possible answer. Consider, as an example, the stimuli used by Téglás et al. (2007): a lottery-like container with three yellow objects and one blue one randomly bouncing inside it (Fig. 1.1A). One can consider it simply as it is—a container with four moving objects. However, the scene can also be represented in a modal way. Beyond its "face" appearance, the scene also individuates a series of logically possible future states of affairs: one in which a blue object exits the container and three in which a yellow object exits (Fig. 1.1B). We need no experience to conceive of such possibilities, provided that we can represent the logical space defined by the scene, compatible with some basic properties of our physical world such as object permanence and solidity. This modal nature of scenes and objects, we believe, was behind Wittgenstein's intuition that "the world is defined by the facts in logical space": metaphysically, a fact is already located in a logical space. Psychologically, we suggest, a fact is conceived as already carving possible future worlds that are compatible with it.

Thus, suppose that when infants look at a scene, not only do they represent the events and the classes of objects it contains (Fig. 1.1A) but they also construct its possible future outcomes (Fig. 1.1B). Suppose further that such possible outcomes can be coded by an appropriate numerical representation (Fig. 1.1C)—whether it be arrays of individual possible occurrences or a representation of the ratio between classes of possible events, regardless of their precise number. Then, under the assumption that all such logically possible outcomes are equiprobable, infants could also represent and estimate the probability that a single outcome (such as "a blue object exits the container") will occur (Fig. 1.1E) by comparing the number of

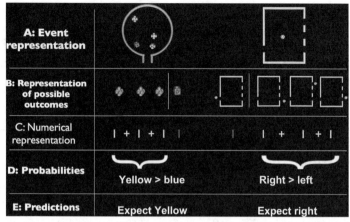

**Figure 1.1** From possibilities to probabilities. A representation of how infants might reason about the probability of a single future event. When inspecting a scene (A), infants create a modal representation of it, hence representing its possible future outcomes (B). If this representation can access infants' numerical systems (C), the probability of the next future outcome can be computed independently of any experience (D). Such a computation can be the basis for predicting the next more likely single outcome (E). The scenes are schematic reproductions of the kinds of events presented to 12-month olds and older children in the studies described in the article (Téglás et al., 2007). In the first scene, the number of objects of different classes affords the cue to compute possible next states of affairs. In the second scene, the frame containing the single object offers the cue to project possible future outcomes. For color version of this figure, the reader is referred to the online version of this book.

possible outcomes in which the events of each kind take place (Fig. 1.1D). In short, we propose that a logical sense of possibility is the foundation of an intuition of the probability of single future events.

That the psychological concept of probability may derive from the concept of possibility was proposed by Johnson-Laird, Legrenzi, Girotto, Legrenzi, and Caverni (1999) within the framework of the mental model theory (Johnson-Laird, 1983). Technically, their theory of modal reasoning was an extension of the mental models' theory of propositional reasoning (Johnson-Laird, Byrne, & Schaeken, 1992). The soundness of this theory can be doubted (Bonatti, 1994; O'Brien, Braine, & Yang, 1994) and with it the soundness of its modal version. However, the intuition that the concept of probability depends on the concept of possibility is independent of the particular implementation that the theory of mental models gave to it and, in our opinion, remains entirely valid.

The view that the possibilities afforded by the logical space circumscribed by the scene, and not past familiarity with its outcomes, is at the basis of our intuitions of probability predicts that infants will have expectations about future events independently of frequency computations or of the relation between populations and samples. Furthermore, the view predicts that, all other things being equal, an intuition of probability will be unaffected by biases. All these, of course, must be proved.

## 5. INFANTS' EXPECTATIONS ABOUT THE PROBABLE FUTURE

There is a difficulty we must examine, before seeing how the theory might work. Is it possible to even get the idea of studying infants' intuitions about possibilities and probabilities off the ground? One immediate objection that would make our proposal not viable can be quickly formulated as follows: how could infants even figure out the space of logical possibilities? How are they supposed to identify what may be going to happen next? Will all objects exit the container? Only one? Perhaps two? Or will they all disappear or fly away? In principle, every scene is compatible with an infinite set of possibilities, out of which only few are relevant for the appropriate predictions. If we can speak and understand language, then delimiting the space is very simple: we can just tell what the relevant space is. We can ask, "What is the probability that the next object that comes out will be blue?," thus selecting some among the many possible relevant outcomes within a scene that must be considered in order to answer the question. Language is a very powerful tool that acts as selector for the relevant problem space. We have no such luxury with infants. They observe the world as it is, not as we describe it, and world scenes per se contain no explicit cue to the information relevant to constrain the space over which to reason about future events.

While ultimately general solutions to such questions are as hard as the frame problem, if infants can be cued to attend to a relevant solution space, then the problem is not unsolvable. Indeed, research in our laboratory suggests that an appropriate familiarization can be used (and must be used) to focus infants' attention to the relevant outcomes (Téglás & Bonatti, 2008). Thus, if infants are familiarized with one particular outcome among the many possible outcomes of a scene (in our example, if they are familiarized with a lottery-like scene in which one and only one object exits the device), then they will reason about the probability of the expected outcome. If, instead, infants are familiarized with the same situation, but no final outcome is ever shown, then they will not focus on the outcome of interest during the test phase and they will not form probabilistic expectations related to it. Infants must be cued to the relevant outcomes of a scene in order to reason about its possible future continuations. Also this behavior is entirely rational: if there is no way to represent the logical space of possible outcomes, then there is no way to predict which outcome will be more likely. Of course, the familiarization must give information about what kind of outcome to expect in the test scenes but not about its probabilities. In the case of the studies by Téglás and his colleagues, for example, infants were familiarized with four lottery-like scenes that contained objects of two classes of equal cardinality, so that the exit of an object of either one or the other class was equiprobable. In each of these familiarization movies, they saw one object (always a different one) exiting the container. Thus, although infants were familiarized with the outcomes of the scenes, they did not possess information leading them to expect one particular outcome. It could be said that also these familiarizations count as "previous experience" and, therefore, that frequentists are right that reasoning about the future requires past experience. We do not feel that this counter-objection describes the situation correctly. All the previous experience given in the experiments we described contains no information to bias infants to expect one particular outcome. Thus, these observations cannot be the basis of infants' responses when they are presented with the test situations, in which the class distribution of objects inside the containers is unbalanced. If anything, this brief familiarization might be used by infants to form expectations about the equiprobability of outcomes. Hence any outcome in the test phase (whether being the exit of an object of the most numerous class, or an object of the less numerous class) should appear as equally surprising. This is not, however, how infants react.

Here, we will not pursue the interesting question about the relation between experience, reasoning, familiarization, and test in experiments any further. In this context, we only want to make the point that infants can be cued into the dimension of what constitutes a relevant outcome, even without language. Language, we submit, is a useful tool to trim the infinite amount of possible continuations of a scene to the relevant class of outcomes. In this property resides its power to help us reason. But it is by no means necessary to reason logically or probabilistically. Provided that infants are cued into the dimension that makes a particular outcome the relevant one, then we can also probe how and whether they represent the relevant future possibilities.

In the experiments by Téglás et al., infants were first primed to the relevant solution space by movies that showed one single object exiting the container—a condition for the experiments to succeed. Then they saw movies terminating with the "probable" and "improbable" outcomes we described (Fig. 1.2, Scene A). As recalled, infants looked significantly longer at the improbable outcome, when the single object exited the container after an occlusion period, than at the more probable outcome in which one of the three identical objects exited. Importantly, Téglás et al. also showed that when a bar in the middle of the frame made it physically impossible for the three identical objects to reach the exit, infants inverted their preferences, looking longer at events in which one of them would exit (Fig. 1.2, Scene B). According to the theory of intuitive probability we are proposing, without the need to previously experienced distributions, infants naturally expect the more probable outcome based on the possible logical outcomes

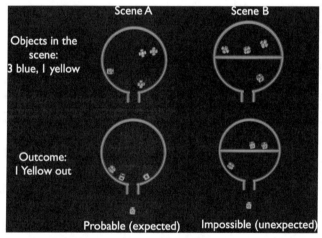

**Figure 1.2** From probabilities to impossibilities. Both scenes have the same outcome: a yellow cubic object exits the container. However, in Scene A, the outcome is the most probable one, whereas in Scene B, it is impossible. Infants look at the outcome of Scene B longer when they find a cubic yellow object than when they find the single blue object, but look at the outcome of Scene A longer when they find the single blue object than when they find a cubic yellow object (Téglás et al., 2007). However, the configurational and low-level perceptual properties of the outcomes of Scenes A and B are highly similar. This inversion in looking pattern suggests that infants can consider the probability of an outcome just as efficiently as they consider its physical possibility, and are able to use the most efficient cues afforded by a scene to ground their expectations. For interpretation of the references to color in this figure legend, the reader is referred to the online version of this book.

of a scene. In the case of the simple lottery experiment, the (relevant) possible outcomes are the single outcome case in which a blue object exits the container and the three outcomes in which a yellow object exits. When a bar blocks the exits of the three yellow objects, then the only possible outcome is that in which a blue object exits the container. The computation we sketched above predicts exactly the pattern of inversion in looking time found by Téglás et al. (2007).

The fact that infants inverted their looking behavior when they saw the container with or without a bar in the middle also allows us to drive home another point concerning the relation between reasoning and biases at the origin of cognition. We know little of what a bias could be in an infant mind. However, if low-level factors such as perceptual grouping, or possible least effort strategies such as tracking the minimal number of objects, or intrinsic preferences such as a penchant for single-object outcomes count as proto-heuristics, then the inversion in looking patterns excludes that infants' reactions could be due to them. Of course the fact that infants' responses are not led by such proto-heuristics does not exclude that other, more complex problems require solutions based on heuristics. For example, the problems tested by Tversky and Kahneman, where the effect of heuristics appears, are far more complex than those studied by Téglás et al. (2007). Because it is almost impossible to test the same problems with 12-month-old infants, the issue is difficult to explore. However, the results of Téglás et al. at least suffice to establish that simple heuristics that could play a role in infants' reactions do not necessarily lead infants' reasoning astray. Thus, they open the possibility that the heuristics and biases present in adult reasoning are not immutable features of the human mind as the dual process theory holds. Instead, they may be spurious by-products of complex interactions between experience and mental mechanisms during development, rather than the product of our evolutionary history. Their explanation can be approached developmentally by studying their origins and the conditions under which they are formed.

## 6. INTUITIVE STATISTICS AND LOGICAL INTUITIONS OF PROBABILITIES: CONFLICTING OR COMPLEMENTARY EXPLANATIONS?

We proposed to explain the result of Téglás et al. by assuming that infants represent the (relevant) logically possible outcomes of a scene and, from them, form expectations about the most probable next future event. However, other alternative explanations are possible. In particular, we see an account along the lines of the theory proposed by Xu and Garcia (2008) that only appeals to intuitive statistics. Such an account would not need to postulate the representation of a space of future possibilities, and it may work equally well.

According to the intuitive probability proposal, infants represent a problem space as a small set of possible, yet never occurred, mutually exclusive events. Instead, an explanation based on intuitive statistics would consider the estimation of the probability of an event not yet encountered in terms of its relationship with an actual, perceived, distribution. Because in lottery experiments by Téglás et al. infants always have the full population in front of them, it could be possible to explain the results in terms of intuitive statistics as follows. Suppose that infants ⌐onsider the objects inside the container (say, three yellow and one blue) as the full population of reference and the exit of one object from the container as a randomly drawn sample extracted from that population. Then, the exit of one yellow object will be less surprising because it would be considered as the draw of a one-object sample that better matches the distribution of the population than the draw of a one-object sample that contains the only existing blue object. Such reasoning does not require that infants conceive the space of the relevant possible outcomes. The full population is in front of them and they can directly compare the sample to the population distribution. This explanation might also account for the inversion of looking time between the situation in which every object could fall out of the container and the situation in which a bar blocked the yellow objects from reaching the exit. It might be possible to think that, when the bar isolates the three yellow objects, infants think that the population distribution from which the sample is drawn changes and consists only of the single blue object. Accordingly, they form the expectation that the one-object sample must be blue because it corresponds to the full population, which, again, infants have in front of them.

Data collected by Denison and Xu (2010) seem to support this interpretation. The authors showed 14-month-old infants one transparent jar containing 50 lollipops of two colors, with a ratio of 4:1, and another jar with the same number of lollipops but with the ratio between colors inverted. The authors first established what color each individual infant preferred. Then, they presented the two jars to infants and two empty cups. After infants saw the content of the jars, one lollipop from the first jar was put in one of the cups and a lollipop from the second jar was put in the second cup. The action was executed in such a way that infants could see from what jar the lollipops were drawn but not the lollipops' colors. Finally, infants were left free to grab the cup they preferred. Denison and Xu found that infants chose the cup containing the lollipop taken from the jar with the higher proportion of lollipop of their favorite colors. This result does not have a straightforward interpretation in terms of the theory we proposed. It is arguably implausible to suppose that infants solve the task by relating the two possible outcomes (a pink lollipop or a black lollipop) to the space of logically possible outcomes afforded by the objects present in the scene. Representing such logical space would involve representing a set of distinct, mutually exclusive, possible events that is just too big to be represented.

However, other results seem easier to account for in the framework we propose but do not have a straightforward explanation in terms of intuitive statistics, insofar as this explanation requires a computation based on a perceived population distribution. Téglás et al. (2007) and ) tested infants and children with a second type of scene, which differed in one crucial aspect from the lottery scenes (Fig. 1.1, right). It presented a ball bouncing inside a box with one hole in a vertical wall and three holes in the opposite vertical wall. After some time in which infants and children could see the ball freely bouncing inside, an occluder covered the box. Care was taken to ensure that the position and last trajectory of the ball right before the occlusion was uninformative about the side from which it would eventually exit. Finally, the ball exited the box from one of the sides. ) showed that 12-month-old infants looked longer at the improbable exit (the one-hole side) than at the probable exit. Likewise showed that children react faster when they have to guess that the ball will exit the three-hole side.

Just as the lottery scene, this kind of scene individuates four logically possible outcomes. The ball can exit from the only hole on the one side or else from the upper, the middle, or the lower holes on the other side. Thus, according to our theory of intuitive probability, reasoners should expect the ball to exit from the three-hole side, rather than from the one-hole side because one kind of events (say, exiting from the left side) occurs in three possible future continuations of the scene whereas another kind of events (say, exiting from the right side) only occurs in one possible future continuation. Indeed, infants and children behaved as predicted by our theory. However, is it possible to make the same prediction in terms of an intuitive statistics theory? We do not find it that simple. According to this theory, the ability to estimate the probability of a future single event's probability is derivative of the ability to grasp the relation between a sample and a perceived population. However, in the case of the ball in the box, there is no perceivable population distribution of which the exit of the ball from a particular side is a sample. Whatever happens, it happens only in the mind of the observer: if infants and children anticipate where the ball will exit, they do it by constructing a problem space of mental possibilities, on the basis of which they form their intuitions of the probability of future outcomes.

## 7. INFANT RATIONALITY AND SIMULATIONS: YET A THIRD ALTERNATIVE?

Recently Téglás et al. (2011) showed that infants' probabilistic reasoning abilities are even more sophisticated than what we have been discussing so far. As we recalled, any scene contains multiple kinds of information. An optimal reasoner should be able to decide which ones are relevant in a particular situation, as well as weight their relevance for the problem at hand. Furthermore, such evaluations must adapt dynamically because small changes in a developing situation can change their relative importance. Téglás et al. (2011) operationalized the investigation on infants' abilities to weight and integrate different changing cues in their predictions about future events by modifying crucial aspects of the scenes tested by Téglás et al. (2007). Infants were always presented with simple situations in which three yellow and one blue object bounced inside a lottery-like container. However, first, the objects of either categories could be either far or distant from the exit before the occluder covered the content of the box (Fig. 1.1). Second, the length of the occlusion separating the last moment in which the objects were visible before the occlusion and the first moment in which one of the object exited the container varied. Thus, the experiments varied the relevance of two cues: how distant an object is from the exit and how many objects of different classes are in the container.

The logic of these experiments was as follows. When objects cannot be seen for a very short time because an extremely short occlusion hides them from sight, then the distance of an object from the exit, and not its class membership, should be the most relevant cue to predict the next future outcome. Indeed, it would be almost impossible in an extremely short time for a distant object to exit the container; so, infants should expect that the first object to exit the container is the one that was closest to the exit before the short occlusion, regardless of its class membership. On the other hand, when the objects cannot be seen for a long period, because they keep moving inside the container, their locations prior to the occlusion is irrelevant. Surely, they changed positions many times during the occlusion period and hence where they were the last time one could see them is not predictive of where they will be after the occlusion. However, the shape and color of the object do not change. Thus, in this case, only the class membership of the objects (whether they belong to the most represented or to the less represented class) should matter. Thus, an optimal rational prediction of the outcomes should consider at least two aspects of the situation: the number of objects per category and the relative distance of the objects from the exit. Moreover, the relative importance of these two factors should vary depending on the length of the occlusion. Indeed, as indicated by their looking time at the final outcomes, infants only considered the relative distance of the objects from the exit, but not their categories or category distribution, when the occlusion was 0.04-s long. When the occlusion increased to 1 s, they considered both factors. Finally, when the occlusion was 2-s long, they only considered the category membership of the objects, but not their distance from the exit, to form their expectations. Thus, infants behaved as optimal rational agents. Téglás et al. (2011) also specified the formal way in which infants can be said to be optimal rational agents. They proposed a probabilistic model in which a Bayesian ideal observer equipped with basic knowledge of an objects' physical properties quantitatively predicts infants' looking behavior. Intuitively, the model simulates the possible trajectories of the objects as temporal series of possible world states, where the expectation of an outcome (i.e. one blue object exits first at a given time) is a function of how many trajectories are compatible with that outcome. The model fits impressively well with the infants' looking times in this as well as in many other studies, opening the possibility that a Bayesian inference system could be part of the explanation of many known results in infants' cognition of objects and events in the world.

Is the explanation proposed by Téglás et al. (2011) yet a third theory of infants' reasoning about the uncertain future? The fact that the model uses the simulation of physical trajectories to make its prediction may suggest that infants' expectations are based on simulation mechanisms reproducing object trajectories analogically, a view akin to a mental model theory of mental processes. Although this is a possibility, it is in no way mandated by the model proposed by Téglás et al. (2011). Such a model does not carry any commitment to the format of the internal representations on the basis of which infants form their expectations. That is, it is compatible both with a view of mental processes that takes seriously the existence of "analog simulations" in the mind or else with a view that conceives simulations as knowledge-based symbol manipulations. The case is no different from the debate about the nature of imagery (Pylyshyn, 1973, 1980, 2002, 2007).

Although the exact format of the internal representation underlying infants' abilities at integrating different information cannot be established, adult data suggest that humans are extremely poor at reconstructing in imagination quite simple dynamical scenes, giving chronometric and explicit responses that seem incompatible with the presence of an underlying analog simulation (Levillain & Bonatti, 2011). These data would seem to cast doubts about the existence of analog simulations in infants as well.

Our point, in this context, is that the Bayesian model elaborated by Téglás et al. (2011) does not force upon us a theory that assumes the existence of mental analog simulations. Indeed, the details of the simulations are not so important. Téglás et al. showed that the simulations needed to account for infants' behavior can be dramatically curtailed—from several thousands to four—without loss of predictability (Téglás et al., 2011, supplementary material). The resilience of the model under severe resource limitations suggests that the specific details of the simulations are not what that carries its explanatory power but, rather, the ability to represent alternative situations and conceive their possible outcomes. What, instead, cannot be eliminated or reduced from the model is the presence of a sophisticated inference device incorporating logical operations about real and possible future states (Perfors, Tenenbaum, Griffiths, & Xu, 2011). The postulation of the existence of this particular representational ability, which is highly consistent with the theory we proposed, is what we believe will become one of the major focuses of research in the next years.

## 8. WHAT ABOUT "EXPERIENCED FREQUENCIES"?

We have discussed two theories about intuitive understanding of probabilities, and we have tried to speculate about how they could account for some results about infants' probabilistic reasoning. We have shown that they can both predict some of the existing data but also that both have difficulties at predicting other data. The discussion may suggest that infants may have access to different computations that both allow, in certain cases, to predict the probability of single future events. Infants can predict a future event by seeing it as a sample of a perceived distribution. They can also predict a future event representing a space of logically possible outcomes and locating it inside that space. Further research is needed to explore this possibility. However, one point that the data and the explanations we presented should drive home is that infants' reasoning about the probable future cannot be explained on the basis of elementary perceptual biases nor on the basis of simple frequency mechanisms. To which we finally turn.

Both our proposal and the intuitive statistics theory postulate computational mechanisms that cannot be reduced to the ubiquitous frequency detection abilities that have been often documented in infants and adults. What, then, is the role of the "encountered frequency" of events that, according to the frequentist theory, are at the basis of our reasoning about distributions? We do not know whether and how infants integrate frequency information potentially in conflict with their initial intuitions of probability, but Téglás et al. explored this issue at least in 5-year olds. Children were shown situations where a ball inside a container with three exits on one side and one exit on the other side bounces randomly, eventually exiting the container (Fig. 1.1, right). The intuitive probability afforded by the device should lead one to predict a more likely exit from the three-exit side. However, by repeatedly presenting a scene ending with the ball exiting from the one-exit side, a conflict between a priori probability afforded by the situation and actual frequency of outcomes arose. Children had to press a button when the ball exited the container after an occlusion period that obliged them to react from their representations of the scene. Before their responses, they were also asked to give explicit judgments about what outcome they thought more likely. Finally, after being exposed for a while to the actual frequencies of outcomes, they were asked again an explicit judgment about what outcome occurred most.

Initially, both children's motor responses and their explicit judgments were influenced by the intuition that the ball had more chances to exit from the three-exit side. Also, after experiencing the frequencies of outcomes, when such frequency conflicted with the initial intuitions, children motor responses adapted to the distribution: after some time, children reacted faster when the ball exited the one-hole side. However, their explicit judgments did not adapt to frequencies. Even after seeing the ball exiting the one-exit side 75% of the time, children maintained that the ball was more likely to exit the three-hole side, as if the main factor determining their explicit judgments were, not their experience with the outcomes, but the representation of the logical possibilities afforded by the scene. So frequency does have an effect, but not where the frequentists would predict it. In our experiments, it affected motor responses, but not judgments about probabilities. That is, experience molds the way we act, but not necessarily the way we think.

## 9. THE FUTURE OF PREDICTIONS ABOUT THE FUTURE

The theory we proposed asks us to seriously consider the possibility that infants are little logicians, who can create logical representations of situations and make inferences from them in a rational way. Infants do seem to use abstract logical operators when acquiring rules (Marcus, Vijayan, Rao, & Vishton, 1999), creating representations of sets (Feigenson & Halberda, 2004), or learning words (Halberda, 2003). And by now there is good evidence that toddlers spontaneously engage in a form of exploratory play that can be described as a kind of rational hypothesis testing and confirmation (Bonawitz et al., 2010; Cook, Goodman, & Schulz, 2011; Gweon & Schulz, 2011; Schulz, Standing, & Bonawitz, 2008), suggesting the presence of very advanced logical representations needed to formulate and test hypotheses. But researchers have just begun to scratch the surface of the problem of determining the nature of infants' logical representations, and evidence to inform us about the existence, the format, and the extent of such representations is entirely lacking. Equally poor is our understanding of the relation between the representations of future possibilities afforded by a scene and infants' different systems for representing quantities. These are questions that we find fascinating and that will draw our attention in the coming years.

Yet, even in the current defective state of knowledge, we now know that infants can predict the uncertain future far better than a picture of early cognition as a collection of different encapsulated systems would suggest. This conclusion does not square with most theories about human reasoning and certainly seriously puts into question the currently popular dual process approach to human reasoning. There is an empirical and theoretical space that most of that literature missed. It demands to be explored and perhaps will help us tell a piece of the story about the inventiveness of human thought.

## ACKNOWLEDGMENTS

The research was supported by the Ministerio de Ciencia e Innovación PSI2009-08232PSIC grant to LLB, by Consolider Ingenio 2010 Program (CSD2007-00012) of the Spanish Ministry of Economy and Competitiveness, by the Secretaria de Universitats i Recerca del Departament d'Economia i Coneixement of the Generalitat de Catalunya (2011 FIB_000695), and by the Hungarian Science Foundation (OTKA NK83997) grant. We thank Kimberly Brink, Fei Xu, Gergo Csibra, and Tamar Kushnir for their comments on a first version of the manuscript.

# REFERENCES

Amati, D., & Shallice, T. (2007). On the emergence of modern humans. *Cognition, 103*(3), 358–385.

Baillargeon, R., Spelke, E. S., & Wasserman, S. (1985). Object permanence in five-month-old infants. *Cognition, 20*(3), 191–208.

Bonatti, L. (1994). Propositional reasoning by model? *Psychological Review, 101*(4), 725–733.

Bonawitz, E. B., Ferranti, D., Saxe, R., Gopnik, A., Meltzoff, A. N., Woodward, J., et al. (2010). Just do it? Investigating the gap between prediction and action in toddlers' causal inferences. *Cognition, 115*(1), 104–117.

Braine, M. D. S., O'Brien, D. P., Noveck, I. A., Samuels, M. C., Lea, R. B., Fisch, S. M., et al. (1995). Predicting intermediate and multiple conclusions in propositional logic inference problems: further evidence for a mental logic. *Journal of Experimental Psychology: General, 124*(3), 263–292.

Carruthers, P. (2002). The cognitive functions of language. *Behavioral and Brain Sciences, 25*(6), 657–726.

Cook, C., Goodman, N. D., & Schulz, L. E. (2011). Where science starts: spontaneous experiments in preschoolers' exploratory play. *Cognition, 120*(3), 341–349.

Cosmides, L. (1989). The logic of social exchange: has natural selection shaped how humans reason? Studies with the Wason selection task. *Cognition, 31*(3), 187–276.

Cosmides, L., & Tooby, J. (1996). Are humans good intuitive statisticians after all? Rethinking some conclusions from the literature on judgment under uncertainty. *Cognition, 58*(1), 1–73.

De Neys, W. (2012). Bias and conflict: a case for logical intuitions. *Perspectives on Psychological Science, 7*(1), 28–38.

De Neys, W., & Franssens, S. (2009). Belief inhibition during thinking: not always winning but at least taking part. *Cognition, 113*(1), 45–61.

De Neys, W., & Schaeken, W. (2007). When people are more logical under cognitive load: dual task impact on scalar implicature. *Experimental Psychology, 54*(2), 128–133.

Denison, S., & Xu, F. (2010). Twelve- to 14-month-old infants can predict single-event probability with large set sizes. *Developmental Science, 13*(5), 798–803.

Evans, J. St. B. T. (1989). *Bias in human reasoning: Causes and consequences.* Hillsdale, NJ: Lawrence Erlbaum Associates, Inc.

Evans, J. St. B. T. (2003). In two minds: dual-process accounts of reasoning. *Trends in Cognitive Sciences, 7*(10), 454–459.

Evans, J. St. B. T. (2008). Dual-processing accounts of reasoning, judgment, and social cognition. *Annual Review of Psychology, 59*, 255–278.

Feigenson, L. (2005). A double-dissociation in infants' representations of object arrays. *Cognition, 95*(3), B37–b48.

Feigenson, L., & Carey, S. (2005). On the limits of infants' quantification of small object arrays. *Cognition, 97*(3), 295–313.

Feigenson, L., Dehaene, S., & Spelke, E. (2004). Core systems of number. *Trends in Cognitive Sciences, 8*(7), 307–314.

Feigenson, L., & Halberda, J. (2004). Infants chunk object arrays into sets of individuals. *Cognition, 91*(2), 173–190.

Fiser, J., & Aslin, R. N. (2002). Statistical learning of new visual feature combinations by infants. *Proceedings of the National Academy of Sciences of the United States of America, 99*(24), 15822–15826.

Gergely, G., & Csibra, G. (2003). Teleological reasoning in infancy: the naïve theory of rational action. *Trends in Cognitive Sciences, 7*(7), 287–292.

Gergely, G., Nádasdy, Z., Csibra, G., & Bíró, S. (1995). Taking the intentional stance at 12 months of age. *Cognition, 56*(2), 165–193.

Gigerenzer, G., & Hoffrage, U. (1995). How to improve Bayesian reasoning without instruction: frequency formats. *Psychological Review, 102*(4), 684–704.

Gilovich, T., Vallone, R., & Tversky, A. (1985). The hot hand in basketball: on the misperception of random sequences. *Cognitive Psychology, 17*(3), 295–314.

Griffiths, T. L., Kemp, C., & Tenenbaum, J. B. (2008). Bayesian models of cognition. In R. Sun (Ed.), *The Cambridge Handbook of Computational Psychology* (pp. 59–100). Cambridge: Cambridge University Press.

Griffiths, T. L., & Tenenbaum, J. B. (2006). Optimal Predictions in Everyday Cognition. *Psychological Science, 17*(9), 767–773.

Gweon, H., & Schulz, L. (2011). 16-Month-olds rationally infer causes of failed actions. *Science, 332*(6037), 1524.

Halberda, J. (2003). The development of a word-learning strategy. *Cognition, 87*(1), B23–B34.

Hauser, M. D., Newport, E. L., & Aslin, R. N. (2001). Segmentation of the speech stream in a non-human primate: statistical learning in cotton-top tamarins. *Cognition, 78*(3), B53–B64.

Hume, D. (2000). *An enquiry concerning human understanding.* Kitchener, ON: Batoche.

Johnson-Laird, P. N., Legrenzi, P., Girotto, V., Legrenzi, M. S., & Caverni, J.-P. (1999). Naive probability: a mental model theory of extensional reasoning. *Psychological Review, 106*(1), 62–88.

Johnson-Laird, P. N. (1983). *Mental models.* Cambridge, MA: Harvard University Press.

Johnson-Laird, P. N., Byrne, R. M., & Schaeken, W. (1992). Propositional reasoning by model. *Psychological Review, 99*(3), 418–439.

Kahneman, D., & Tversky, A. (1972). Subjective probability: a judgment of representativeness. *Cognitive Psychology, 3*(3), 430–454.

Kushnir, T., Xu, F., & Wellman, H. M. (2010). Young children use statistical sampling to infer the preferences of other people. *Psychological Science, 21*(8), 1134–1140.

Lea, R. B., & Mulligan, E. J. (2002). The effect of negation on deductive inferences. *Journal of Experimental Psychology: Learning, Memory, and Cognition, 28*(2), 303–317.

Lea, R. B., O'Brien, D. P., Fisch, S. M., & Noveck, I. A. (1990). Predicting propositional logic inferences in text comprehension. *Journal of Memory and Language, 29*(3), 361–387.

Levillain, F., & Bonatti, L. L. (2011). A dissociation between judged causality and imagined locations in simple dynamic scenes. *Psychological Science, 22*(5), 674–681.

Marcus, G. F., Vijayan, S., Rao, S. B., & Vishton, P. M. (1999). Rule learning by seven-month-old infants. *Science, 283*(5398), 77–80.

Mithen, S. J. (1996). *The prehistory of the mind: a search for the origins of art, religion and science.* London: Thames and Hudson.

O'Brien, D. P., Braine, M. D. S., & Yang, Y. (1994). Propositional reasoning by mental models? Simple to refute in principle and in practice. *Psychological Review, 101*(4), 711–724.

Perfors, A., Tenenbaum, J. B., Griffiths, T. L., & Xu, F. (2011). A tutorial introduction to Bayesian models of cognitive development. *Cognition, 120,* 302–321.

Piaget, J., Chomsky, N., & Piatelli-Palmarini, M. (1980). *Language and learning: the debate between Jean Piaget and Noam Chomsky.* Cambridge, MA: Harvard University Press.

Pylyshyn, Z. W. (1973). What the mind's eye tells the mind's brain: a critique of mental imagery. *Psychological Bulletin, 80*(1), 1–24.

Pylyshyn, Z. W. (1980). Computation and cognition: issues in the foundations of cognitive science. *Behavioral and Brain Sciences, 3*(1), 111–169.

Pylyshyn, Z. W. (2002). Mental imagery: in search of a theory. *Behavioral and Brain Sciences, 25*(2), 157–238.

Pylyshyn, Z. W. (2007). *Things and places: How the mind connects with the world.* Cambridge, MA: MIT Press.

Reverberi, C., Bonatti, L. L., Frackowiak, R. S., Paulesu, E., Cherubini, P., & Macaluso, E. (2012). Large scale brain activations predict reasoning profiles. *Neuroimage, 59*(2), 1752–1764.

Reverberi, C., Pischedda, D., Burigo, M., & Cherubini, P. (2012). Deduction without awareness. *Acta Psychologica, 139*(1), 244–253.

Reverberi, C., Shallice, T., D'Agostini, S., Skrap, M., & Bonatti, L. L. (2009). Cortical bases of elementary deductive reasoning: inference, memory, and metadeduction. *Neuropsychologia, 47*(4), 1107–1116.

Saffran, J. R., Aslin, R. N., & Newport, E. L. (1996). Statistical learning by 8-month-old infants. *Science, 274*(5294), 1926–1928.

Schulz, L. E., Standing, H. R., & Bonawitz, E. B. (2008). Word, thought, and deed: the role of object categories in children's inductive inferences and exploratory play. *Developmental Psychology, 44*(5), 1266–1276.

Sloman, S. A. (1996). The empirical case for two systems of reasoning. *Psychological Bulletin, 119*(1), 3–22.

Southgate, V., & Csibra, G. (2009). Inferring the outcome of an ongoing novel action at 13 months. *Developmental Psychology, 45*(6), 1794–1798.

Spelke, E. S. (2003). What makes us smart? Core knowledge and natural language. In D. Gentner, & S. Goldin-Meadow (Eds.), *Language in mind: Advances in the study of language and thought* (pp. 277–311). Cambridge, MA: MIT Press.

Spelke, E. S., Breinlinger, K., Macomber, J., & Jacobson, K. (1992). Origins of knowledge. *Psychological Review, 99*(4), 605–632.

Stanovich, K. E., & West, R. F. (2000). Individual differences in reasoning: implications for the rationality debate? *Behavioral and Brain Sciences, 23*(5), 645–726.

Téglás, E., & Bonatti, L. L. (2008). Probability triggers the eye: reasoning about uncertain events in 12-month-old infants. *In: Proceedings from International Conference of Infant Studies*. Vancouver, CA.

Téglás, E., Girotto, V., Gonzalez, M., & Bonatti, L. L. (2007). Intuitions of probabilities shape expectations about the future at 12 months and beyond. *Proceedings of the National Academy of Sciences of the United States of America, 104*(48), 19156–19159.

Téglás, E., Vul, E., Girotto, V., Gonzalez, M., Tenenbaum, J. B., & Bonatti, L. L. (2011). Pure reasoning in 12-month-old infants as probabilistic inference. *Science, 332*(6033), 1054–1058.

Tenenbaum, J. B., Griffiths, T. L., & Kemp, C. (2006). Theory-based Bayesian models of inductive learning and reasoning. *Trends in Cognitive Sciences, 10*(7), 309–318.

Toro, J. M., & Trobalón, J. B. (2005). Statistical computations over a speech stream in a rodent. *Perception & Psychophysics, 67*(5), 867–875.

Tversky, A., & Kahneman, D. (1974). Judgment under uncertainty: heuristics and biases. *Science, 185*(4157), 1124–1131.

Tversky, A., & Kahneman, D. (1981). The framing of decisions and the psychology of choice. *Science, 211*(4481), 453–458.

Tversky, A., & Kahneman, D. (1993). Belief in the law of small numbers. In C. Keren, & C. Lewis (Eds.), *A handbook for riala attalysis ill the behavioral sciellces: Methodological issues* (pp. 341–349). Hillsdale, NJ: Erlbaum.

Wason, P. C. (1968). Reasoning about a rule. *Quarterly Journal of Experimental Psychology A, 20*(3), 273–281.

Woodward, A. L. (1998). Infants selectively encode the goal object of an actor's reach. *Cognition, 69*(1), 1–34.

Woodward, A. L. (1999). Infants' ability to distinguish between purposeful and non-purposeful behaviors. *Infant Behavior & Development, 22*(2), 145–160.

Xu, F., & Denison, S. (2009). Statistical inference and sensitivity to sampling in 11-month-old infants. *Cognition, 112*(1), 97–104.

Xu, F., & Garcia, V. (2008). Intuitive statistics by 8-month-old infants. *Proceedings of the National Academy of Sciences of the United States of America, 105*(13), 5012–5015.

Xu, F., & Spelke, E. S. (2000). Large number discrimination in 6-month-old infants. *Cognition, 74*(1), B1–B11.

# CHAPTER TWO

# Probabilistic Inference in Human Infants

## Stephanie Denison[1] and Fei Xu

Department of Psychology, University of California, Berkeley, Berkeley, CA, 94720, USA.
[1]Corresponding author: E-mail: smdeniso@berkeley.edu

## Contents

## Abstract

In this chapter, we review empirical evidence in support of infants' ability to make rudimentary probabilistic inferences. A recent surge of research in cognitive developmental psychology examines whether human learners, from infancy through adulthood, reason in ways consistent with Bayesian inference. However, when exploring this question an important first step is to identify the available inference mechanisms and computational machinery that might allow infants and young children to make inductive inferences. A number of recent studies have asked if infants may be "intuitive statisticians," making inferences about the relationship between samples and populations in both looking-time and choice tasks. Furthermore, infants make these inferences under a variety of sampling conditions and integrate prior domain knowledge into their probability calculations. The competences demonstrated in the reviewed experiments appear to draw on an intuitive

*Advances in Child Development and Behavior*, Volume 43
ISSN 0065-2407,
http://dx.doi.org/10.1016/B978-0-12-397919-3.00002-2
27

probability notion that is early emerging and does not appear to be available for conscious reflection.

## 1. INTRODUCTION

What is the nature of early learning in infants and young children? What kinds of learning mechanisms are responsible for the rapidly developing knowledge—about objects, people, causality, and numbers—that we see in infancy and beyond? Are we rational learners and can rational computational models capture human behavior? These questions have been of great interest to psychologists for many decades. In this paper, we focus on a body of new empirical evidence from infants that tries to answer some of these questions.

The ability to make accurate inductive inferences based on limited data has implications for the longstanding debates in cognitive developmental psychology concerning the initial state of human learners and the learning mechanisms that can support conceptual development (e.g. Carey, 2009; Elman et al., 1996; Hirschfeld & Gelman, 1994; Smith, 2001; Spelke, 1994). Throughout the history of developmental psychology, these debates have divided developmental theorists into two opposing groups. One group, the nativists, tends to grant the human infant a great deal of initial conceptual knowledge. This theoretical outlook is usually coupled with the assumption that limited learning mechanisms need to be posited to support conceptual development and that many developmental changes may be accounted for by brain maturation. The other group, the empiricists, tends to posit that human infants start out with only perceptual primitives and that they lack initial conceptual knowledge. This theoretical commitment is typically paired with the assumption that associative learning mechanisms are responsible for the accumulation of conceptual knowledge and conceptual change. Furthermore, developmental psychologists who fall in the nativist camp, positing early conceptual knowledge and minimal learning, tend to advocate domain-specific learning mechanisms. Conversely, those who fall in the empiricist camp, positing early perceptual processing and a large role for learning, tend to advocate data-driven, domain-general learning mechanisms.

Traditionally, developmental psychologists have taken a strong stance on both these debates, placing themselves clearly on one side of the theoretical fence or the other. However, as both sides have provided more and more evidence in favor of their respective viewpoints, it has become increasingly clear that some philosophies from both camps are likely to have merit, while other aspects continually lack explanatory power for some phenomena. Take, for example, the domain of word learning, where a satisfying theory must account for a number of known phenomena. Empiricist accounts of word learning (e.g. Colunga & Smith, 2005; Regier, 2003, 2005) account reasonably well for the fact that children are capable of learning words at multiple levels of taxonomic hierarchies (e.g. they learn words such as animal, dog, and poodle). However, they have difficulty dealing with the fact that children are able to learn the meaning of new words after observing very small numbers of exemplars, a phenomenon called fast mapping, as the learning mechanisms typically posited by these accounts require a large number of object and label pairings to acquire new words. Conversely, more nativist approaches to word learning, which posit a number of innate constraints, can account for fast mapping but they have difficulty accounting for how children acquire words at multiple levels of a taxonomy (e.g. Markman, 1989; Siskind, 1996). Thus, both nativist and empiricist approaches appear to deal quite readily with some aspects of word learning, but others simply cannot be explained. Unfortunately, the problem with confessing that both camps get parts of the argument right, and parts of the argument wrong, is that this can be viewed as theoretical fence sitting, which is typically frowned upon in science. Nonetheless, these strong dichotomies are dissatisfying to many developmentalists. This is likely due to the fact that everyone believes that there is some innate knowledge, they just might disagree over how structured or advanced it is, and everyone believes there is some role for learning but, again, they might disagree over how central the learning mechanisms are to the story of development.

Recently, a theoretical framework that offers a middle ground between nativism and empiricism, termed rational constructivism, has been introduced (Xu, 2007; Xu, Dewar, & Perfors, 2009; Xu & Griffiths, 2011). One central focus of rational constructivism is to explore the role of domain–general inductive inference mechanisms in development. Inductive inference mechanisms may provide a more satisfying account of explaining how it is that children make rapid inferences from sparse data. They do not require that the learner bring a great deal of initial conceptual knowledge to any given task, but they can account for the rapid and accurate inferences that young children make with limited and imperfect data. In fact, it has been suggested that some of the early constraints that young learners use to guide their inferences in domains such as word learning may be acquired through these learning mechanisms (Dewar & Xu, 2010; Griffiths, Chater, Kemp, Perfors, & Tenenbaum, 2010; Kemp, Perfors, & Tenenbaum, 2007; Smith, Jones, Landau, Gershkoff-Stowe, & Samuelson, 2002). The inductive inference mechanisms central to rational constructivism are Bayesian in nature, allowing a role for both prior knowledge and input data in driving conceptual growth and thus bridging the nativist–empiricist divide to provide an explanation for learning and development in early childhood. Inductive inference mechanisms based on Bayesian principles assume that the learner makes educated guesses about the probabilities of a set of hypotheses, and these degrees of belief can be updated when additional pieces of evidence are acquired. They allow the learner to make inductive leaps based on minimal amounts of stochastic data—data similar in kind to the type of input that humans receive in the real world.

The purpose of this chapter is to explore how inductive inference gets off the ground in early infancy. If Bayesian inference is a good candidate to drive learning in early childhood and throughout the lifespan, an important first step is to identify the computational machinery that might allow infants and young children to make inferences of this nature. Although young children appear to make inductive inferences in ways that are consistent with Bayesian inference, the question of when these mechanisms come online and whether or not they are available in early infancy remain largely unknown. One central prerequisite to computing Bayesian inference, or approximations to Bayesian inference, is the ability to reason about probabilities and probabilistic data. In this chapter, we review research that explores the developmental origins of probabilistic inference in human infants. Do untutored infants have intuitions about probability that could serve as a prerequisite to later inductive inference? Can they make inductive inferences based on incomplete data to make generalizations from samples to populations and vice versa? These questions become even more interesting to consider when we think about the wealth of research suggesting that adults often struggle to make inferences in contexts that involve these basic probability computations (Tversky & Kahneman, 1974, 1981). In this chapter, we review evidence mainly from our laboratory suggesting that infants are capable of making probability computations in a variety of contexts (see also Cesana-Arlotti, Teglas, & Bonatti, 2012). We then discuss the implications of these findings to traditional views of development and the more mature states of cognitive reasoning in children and adults.

## 2. EMPIRICAL EVIDENCE FOR PROBABILISTIC INFERENCE IN INFANCY

### 2.1. Rudimentary Probabilistic Inferences

We begin by reviewing the available evidence suggesting that infants may be "intuitive statisticians." There exists a long history of investigating probabilistic reasoning in young children, beginning with Piaget and extending to contemporary researchers in both psychology and education. In Piaget's original experiments, he asked whether or not young children had intuitions about quantitative proportions and randomization by assessing their ability to make an inference about the likely contents of a sample, based on the composition of a population (Piaget & Inhelder, 1975). He showed 5- to 12-year-old children various distributions of two colors of tokens being placed in an opaque bag. He then simply asked the children which color they would be "most likely" to draw if they reached into the bag and pulled out just one token. In this task, children below the age of 7 did not systematically rely on the proportions of colored tokens to make their guesses and they did not appear to understand the concept of randomness. Children instead provided responses based on inappropriate elements such as idiosyncratic properties of the two colors; for example, "I'll get red because I like red." or an incorrect intuition of randomness, for example, "I'll get red because red went first."

Piaget's conclusions have not gone unchallenged over the past 60 years. Yost, Siegel, and Andrews revisited Piaget's question in their 1962 paper and found that 5-year-old children can succeed at analogous problems when the task is made more appropriate for a young age group. In particular, they found that children will provide correct answers at higher than chance levels when the verbal demands of the task are reduced. Convergent findings have been reported in subsequent experiments examining simple relationships between samples and populations with 4- and 5-year-old children (Acredolo, O'Connor, Banks, & Horobin, 1989; Goldberg, 1966; Reyna & Brainerd, 1994). In addition to the evidence suggesting that preschool-aged children can make rudimentary probabilistic computations, more recent experiments have revealed that slightly older children, beginning at around ages 6 and 7, can make very sophisticated inferences about the likely outcomes of uncertain events based on probability in a variety of contexts. For example, children make accurate probabilistic inferences in tasks involving complex judgments of expected values (Schlottmann & Anderson,

1994) and in tasks that require judgments based on the integration of prior probabilities and additional information (Girotto & Gonzalez, 2008; Gonzalez & Girotto, 2011).

Recently studies have begun investigating probabilistic inference in infancy. Three experiments, all employing the violation of expectation (VOE) looking-time paradigm, have investigated rudimentary probabilistic inference in infants' during the first year of life. The VOE looking-time paradigm capitalizes on the fact that infants look longer at events that they find unusual or surprising—events that violate their expectations. In a typical VOE experiment using visual displays, infants begin by looking at displays to become familiarized or habituated to the stimuli that will be used in the experimental session. Infants are then shown test trials, during which events that are more or less probable are shown, and infants' looking times are recorded. The basic intuition is that infants should look longer at an outcome event that is less probable than one that is more probable.

Teglas, Gonzalez, Girroto, and Bonatti (2007) used the VOE looking-time paradigm to ask whether 12-month-old infants could engage in probabilistic inference. In particular, they were interested in whether or not infants can make inferences about single-event probability, which in their paradigm requires the individual to observe a population of objects and reason about the likely outcome when just a single, random object is removed. Infants were familiarized to a lottery machine device displayed on a computer screen, containing four objects, in a 3 yellow to 1 blue ratio. On test trials, the machine was briefly occluded and infants were shown two alternating outcomes: either one of the yellow objects appeared to have exited from a chute in the bottom of the machine or the blue object exited from the chute. As a group, infants looked longer at the events in which the blue object exited the chute, suggesting that they found this outcome less probable. This suggests that 12-month-old infants realize that when a single object is randomly drawn from a 3:1 distribution, the object drawn is more likely to be of the majority kind.

Other studies have explored probabilistic inference in infancy by examining whether or not infants can reason about the relationship between large populations of objects and multiobject samples. Xu and Garcia (2008) tested 8-month-old infants' abilities to make generalizations from small samples to larger populations using a VOE looking-time experiment with a live experimenter and live objects. The experiment began with infants viewing familiarization trials, during which an experimenter placed a single, covered box on the stage, shook it back and forth, and removed the cover to show the infants the contents of the box—a large collection of Ping-Pong balls. On alternating trials, the population of balls in the box was either in a 9:1 red to white balls' ratio or a 9:1 white to red balls' ratio, but these large boxes appeared identical when the covers were closed. This familiarization was followed by test trials, during which the experimenter again took out a large covered box and placed it on the stage, shook it back and forth a couple of times, closed her eyes, reached into the box, and removed a sample. After removing the sample, the experimenter removed the cover on the box to reveal the population, always consisting of mostly red balls for one group of infants or mostly white balls for the other group. On alternating trials, the sample removed from the box consisted of either four red and one white Ping-Pong balls or four white and one red Ping-Pong balls (see Fig. 2.1). Infants looked longer at the 4:1 white to red ball samples if

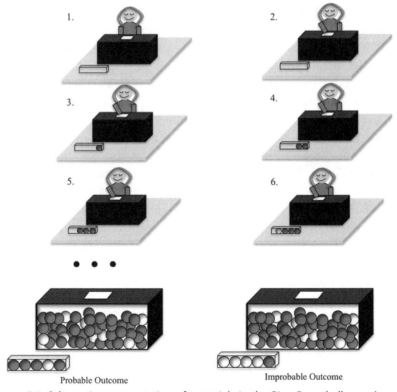

**Figure 2.1** Schematic representation of test trials in the Ping-Pong ball experiments. *Adapted from Xu and Garcia (2008).* For color version of this figure, the reader is referred to the online version of this book.

they were in the group that was shown the mostly red box and they looked longer at the 4:1 red to white ball samples if they were in the group that was shown the mostly white box. Thus, infants in this experiment were able to assess what a population is likely to consist of, based on a small random sample.

In a second experiment, Xu and Garcia (2008) demonstrated that infants could also make this inference in the reverse direction. The experimenter began by showing infants the open box filled with mostly red Ping-Pong balls for one group and mostly white Ping-Pong balls for the other group and then closed the box. She then removed the 4:1 red to white or white to red samples from the box on alternating trials. Infants in this experiment looked longer at the less probable 4:1 white to red ball samples being drawn from the mostly red population and the 4:1 red to white ball samples from the mostly white population. Therefore, in this case, similarly to the lottery machine experiment but with large numbers of objects, when infants were shown the population from which a sample was to be drawn, they expected that sample should be representative of the population.

As with most looking-time experiments, alternatives to the interpretation that infants produce this looking pattern because they are making probabilistic inferences are possible. One might wonder whether infants are making probability computations in these experiments or instead reacting to the perceptual differences between the samples and populations. It is possible that infants looked longer at the four white and one red ball samples being drawn from the mostly red box because the sample and box are more different in appearance, and potentially more interesting to look at, than in the outcome displaying the four red and one white sample drawn from the mostly red box. To control for this possibility, a second set of experiments were run with additional groups of 8-month-old infants (Xu & Garcia, 2008). In these experiments, infants saw the exact same familiarization trials but on test trials, the experimenter eliminated the sampling relationship between the large box and the small sample container. Infants saw the closed box being placed on the stage and then the experimenter removed a sample, not from the box but from her pocket, placed it in the container, and then removed the cover on the box. Thus, infants saw the exact same outcomes during the timed portion of the test trials as in the original experiments, but the sample did not originate from the large box. In these experiments, 8-month-old infants did not look reliably longer to either outcome, suggesting that infants in the original experiments were not reacting to the perceptual differences in the scene but instead to what is probable and improbable given the distribution of balls in the population.

The two sets of experiments reviewed here suggest that 12-month-old infants can make single-event probabilistic inferences and that 8-month-old infants can make inferences from samples to populations and vice versa.

What about younger infants? It seems plausible that younger infants could compute probabilities, given evidence revealing sensitivity to statistical input from newborns to 8-month-olds in domains such as phoneme discrimination, word segmentation, and visual pattern learning (e.g. Aslin, Saffran, & Newport, 1998; Bulf, Johnson, & Valenza, 2011; Kirkham, Slemmer, & Johnson, 2002; Maye, Werker, & Gerken, 2002; Saffran, Aslin, & Newport, 1996). Additionally, Sobel and Kirkham (2006, 2007) have found that 8-month-old, but not 5-month-old, infants can reason about conditional probabilities with visual displays. Thus, it is unclear as to how infants in the first 6 months of life would fare in a probabilistic inference experiment similar to the ones reported in this review.

To test whether or not infants younger than 8 months can make generalizations from samples to populations, Denison, Reed, and Xu (2012) conducted an experiment designed to test 4.5- and 6-month-old infants' probability intuitions. The experimental procedure was structured to keep processing demands minimal but to also control for a potential confound in the lottery machine and Ping-Pong ball experiments described above. Denison et al. used displays that always consisted of two complementary population boxes with 4:1 and 1:4 ratios of pink and yellow balls in each box. Thus, in this experiment, unlike in Xu and Garcia (2008) and Teglas et al. (2007), the amount of each color (e.g. pink vs. yellow) present in the population containers was always equivalent.

Infants were first familiarized to a scene with two large boxes placed side-by-side on a stage with, for example, the box on the right containing a 4:1 pink to yellow balls' ratio and the box on the left containing a 4:1 yellow to pink balls' ratio. On test trials, the two boxes were again placed on the stage, with covers, and the experimenter shook each box, reached into the box on the right to remove a sample of balls and placed them in a container in between the two boxes. She then mimicked this sampling action with the box on the left to draw infants' attention to each box equally. Finally, the experimenter revealed the contents of the boxes simultaneously and the infants' looking times were recorded. On alternating trials, the sample removed was either four pink and one yellow balls (i.e. the more probable sample) or four yellow and one pink balls (i.e. the less probable sample) from the mostly pink box. In this experiment, 6-month-old infants looked reliably longer at the less probable 4:1 yellow to pink ball samples being drawn from a mostly pink box, but 4.5-month-olds looked approximately equally at both samples. Thus, it appears that 6-month-old infants have intuitions about the relationship between samples and populations, but this competence was not found in 4.5-month-olds.

Although the presence of the two population boxes equates the amount of pinkness and yellowness in the scene, it is still possible that infants only paid attention to the box from which the sample had been drawn. Frame-by-frame coding analyses of the test trials provided support against this alternative interpretation of the 6-month-olds' looking behavior and also insights into the possible reason why 4.5-month-olds failed. The coder broke down the infants' scanning behavior to assess the duration of time that each infant looked at three different portions of the stage: 1) The box on the right (i.e. the box from which the sample was drawn), 2) the box on the left (i.e. the box that the experimenter mimicked the sampling with), and 3) the sample itself. This coding revealed that 6-month-old infants spent approximately equal amounts of time scanning the two boxes and the sample during the test trials. Thus, 6-month-olds attended to the entire scene. These analyses suggest that it was unlikely that infants simply ignored the second, complementary population box and then reacted to the perceptual features of each sample compared to the sampled box to produce their differential looking times. The 4.5-month-old infants, on the other hand, produced a somewhat surprising pattern of scanning behavior. While the population contents were still hidden and the experimenter was performing the sampling and the mimicked sampling, the 4.5-month-olds attended significantly more to the *unsampled* population box than to the box from which the sample was drawn. In order to make accurate probabilistic inferences, infants must track where samples are drawn from, and this may be an ability that 4.5-month-old infants lack. Perhaps the 6-month-old infants were able to scan the scene and extract the relevant information for making generalizations whereas the 4.5-month-olds were not yet able to hone in on the most pertinent components of a scene to make an accurate probabilistic inference. Infants at this age may not realize that it is necessary to attend to the source from which a sample is drawn in order to make accurate generalizations. Future experiments are needed to explore this possibility more directly. If these inferential abilities only come online at around 6 months of age, they may not be responsible for the acquisition of the domain knowledge we see in very young infants (e.g. Baillargeon, 2008).

However, the jury is still out on this since it is not clear if the current methodology is the best way to uncover such competence in infants younger than 6 months.

In sum, these new findings provide strong support for rudimentary probabilistic inference in infants as young as 6 months of age. These experiments challenge the view that it is not until at least 4 years of age that children are capable of making such inferences. These initial findings raise many interesting questions about early inductive learning abilities. In the next section, we consider two of them in some detail: how sophisticated is this ability in infants? In particular, do infants understand the difference between random sampling and nonrandom sampling, a critical component of probabilistic inference? Can infants integrate domain knowledge in their probabilistic computations, a critical question in understanding the nature of these learning mechanisms?

## 2.2. Integrating Domain-Specific Constraints on the Sampling Process

Probabilistic inferences are often only valid if we assume random sampling. In the experiments presented in the previous section, it is assumed that infants were reasoning based on the principle of random sampling. However, the inferences that infants make should be quite different if the experimenter does not remove a sample at random but instead removes a sample to illustrate a goal or preference for particular objects or to teach the learner something about a subset of the objects. In cases where the agent is not drawing out objects at random, the sample should likely reflect the agent's goals and not necessarily the composition of the distribution. Are infants sensitive to some of the cues that indicate either random or nonrandom sampling?

Additionally, recall that the motivation for examining probabilistic inference in infancy was to reveal whether or not probabilistic inference is a viable domain-general inductive inference mechanism that can be used to acquire domain knowledge. If computations that involve probability are meant to be part of a domain-general learning mechanism that can support the accumulation of domain knowledge, these computations should be integrated with domain knowledge early on. Thus, the following experiments examine whether or not infants can integrate domain knowledge with probabilistic inference early in infancy. When infants make probabilistic computations, do they do so in a purely bottom–up, data-driven way, making automatic inferences about populations based on samples and vice versa? Or, is this a top-down process, in which human learners can integrate their substantive domain knowledge in order to influence the output of their probabilistic computations?

### 2.2.1. Integrating Psychological Constraints with Probabilistic Inference

Xu and Denison (2009) designed a study to address whether or not preverbal infants make one of the key assumptions necessary for correct probabilistic inference—random sampling—and if this assumption can be overturned in light of relevant evidence; 11-month-old infants were tested in an experiment similar in design to Xu and Garcia (2008). Infants were assigned to one of three conditions in which two variables pertaining to an agent drawing samples from a box were manipulated. The first variable manipulated was whether or not an experimenter demonstrated a goal for obtaining particular colored Ping-Pong balls. Thus, infants in a *random sampling* condition saw that the experimenter did not have a specific goal for obtaining a particular color of balls but infants in *nonrandom sampling* and *blindfolding* conditions saw that the experimenter had a goal for collecting, for example, white Ping-Pong balls rather than red balls. The second variable that was manipulated was whether or not the experimenter had visual access to the population from which she was sampling during test trials. In the random sampling condition, the experimenter turned her head and closed her eyes during sampling; in the nonrandom sampling condition, the experimenter looked into the box during sampling; and in the blindfolding condition, the experimenter was blindfolded during sampling. The experimenter always drew out alternating samples of either five white or five red balls from the large covered box that was revealed to contain a large population of mostly red balls.

Infants in the random sampling condition provided a looking pattern that replicated Xu and Garcia (2008); they looked longer when the five white ball samples was drawn from the mostly red box as this sample was less probable than the five red ball samples. Infants in the nonrandom sampling condition looked longer at the five red ball samples as this sample was incongruent with the experimenter's goal. Thus, the infants in the nonrandom sampling condition made inferences based on the experimenter's goals, even though this goal conflicted with the base rate of balls in the population box. Finally, infants in the blindfolding condition looked longer at the five white ball samples. These infants apparently realized that, although the experimenter expressed a goal for obtaining white balls, she could not act on this goal because her visual access was blocked, and thus, she was forced to draw a random sample. Overall, infants in this experiment flexibly took into account sampling conditions and integrated substantive domain knowledge about agents into probabilistic inference: If a person has a specific goal and has the means (i.e. visual access) to act on that goal, infants expect sampling behavior to reflect that agent's goals. On the other hand, if a person has a goal but lacks control over their sampling choices due to blocked visual access, they assume that the sample should reflect the distribution.

Adding to the literature on infants' abilities to consider the sampling process in probabilistic inference, Gweon, Tenenbaum, and Schulz (2010) examined whether or not 15-month-old infants can use probabilistic data to make accurate object property generalizations. In their study, infants in one condition saw a box containing a large population of rubber balls in a 4:1 blue to yellow ratio and infants in a second condition saw a population with the opposite ratio. For all infants, the experimenter removed three blue balls from the box and demonstrated that they had the property of squeaking. The question is, does the infant think that the yellow balls should also squeak? The experimenter gave a yellow ball to the infant and then measured how persistent the infant was in trying to make the yellow ball squeak. They found that infants in the *mostly blue population* condition were more likely to think that the yellow balls should squeak than infants in the *mostly yellow population* condition. This is because infants correctly inferred that the sample was more likely to have been intentionally removed to reveal a property specific to blue balls in the case where the blue balls were in the minority, but balls might have been drawn randomly in the case where blue balls were in the majority. That is, in the former case, the experimenter appeared to be sampling to demonstrate that the blue balls had a special property, but in the latter case, she was likely sampling from the entire contents of the box and so she was not intentionally demonstrating that only the blue balls had the special property.

The results of these two studies suggest that 11- and 15-month-old infants use both their knowledge about agents and their probabilistic inference capabilities in probabilistic reasoning and property induction tasks. Infants were able to make generalizations based either on the probability of obtaining particular samples based on the contents of a population or on psychological constraints placed on the person removing the samples.

### 2.2.2. Integrating Physical Constraints in Probabilistic Inference

In addition to providing evidence for sensitivity to sampling conditions, infants' performance in the previous experiments highlights a sophisticated ability to integrate domain knowledge regarding agents in probabilistic inference. Parallel results—in fact, even more complex and nuanced—have been found in the domain of naive physics in four studies.

The following experiments shed light on two important questions about infants' probabilistic inference abilities: First, they provide evidence for integration between probabilistic reasoning and substantive domain knowledge in a second domain. The development of naive physics in infancy has been heavily studied over the past 30 years. Research suggests that infants possess a wealth of knowledge about the typical behavior of physical objects: They understand basic principles, realizing that objects behave in accord with the core principle of persistence—which includes concepts such as solidity, continuity, cohesion, and boundedness (Baillargeon & Carey, in press; Spelke, Breinlinger, Macomber, & Jacobson, 1992; Spelke, Phillips, & Woodward, 1995). Additionally, as infants' knowledge of naive physics progresses within the second half of the first year, they apply these core principles in increasingly sophisticated ways when reasoning about complex physical events such as occlusion, covering, support, and containment (see Baillargeon, 2008; Baillargeon & Carey, in press, for reviews). Thus, the domain of naive physics appears a good place to examine more complex abilities that infants might have for integrating knowledge in probabilistic inference.

Second, the following experiments on probabilistic inference and naive physics help to elucidate the strategy that infants might use to make probabilistic inferences. One possibility, consistent with all of the findings demonstrated thus far, is that infants make true, analytically valid probability computations or estimations when faced with random sampling events in these tasks. A second possibility is that infants might employ a reasoning heuristic to make these inferences, such as the representativeness heuristic. The representativeness heuristic, in the context of these infant experiments would simply translate to: "if a random sampling event is encountered, I expect the distribution of the sample to reflect the distribution of the population in terms of perceptual features." Thus, infants might either be making quite sophisticated probabilistic inferences or they might be using a mental shortcut to quickly assess the likely contents of a population based on a sample (or vice versa). As with all heuristics, if infants are using the representativeness heuristic to make judgments in these tasks, they should make some predictable errors in cases where this heuristic breaks down and does not provide a correct probabilistic estimation. The following experiments begin to tease apart these two possibilities.

The first piece of evidence to suggest that infants can integrate their knowledge regarding the behavior of physical objects with probabilistic inference comes from the lottery machine experiments conducted by Teglas et al. (2007), reviewed above. Recall that infants used distributional information to infer that one of the more numerous yellow objects was more likely to exit the machine on a single draw than the blue object. Infants in a second experiment were shown that a physical barrier existed inside the machine and that the three yellow objects were placed above the barrier and the single blue object was placed below. This second group of infants used their knowledge of naive physics, rather than distributional information to reason that the blue object was now the more probable object to exit the machine as objects cannot pass through solid barriers. These results suggest that 12-month-old infants can appropriately use either probability information or their knowledge of naive physics when making an inference about the likely outcome of an event.

In Teglas et al. (2007) and Xu and Denison (2009), infants were able to assess when to use ratio information and when to use domain-specific knowledge regarding naive physics or naive psychology to make an inference. These abilities are impressive as infants used very subtle cues—the presence or absence of a physical barrier and an agent's perceptual access to a scene—to infer whether or not they should compute probabilities or instead make a judgment using physical or psychological knowledge, respectively. However, these experiments did not require infants to fully *integrate* domain-specific knowledge in statistical inference—that is, infants were required to use one knowledge source or the other but not both simultaneously.

Using a paradigm similar to Xu and Garcia (2008) and Xu and Denison (2009), Denison and Xu (2010a) tested whether or not 11-month-old infants can integrate their knowledge of cohesion—the fact that objects do not spontaneously merge together or break apart—to exclude a portion of objects in a population from their probability computations. This experiment had two conditions, a *movable* condition and a *nonmovable* condition. In the nonmovable condition, infants were shown through a variety of demonstration trials that green balls with Velcro strips have the property of

getting stuck to the insides of boxes and containers. Following demonstrations, on test trials, infants watched an experimenter sample four yellow
and one red balls or four red and one yellow balls, on alternating trials, from
a box containing a 5:4:1 ratio of green to red to yellow balls. Infants looked
longer at the 4:1 yellow to red ball samples than the 4:1 red to yellow ball
samples. These infants appeared to apply the constraint that green balls stick
to boxes, rendering them unavailable for sampling. They then presumably
computed probabilities over the remaining sets of balls, reasoning that
obtaining the 4:1 yellow to red ball samples from the 5:4:1 green to red to
yellow population was less probable than the 4:1 red to yellow ball samples.
Furthermore, another group of 11-month-old infants were tested in
a movable condition, during which they were not shown that green balls
with Velcro were stuck inside boxes. These infants looked for the same (and
relatively long) amounts of time at the two samples on test trials. This finding
suggests that when two samples are both highly unlikely to be drawn
randomly from a population, infants are not capable of discriminating which
is less likely as both appear to violate their expectations. This rules out the
potential alternative interpretation of the looking pattern of infants in the
nonmovable condition, suggesting that they did not ignore the physical
constraint and simply compute which of two extremely low probability
events was more probable, rather they applied the constraint and computed
over remaining sets of balls.

Teglas et al. (2011) recently tested an even more challenging ability for
integration in 12-month-old infants, using the lottery machine paradigm to
assess whether infants could integrate spatiotemporal information in probabilistic inference. To make an inference about which color object was most
likely to exit the chute in this experiment, infants were required to integrate
the ratio of three yellow to one blue objects with two pieces of spatiotemporal information, which were systematically varied across infants: the
duration of occlusion before an object exited the chute (i.e. the objects were
occluded for 0, 1, or 2 s) and the physical arrangement of the objects in the
machine (i.e. the relative proximity of the yellow objects vs. the blue object
to the chute at time of occlusion). Remarkably, infants' looking times in this
experiment were of a graded nature, suggesting that they correctly integrated spatiotemporal information with the number of objects of each type.
Essentially, as occlusion time was varied from brief to relatively long, infants
placed less importance on proximity to the chute and more importance on
the ratio of blue to yellow objects and vice versa. This experiment suggests
that infants can put together information about the interaction of the

physical arrangement of objects, occlusion time, and the ratio of objects when making a prediction about a future event. This finding adds to the evidence in favor of infants' ability to combine probability information with substantive domain knowledge.

Findings from Denison and Xu (2010a) and Teglas et al. (2011) suggest that infants can integrate knowledge of naive physics in probabilistic inference. However, neither of these experiments definitively demonstrates that infants can use domain knowledge to adjust the base rate of populations when making probabilistic inferences. Evidence demonstrating that infants use physical knowledge to alter the base rates of a population to make probabilistic inferences would provide strong support for the claim that infants' probability computations and domain-specific knowledge are truly integrated. In addition, requiring infants to fully integrate their knowledge of naive physics may allow for an empirical test of whether infants make probability computations in these tasks or instead use a version of the representativeness heuristic. To be clear about the distinction between these alternatives, the representativeness heuristic states that, when one attempts to infer whether an object, person, or event belongs to or is an exemplar of a particular category, that object should have similar surface features to that category in general (Tversky & Kahneman, 1974). It is straightforward to see how this heuristic could apply to the infant probabilistic inference experiments reviewed here; infants could simply use the representativeness heuristic to judge whether a sample is perceptually similar to a population to make a quick inference about the likelihood of a particular outcome. As in the case of adult reasoning, this heuristic often serves as a useful shortcut but it does not always result in correct inferences as its use often results in biased judgments.

Although the results from Denison and Xu (2010a) can be interpreted as an argument against the use of this heuristic, an alternative interpretation of infant performance that includes representativeness is also plausible. Adults can select attention to up to three sets of elements within a large array (e.g. Alvarez & Cavanagh, 2004; Halberda, Sires, & Feigenson, 2006), and infants in this experiment may have selected attention to two of the sets in the population box—the red and yellow balls—filtering out the green balls and then simply compared the perceptual features of the population box to the samples to make judgments.

In a recent series of experiments, Denison, Trikutam, and Xu (2012) used a design similar to Denison and Xu (2010a) to directly address the question of whether infants rely on probability computations or representativeness in these tasks. The manipulation required infants to rapidly learn either a probabilistic physical constraint in one experiment or a deterministic constraint in a second experiment and apply it in probabilistic inference. Infants in these experiments saw two sets of Ping-Pong balls—red balls with no distinctive markings and green balls with Velcro strips. Although all the green balls were identical in appearance, the data given to the infants on demonstration trials were varied across the two experiments to illustrate that the physical property of movability applied probabilistically to the green balls in the first experiment (c. 80% of the balls were immovable from boxes) and deterministically to the set in the second experiment (all green balls were immovable). In both experiments, the test trials consisted of a large closed box being placed on stage and an experimenter removing, on alternating trials, samples consisting of four green and one red balls or four red and one green balls. The population revealed in the box contained a 3:1 ratio of green to red balls.

In the *Probabilistic Constraint* experiment, if infants realize that the majority of green balls get stuck in boxes, and integrate this with the distribution of balls in the box, they should think the 4:1 green to red ball samples unlikely and unexpected, looking longer at it regardless of the fact that this sample looks nearly identical to the population. This is because most of the green balls but not all are unavailable for sampling. If infants cannot identify and integrate the constraint, or if they apply the representativeness heuristic when attending to the final outcomes, they should find the 4:1 red to green ball samples unexpected and look longer at it as this would be judged to be unlikely in both these cases. In the *Deterministic Constraint* experiment, infants should reason that both samples are unlikely, given the demonstration trials they observed (see Fig. 2.2 for a representation of the predictions).

Infants in the Probabilistic Constraint experiment looked longer at the 4:1 green to red ball samples than the 4:1 red to green ball samples. This suggests that infants were able to integrate a stochastic physical constraint rule in probabilistic inference, using the physical constraint placed on a subset of green balls to adjust the base rate of balls available for sampling in their probabilistic computations. Thus, infants in this experiment appeared to rely on true probability computations to make judgments, not falling pray to the representativeness heuristic to make quick, but in this case incorrect, judgments. Infants in the Deterministic Constraint experiment looked about equally at the two outcomes, suggesting that they found both samples unexpected, given that no green balls were available for sampling.

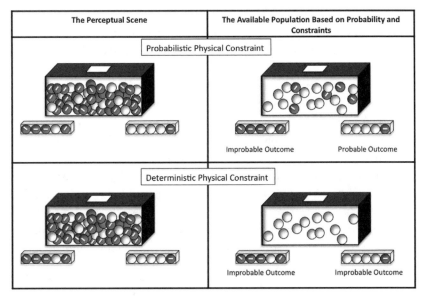

**Figure 2.2** Predictions for the test trials in the Probabilistic and Deterministic Constraint experiments. *From Denison, Trikutum, and Xu (2012).*

Collectively, the findings from these four studies suggest a surprisingly complex ability to make probabilistic inferences that require integration of naive physics by the end of the first year. Infants are capable of discerning whether they should rely on distributional information or physical constraints when making inferences about the likely outcome of future events (Teglas et al., 2007). They can also integrate predictions from distributional information and predictions from spatiotemporal information when making these inferences (Teglas et al., 2011). Finally, infants appear to rely on accurate probabilistic computations and not representativeness when constraints imposed by naive physics are used to alter the base rate of a probability computation (Denison & Xu, 2010a; Denison et al., 2012).

### 2.2.3. Summary of Infants' Abilities to Integrate Constraints

The results of the experiments reported in this section suggest that infants can integrate probabilistic inference with substantive domain knowledge when making judgments about the likely outcomes of future events. Infants flexibly use either their knowledge of agents and physical object properties or distributional information in the populations and samples, or both simultaneously to make inferences, suggesting that early probabilistic computations are integrated with substantive domain knowledge. Together, these findings demonstrate that probability computations in infancy do not unfold automatically. When faced with a situation in which infants must make generalizations from samples to populations, they make these computations by considering potential constraints that might be placed on the generative process. This integration with domain knowledge suggests that probabilistic inference is a good candidate for use in a domain-general inductive inference mechanism that could help build early emerging domain knowledge.

While infants learn a great deal through observing other people's actions, they also use their own actions as a means for learning, through activities such as object manipulation, play, and search. In the following section, we discuss recent work that explores whether or not infants can use their probabilistic computations to guide prediction and action in a choice task.

## 2.3. Infants Use Probability Calculations to Make Predictions That Guide Their Actions

So far, almost all the experiments we have reviewed employ the VOE method with infants. One ambiguity in using looking-time methods is that it is difficult to assess whether or not infants can make predictions about the likely outcome of events or if they can only judge the events post hoc. A second ambiguity is that the interpretation of looking-time data can be controversial, as lower level interpretations of the findings are often plausible, as opposed to rich interpretations regarding conceptual knowledge. Because of these ambiguities and because looking time is by nature an indirect measure of conceptual knowledge (Aslin, 2007), the following experiments serve to provide converging evidence of probabilistic inference in infancy using a novel methodology. Furthermore, the experiments detailed below will also tease apart one final important confound in all the previously discussed experiments. In all cases examined thus far, infants could rely on a simple heuristic that compares absolute quantities: if the lottery machine has three blue objects and one yellow object, it is more probable to get a blue one on a single random draw because three is more than one (Teglas et al., 2007, 2011); if one box has 40 green and 10 red balls and the other has 10 green and 40 red balls, then it is more probable to get a green ball from the first box than the second on a random draw because 40 is more than 10. A true understanding of probability is based on proportions since probability is an intensive quantity (Bryant & Nunes, 2012). For example, if one gumball machine contains 12 pink and many candies of other colors and the other 12 pink and a few candies of other colors, even though the number of pink gumballs is the same in the two machines, it is the proportion of pink ones in each jar that determines which one is more likely to yield a pink one—the one you want—when you insert a quarter into a machine. The experiments that follow present infants with versions of this question, providing the first unequivocal test of probabilistic reasoning based on proportion in infancy.

The general procedure used in the following experiments was modeled after a methodology created by Feigenson, Carey, and Hauser (2002). Infants begin by completing a preference trial, during which the experimenter shows the infant two objects—one attractive pink lollipop, decorated with silver sparkles and stars and one unadorned black lollipop. These objects are placed about a meter apart on the floor and the infant is allowed to crawl or walk toward the lollipop of their choice and this is considered their preference. Most infants (but not all) prefer the pink lollipop during this trial. Next infants complete a test trial. The experimenter brings out two large transparent jars each containing different distributions of pink and black lollipops. The ratios of pink:black lollipops differ depending on the experiment but, in general, one jar always has a more favorable ratio of the infants' preferred to nonpreferred (or in one experiment, neutral) lollipops. After showing infants these two populations, the experimenter places covers over the populations and then removes, one at a time, a single lollipop from each population, doing so in such a way that the infant can see that a single object is being drawn, indicated by the single lollipop stick, but the color of that object is always occluded by the experimenter's hand. Each of these lollipops is then placed in separate cups with covers and infants are permitted to crawl or walk toward and search in a cup of their choice. If infants understand that the population with a more favorable ratio of preferred to nonpreferred objects is most likely to yield a preferred object on a single draw, they should search in the location from which a sample from this jar is placed (see Fig. 2.3).

In the first experiment, 10- to 12-month-old infants were tested in a procedure with complementary 3:1 populations of pink and black lollipops, with the number of preferred lollipops for each individual infant controlled across populations. Infants were first given a preference trial between a black and a pink lollipop. Then they completed a test trial with populations that were based on their individual preferences: If the infant

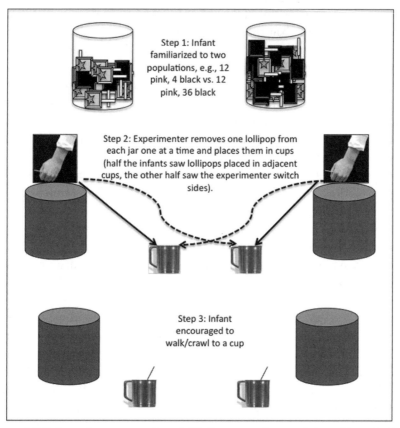

**Figure 2.3** Schematic representation of all lollipop experiments. *Adapted from Denison and Xu (2010b).* For color version of this figure, the reader is referred to the online version of this book.

preferred a pink lollipop, he/she saw one population containing a 12:4 ratio of pink to black lollipops and a second population containing a 12:36 ratio of pink to black lollipops; if the infant preferred a black lollipop, he/she saw populations with the opposite ratios. Thus, the number of preferred or *target* lollipops was equated across populations and the number of nonpreferred lollipops was varied to alter the proportions. This experiment requires that infants reason about the difference in proportion of target objects between the two competing populations and not just the absolute quantity of target objects compared across each population. Thus, if infants search based on comparisons of absolute quantity of target objects, they should perform at chance in this experiment. If they instead make their choices based on the comparison of the two proportions across populations, they should search in the location containing a sample from the 12:4 preferred to nonpreferred lollipops. Infants in this experiment searched in the 12:4 location more often than would be expected by chance.

When absolute quantity of target objects is equated across populations, infants make a judgment based on proportions, suggesting that when they are prevented from making an inference based on quantity, they correctly use proportional information to make a judgment. However, this does not inform us as to how infants would make judgments if absolute quantity and proportional information were in conflict. In a second experiment, infants were shown one population with a ratio of 16:4 preferred to nonpreferred lollipops and a second population with a ratio of 24:96 preferred to non-preferred lollipops. If infants rely on a quantity heuristic in this experiment, they should search in the location with a sample from the 24:96 population as 24 target items is greater than 16 target items. If they instead correctly make judgments based on comparisons of proportions of preferred to nonpreferred lollipops, they should search in the location with a sample from the 16:4 population as this is more likely to yield a preferred object. Infants in this experiment used comparisons of proportional information and not absolute quantity as they searched in the 16:4 location at higher than chance levels. Thus, even when infants could use a quantity heuristic, they instead use proportional information to make a more accurate probabilistic inference.

Although these two experiments suggest that infants are unlikely to be using a quantity heuristic to compare absolute numbers of target objects to make probabilistic inferences, one additional confound remains. It is possible that infants use a different quantity heuristic to guide their search. Infants could use comparisons of absolute quantities of nonpreferred objects to make inferences by avoiding nonpreferred items in all the experiments discussed so far. That is, in the previous two experiments, the cup with the higher probability of containing a preferred lollipop always coincided with a population containing a lower absolute number of nonpreferred lollipops. Thus, a third experiment was designed such that infants could not use comparisons of absolute quantity of either preferred or nonpreferred lolli-pops to make judgments. This experiment involved two additional exper-imental phases, a familiarization phase at the beginning of the experiment and a posttest at the conclusion. First, infants were briefly familiarized to three different lollipops: pink, green, and black. During the preference phase, infants again chose between a decorated pink lollipop and a plain black lollipop. On test trials, the infants saw populations with containers of pink, black, and green lollipops, with the pink and black being either the preferred or nonpreferred object (according to the individual infant's preference trial) and the green lollipops serving as neutral objects. The distributions consisted of a ratio of 8:12:2 preferred to nonpreferred to neutral lollipops versus a ratio of 8:8:64 preferred to nonpreferred to neutral lollipops. In this case, if infants are motivated by increasing their likelihood of obtaining a preferred lollipop, and they achieve this based on comparisons of proportions, they should choose the one lollipop drawn from the 8:12:2 population as this population is more likely to yield a preferred lollipop than the 8:8:64 population (8/22 vs. 8/80). If infants are instead motivated by *avoiding* nonpreferred lollipops, either based on comparisons of absolute quantity (8 vs.12) or proportions (12/22 vs. 8/80), they should choose the lollipop drawn from the 8:8:64 population. Finally, if infants make choices based on comparisons of absolute quantity of preferred lollipops across populations (8 vs. 8), they should perform at chance. Infants should only make the inference to search in the location containing a sample from the 8:12:2 location if they are a) motivated by increasing the probability of obtaining a preferred lollipop and b) reasoning based on comparisons of proportions of preferred lollipops to all other lollipops across the populations ($8/22 = 0.36$ vs. $8/80 = 0.10$). On the test trial, the experimenter did not allow infants to see inside the cup that they chose, and the experiment concluded with a final posttest. In this posttest, the preference trial was repeated (with sides of the lollipops counterbalanced) to ensure that infants did in fact continue to prefer the same lollipop that they originally chose.

Infants in this experiment chose the sample from the 8:12:2 population more often than would be expected by chance. Thus, infants appear to use proportional information and not comparisons of absolute quantities of either preferred or nonpreferred objects to guide their choices in this task. Additionally, over 90% of infants continued to prefer the lollipop that they had originally chosen on the preference posttest. Together, the results of these three experiments demonstrate that infants can accurately navigate the world by using probabilistic computations to guide their search for desired objects. This ability to reason based on proportions, rather than absolute quantities, is the hallmark of true probabilistic inference.

## 2.4. Summary and Discussion of the Infant Empirical Work

We have reviewed three bodies of research suggesting that infants engage in probabilistic inference. In the experiments investigating rudimentary probabilistic inference in infancy, we see that infants as young as 6 months can make basic generalizations from samples to populations and vice versa with large numbers of objects (Denison et al., in press; Xu & Garcia, 2008). It is also true that infants can make judgments about the likely outcome of a single sampling event when the population is known, with numbers of objects within the limits of object tracking (Teglas et al., 2007). Beyond this, infants can integrate distributional information with substantive domain knowledge (Denison & Xu, 2010a; Denison et al., in preparation; Gweon et al., 2010; Teglas et al., 2011; Xu & Denison, 2009); 11- and 15-month-old infants can flexibly use either psychological and physical knowledge or probability information to make inferences in contexts that involve sampling from a distribution. They can also fully integrate knowledge of naive physics in probabilistic inference, relying on accurate probability computations and not representativeness when these two inference strategies conflict. Finally, the experiments examining single-event probabilistic inference in a choice task reveals three additional pieces of evidence in favor of infants' abilities to make probabilistic inferences: infants can use probability information to guide search and to fulfill their own desires, and they do not do this by making comparisons of absolute quantities but rather by accurately computing and comparing proportions within and across populations.

## 3. IMPLICATIONS AND CONCLUSIONS

The evidence reviewed above in support of probabilistic inference in young infants suggests that human learners may have an intuitive notion of probability. This ability may provide the foundation for inductive inference across a variety of domains beginning early in development. Thus, the evidence reviewed here suggests that infants, beginning at least by 6 months, possess one of the key prerequisite abilities for an inductive inference mechanism based on the principles of rational Bayesian inference. Infants' capacity to go beyond the data given to make generalizations from samples to populations and vice versa helps to reveal how it is that young children are so proficient at learning from limited data.

One important question left open is whether infants are computing probabilities over discrete, individual objects or over continuous regions of color. In studies on numerical reasoning, researchers carefully disentangle whether infants or nonhuman animals use discrete (e.g. number of elements in a visual–spatial array or number of sounds in a sequence) or continuous quantities (e.g. the total area covered by all the elements in a visual–spatial array or the total duration of a sound sequence) in their computations. This, of course, is because only evidence for the former would constitute evidence for representations of number (Brannon, Abbott, & Lutz, 2004; Lipton & Spelke, 2003; Xu & Spelke, 2000). Estimating probabilities is interestingly different: one can estimate proportions using either discrete or continuous quantities. For example, if there are about four red balls in a jar of about 20 total, the proportion of red ones is 0.2 and if I make a single random draw from the jar, the probability of drawing a red one is also 0.2. Likewise, if the length of a straight line is about the length of my hand and the red part of the line is about the length of my middle finger, the proportion of red in the full segment is about 0.4. If I drop a small object on the line, the probability of it landing on the red segment is about 0.4. Even though current experiments cannot disentangle these two possibilities, it does not detract from the finding that infants can compute probabilities. Additionally, it seems more likely that infants in most of these experiments were reasoning about the proportions of individual objects and not continuous quantities, given much evidence suggesting that young infants can reason about discrete objects but not continuous quantities (e.g. Feigenson, Carey, & Spelke, 2002; Huntley-Fenner, Carey, & Solimando, 2002; Rosenberg & Carey, 2009, though see Hespos, Ferry, & Rips, 2009). Take, for example, the experiment suggesting that infants can integrate both probabilistic and deterministic physical constraints in probabilistic inference. Much of infants' knowledge of naive physics, including the understanding of cohesion, does not translate to continuous arrays like piles of sand (Spelke & Born, 1993). Thus, it seems unlikely that infants would be able to integrate such a rule in their probability computations if they were not computing over objects. Regardless, future studies should investigate whether infants are able to compute probabilities using both discrete and continuous variables. In fact, some evidence suggests that older children perform better at proportional reasoning when dealing with continuous rather than discrete quantities (Boyer, Levine & Huttenlocher, 2008; Jeong, Levine, & Huttenlocher, 2007; Spinillo & Bryant, 1999). It is an open question as to whether or not infants would perform better with one stimuli type or the other.

The work on infant probabilistic reasoning reported here has implications for the large body of literature investigating rational inference in human adults, adding to a growing body of research suggesting that human reasoning may not be as irrational as was once thought (Chater & Oaksford, 2008; Gigerenzer, 2000; Gigerenzer & Gaissmaier, 2011; Griffiths &

Tenenbaum, 2006; Tenenbaum, Kemp, Griffiths, & Goodman, 2011). In the classic experiments by Tversky and Kahneman (1974, 1981) examining adult reasoning, they found that people often use mental shortcuts such as the availability heuristic or the representativeness heuristic to make judgments under uncertainty and that use of these heuristics often result in biased, incorrect inferences. The findings reported in the infant experiments here suggest that infants do not begin by relying on representativeness or similarity heuristics in making probabilistic inferences in cases where accurate analytical reasoning and heuristic reasoning should produce conflicting results. According to these findings, the use of heuristics may be a later-developing phenomenon—the accumulation of factual knowledge may be the source of these heuristics and they may indeed provide useful shortcuts in real-life situations (Kokis et al., 2002). Further exploration of heuristic reasoning in infancy and early childhood is needed to investigate whether or not young learners can rely on heuristics under appropriate circumstances to increase efficiency when a full analysis of probabilities is not required.

## 4. FUTURE DIRECTIONS

We have reviewed a growing body of evidence suggesting that sophisticated probabilistic inference abilities are present early in infancy. Future work with infants should continue to focus on a number of questions left open from the experiments reported here. First, future studies should continue to explore the age at which this ability comes online. Are infants younger than 6 months really incapable of making inferences between samples and populations or might a different task reveal competence at earlier ages? If infants younger than 6 months cannot compute or estimate probabilities, this will surely have implications for the kind of learning that could possibly take place within the first 6 months and for how the ability to make probabilistic inferences comes to be.

Second, future work should explore whether or not infants can use sampling information to acquire new knowledge early in infancy in domains such as naive physics and psychology. The work reported here suggests that the ability to compute probabilities is integrated with substantive domain knowledge early on in infancy. If making generalizations from samples to populations is truly a mechanism for learning or a prerequisite to inductive inference in infancy, the next step is to examine whether young infants can use sampling information to learn a new rule in a specific domain. For example, infants should be able to use the information gained from observing a small number of instances of physical events to make generalizations that allow them to establish rules in naive physics that they have not yet acquired. Recent work suggests that older infants and preschoolers are capable of using sampling information to infer that an agent has a preference for a particular object (Kushnir, Xu, & Wellman, 2010; Ma & Xu, 2011). It remains to be seen if younger infants can use sampling information to make similar inferences.

Finally, probabilistic inference may be linked to the two known systems used for quantitative reasoning throughout the lifespan. That is, in the experiments that examine probabilistic inference with large populations and multiobject samples (e.g. Xu & Garcia, 2008), approximate numerosities are likely provided by the analog magnitude system to establish ratio information. In the lottery machine experiments, object files, which can be used to track quantity, are likely involved in allowing infants to recognize which of two object types is more numerous in each set, allowing an estimate of which object type is most likely to be sampled on a random draw. If these two systems for reasoning about quantity provide the input to probabilistic computations, predictable limits should be encountered in probabilistic reasoning, mirroring those found in numerical reasoning (see Feigenson, Dehaene, & Spelke, 2004). It will be interesting to examine how numerical reasoning interacts with probabilistic inference in future studies.

In conclusion, the empirical work reviewed in this chapter reveals that notions of probability and randomness are available to children far earlier in development than was first posited. The picture of the young child's probability concept has changed dramatically over the past 60 years as researchers have revealed competences in infants that were not initially credited to children until they reached the first or second grade.

The broad finding that infants can make generalizations from samples to populations provides important insight into classic debates concerning the initial cognitive state of the human infant and the learning mechanisms that are available to support conceptual change. The empirical results reviewed in this chapter indicate that probabilistic inference may be an innate learning mechanism that is the foundation for later learning, and such domain-general learning mechanisms may give rise to domain-specific knowledge (Teglas et al., 2007; Xu & Griffiths, 2011). Future work will not only explore further the nature and limits of early probabilistic reasoning but also how this kind of learning mechanism may be used to construct new concepts and new knowledge.

# REFERENCES

Acredolo, C., O'Connor, J., Banks, L., & Horobin, K. (1989). Children's ability to make probability estimates: skills revealed through application of Anderson's functional measurement methodology. *Child Development, 60,* 933–945.

Alvarez, G. A., & Cavanagh, P. (2004). The capacity of visual short-term memory is set both by visual information load and by number of objects. *Psychological Science, 15*(2), 106–111.

Aslin, R. N. (2007). What's in a look? *Developmental Science, 10,* 48–53.

Aslin, R., Saffran, J., & Newport, E. (1998). Computation of conditional probability statistics by 8-month-old infants. *Psychological Science, 9,* 321–324.

Baillargeon, R. (2008). Innate ideas revisited: for a principle of persistence in infants' physical reasoning. *Perspectives on Psychological Science, 3*(1), 2–13.

Baillargeon, R., & Carey, S. (in press). Core cognition and beyond: the acquisition of physical and numerical knowledge. In S. Pauen & M. Bornstein (Eds.), Early childhood development and later achievement. London: Cambridge University Press.

Boyer, T. W., Levine, S. C., & Huttenlocher, J. (2008). Development of proportional reasoning: where young children go wrong. *Developmental Psychology, 33*(5), 1478–1490.

Brannon, E. M., Abbott, S., & Lutz, D. J. (2004). Number bias for the discrimination of large visual sets in infancy. *Cognition, 93,* B59–B68.

Bryant, P., & Nunes, T. (2012). *Children's understanding of probability: A literature review.* London, England: Nuffield Foundation.

Bulf, H., Johnson, S. P., & Valenza, E. (2011). Visual statistical learning in the newborn infant. *Cognition, 121,* 127–132.

Carey, S. (2009). *The origins of concepts.* New York, New York: Oxford University Press.

Cesana-Arlotti, N., Teglas, E., & Bonatti, L. (2012). The probable and the possible at 12 months: intuitive reasoning about the uncertain future. In T. Kushnir, & F. Xu (Eds.), *Advances in child development and behavior: Rational constructivism in cognitive development.* Waltham, MA: Academic Press.

Chater, N., & Oaksford, M. (Eds.). (2008). *The probabilistic mind: Prospects for Bayesian cognitive science.* Oxford: Oxford University Press.

Colunga, E., & Smith, L. B. (2005). From the lexicon to expectations about kinds: the role of associative learning. *Psychological Review, 112,* 347–382.

Denison, S., & Xu, F. (2010a). Integrating physical constraints in statistical inference by 11-month-old infants. *Cognitive Science, 34,* 885–908.

Denison, S., & Xu, F. (2010b). Twelve- to 14-month-old infants can predict single-event probability with large set sizes. *Developmental Science, 13,* 798–803.

Denison, S. Reed, C., & Xu, F. (2012). Probabilistic reasoning in very young infants: evidence from 4.5- and 6-month-olds. *Developmental Psychology*, April 2012, doi:10.1037/a00282728.

Denison, S., Trikutum, P. & Xu, F. (June, 2012). Integrating physical constraints in probabilistic inference. Paper presentation at the International Conference on Infant Studies. Minneapolis, MInnesota.

Dewar, K., & Xu, F. (2010). Induction, overhypothesis, and the origin of abstract knowledge: evidence from 9-month-old infants. *Psychological Science, 21,* 1871–1877.

Elman, J., Bates, E., Johnson, M., Karmiloff-Smith, A., Paris, D., & Plunkett, K. (1996). *Rethinking innateness: A connectionist perspective on development.* Cambridge, MA: The MIT Press.

Feigenson, L., Carey, S., & Hauser, M. (2002). The representations underlying infants' choice of more: object files versus analog magnitudes. *Psychological Science, 13*(2), 150–156.

Feigenson, L., Carey, S., & Spelke, E. S. (2002). Infants' discrimination of number vs. continuous extent. *Cognitive Psychology, 44*, 33–66.

Feigenson, L., Dehaene, S., & Spelke, E. (2004). Core systems of number. *Trends in Cognitive Sciences, 8*(7), 307–314.

Gigerenzer, G. (2000). *Adaptive thinking: Rationality in the real world.* New York: Oxford University Press.

Gigerenzer, G., & Gaissmaier, W. (2011). Heuristic decision making. *Annual Review of Psychology, 62*, 451–482.

Girotto, V., & Gonzalez, M. (2008). Children's understanding of posterior probability. *Cognition, 106*(1), 325–344.

Goldberg, S. (1966). Probability judgments of preschool children: task conditions and performance. *Child Development, 37*, 158–167.

Gonzalez, M., & Girotto, V. (2011). Combinatorics and probability: six- to ten-year-olds reliably predict whether a relation will occur. *Cognition, 120*, 372–379.

Griffiths, T. L., & Tenenbaum, J. B. (2006). Optimal predictions in everyday cognition. *Psychological Science, 17*, 767–773.

Griffiths, T. L., Chater, N., Kemp, C., Perfors, A., & Tenenbaum, J. B. (2010). Probabilistic models of cognition: exploring representations and inductive biases. *Trends in Cognitive Sciences, 14*, 357–364.

Gweon, H., Tenenbaum, J. B., & Schulz, L. E. (2010). Infants consider both the sample and the sampling process in inductive generalization. *Proceedings of the National Academy of Sciences of the United States of America, 107*(20), 9066–9071.

Halberda, J., Sires, S., & Feigenson, L. (2006). Multiple spatially overlapping sets can be enumerated in parallel. *Psychological Science, 17*(7), 572–576.

Hespos, S. J., Ferry, A., & Rips, L. (2009). Five-month-old infants have different expectations for solids and substances. *Psychological Science, 20*(5), 603–611.

Hirschfeld, L., & Gelman, S. (1994). *Mapping the mind: domain specificity in cognition and culture.* New York: Cambridge University Press.

Huntley-Fenner, G., Carey, S., & Solimando, A. (2002). Objects are individuals but stuff doesn't count: perceived rigidity and cohesiveness influence infants' representations of small groups of discrete entities. *Cognition, 85*, 203–221.

Jeong, Y., Levine, S. C., & Huttenlocher, J. (2007). The development of proportional reasoning: effect of continuous versus discrete quantities. *Journal of Cognition and Development, 8*(2), 237–256.

Kemp, C., Perfors, A., & Tenenbaum, J. B. (2007). Learning overhypotheses with hierarchical Bayesian models. *Developmental Science, 10*(3), 307–321.

Kirkham, N., Slemmer, J., & Johnson, S. (2002). Visual statistical learning in infancy: evidence of a domain general learning mechanism. *Cognition, 83*, B35–B42.

Kokis, J., Macpherson, R., Toplak, M., West, R. F., & Stanovich, K. E. (2002). Heuristic and analytic processing: age trends and associations with cognitive ability and cognitive styles. *Journal of Experimental Child Psychology, 83*, 26–52.

Kushnir, T., Xu, F., & Wellman, H. (2010). Young children use statistical sampling to infer the preferences of others. *Psychological Science, 21*, 1134–1140.

Lipton, J., & Spelke, E. (2003). Origins of number sense: large number discrimination in 6-month-old infants. *Psychological Science, 14*, 396–401.

Ma, L., & Xu, F. (2011). Young children's use of statistical sampling evidence to infer the subjectivity of preferences. *Cognition, 120*(3), 403–411.

Markman, E. M. (1989). *Categorization and naming in children.* Cambridge, MA: MIT Press.

Maye, J., Werker, J., & Gerken, L. (2002). Infant sensitivity to distributional information can affect phonetic discrimination. *Cognition, 82*(3), B101–B111.

Piaget, J., & Inhelder, B. (1975). *The origin of the idea of chance in children.* London, England: Routledge and Kegan Paul. (Translation of original work 1951).

Regier, T. (2003). Emergent constraints on word-learning: a computational review. *Trends in Cognitive Science, 7*, 263–268.

Regier, T. (2005). The emergence of words: attentional learning in form and meaning. *Cognitive Science, 29*, 819–866.

Reyna, V. F., & Brainerd, C. J. (1994). The origins of probability judgment: a review of data and theories. In G. Wright, & P. Ayton (Eds.), *Subjective probability* (pp. 239–272). New York, New York: Wiley.

Rosenberg, R. & Carey, S. Infants' representations of material entities. In B. H. Hood & L. R. Santos (Eds.), *The origins of object knowledge*. Oxford: Oxford University Press.

Saffran, J., Aslin, R., & Newport, E. (1996). Statistical learning by 8-month-old infants. *Science, 274*, 1926–2928.

Schlottmann, A., & Anderson, N. H. (1994). Children's judgments of expected value. *Developmental Psychology, 30*(1), 56–66.

Siskind, J. M. (1996). A computational study of cross-situational techniques for learning word-to-meaning mappings. *Cognition, 61*, 39–91.

Smith, L. B. (2001). How domain-general processes may create domain-specific biases. In M. Bowerman, & S. Levinson (Eds.), *Language acquisition and conceptual development* (pp. 101–131). London: Cambridge University Press.

Smith, L. B., Jones, S. S., Landau, B., Gershkoff-Stowe, L., & Samuelson, L. (2002). Object name learning provides on-the-job training for attention. *Psychological Science, 13*, 13–19.

Sobel, D. M., & Kirkham, N. Z. (2006). Blickets and babies: the development of causal reasoning in toddlers and infants. *Developmental Psychology, 42*, 1103–1115.

Sobel, D. M., & Kirkham, N. Z. (2007). Bayes nets and babies: infants' developing statistical reasoning abilities and their representation of causal knowledge. *Developmental Science, 10*(3), 298–306.

Spelke, E. S. (1994). Initial knowledge: six suggestions. *Cognition, 50*(1), 431–445.

Spelke, E. S., & Born, W. S. (1983). *Visual perception of objects by three-month-old infants.* Unpublished manuscript.

Spelke, E., Breinlinger, K., Macomber, J., & Jacobson, K. (1992). Origins of knowledge. *Psychological Review, 99*(4), 605–632.

Spelke, E. S., Phillips, A., & Woodward, A. L. (1995). Infants' knowledge of object motion and human action. In D. Sperber, D. Premack, & A. J. Premack (Eds.), *Causal cognition: A multidisciplinary debate* (pp. 44–78). Oxford: Clarendon Press.

Spinillo, A. G., & Bryant, P. (1999). Proportional reasoning in young children: part-part comparisons about continuous and discontinuous quantity. *Mathematical Cognition, 5*(2), 181–197.

Teglas, E., Vul, E., Girotto, V., Gonzalez, M., Tenenbaum, J. B., & Bonatti, L. L. (2011). Pure reasoning in 12-month-old infants as probabilistic inference. *Science, 332*, 1054–1058.

Teglas, E., Girotto, V., Gonzalez, M., & Bonatti, L. L. (2007). Intuitions of probabilities shape expectations about the future at 12 months and beyond. *Proceedings of the National Academy of Sciences of the United States of America, 104*, 19156–19159.

Tenenbaum, J. B., Kemp, C., Griffiths, T. L., & Goodman, N. D. (2011). How to grow a mind: statistics, structure, and abstraction. *Science, 331*, 1279–1285.

Tversky, A., & Kahneman, D. (1981). The framing of decisions and the psychology of choice. *Science, 211*(4481), 453–458.

Tversky, A., & Kahneman, D. (1974). Judgment under uncertainty: Heuristics and biases. *Science, 185*(4157), 1124–1131.

Xu, F. (2007). Rational statistical inference and cognitive development. In P. Carruthers, S. Laurence, & S. Stich (Eds.), *The innate mind: foundations and the future*, Vol. 3 (pp. 199–215). New York, New York: Oxford University Press.

Xu, F., & Denison, S. (2009). Statistical inference and sensitivity to sampling in 11-month-old infants. *Cognition, 112*, 97–104.

Xu, F., Dewar, K., & Perfors, A. (2009). Induction, overhypotheses, and the shape bias: some arguments and evidence for rational constructivism. In B. M. Hood, & L. Santos (Eds.), *The origins of object knowledge* (pp. 263–284). New York, New York: Oxford University Press.

Xu, F., & Garcia, V. (2008). Intuitive statistics by 8-month-old infants. *Proceedings of the National Academy of Sciences of the United States of America, 105*, 5012–5015.

Xu, F., & Griffiths, T. L. (2011). Probabilistic models of cognitive development: towards a rational constructivist approach to the study of learning and development. *Cognition, 120*(3), 299–301.

Xu, F., & Spelke, E. S. (2000). Large number discrimination in 6-month-old infants. *Cognition, 74*, B1–B11.

Yost, P. A., Siegel, A. E., & Andrews, J. M. (1962). Nonverbal probability judgments by young children. *Child Development, 33*, 769–780.

# CHAPTER THREE

# Reasoning about Instrumental and Communicative Agency in Human Infancy

## György Gergely*[,1] and Pierre Jacob**

*Department of Cognitive Science, Cognitive Development Center, Central European University, 1015 Budapest, Hattyú u. 14, Hungary
**Institut Jean Nicod, UMR 8129, CNRS/ENS/EHESS, ecole Normale Supérieure, 29, rue d'Ulm, 75005 Paris, France
[1]Corresponding author: E-mail: gergelygy@ceu.hu

## Contents

## Abstract

Theoretical rationality and practical rationality are, respectively, properties of an individual's belief system and decision system. While reasoning about instrumental actions complies with practical rationality, understanding communicative actions complies with the principle of relevance. Section 2 reviews the evidence showing that young infants can reason about an agent's instrumental action by representing her subjective motivations and the episodic contents of her epistemic states (including false beliefs). Section 3 reviews the evidence showing special sensitivity in young human infants to some ostensive behavioral signals encoding an agent's communicative intention. We also address the puzzle of imitative learning of novel means actions by 1-year olds and argue that it can be resolved only by assuming that the infant construes the model's demonstration as a communicative, not an instrumental, action. Section 4 reviews the evidence for natural pedagogy, a species-unique social communicative learning mechanism that exploits human infants' receptivity to ostensive–communicative signals and enables infants to acquire kind-wide generalizations from the nonverbal demonstrations of communicative agents. We argue that the essentialist bias that has been shown to be involved in children's concepts of natural kinds also applies to infants' concepts of artifacts. We further examine how natural pedagogy may also boost inductive learning in human infancy.

# 1. INTRODUCTION: THE MANY FACES OF HUMAN REASON

Philosophers draw a basic distinction between practical and theoretical rationality. While practical rationality is a property of an agent's decision system, theoretical rationality is a property of an agent's belief system. An agent's decision is rational if it selects an action that is likely to maximize the agent's utility function (i.e. the agent's desire or preference about, e.g., commodities) in light of her beliefs (about, e.g., the prices of commodities). A belief is deemed rational if its content stands in deductive and/or inductive relations to the contents of other accepted beliefs, which warrant its acceptance (cf. Davidson, 1980, 2004 and Dennett, 1978, 1987).

The human ability to entertain *reasons for believing*, however, is not restricted to theoretical rationality so defined. Humans evolved species-specific ways to acquire beliefs based on *communication* (Recanati, 2001; Sperber, 1997). As a result, they are unique in their evolved capacity to create, transmit, maintain, and stabilize across generations an increasing body of cultural beliefs ranging over technology, social traditions, history, religion, the law, the arts, science, and mathematics. To simplify, humans can accept a culturally transmitted belief for one of two reasons (or both): its *content* or the *authority* of its source (Sperber, 1997, 2001, Sperber et al., 2010).

To accept a culturally transmitted belief on account of its content is to grasp its deductive relations to the contents of other beliefs and/or its inductive relations to the evidence, in accordance with the principles of theoretical rationality. A culturally transmitted belief can also be accepted on account of the authority of its source. We shall call *deferential* such culturally transmitted beliefs (Recanati, 1997). A deferential belief can be accepted either because its source is known, remembered, and judged to be reliable (or trustworthy) or because it is taken to be shared common knowledge among members of one's community. When accepted by deference to the authority of its source, the content of a culturally transmitted belief may to a large extent remain cognitively *opaque* to the individual who subscribes to it. In some cases, further cognitive processing may make the opaque content of a deferentially acquired belief more transparent by tracking its inferential connections to the contents of other beliefs and to later acquired relevant evidence. In human adult social life, deferential beliefs are ubiquitous, and so are beliefs whose contents may remain cognitively opaque to the individuals who accept them throughout their lives.

Since it is based on trust (i.e. judgments about the authority of their source), the acceptance of deferential beliefs is not entirely groundless or unjustified. To accept a deferential belief is to fulfill the informative intention of an agent who performed a communicative action in accordance with the principle of *relevance* (cf. Sperber & Wilson, 1995, 2012; Wilson & Sperber, 2002). On the approach by Sperber & Wilson (1995), a piece of communicated information is said to be more relevant than a competing one if by attending to the former the addressee of the communicative act can derive more cognitive benefit than by attending to the latter. The cognitive benefit of a relevant piece of information is in turn conceptualized in terms of a trade-off between the cognitive effects produced by the novel implications arrived at and the cognitive effort devoted to processing these implications.

From birth on, human infants are exposed to two basic kinds of intentional agency: *instrumental* and *communicative* agency (Gergely, 2010). While they observe agents perform instrumental actions as a means to satisfy their subjective desires and preferences, infants are also the recipients of the actions of agents with communicative intentions whose fulfillment depends on their being recognized by their addressees. Making sense of an agent's noncommunicative instrumental action requires the third-personal ascription to the agent of a goal or intention to achieve some desirable outcome in light of her beliefs about the world, in accordance with the principle of practical rationality (Dennett, 1987; Fodor, 1992). By contrast, when being addressed by an agent's ostensive–communicative action, infants must make sense of the agent's communicative intention (Csibra, 2010) to enable inferences to the intended meaning, in accordance with the principle of relevance (Sperber & Wilson, 1995).

Recent evidence shows that surprisingly even before the end of their first year, human infants are able to ascribe and represent both the subjective motivations and episodic (or context bound) contents of epistemic states of agents of instrumental actions. There is also significant evidence indicating that preverbal infants are uniquely receptive to ostensive signals by which communicative agents make manifest that they have a communicative

intention. Further evidence suggests that this evolved receptivity to ostensive signals supports an early social learning mechanism (*natural pedagogy*),
whereby preverbal infants are able to interpret some of the nonverbal deictic
actions and demonstrations of communicative agents as referring to a kind
and displaying a property of the kind. If so, then infants can form some
general deferential beliefs about the world from their interpretation of
communicative agency. Clearly, this social learning mechanism could not
work unless the reception of ostensive signals induced an attitude of basic
epistemic trust in the infants toward their communicative informants
(Gergely, Egyed, & Király, 2007).

We have two main goals in this chapter. Our first goal is to argue that
much of early social cognition of human infants is shaped by the different
types of inferential constraints imposed by the principle of practical rationality and the principle of relevance on interpreting acts of instrumental and
communicative agency. Our second goal is to examine the scope and limits
of the trust-based communicative learning system of natural pedagogy that
underlies the fast intergenerational transfer of knowledge about the world by
enabling human infants to acquire deferential beliefs about kinds. We shall
argue that natural pedagogy enables infants to fast learn generalizations about
artifact kinds. As natural pedagogy is a social cultural learning mechanism
based on the principle of relevance, it may interact in subtle and complex
ways with the inductive and statistical principles, which underlie belief
formation based on theoretical rationality (cf. Section 4.3).

In Section 2, we review recent developmental evidence showing that
young infants can represent the subjective motivations and episodic belief
contents of agents of instrumental actions. In Section 3, we review the
evidence showing the early sensitivity of human infants to ostensive–
communicative agency and we address the puzzle of imitative learning. In
Section 4, we review evidence showing the early presence of natural
pedagogy as a means to learn about artifact and social kinds in human infancy.
We further examine the question of how relevance-based processes at work
in natural pedagogy combine with principles of statistical inference that have
recently been shown to help young children learn about causal relationships.

## 2. THIRD-PERSONAL REASONING ABOUT INSTRUMENTAL AGENCY IN YOUNG INFANTS

Following the famous paper by Premack and Woodruff (1978), much
developmental research on the ontogenesis of theory of mind in human

children has focused on the emerging ability to pass the standard elicited false belief task (cf. Wimmer & Perner, 1983). In this task, a participant who knows the location of some object is asked to predict where an agent with a false belief about its location will look for it. Two decades of intense developmental research showed that not until they are in their fourth year are human children able to pass the standard false belief tasks (Wellman, Cross, & Watson, 2001).

However, starting with the seminal paper by Onishi and Baillargeon (2005), recent evidence has shown that before they reach their second year, human infants are able to ascribe epistemic states, including false beliefs, to others (see Caron, 2009; Gergely, 2010; Jacob, in press, for reviews). Exploitation of the violation-of-expectation and other paradigms has enabled developmental psychologists to reduce some of the cognitive demands that passing the standard false belief tasks required (such as language understanding, pragmatic competence and inhibitory control). Furthermore, the picture supported by our review of the recent developmental evidence is hard to square with the widespread assumption that infants start with a "simple" desire psychology before they can move to a belief–desire psychology, as was suggested by Wellman (1990) and others.

## 2.1. Ascribing Motivational States to Others

There is evidence that before the end of their first year, infants can track others' subjective motivations. In a series of studies applying violation-of-expectation looking paradigms, Csibra, Gergely, and collaborators have shown that infants look longer when an agent selects a less efficient instead of a more efficient action alternative as a means to achieving a goal state in the presence of some situational constraint (Csibra, Bíró, Koós, & Gergely, 2003; Csibra, Gergely, Bíró, Koós, & Brockbank, 1999; Gergely, Nádasdy, Csibra, & Bíró, 1995). Overall, the findings of Csibra and Gergely strongly suggest that infants interpret observed instrumental actions by evaluating the *efficiency* of the agent's action as a means to achieve a goal, in light of relevant situational constraints (cf. Gergely & Csibra, 2003).

In a two-object choice paradigm, Woodward (1998) showed young infants a human hand repeatedly reach for and contact one of two toys. After the locations of the toys were switched, infants looked longer when the hand reached for the new toy at the old location rather than the old toy at the new location. No such differential looking was found, however, in infants between 6 and 12 months of age if either the agent was a rigid rod or the hand approach was unfamiliar as it ended by contacting the object with the back-of-the-hand (Woodward, 1998, 1999). Woodward interpreted her findings as evidence that young infants ascribe goals only to agents whose perceptual appearance bears a strong similarity to their own bodily appearance and whose movements they can map onto their own motor repertoire. This view of goal ascription has been argued to support the widely shared assumption that, unlike inferring others' epistemic belief states, the ascription of motivational states (such as goals, intentions, or emotions) to an agent can be accomplished by cognitively less demanding automatic and noninferential processes of direct perceptual–motor matching and motor resonance induced by the perceptual similarity of the observed behaviors of others to familiar action schemes already present in the infant's motor repertoire (cf. Meltzoff, 2005; Tomasello, 1999; Rizzolatti & Craighero, 2004).

Further findings have shown, however, that neither of these conditions is necessary nor sufficient for ascribing a goal to an agent by young infants. First, Király, Jovanovic, Aschersleben, Prinz, and Gergely (2003) and Jovanovic et al. (2007) have shown that if 8- and even 6-month olds are first familiarized with one of two toys being repeatedly not only contacted but also slightly displaced by the unfamiliar back-of-the-hand action, then they look longer in the test if the back-of-the-hand action displaces a novel toy at the old location instead of the same toy now at the new location. Second, Biro and Leslie (2007) have shown that if 6-month olds see a rigid rod approach one of two targets from several different angles, repeatedly pick it up by contacting three different parts of the toy (cues of equifinal variations of behavior), then they look longer if the rod performs the same action on a different target at the old location rather than on the same target at a different location. Luo and Baillargeon (2005) report a study in which 5-month olds first saw a self-propelled box repeatedly move to and contact one of two targets. During the test phase, 5-month olds looked longer when the box moved to contact the novel object at the old location rather than the old target at the new location.

These (and other) findings show that motor familiarity with the agent's action and perceptual similarity between the agent's and the infants' bodies are not necessary for interpreting an agent's action as goal directed. This is in line with studies by Gergely and Csibra (2003) that demonstrated early goal attribution even to animated abstract two-dimensional (2D) figures as long as they showed efficient goal approach. In fact, 6- and 9-month olds can interpret a wide range of unfamiliar objects (such as a robot, a box, abstract

2D figures, and even biologically impossible hand actions, see Southgate, Johnson, & Csibra, 2008) as goal-directed agents as long as their behaviors exhibit rational sensitivity to relevant changes in their situational constraints by modifying their target-directed approach contingently and in a justifiable manner obeying the principle of rational (efficient) action (Bíró & Leslie, 2007; Csibra, 2008; Csibra et al., 1999, 2003; Gergely, 2003; Gergely et al., 1995; Hernik & Southgate, 2012; Kamewari, Kato, Kanda, Ishiguro, & Hiraki, 2005; Luo & Baillargeon, 2005; Wagner & Carey, 2005; Southgate et al., 2008). Furthermore, the evidence shows that if in Woodward's object-choice paradigm during the familiarization trials infants see an agent repeatedly move to the same object in the absence of a competing target, then they do not look longer when the agent moves to contact a novel target at the old location rather than the old object at a new location in the test trials (Luo & Baillargeon, 2005; Hernik & Southgate, 2012). This strongly suggests that what Woodward's object–choice paradigm tests is not goal-ascription proper but instead the ascription of a contrastive preference (i.e. a subjective disposition) to the agent (cf. Gergely, 2010; Jacob, 2012, for further analysis).

In sum, the evidence reviewed above reveals that very young infants ascribe goals and preferences to the agent of an instrumental action. In accordance with the principle of practical rationality, the agent should be expected to execute an instrumental action that will increase the probability that she will satisfy her motivation in light of what she believes. The question arises: do infants expect an agent to perform an instrumental action, not only as a function of her motivations but also as a function of what she believes?

## 2.2. Ascribing Epistemic States to Others

In the last decade, a number of studies have offered new evidence that before the end of their second year, human infants are able not only to ascribe motivations to others but also to represent the contents of others' false beliefs and to ascribe to others false beliefs that they do not share. For example, Buttelmann, Carpenter, and Tomasello (2009) found that the helping behavior of 25- and 18-month olds is reliably modulated by their ability to ascribe to the agent of an unsuccessful attempt at retrieving a toy from one of two boxes either a true or a false belief about the location of the toy (for further evidence showing false belief ascription by 24- and 18-month olds, see Southgate, Senju, & Csibra, 2007 and Southgate, Chevallier, & Csibra, 2010).

Further important studies using the nonverbal violation-of-expectation looking paradigm provided initial evidence that even 13- and 15-month olds are able to ascribe false beliefs to others. In the experiment by Onishi and Baillargeon (2005), 15-month olds saw an agent motivated to find a toy and reach for it in either a green or a yellow box. Onishi and Baillargeon compared four conditions, in each of which the infants knew the true location of the toy: the infants could see the agent reach for the toy in either the green or the yellow box while the toy was either in that location or not. They found that infants looked reliably longer when they saw the agent reach for the toy either in the wrong location while she had a true belief about the toy's location or in the right location while she had a false belief. Surian, Caldi, and Sperber (2007) further reported that 13-month olds look longer at test trials in which an agent retrieves its preferred food when it is hidden from the agent's (but not the infant's) view by a high barrier than when it is visible to the agent and they also look longer when the food hidden from the agent's view by a barrier has been placed there in the agent's absence than in the agent's presence. Kovács, Téglás, and Endress (2010) provide further intriguing evidence that even 7-month olds automatically track and represent others' true and false beliefs.

Further evidence making use of the Woodward choice-based preference attribution paradigm suggests that even before the end of their first year, human infants modulate their ascription of preferences as a function of the content of the epistemic state ascribed to the agent. For example, in the familiarization trials, Luo and Baillargeon (2007) showed 12.5-month olds an agent repeatedly reach for the same object either when she knew that there was another object present or when she did not (while the two objects were visible to the infants all along). Infants looked longer when the agent selected the alternative object when it was made visible during the test phase, only if she had already known that there was another object present from having seen it put there earlier during the familiarization phase. Going one step further, Luo (2011) addressed the question whether 10-month olds would ascribe a preference to an agent when she *falsely believed* there to be either two objects or only one present. She found that 10-month olds did ascribe a preference to an agent if she mistakenly believed that two objects were present on the stage, while unbeknownst to her, a hand removed one of the objects from the side that was hidden from the agent's view but not from the infant's view. But they did not ascribe a preference to the agent when she knew that there was only one object present. Conversely, infants failed to ascribe a preference to the agent if she mistakenly believed that only one object was present on the stage, while unbeknownst to her, a human hand added on the stage a second object that was hidden from the agent's view, but not from the infants' view. Infants, however, did ascribe a preference to the agent when she knew that there were two objects present.

In all the scenarios previously reviewed showing that before the end of their first year human infants are able to ascribe false beliefs to an agent, the agent's action is directed toward some target and it depends on both the agent's epistemic state and her motivation. In the experiment by Onishi and Baillargeon (2005), the infants seem to take the agent's motivation to find an object as background information (from the familiarization trials) and they look longer in the test trials when the agent fails to act in accordance with the content of her true or false belief. Conversely, in the Woodward choice-based design exploited by Luo (2011), the infants seem to extract from the familiarization trials, as background information, the content of the agent's epistemic state as a condition for ascribing a preference to the agent and they look longer in the test trials only when the agent with a preference fails to act in accordance with it.

## 3. SECOND-PERSONAL UNDERSTANDING OF COMMUNICATIVE AGENCY IN YOUNG INFANTS

The evidence reviewed in Section 2 shows that young human infants can ascribe motivations and epistemic states to agents of instrumental action, in accordance with the principle of practical rationality. We now turn to developmental research demonstrating human infants' species-unique preparedness to recognize and interpret nonverbal *communicative actions* that are ostensively addressed to them. While a third-person observer expects an agent to execute an instrumental action in accordance with the principle of practical rationality, an addressee of an ostensive–communicative act expects the communicative agent to act in accordance with the principle of relevance (cf. Sperber & Wilson, 1995).

### 3.1. Preverbal Infants' Receptivity to Ostensive Referential Communication

Sperber and Wilson (1995) call *ostensive* stimuli the signals whereby an agent makes manifest to an addressee her communicative intention to manifest some new relevant information for the addressee (i.e. her informative intention). Right after birth, infants display species-specific sensitivity to, and preference for, some nonverbal ostensive behavioral signals, such as eye contact, infant-directed speech or motherese, and infant-contingent distal responsivity (see Csibra, 2010; Csibra & Gergely, 2009, for reviews).

Recent evidence shows that from very early on these ostensive signals generate a *referential expectation* in infants (Csibra & Gergely, 2006, 2009). Senju and Csibra (2008) report that 6-month olds followed an agent's gaze shift to one of two objects but only if it had been preceded by ostensive signals (either eye contact or infant-directed speech) addressed to the infant. In a study by Csibra and Volein (2008), after the agent produced ostensive signals, 12- and 8-month olds followed her gaze shift to one of two locations hidden from the infants' view by occluders. When the occluders were removed, an object was revealed either at the location where the agent had looked or at the other location. Infants at both ages looked longer at the empty location if the agent had looked at it than if she had not, showing that they expected the agent to look at a location occupied by a referent object rather than at an empty location. Furthermore, Deligianni, Senju, Gergely, and Csibra (2011) in an automated eye tracker-based study used an infant-induced contingent reactivity paradigm to demonstrate that 8-month olds gaze follow an unfamiliar object's bodily orientation response toward one of two targets, but only if the object had been reacting contingently before (producing self-propelled body movements such as tilting) to being looked at by the infant (see also Movellan & Watson, 2002; Johnson, Slaughter, & Carey, 1998, for similar results with 10- and 12-month olds).

Recent studies also provide converging evidence that when engaged in an ostensive–communicative interaction with an adult (such as joint play with objects), 12- and 18-month olds show early competence in drawing correct pragmatic inferences that enable them to identify the intended referent out of a number of alternative objects present when interpreting a communicator's ambiguous ostensive referential pointing gesture (e.g. Moll & Tomasello, 2004; Tomasello & Haberl, 2003). As shown by Southgate et al. (2010), in a communicative interactive context, 18-month olds can even correctly infer on pragmatic grounds the intended referent of another's false belief based pointing gesture. In this study, an adult ostensively engaged 18-month olds in a joint play activity with new toys. She placed the two novel unnamed objects in two separate boxes and then temporarily left the room. In her absence, a second experimenter switched the objects so that now they were each in opposite boxes. Shortly after, the first experimenter returned to continue their game apparently ignorant about the toys having been switched. Ostensively communicating to the infant, she pointed to one of the two (closed) boxes to request the baby to give her the toy from the box that she (falsely) believed to contain the intended object. In this communicative episodic context, infants were able to infer that the intended referent of the pointing gesture was not the object actually in the designated box, but the toy in the other box. Accordingly, they opened the *other* box (not the one the requester was pointing at) to give her the object that she meant to request by her false belief-based pointing gesture (cf. Buttelmann et al., 2009).

Furthermore, by the time they are 12-month-old, human infants are not only able to referentially understand another's communicative pointing but they also start to actively use ostensive referential pointing themselves to establish shared attention with the adult over a specific referent object to fulfill different types of communicative functions such as requesting the object from the adult (protoimperative pointing, see Bates, Camaioni, & Volterra, 1975), sharing with the adult their currently felt subjective motivational attitude toward the specific referent, such as liking and positive interest (proto-declarative pointing, see Liszkowski, Carpenter, Henning, Striano, & Tom-asello, 2004; Tomasello, Carpenter, & Liszkowski, 2007), or inquiring to receive new and relevant information about the novel object and its kind (protointerrogative pointing, see Begus & Southgate, 2012; Southgate, van Maanen, & Csibra, 2007; Kovács, Tauzin, Téglás, Csibra, & Gergely, 2012).

In sum, the evidence shows that human infants are prepared from the start to recognize nonverbal ostensive referential signals and action–demonstrations addressed to them as encoding another's communicative intention to manifest new information about the referent (the informative intention) that is relevant for the addressee. As Csibra (2010) has argued, very young infants might well be in a position similar to that of a foreign addressee of a verbal communicative act, who is unable to retrieve a speaker's informative intention for lack of understanding the meaning of the speaker's utterance. Nonetheless, the foreign addressee may well recognize being the target of the speaker's communicative intention on the basis of the speaker's ostensive behavior. Furthermore, ostensive signals to which preverbal human infants have been shown to be uniquely sensitive can plausibly be said to *code* the presence of an agent's communicative intention. If so, then little (if any) further work is left for preverbal infants to infer the presence of a speaker's communicative intention after receiving ostensive signals.

Finally, in all the studies reviewed above, the communicative interactions were cooperative actions involving shared goals of immediate episodic relevance. Infants were able in such contexts to disambiguate the referent of the communicator's nonverbal deictic referential action, even when the deictic gesture was based on false belief (about, e.g., the location of the intended referent). Crucially, in the episodic context of joint actions where communicator and addressee have shared goals and common knowledge about a restricted set of relevant familiar individual objects, nonverbal deictic pointing owes its referential success to the fact that it directs the other's attention to the particular intended referent by highlighting its *spatial location* (which is one of its typically transient and episodic properties). The fact that nonverbal deictic gestures are anchored in a socially shared episodic context seems to impose severe restrictions on their referential scope—a limitation emphasized by Tomasello (2008) when he points out that "the almost complete dependence of pointing on common ground between communicator and recipient is thus both its strength and its weakness" (pp. 202–203).

However, in apparent contrast to this assumption, a recent study by Egyed, Király, and Gergely (2012) demonstrates the special power of ostensive signals to induce a *nonepisodic* interpretation of a communicative agent's object-directed emotion gestures as conveying relevant information about motivational dispositional properties such as *preferences that are socially shared* and, as such, can be generalized and attributed to other agents who are not part of the shared episodic context. 18-month olds saw an adult agent display a positive and a negative object-directed facial–vocal emotional expression (liking vs. disgust), one directed toward a novel object on her left, the other toward another unfamiliar object on her right. In the ostensive–communicative condition, before displaying her object-directed emotional expressions, the agent first ostensively addressed the infant. In the noncommunicative demonstration context, the agent neither looked at nor talked to the infant before displaying her pair of object-directed emotion expressions. After the first agent left the room, a new agent came in and without looking at either object, she requested the infant to give her one of them. In the ostensive–communicative condition, but *not* in the noncommunicative observation condition, infants reliably gave to the second agent the object toward which the first experimenter had emoted positively. Finally, in the noncommunicative condition, infants reliably gave to the first agent the object that had been the target of her own positive emotional expression. In the latter case, the application of the principle of practical rationality to an object-directed action would require the ascription to the agent of a person-specific subjective motivational state of contrastive preference for one over the other of the two objects. Application of the principle of relevance triggered by the presence of ostensive cues, however, induced in infants the assumption that the relevance of the contrastive preference displayed toward the two objects *goes beyond the episodic situation* and demonstrates a socially shared dispositional property that can be relevantly *generalized* to other members of one's social group as well.

## 3.2. A Puzzle about Imitative Learning

A number of psychologists, including Tomasello and colleagues, have taken imitation to be a process that both complies with the principle of practical rationality and also underlies cultural learning, i.e. the intergenerational transmission of cultural knowledge (cf. Tomasello, 1996, 1999; Tomasello, Kruger, & Ratner, 1993; Tomasello, Carpenter, Call, Behne, & Moll, 2005; Buttelmann, Carpenter, Call, & Tomasello, 2007). In particular, Tomasello et al. (1993) have hypothesized that, unlike blind mimicry, *true* imitation requires the imitator to construe the agent's intention as a rational choice of an action plan, i.e. as an efficient means toward achieving her goal, in accordance with the principle of practical rationality. The question is: to what extent can the rational imitation model account for imitative learning, i.e. human children's ability to interpret and reproduce an agent's selection of some novel action as a means to achieving her goal. As Gergely, Bekkering, and Király (2002) have noticed, the question is made pressing by Meltzoff's (1988) study in which 14-month olds observed an adult model perform an unusual head action whereby she turned on a magic light box by leaning forward and applying her forehead to the box. Meltzoff (1988) reports that after a week delay, 67% of the infants who had watched it imitatively reproduced the agent's odd head action. On the face of it, this result is a puzzle for the rational imitation approach because the model's head action can hardly be evaluated as an efficient means to achieve the goal of turning the light on.

To address this puzzle, Gergely et al. (2002) had 14-month olds watch a model perform the odd head action as a means to switching on a light box in one of two contexts: in the hands–occupied context, the model first pretended that she was chilly, covered her shoulders with a blanket, and used her hands to hold the blanket around her shoulders, before demonstrating the odd head action. In the hands-free context, she also pretended to be chilly, covered her shoulders with a blanket, and tied a knot on it thereby freeing her hands, which she ostensibly placed unoccupied on the table, before demonstrating the odd head action. Gergely et al. (2002) found that while in the hands-free context, 69% of the children replicated the odd head action, in the hands-occupied condition, only 21% of them did. Instead, in the hands-occupied context, infants freely used their own hands. (For further confirmation of the influence of social communicative contexts on selective imitation in 12- and 14-month olds, cf. Buttelmann, Carpenter, Call, & Tomasello, 2008; Király, 2009; Király, Csibra, & Gergely, 2004; Király, Csibra, & Gergely, 2012, Király, Egyed, & Gergely, 2012; Schwier, van Maanen, Carpenter, & Tomasello, 2006; Zmyj, Daum, & Aschersleben, 2009.)

While the model's choice of the head action seems rational in the hands-occupied context, so does the infants' choice to (nonimitatively) emulate the agent's goal by selecting a more efficient means action available to them (whose hands were unoccupied). So far this is in accordance with the rational imitation model, which assumes "that infants take into account the constraints on the demonstrator—the reasons why she acted the way she did—as well as the constraints on themselves and then choose an action themselves rationally" (Buttelmann et al., 2008, p. 625).

But the puzzle is: why did the majority of infants reenact the experimenter's odd head action in the hands-free context when both the model and the infant could have used their own free hands and thereby select a more efficient means?[1] In answer to this question, Tomasello and colleagues have proposed a slightly different version of the rational imitation model: they have surmised that the more an agent's action is construed as displaying the *freedom* of the agent's choice, the more the infants are likely to reproduce the model's action. Arguably, the agent's selection of the head action as a means to switching on the light box reflects the infant's sensitivity to the agent's freedom of choice in the hands-free condition, where her decision to perform the odd head action was less constrained by the external circumstances than in the hands-occupied condition (cf. Buttelmann et al., 2007). On this version of the rational imitation model (as well as on the initial "rational imitation" hypothesis by Gergely et al., 2002), infants reproduced the agent's unexpected head action as a way of figuring (learning) what the agent's reason for his action was.

## 3.3. Solving the Puzzle about Imitative Learning

If, however, the agent's goal is to switch on the light, then there is no way that by performing the head action (rather than by using their own hands),

---

[1] In fact, in the hands-free context, all infants performed at least one (and typically more) nonimitative hand actions to emulate the goal by using their hand to touch the light box before reenacting the odd head action (cf. Gergely et al., 2002; Király, Csibra, & Gergely, 2012; Király, Egyed, & Gergely, 2012; Paulus, Hunnius, Vissers, & Bekkering, 2011).

an imitator could discover to what extent it is an efficient means to achieve the agent's goal, in accordance with the principle of practical rationality. Nor could performing the head action allow an imitator to discover to what extent the head action is a more efficient means to achieve the agent's goal in the hands-free than in the hands-occupied context. But infants imitated the head action far more often in the hands-free than in the hands-occupied context. Furthermore, as Gergely and Csibra (2005, 2006) have pointed out, no version of the rational imitation model could explain the later findings of Király, Csibra, & Gergely (2012; Király, Egyed, & Gergely, 2012; Király et al. 2004) showing that only when the head-touch actions are demonstrated by a communicative agent addressing the infants from a second-person perspective by ostensive referential gestures did infants selectively imitate the head action more in the hands-free than in the hands-occupied context. In fact, when infants observed a noncommunicative agent perform the head-touch actions in the hands-free condition, they tended not to reproduce the head action at all showing significantly less head-touch reenactment than in the corresponding hands-free context of the communicative demonstration condition.[2] Other studies also found that the presence of social communicative demonstration context exerts a powerful modulating effect on imitative reenactment inducing selective imitation in ostensive contexts with much reduced imitation of the same actions observed in third-person noncommunicative contexts (cf. Brugger, Lariviere, Mumme, & Bushnell, 2007; Király, 2009; Nielsen, 2006; Southgate, Chevallier, & Csibra, 2009).

Following Gergely and Csibra (2005, 2006) and Király, Csibra, & Gergely (2012; Király, Egyed, & Gergely, 2012; Király et al., 2004), we therefore suggest that the mistaken assumption made by advocates of the rational imitation model is that even when they are provided with ostensive cues, infants interpret the agent's head action as an instrumental action to be performed in accordance with the principle of practical rationality. If addressed by ostensive signals, infants do not stand to the agent's head action as third-personal observers of an instrumental action. Instead, the reception of ostensive cues automatically causes the infants to assume that the agent is performing a communicative action, and they interpret the agent's action demonstration from an addressee's second-personal perspective. As a result, they expect the communicative agent to demonstrate for them something

[2] This finding has recently been replicated using a modified procedure by Király, Egyed, & Gergely (2012), in response to a potential methodological criticism by Paulus et al. (2011).

novel and relevant to be reproduced, in accordance with the principle of relevance.

Following her production of ostensive cues, in the hands–occupied context, the model first demonstrated to the infants that her hands were occupied with holding the blanket covering her shoulders when she proceeded to perform the odd head action to illuminate the touch-sensitive lamp in front of her. What the infants therefore learnt from the model's head action was that the unfamiliar artifact on the table is a lamp that can be operated by contact and that they could (and ought to) turn on the lamp by making contact with it using an instrumental action appropriate for the purpose. But in the hands-free context, after having tied a knot on the blanket, the demonstrator conspicuously placed her now free hands at rest next to the touch-lamp calling the infants' attention to the relevance of the fact that her hands are now available for alternative instrumental use. What the infants therefore learnt from the model's head action was that they could (and ought to) turn on the light box by applying their head, instead of their hands. In brief, infants apparently interpreted the agent's ostensive signals as cues indicating a pedagogical context and so they learnt to perform the odd head action, thereby acquiring a deferential belief about the normative manner or social expectation as to how one "ought to" operate the touch lamp. This finding further suggests that the process whereby infants learnt to perform the odd head action was not based on the assumption that this action was the most efficient causal alternative to bring about the effect. Instead, they may have encoded the demonstrated head action as socially relevant shared knowledge about a normatively expected way of executing the skill.

## 4. ENDURING RELEVANCE AND RATIONALITY

Since relevance is a property of a communicative action, it must be recognized as such by the recipient of the communication to whom it is ostensively addressed (i.e. from a second-person perspective). Practical rationality is a property of an agent's decision to perform a particular instrumental action to achieve her episodic goal, in the most efficient manner available. This property is recognized by the interpreter observing the instrumental action from a third-person perspective inducing the expectation that the action chosen by the agent will be the most efficient one to enable her to fulfill her desire in the light of her beliefs. An agent's belief is taken to be theoretically rational when its content stands in deductive or inductive relations to the contents of other accepted beliefs, which warrant its acceptance. The warrant underlying the theoretical rationality of beliefs can also be computed from a third-person perspective. Inductive learning is the process whereby humans in general and human children in particular form new beliefs and update their older beliefs. In what follows, we shall examine novel evidence showing how an addressee's presumption of the relevance of an agent's communicative action can considerably support inductive learning in human infancy.

## 4.1. The Puzzle of Deictic Reference to Kinds

While experiments reviewed in Section 3.1 show that preverbal human infants are able to disambiguate the intended referents of deictic pointing in the episodic context of joint actions, further experiments indicate that the reception of ostensive signals can also prepare preverbal human infants to receive *nonepisodic* information about the referent of an agent's communicative action. The study by Egyed et al. (2012) on preference attribution discussed at the end of Section 3.1 above provided a first example of this phenomenon (cf. Gergely et al., 2007). Here, we shall review further recent studies showing that when ostensively cued in an appropriate nonfamiliar context, infants can interpret an agent's deictic referential action as intended to refer to a kind, not merely an individual. Since deictic reference performed by pointing by its very nature individuates its referent by highlighting its spatial position (which is a transient and episodic property of particular objects), this raises the puzzle of deictic reference to kinds.

In fact, the evidence suggests that the reception of ostensive signals can trigger in infants two broad kinds of expectation about an agent's subsequent nonverbal communicative action. In the context of a joint (cooperative or competitive) action, in which agents have a shared episodic goal and share common knowledge about a restricted set of familiar objects and the surrounding situational constraints, infants have been shown to expect a communicative agent to convey relevant episodic information (Tomasello, 2008). In such contexts, the reception of ostensive signals generates an expectation of *local* relevance: infants' expectation of local relevance enables them to determine the intended referent of the communicator's deictic referential act required for fulfilling the shared episodic goal. As the discussion of imitative learning showed, however, lacking the context of a shared episodic goal and a set of familiar objects, however, the reception of ostensive signals triggers a presumption of *enduring* relevance. As we shall now argue, when ostensively cued in the presence of novel unfamiliar objects, infants expect to be taught relevant nonepisodic information about kinds. They expect the communicator's referential action to apply to a kind (not an object) and her subsequent demonstration to display a nonepisodic (or enduring) property of the kind.

In a study by Yoon, Johnson, and Csibra (2008) about change detection in a communicative or a noncommunicative context, 9-month olds saw an object which was either the target of an agent's instrumental (noncommunicative) reaching action or was demonstrated by the agent's communicative act using referential pointing ostensively addressed to the infant. Then a screen came down to briefly occlude the object which either changed it's spatial position or its visual features before being revealed to the infant again. Infants looked longer at a change of the object's location than at a change of the object's visual features in the noncommunicative instrumental action condition but they showed the opposite looking pattern in the communicative action condition. Clearly, while a target's temporary location is relevant to predicting and explaining an agent's instrumental action directed to it, the visual features of the object highlighted by the ostensive referential pointing gesture are more likely to be nonepisodic properties relevant for reidentifying it under new circumstances, learning about its kind and classifying it under a sortal concept.

Years ago, Piaget (1954) reported the classical A–not–B *perseveration* error phenomenon whereby infants between 8 and 12 months are engaged in an episodic hide-and-search game in which an adult repeatedly hides a toy under one (A) of two opaque containers (A and B) in full view of the infant. After each hiding event, the infant is allowed to retrieve the object. During test trials where the demonstrator places the object repeatedly under container B, infants continue to perseveratively search for it under container A where it had been previously hidden. Topál, Gergely, Miklósi, Erdőhegyi, and Csibra (2008) compared three conditions. In the first communicative condition, 10-month olds received ostensive signals before and while the adult played the hide-and-search game. In the second noncommunicative condition, the agent presented the hiding actions without any ostensive signals directed to the infant. In the third nonsocial condition, the agent was hidden behind a curtain while her hands were baiting the containers, and therefore, she was not visible to the infants at all. Topál et al. (2008) report that 86% of the infants committed the A-not-B perseverative error in the communicative condition (replicating previous findings), but this error rate sharply dropped in the noncommunicative and the nonsocial conditions. Topál et al. (2008) argue that when they fall under the spell of ostensive–communicative signals, 10-month olds are fooled into misinterpreting the episodic hide-and-search game as being a communicative teaching demonstration about some nonepisodic property—exemplified by the manifested action—that relates the toy and one of a pair of containers spatially individuated by the demonstrator's deictic referential actions. In sum, while hiding events in the standard A-not-B task can be (and has been) interpreted as conveying episodic information about the referent's current location ("the target object is now under container A"), these results suggest that due to the presence of ostensive signals, infants interpreted them as communicative actions manifesting relevant information for them to acquire about some generalizable normative property of the referent kind (e.g. "Container A is where this (kind of) object belongs to/should be placed in/should be looked for", see also Topál, Gergely, Erdőhegyi, Csibra, & Miklósi, 2009).

While the evidence reviewed so far indicates that the presence of ostensive cues generates referential expectations in preverbal human infants, further evidence shows that ostensive signals also cause infants to expect a communicative agent's display of an object to refer to a *kind*. Futó, Téglás, Csibra, and Gergely (2010) exploited the object-individuation paradigm by Xu and Carey (1996) to investigate the ability of 10-month olds to represent objects in terms of their kinds. After infants were familiarized to seeing two distinct objects (e.g. a truck and a teddy bear) emerge one at a time from behind a screen and never simultaneously, the screen was removed, and infants either saw the two objects or only one. Xu and Carey (1996) reported that while 12-month olds looked longer when they saw only one object, 10-month olds looked equally at the two events. In other words, 10-month olds did not yet rely on feature-based information to individuate objects in this task. Further evidence showed that when each of the two objects were named by one of two distinct verbal labels when separately visible, even 9-month olds looked longer at the single object event than at the two objects event (Xu, 2002, 2005, 2007).

The goal of the three experiments by Futó et al. (2010) was to test whether communicative ostensive signals could play the same role as verbal labeling in enabling 10-month olds to rely on property information in an object-individuation task. In the first experiment, the selected objects were two novel artifacts, one with a handle and the other with a dial, and the relevant properties to be displayed by the agent's nonverbal communicative actions were kind-relevant functional properties. In the communicative function demonstration condition, before receiving two familiarization trials, 10-month olds were first ostensively greeted by infant-directed speech (while the artifacts were still hidden behind the screen). During the familiarization trials, the infants saw the agent, which was a human hand, separately display each artifact on either one or the other side of the screen and perform a different function demonstration on each of them: the hand pulled the handle on one artifact, which produced flashes of light as a result, or turned the dial on the other artifact, which produced a melodic sound effect. Finally, the hand pulled back each of the objects behind the screen. After two such familiarization trials, the infants received two test trials: while the first was identical to the familiarization trials, during the second, the hand removed the screen and revealed either both of the objects or only one. Infants looked reliably longer when only one object was revealed rather than two.

In a second experiment, Futó et al., (2010) removed one of two parameters: in the non-ostensive condition, infants heard a synthesized nonspeech sound transform of the original ostensive greeting in infant-directed speech before the familiarization trials. In the no-intervention condition, the hand that had pulled out the objects from behind the screen withdrew from sight without performing the function demonstration on them, and infants instead saw either the handle or the dial move by itself while the object was simultaneously emitting either light or sound. Infants looked equally long at the one-object and at the two-object events in the test trials in both the non-ostensive and the no-intervention conditions.

In a third experiment, Futó et al., (2010) reproduced the familiarization and test trials of the first experiment (with ostensive greeting and manual intervention present). However, instead of using two distinct novel artifacts, the very same single artifact was presented on each side, which, however, had two instead of just one manipulanda protruding from it (a handle and a dial). So the two different function demonstrations by the hand producing either the light or the sound effect were demonstrated on the same artifact in alternation, at either side of the screen. Infants looked longer in the test trials when they saw the same single object (with both the dial and the handle) than when they saw two distinct novel objects (neither of which they had seen during familiarization), one with only a handle and the other with only a dial on it.

In the first experiment, infants took the communicative agent to be referring to a kind of artifact and they interpreted the agent's subsequent manual demonstration of the function of the object to display a generic (nonepisodic) functional property of the kind in question. (This is the puzzle of deictic reference to kinds.) They must have further assumed that two distinct functional properties such as producing a light versus a sound upon manipulation could not serve at the same time as kind-defining properties of a single kind of artifact. As a result, they looked longer when they saw only one object rather than two in the test trials. In other words, if preceded by ostensive cues, then an agent's referential action and communicative demonstration were interpreted by the 10-month olds as manifesting kind-specifying functional properties leading them to infer the presence of *two* different artifact kinds that the referent objects must have belonged to.

In the second experiment, lack of ostensive cues failed to trigger the expectation that the agent's deictic demonstrative actions would make reference to kinds rather than referring to an individual object. So even though the hand demonstrated two different actions resulting in alternative effects on the two objects, infants did not interpret these demonstrations as referring to two separate artifact kinds. As a result, they looked equally long when seeing one versus two objects present behind the screen during the test. In the no-manual intervention condition, the handle and the dial on the artifacts were shown to move on their own simultaneously producing light versus sound. Here, infants could not interpret these contingent behaviors as functional properties, and so in spite of the preceding ostensive signals, they could not make sense of the agent's referential action as referring to a kind of artifact, in the absence of a subsequent manual action–demonstration that could have identified the predicated artifact function.

Furthermore, the third experiment suggests that the infants were so strongly cued toward interpreting the agent's communicative action as referring to a kind that when the agent demonstrated that a single artifact could produce both light and a sound, they were fooled into assuming that only two distinct kinds could exhibit two distinct functional properties. This is shown by the fact that they looked longer when seeing during test the single object that they had seen during the familiarization events than when seeing two novel objects whose features only partially matched those of the one seen during familiarization.

Assuming that infants are able to represent the content of a communicative intention (as we argued in Section 3.1 that they are), then they should expect the nonverbal action of a communicative agent to be relevant. Furthermore, what the above findings suggest is that, in the presence of ostensive signals, an agent's referential action and demonstration upon a novel object and/or property cue infants' expectation of relevance: infants expect the information conveyed by the communicative agent to be about enduring properties of an artifact *kind*. *Natural pedagogy* is the name given by

Csibra and Gergely (2009) to the social learning mechanism enabling infants to acquire kind-wide generalizations on the basis of their interpretation of the ostensive nonverbal referential actions and demonstrations of communicative agents. In the presence of ostensive signals, an agent's referential action and demonstration are interpreted as displaying the property of a kind (i.e. as teaching a kind-wide generalization).

Clearly, preverbal human infants have no means at their disposal for assessing the trustworthiness of their informants. Consequently, general deferential beliefs about kinds formed by preverbal human infants can only be based on blindly trusting their informants. New evidence suggests both that natural pedagogy enables preverbal human infants to acquire generalizations about kinds of artifacts and also that the essentialist bias documented in young children's concepts of natural kinds extends to their concepts of artifact kinds.

## 4.2. The Scope of Psychological Essentialism in Infancy

Essentialism is the idea that entities of various kinds have essential causal properties which are not directly observable but are responsible for the observable features of the entities that bear them. Psychological essentialism is the view accepted by many psychologists that essentialism underlies human children's conceptual development in various cognitive domains. The essential property is construed as a "causal placeholder" (Gopnik & Nazzi, 2003). While developmental psychologists have adduced much evidence for psychological essentialism in early childhood with respect to physical, chemical, and especially biological kinds (Gelman, 2003), it has been also argued that naive essentialism is likely to be domain specific being restricted to young children's natural kind concepts, and that it initially does not apply to their understanding of artifacts (e. g., Brandone & Gelman, 2009). But as we shall first argue in this section, very recent evidence suggests that preverbal infants are prone to interpret nonverbal referential actions in accordance with psychological essentialist assumptions about artifact kinds as well (Futó et al., 2010).

The findings by Futó et al., (2010) strongly suggest that preverbal infants can learn generalizations about artifact kinds from a sequence of nonverbal actions performed by a communicative agent. As philosophers and psychologists have emphasized, to categorize objects into *kinds* is to assume that they share some common unknown unobservable underlying properties that cause them to have superficial observable properties that can be perceptually detected. As a result, one should not expect the truth of a generalization about some property of a kind to be easily dismissed by negative evidence based on the superficial observable properties of objects falling under the relevant kind. This is exactly what a recent experiment with older children shows.

In a study by Butler and Markman (2012), 4-year olds were presented with 11 wooden blocks and taught their name, i.e. 'blicket'. Only 1 out of 11 blickets had a (nonvisible) magnetic tape on one end. Then the children were shown the novel property of the magnetic blicket: by applying the blicket with magnetic tape to paper clips, the experimenter picked up the paper clips, in three distinct conditions. In the pedagogical condition, the children were informed that they would be taught something novel and interesting before the magnetic property of the blicket was demonstrated. In the accidental condition, the experimenter accidentally dropped the magnetic blicket onto the paper clips. In the intentional condition, the experimenter deliberately placed the magnetic blicket onto the paper clips without, however, ostensively addressing the infants. In all three conditions, after her demonstration, the experimenter placed all 11 blickets on the table and encouraged the children to play with them. Butler and Markman (2012) found that children's persistence in exploring the magnetic property of blickets in the face of mounting negative evidence (that they themselves generated as they were trying out the rest of the non-magnetic blickets in front of them) was remarkably stronger in the pedagogical than in either the accidental or the intentional condition.

Arguably, this study shows that in the pedagogical condition (and only in this condition), children took the generalization about the magnetic property of blickets to have generic content, i.e. they took the demonstrated magnetic property of blickets to be a property of a kind of objects. If resistance to counterevidence is taken as a signature of the generic content of kind-wide generalizations, then one may interpret 10-month olds' perseveration in the A-not-B task investigated by Topál et al. (2008, 2009) as providing such evidence. In the ostensive–communicative condition of that study, the high rate of erroneous perseverative search under the (now empty) container A during the B-hiding trials did not decrease across the three B trials even though these provided clear cases of counterevidence. Infants may have interpreted the A-hiding demonstration as displaying a relevant property of the kind of action executed (placing the toys into container A) and thereby carrying social normative implications, which were violated but not modified by the B-hiding events. This signature of kind-wide generalizations seems also displayed by 14-month olds' selective imitative learning of novel means as demonstrated by Gergely et al. (2002).

In response to the ostensively demonstrated model's head action, the infants' strong inclination to reenact this opaque, odd, and apparently nonrational means action (in the hands-free context) was quite uninhibited by the availability of the negative evidence, which infants spontaneously produced by concomitantly performing hand actions that successfully turned the light box on in a more efficient way.

Leslie (2007) has argued that generics in natural languages ("birds fly"), which contain no explicitly encoded quantifiers, have peculiar semantic properties that make them strongly resistant to counterevidence and furthermore that humans are biased toward making kind-wide generalizations with such a peculiar generic content. Arguably, the causal essentialist construal of kinds can provide an explanation for why generalizations about kinds should not be easily dismissed by putative negative evidence based on the observable features of instances of kinds. In the case of natural kinds, for example, according to biological essentialism, it is in the biological nature of tigers to be striped, a tiger that fails to be striped is a defective tiger, but it is not a counterexample to the essentialist claim that being striped is caused by some unknown essential biological property of tigers (cf. Atran, 1990). While being striped (which is observable) is taken to be caused by some biological unobservable essential property of tigers, it is *not* itself an essential biological property of tigers. Conversely, being deprived of observable stripes is not counterevidence to the presumed presence of an underlying essential biological property that causes tigers to be striped in *normal* conditions.

What the evidence previously reviewed shows is that young children also make essentialist assumptions about *artifact* and *social* kinds. Furthermore, it also shows that preverbal human infants can learn generalizations about artifact and social kinds from the nonverbal actions of communicative agents. Nonverbal demonstrations seem well suited for conveying generic (nonepisodic) information about artifact kinds as well as some social kinds. For example, in the experiments by Futó et al., (2010), the two-step communicative action involved a pair of referential act and a demonstration whose function was to display the property predicated of the ostensively referred kind of artifact (e.g. produce either a melodic sound or a flash of light). Arguably, the essentialist construal of artifact and social kinds by preverbal human infants is promoted by their irresistible tendency to epistemically trust their communicative informants. Because they accept the information conveyed by communicative agents on trust, infants might assume not merely that the observable features of man-made tools and human actions and practices demonstrated to them are caused by some deep underlying essential properties, but that they *must* be so caused. Why should trustworthy informants take the trouble to display the properties of artifact and/or social kinds by means of their nonverbal communicative actions for infants' benefit if they did not thereby convey either the functional properties of *normal* (i.e. non-defective) artifacts or the *norms* with which the actions of human agents *ought* to comply? Furthermore, the ascription of functions to both natural and artifact kinds involves or carries *normality* assumptions. Just as it is the function of a normal mammalian heart to pump blood, it is also the function of a normal chair to afford the possibility of sitting on it. A mammalian heart that fails to pump blood is a defective heart whose biological function is to pump blood. Even if poorly designed (or damaged), a chair has the (intended) function to enable humans to sit on it.[3]

As emphasized by Csibra and Gergely (2006), human infants are borne into a world populated with man-made artefacts whose causal and functional properties as well as appropriate manner of use are epistemically larely opaque to them. This epistemic opacity may encourage infants to assume, in accordance with the essentialist bias, that the surface-observable properties of man-made tools result from their underlying essential properties (e.g. their intended function). This could provide a further reason for why the essentialist bias in young human children extends to artifact kinds.

Finally, normality assumptions are also carried by ascriptions of functional properties to social kinds: if an individual fails to comply with social norms (e.g. take his hat off his head as he walks into a church), we take the individual's behavior to be defective (or the individual to defect from the relevant norms), not to be a counterexample to the veracity of the social norms. Arguably, the findings by Gergely et al. (2002) on imitative learning and by Topál et al. (2008, 2009) on the A-not-B task show how the reception of ostensive signals cues human infants into interpreting an episodic demonstration as a teaching session from which they learn a social *norm* about either how to act in the presence of a novel artifact or which of a pair of containers is supposed to contain a toy.

---

3 Millikan (1984, 1993) and Neander (1995) have stressed the pervasiveness of *normality* assumptions in the ascription of functional properties to biological kinds and the non-prescriptive *normative* implications of the ascription of functional properties to biological kinds. Of course, this unified view of the ascription of functional properties (to natural and artifact kinds) builds on a scientific Darwinian view of biological functions, which should not be imputed to preverbal human infants.

## 4.3. Natural Pedagogy and Bayesian Inductive Learning

In this final section, we turn to recent probabilistic Bayesian computational models of rational causal inductive learning that emphasize human infants' remarkable sensitivity to statistical patterns of evidence as the primary basis for constructing coherent, abstract, and causal representations of the world in different knowledge domains. Some recent Bayesian computational models of statistical inductive inferences in young children provide clear evidence for the power of ostensive pedagogical demonstrations in inducing, informing, and constraining the scope of inductive inferential generalizations drawn by preschoolers. For example, Bonawitz et al. (2011) have argued that "children are more likely both to learn demonstrated material and to generalize it to novel contexts in teaching than in non-teaching situations" (p. 326), in accordance with the natural pedagogy approach. Buchsbaum, Gopnik, Griffiths, and Shafto (2011) have also showed that a demonstrator's peda-gogical stance has a significant effect on children's decisions whether to imitate part or all action sequences demonstrated to them.

Several recent studies, however, provide suggestive evidence that even much younger infants seem to possess sensitivity to purely statistical infor-mation that entails random versus selective sampling by an agent and that they can rely on such statistical information to spontaneously constrain the kind of inferential generalizations they draw from the observed evidence (e.g. Gweon, Tenenbaum, & Schulz, 2010; Ma & Xu, 2011; Kushnir, Xu, & Wellman, 2010). For example, Gweon et al. (2010) argued that different inferences are licensed if samples are drawn randomly from the whole population (*weak sampling*, i.e. an agent chooses items at random from the population, independent of their properties) than if they are drawn selectively only from the property's extension (*strong sampling*, i.e. the agent samples items selectively, depending on their relevant properties). As they point out, "weak sampling provides a less powerful constraint on induction (as both positive and negative evidence will be necessary to constrain inferences generalizing to subpopulations)," while "even a few samples of positive evidence … can constrain inductive generalizations to subpopulations or kinds" (p. 9066) under the assumption of strong sampling by the agent.

In a series of elegant studies, Gweon et al. (2010) explored the hypothesis that there may be "early constraints on what infants assume about rational agents' sampling processes" (p. 9066). In one study, 15-month olds watched as an adult glanced into a transparent box in front of them (containing a population of blue and yellow balls), pulled out a blue ball, squeezed it so that it squeaked, and then set it on the table. The experimenter repeated this until she pulled out the sample of blue balls (three, two, or just one) tested in the given conditions. Then, after a brief pause, she went on to pull out a yellow ball and put it in front of the child saying, "Here you go, you can go ahead and play." Across different (random vs. selective) sampling conditions, infants saw exactly the same sequence of demonstrations while the distribution of the population from which the agent sampled the balls was varied in a way that was transparent to the infants. For example, in a random sampling condition, a sequence of three blue balls were sampled from a transparent box which (visibly to the infant) contained a majority (75%) of blue and only a minority (25%) of yellow balls, while in the strong sampling condition the three blue balls were drawn identically but this time from a transparent box that contained only a minority (25%) of blue balls and 75% of yellow balls. The question of interest was the degree to which infants would differentially generalize the object property (makes sound if squeezed) demonstrated on the three sampled blue balls to the yellow ball as a function of their evaluation of the difference between the sampling conditions. The results showed that while infants constrained their generalization of the squeaking property to the blue balls in the strong sampling condition (with only 33% of them squeezing the yellow ball), they did not do so in the random sampling condition (where 80% tried to squeeze the yellow ball). Based on such results, the authors conclude that "in the absence of behavioral cues to the sampling process, infants make inferences consistent with the use of strong sampling." Thus, they argue that "infants make accurate generalizations from sparse data, in part because their inferences are sensitive to how the sample of evidence reflects the population" (p. 9071).

Other recent studies based on the Bayesian approach have explored the use of statistical evidence in rational inferences about the social world (see Ma & Xu, 2011; Kushnir et al., 2010). For example, Ma & Xu (2011) raised the intriguing question "whether young children can use statistical patterns in the choices that other people make to infer the subjective nature of mental states" (p. 410). They point out that "as a source of motivation that enables an agent's choice of one option over another, preferences are subjective and often person-specific—different people can have different attitudes toward the same entity" (p. 403). In their study, they explored, therefore, whether toddlers can make use of purely statistical sampling evidence as a basis for ascribing to others person-specific subjective preferences different from their own. First, in a baseline condition, the experimenter presented 2-year olds and 16-month olds with two bowls each containing one of two kinds of objects (either boring or interesting toys only). The infants were then asked: "Which one do you like to play with? Just choose one!" The toddlers' choices were taken to indicate their own subjective preference (in fact, most expressed preference for the interesting toys). Second, to assess the infants' prior beliefs about the experimenter's subjective preference, the adult placed one hand, palm facing up, between the two bowls and asked the child: "I like to have a toy to play with. Can I have the one I like?" In general, infants relied on their own preference when judging the experimenter's likely subjective preference: they tended to give her the same kind of (interesting) toy that they themselves had shown a preference for. Third, toddlers saw the adult sample six boring objects in three conditions. In the nonrandom sampling condition, the adult drew six boring objects from a transparent jar containing only 13% boring objects and 87% interesting ones. In one of the random sampling condition (without alternative), the adult drew six boring objects again this time, however, from a transparent jar containing 100% boring objects. In the random sampling condition with an alternative, the adult drew the six boring objects from a transparent jar containing 88% boring objects and only 12% interesting ones. This was followed by a test phase to examine whether the sampling information would affect children's judgment of the experimenter's preference. Immediately after the sampling event, the experimenter asked children about her own subjective preference a second time: "I like to have a toy to play with. Can I have the one I like?" The toddlers' choice of toy to offer from the two bowls (boring or interesting toy) was interpreted as reflecting the person-specific subjective preference that the infant ascribed to the adult (as a function of her previously observed sampling behavior). Ma and Xu (2011) report that 2-year olds used the nonrandom sampling as a cue to the agent's current subjective preference (i.e. for the boring objects), while in both versions of the random sampling condition, they continued to rely on their own preference as the basis for judging the agent's likely preference. The authors report a weaker but similar effect in 16-month olds as well. Based on these results, they conclude "that by age 2 children apprehend the subjectivity of preferences based on sampling evidence alone, in the absence of social–pragmatic cues" (p. 410).

In sum, the studies reviewed above provide intriguing new evidence that when learning from the observed actions of intentional agents human infants show sensitivity to statistical information that is compatible with the assumption of strong sampling by the agent and can rely on such information to induce fast learning as well as to constrain the referential scope of projected inductive generalizations to kinds. The evidence also indicates that the assumption of strong sampling is applied to drive rational inferential learning about different aspects of the physical and social world already by 15- and 20-month-old infant observers (in contrast to conditions where the same evidence is interpreted as involving random sampling).

The core theoretical assumption behind the Bayesian research program of rational inductive learning is the proposal that the early constraints on what infants assume about agents' sampling processes reflect a central property of rational instrumental agency. As Gweon et al. (2010) put it, "considerable work suggests that infants make assumptions about rational agents with respect to intentional goal-directed actions (Gergely & Csibra, 2003; Gergely et al., 1995; Woodward, 1998)" (p. 9070). While they further argue that "it would be very interesting if the assumption that agents were likely to engage in selective sampling were part of this repertoire" (p. 9070), they refer to the body of evidence (reviewed in Section 2) showing that infants expect agents of instrumental actions to choose the most efficient means action available to them to achieve their goal, in accordance with the principle of practical rationality. Is this core assumption correct?

We doubt it on two grounds. On the one hand, we have argued that practical rationality is restricted to the third-person interpretation of the instrumental actions of goal-directed agents and to their expectable choice of efficient means actions to bring about their episodic goals in the world. On the other hand, much evidence reviewed above in this paper shows that infants learn to make generalizations about social and artifact kinds from a second-person perspective from communicative actions addressed to them, while they fail to do so when they observe from a third-person perspective the very same actions performed by a noncommunicative agent. For example, in studies on selective imitative learning of novel means actions, 14-month olds were provided with the same statistical evidence when they observed an adult perform three times in a row an odd and unfamiliar "head action" to contact and illuminate a novel touch-sensitive lamp in the hands-free condition either by a communicative agent ostensively addressing them or by a noncommunicative agent observed from a third-person perspective. The infants only learnt to perform the odd head action in the former but not in the latter condition (Király, Csibra & Gergely, 2012). In the object-individuation study of Futó et al., (2010), 10-month olds were provided with the same statistical evidence in either a communicative or a noncom-municative action–demonstration condition involving six repeated function demonstrations of each of two novel functions on two different artifacts,

respectively. While the demonstrations provided sufficient statistical information of positive evidence to support inductive generalization of the
functional property to the artifact kind, infants showed evidence of kind
assignment only in the communicative ostensive demonstration context. On
this basis, we surmise that infants take strong sampling as part of communicative, not instrumental, agency. We further think that both the studies of
Gweon et al. (2010) and Ma and Xu (2011) corroborate our diagnosis.

For instance, in the study by Gweon et al. (2010), after the experimenter
ostensively addressed the infant, she established joint referential attention, by
removing the cloth covering the transparent box "and drew the child's
attention to its contents by pointing to the window" (p. 9071), thereby
making the statistical composition of the population of balls shared and
relevant contextual background knowledge. In this communicative context,
the infants could interpret the agent's subsequent communicative action–
demonstrations as instances of either weak or selective sampling. In experiments 1–3, infants were therefore in a position to interpret the agent's
action–demonstrations as instances of strong sampling. By contrast, in
experiment 4, which tested the infants' sensitivity to random sampling, the
agent first ostensively called the infants' attention to the fact that the
sampling method she applied to draw the balls was random (i.e. in violation
of the assumption of strong sampling): "rather than pulling the balls out, the
experimenter shook the box upside down to let the balls fall out. Then she
told the child, 'The next one is going to be yours'." (p. 9071).

The same is true of the procedure applied in the study by Ma and Xu
(2011) where before sampling the six boring objects in each condition, the
experimenter "first brought out a jar and directed children's attention to the
objects inside (e.g. 'Look! I have a big jar. There are two kinds of things in it
[Boring 13% condition]/there is only one kind of things in it [Boring 100%
condition]. I am going to get some!')" (p. 405). In fact, following the
sampling demonstrations (and before the test phase), the experimenter
communicatively addressed the infant *once again* to make sure that the
relevant contextual information about the population distribution from
which the sampling evidence had been drawn was shared knowledge: "At
the end of the sampling event, she directed children's attention to both the
population and the sample, "Look! This many (holding the jar), and I got six
of this one (holding the display container)" (p. 405). Furthermore, given the
fact that the statistical evidence presented by the preferential sampling
demonstrations in the study by Ma and Xu (2011) were preceded by strong
ostensive–communicative cues directed to the toddlers, it seems entirely

possible that what their results demonstrate is not merely that toddlers learnt to ascribe to others preferences different from their own on the basis of one individual's strong sampling behavior but that they would even be willing to generalize the other's preference to different agents as well (as is the case in study by Egyed et al., 2012).

## 5. CONCLUDING REMARKS

As the evidence reviewed in Section 2 shows, preverbal human infants are surprisingly able to represent the subjective motivations and the episodic contents of the epistemic states of agents of instrumental actions from a third-person perspective, in accordance with the principle of practical rationality. As the evidence reviewed in Sections 3 and 4 shows, their unique sensitivity to coded ostensive signals makes preverbal human infants surprisingly able to detect the presence of agents' communicative intentions and to interpret nonverbal communicative actions from a second-person perspective.

In Sections 3.2 and 3.3, we argued that in order to solve the puzzle of imitative learning, it is necessary to give up the rational imitation model according to which the model's action is construed as an instrumental action performed in accordance with the principle of practical rationality. Instead, the model's action should be construed as a communicative action whose goal is to teach new and relevant knowledge performed in accordance with the principle of relevance. This finding illustrates the separation between the system underlying infants' early reasoning about the psychological states of instrumental agents and the system whereby they acquire novel and relevant knowledge from communicative demonstrations when addressed by ostensive signals.

In Section 3.1, we reviewed evidence showing that in the context of joint actions where both agents have shared goals and share relevant common knowledge about a restricted set of familiar objects, preverbal human infants are able to disambiguate the intended referents of the nonverbal deictic pointing actions of their communicative partners. By contrast, in Section 4.1, we reviewed evidence showing that preverbal human infants are also prone to acquire deferential (trust based) beliefs about properties of artifact kinds from their interpretation of some of the referential actions and demonstrative displays of nonverbal communicative agents. In Section 4.2, we argued that such deferential beliefs about artifact kinds are formed in accordance with the principle of psychological essentialism. One crucial issue for further research is to investigate in detail what makes infants switch their expectation of relevance from episodic to nonepisodic information and conversely. In Section 4.3, we examined a selective sample of investigations about the ability of young children to make use of statistical inferences and we have argued that these studies are consistent with the idea that infants interpret strong sampling as part of a communicative action. Further work is needed to better understand how natural pedagogy and statistically based inductive learning combine in early infancy.

## ACKNOWLEDGMENTS

We wish to thank Dan Sperber, Willem Frankenhuis, and the two editors for their helpful comments on an earlier draft of this chapter.

## REFERENCES

Atran, S. (1990). *Cognitive foundations of natural history. Towards an anthropology of science.* Cambridge: Cambridge University Press.

Bates, E., Camaioni, L., & Volterra, V. (1975). The acquisition of performatives prior to speech. *Merrill-Palmer Quarterly, 21*, 205–224.

Begus, K., & Southgate, V. (2012), Infant pointing serves an interrogative function. *Developmental Science.* doi:10.1111/j.1467-7687.2012.01160.x.

Bíró, S., & Leslie, A. M. (2007). Infants' perception of goal-directed actions: development through cue-based bootstrapping. *Developmental Science, 10*(3), 379–398.

Bonawitz, E., Shafto, P., Gweon, H., Goodman, N. D., Spelke, E., & Schulz, L. (2011). The double-edged sword of pedagogy: instruction limits spontaneous exploration and discovery. *Cognition, 120*, 322–330.

Brandone, A. C., & Gelman, S. A. (2009). Differences in preschoolers' and adults' use of generics about novel animalsand artifacts: A window onto a conceptual divide. *Cognition, 110*, (2009) 1–22.

Brugger, A., Lariviere, L. A., Mumme, D. L., & Bushnell, E. W. (2007). Doing the right thing: infants' selection of actions to imitate from observed event sequences. *Child Development, 78*, 806–824.

Buchsbaum, D., Gopnik, A., Griffiths, T. L., & Shafto, P. (2011). Children's imitation of causal action sequences is influenced by statistical and pedagogical evidence. *Cognition, 120*, 331–340.

Butler, L. P., & Markman, E. (2012). Preschoolers use intentional and pedagogical cues to guide inductive inferences and exploration. *Child Development, 83*, 1416–1428.

Buttelmann, D., Carpenter, M., Call, J., & Tomasello, M. (2007). Enculturated chimpanzees imitate rationally. *Developmental Science, 10*, F31–F38.

Buttelmann, D., Carpenter, M., Call, J., & Tomasello, M. (2008). Rational tool use and tool choice in human infants and great apes. *Child Development, 79*, 609–626.

Buttelmann, D., Carpenter, M., & Tomasello, M. (2009). Eighteen-month-old infants show false belief understanding in an active helping paradigm. *Cognition, 112*, 337–342.

Caron, A. J. (2009). Comprehension of the representational mind in infancy. *Developmental Review, 29*, 69–95.

Csibra, G. (2008). Goal attribution to inanimate agents by 6.5-month-old infants. *Cognition, 107*, 705–717.

Csibra, G. (2010). Recognizing communicative intentions in infancy. *Mind & Language, 25*, 141–168.

Csibra, G., & Gergely, G. (2006). Social learning and social cognition: the case of pedagogy. In M. H. Johnson, & Y. M. Munakata (Eds.), *Processes of change in brain and cognitive development, attention and performance, XXI* (pp. 249–274).

Csibra, G., & Gergely, G. (2009). Natural pedagogy. *Trends in Cognitive Sciences, 13*, 148–153.

Csibra, G., & Volein, Á (2008). Infants can infer the presence of hidden objects from referential gaze information. *British Journal of Developmental Psychology, 26*, 1–11.

Csibra, G., Bíró, S., Koós, O., & Gergely, G. (2003). One-year-old infants use teleological representations of actions productively. *Cognitive Science, 27*, 111–133.

Csibra, G., Gergely, G., Bíró, S., Koós, O., & Brockbank, M. (1999). Goal attribution without agency cues: the perception of "pure reason" in infancy. *Cognition, 72*, 237–267.

Davidson, D. (1980). *Essays on actions and events*. Oxford: Oxford University Press.

Davidson, D. (2004). *Problems of rationality*. Oxford: Oxford University Press.

Deligianni, F., Senju, A., Gergely, G., & Csibra, G. (2011). Automatized gaze-contingent objects elicit orientation following in 8-month-old infants. *Developmental Psychology, 47*, 1499–1503.

Dennett, D. C. (1978). *Brainstorms, philosophical essays on mind and psychology*. Cambridge, MA: MIT Press.

Dennett, D. C. (1987). *The intentional stance*. Cambridge, MA: MIT Press.

Egyed, K., Király, I., & Gergely, G. (2012). *Communicating shared knowledge without language in infancy*. Manuscript submitted for publication.

Fodor, J. (1992). A theory of the child's theory of mind. *Cognition, 44*(3), 283–296.

Futó, J., Téglás, E., Csibra, G., & Gergely, G. (2010). Communicative Function Demonstration induces kind-based artifact representation in preverbal infants. *Cognition, 117*, 1–8.

Gelman, S. (2003). *The essentialist child*. Oxford: Oxford University Press.

Gergely, G. (2003). What should a robot learn from an infant? Mechanisms of action interpretation and observational learning in infancy. *Connection Science, 13*, 191–209.

Gergely, G. (2010). Kinds of agents: the origins of understanding instrumental and communicative agency. In U. Goshwami (Ed.), *Blackwell handbook of childhood cognitive development* (2nd ed). (pp. 76–105). Oxford: Blackwell Publishers.

Gergely, G., & Csibra, G. (2003). Teleological reasoning about actions: the naïve theory of rational actions. *Trends in Cognitive Sciences, 7*, 287–292.

Gergely, G., & Csibra, G. (2005). The social construction of the cultural mind: imitative learning as a mechanism of human pedagogy. *Interaction Studies, 6*, 463–481.

Gergely, G., & Csibra, G. (2006). Sylvia's recipe: the role of imitation and pedagogy in the transmission of cultural knowledge. In S. Levenson, & N. Enfield (Eds.), *Roots of human sociality: Culture, cognition, and human interaction* (pp. 229–255). Oxford: Berg Publishers.

Gergely, G., Bekkering, H., & Király, I. (2002). Rational imitation in preverbal infants. *Nature, 415*, 755.

Gergely, G., Egyed, K., & Király, I. (2007). On pedagogy. *Developmental Science, 10*, 139–146.

Gergely, G., Nádasdy, Z., Csibra, G., & Bíró, S. (1995). Taking the intentional stance at 12 months of age. *Cognition, 56*, 165–193.

Gopnik, A., & Nazzi, T. (2003). Words, kinds and causal powers: a theory perspective on early naming and categorization. In D. Rakison, & L. Oakes (Eds.), *Early category and concept development: Making sense of the blooming, buzzing confusion"* (p. xxi). New York: Oxford University Press, 303–329.

Gweon, H., Tenenbaum, J. B., & Schulz, L. E. (2010). Infants consider both the sample and the sampling process in inductive generalization. *Proceedings of the National Academy of Sciences of United States of America, 107*(20), 9066–9071.

Hernik, M., & Southgate, V. (2012). Nine-month-old infants do not need to know what the agent prefers in order to reason about its goals: on the role of preference and persistence in infants' goal-attribution. *Developmental Science*, doi:10.1111/j.1467-7687. 2012.01151.x.

Jacob, P. (2012). Sharing and ascribing goals. *Mind & Language, 27*, 200–227.

Jacob, P. (in press). A puzzle about belief ascription. In B., Kaldis (Ed.) *Mind and Society: Cognitive Science Meets the Philosophy of the Social Sciences*. Synthese Philosophy Library, Berlin: Springers.

Johnson, S., Slaughter, V., & Carey, S. (1998). Whose gaze would infants follow? The elicitation of gaze following in 12-month-olds. *Developmental Science, 1*, 233–238.

Jovanovic, B., Király, I., Elsner, B., Gergely, G., Prinz, W., & Aschersleben, G. (2007). The role of effects for infants' perception of action goals. *Psychologia, 50*, 273–290.

Kamewari, K., Kato, M., Kanda, T., Ishiguro, H., & Hiraki, K. (2005). Six-and-a-half-month-old children positively attribute goals to human action and to humanoid-robot motion. *Cognitive Development, 20*, 303–320.

Király, I. (2009). The effect of the model's presence and of negative evidence on infants' selective imitation. *Journal of Experimental Child Psychology, 102*, 14–25.

Király, I., Csibra, G., & Gergely, G. (2004). *The role of communicative-referential cues in observational learning during the second year*. Poster presented at the 14th Biennial International Conference on Infant Studies, May 2004, Chicago, IL.

Király, I., Csibra, G., & Gergely, G. (2012). *Beyond rational imitation: learning arbitrary means actions from communicative demonstrations*. Manuscript submitted for publication.

Király, I., Egyed, K., & Gergely, G. (2012). *Relevance or resonance: inference based selective imitation in communicative context*. Manuscript to be submitted for publication.

Király, I., Jovanovic, B., Aschersleben, G., Prinz, W., & Gergely, G. (2003). Generality and perceptual constraints in understanding goal-directed actions in young infants. *Consciousness and Cognition, 12*, 752–769.

Kovács, Á. M., Téglás, E., & Endress, A. D. (2010). The social sense: susceptibility to others' beliefs in human infants and adults. *Science, 330*, 1830–1834.

Kovács, Á. M., Tauzin, T., Téglás, E., Csibra, G., & Gergely, G. (2012). *Pointing as epistemic request: 12-month-olds point to receive new information about referent*. Manuscript in preparation.

Kushnir, T., Xu, F., & Wellman, H. (2010). Young children use statistical sampling to infer the preferences of others. *Psychological Science, 21*, 1134–1140.

Leslie, S. J. (2007). Generics and the structure of the mind *Philosophical Perspectives, 21*, 375–405.

Liszkowski, U., Carpenter, M., Henning, A., Striano, T., & Tomasello, M. (2004). 12-month-olds point to share attention and interest. *Developmental Science, 7*, 297–307.

Luo, Y. (2011). Do 10-month-old infants understand others' false beliefs? *Cognition, 121*, 289–298.

Luo, Y., & Baillargeon, R. (2005). Can a self-propelled box have a goal? Psychological reasoning in 5-month-old infants. *Psychological Science, 16*, 601–608.

Luo, Y., & Baillargeon, R. (2007). Do 12.5-month-old infants consider what objects others can see when interpreting their actions? *Cognition, 105*, 489–512.

Ma, L., & Xu, F. (2011). Young children's use of statistical sampling evidence to infer the subjectivity of preferences. *Cognition, 120*, 403–411.

Meltzoff, A. N. (1988). Infant imitation after a 1-week delay: long term memory for novel acts and multiple stimuli. *Developmental Psychology, 24*, 470–476.

Meltzoff, A. N. (2005). Imitation and other minds: the like-me hypothesis. In S. Hurley, & N. Chater (Eds.), *Perspectives on imitation: From neuroscience to social science* (pp. 55–77). Cambridge, MA: MIT Press.

Millikan, R. G. (1984). *Language, thought and other biological categories.* Cambridge, MA: MIT Press.

Millikan, R. G. (1993). *White queen psychology and other essays for Alice.* Cambridge, Ma: MIT Press.

Moll, H., & Tomasello, M. (2004). 12- and 18-month-old infants follow gaze to spaces behind barriers. *Developmental Science, 7,* F1–F9.

Movellan, J. R., & Watson, J. S. (2002). The development of gaze following as a Bayesian systems identification problem. UCSD Machine Perception Laboratory Technical Reports 2002.01.

Neander, K. (1995). Misrepresenting and malfunctioning. *Philosophical Studies, 79,* 109–141.

Nielsen, M. (2006). Copying actions and copying outcomes: social learning through the second year. *Developmental Psychology, 42,* 555–565.

Onishi, K. H., & Baillargeon, R. (2005). Do 15-month-old infants understand false beliefs? *Science, 308,* 255–258.

Paulus, M., Hunnius, S., Vissers, M., & Bekkering, H. (2011). Imitation in infancy: rational or motor resonance? *Child Development, 82,* 1047–1057.

Piaget, J. (1954). *The construction of reality in the child.* New York: Basic Books.

Premack, D., & Woodruff, G. (1978). Does the chimpanzee have a theory of mind? *Behavioral and Brain Sciences, 4,* 515–526.

Recanati, F. (1997). Can we believe what we do not understand? *Mind and Language, 12,* 84–100.

Recanati, F. (2001). Modes of presentation: perceptual vs. deferential. In A. Newen, U. Nortmann, & R. Stuhlmann-Laeisz (Eds.), *Building on Frege: New essays on sense, content, and concept* (pp. 197–208). Stanford, CA: CSLI Publications.

Rizzolatti, G., & Craighero, L. (2004). The mirror-neuron system. *Annual Review of Neuroscience, 27,* 169–192.

Schwier, C., van Maanen, C., Carpenter, M., & Tomasello, M. (2006). Rational imitation in 12-month-old infants. *Infancy, 10,* 303–311.

Senju, A., & Csibra, G. (2008). Gaze following in human infants depends on communicative signals. *Current Biology, 18,* 668–671.

Southgate, V., Chevallier, C., & Csibra, G. (2009). Sensitivity to communicative relevance tells young children what to imitate. *Developmental Science, 12,* 1013–1019.

Southgate, V., Chevallier, C., & Csibra, G. (2010). Seventeen-month-olds appeal to false beliefs to interpret others' referential communication. *Developmental Science, 13,* 907–912.

Southgate, V., Johnson, M. H., & Csibra, G. (2008). Infants attribute goals to even biologically impossible actions. *Cognition, 107,* 1059–1069.

Southgate, V., Senju, A., & Csibra, G. (2007). Action anticipation through attribution of false belief by 2-year-olds. *Psychological Science, 18,* 587–192.

Southgate, V., van Maanen, C., & Csibra, G. (2007). Infant pointing: communication to cooperate or communication to learn? *Child Development, 78,* 735–740.

Sperber, D. (1997). Intuitive and reflective beliefs. *Mind and Language, 12,* 67–83.

Sperber, D. (2001). In defense of massive modularity. In E. Dupoux (Ed.), *Language, brain and cognitive development: Essays in honor of Jacques Mehler* (pp. 47–57). Cambridge, MA: MIT Press.

Sperber, D., & Wilson, D. (1995). *Relevance: Communication and cognition* (2nd ed.). Oxford: Blackwell.

Sperber, D., & Wilson, D. (2012). *Relevance and meaning.* Camridge, UK: Cambridge University Press.

Sperber, D., Clément, F., Heintz, C., Mascaro, O., Mercier, H., Origgi, G., et al. (2010). Epistemic vigilance. *Mind & Language, 25,* 359–393.

Surian, L., Caldi, S., & Sperber, D. (2007). Attribution of beliefs to 13-month-old infants. *Psychological Science, 18,* 580–586.

Tomasello, M. (1996). Do apes ape? In C. M. Heyes, & B. G. GalefJr. (Eds.), *Social learning in animals: The roots of culture* (pp. 319–346) New York: Academic Press.

Tomasello, M. (1999). *The cultural origins of human cognition.* Cambridge, MA: Harvard University Press.

Tomasello, M. (2008). *Origins of human communication.* Cambridge: MIT Press.

Tomasello, M., Carpenter, M., Call, J., Behne, T., & Moll, H. (2005). Understanding and sharing intentions: the origins of cultural cognition. *Behavioral and Brain Sciences, 28,* 675–735.

Tomasello, M., Carpenter, M., & Liszkowski, U. (2007). A new look at infant pointing. *Child Development, 78,* 705–722.

Tomasello, M., & Haberl, K. (2003). Understanding attention: 12- and 18-month-olds know what is new for other persons. *Developmental Psychology, 39,* 906–912.

Tomasello, M., Kruger, A., & Ratner, H. (1993). Cultural learning. *Behavioral and Brain Sciences, 16,* 495–552.

Topál, J., Gergely, G., Miklósi, Á, Erdőhegyi, Á, & Csibra, G. (2008). Infants' perseverative search errors are induced by pragmatic misinterpretation. *Science, 321,* 1831–1834.

Topál, J., Gergely, G., Erdöhegyi, Csibra, G., & Miklósi, A. (2009). Differential Sensitivity to Human Communication in Dogs, Wolves, and Human Infants. *Science, 325,* 1269–1272.

Wagner, L., & Carey, S. (2005). 12-month-old infants represent probable ending of motion events. *Infancy, 7,* 73–83.

Wellman, H. M. (1990). *The child's theory of mind. A Bradford book.* Cambridge, MA: MIT Press.

Wellman, H. M., Cross, D., & Watson, J. (2001). Meta-analysis of theory-of-mind development: the truth about false belief. *Child Development, 72,* 655–684.

Wilson, D., & Sperber, D. (2002). Relevance theory. In L. Horn, & G. Ward (Eds.), *Handbook of pragmatics.* Oxford: Blackwell.

Wimmer, H., & Perner, J. (1983). Beliefs about beliefs: representation and constraining function of wrong beliefs in young children's understanding of deception. *Cognition, 13,* 103–128.

Woodward, A. L. (1998). Infants selectively encode the goal object of an actor's reach. *Cognition, 69,* 1–34.

Woodward, A. L. (1999). Infants' ability to distinguish between purposeful and non-purposeful behaviors. *Infant Behavior and Development, 22,* 145–160.

Xu, F. (2002). The role of language in acquiring object kind concepts in infancy. *Cognition, 85,* 223–250.

Xu, F. (2005). Categories, kinds, and object individuation in infancy. In L. Gerschoff-Stowe, & D. Rakison (Eds.), *"Building object categories in developmental time"* (pp. 63–89). Mahwah, NJ: Lawrence Erlbaum.

Xu, F. (2007). Sortal concepts, individuation and language. *Trends in Cognitive Sciences, 11,* 400–406.

Xu, F., & Carey, S. (1996). Infants' metaphysics: the case of numerical identity. *Cognitive Psychology, 30,* 111–153.

Yoon, J. M. D., Johnson, M. H., & Csibra, G. (2008). Communication-induced memory biases in preverbal infants. *Proceedings of the National Academy of Sciences of the United States of America, 105,* 13690–13695.

Zmyj, N., Daum, M. M., & Aschersleben, G. (2009). The development of rational imitation in 9- and 12-month-old infants. *Infancy, 14,* 131–141.

# CHAPTER FOUR

# Can Rational Models Be Good Accounts of Developmental Change? The Case of Language Development at Two Time Scales

## Colin R. Dawson* and LouAnn Gerken[†,1]

*School of information: Science, Technology, and Arts 1040 E. 4th Street University of Arizona, Tucson, AZ 85721-0077, USA
†Department of Psychology 1503 E University Blvd. University of Arizona, Tucson, AZ 85721-0068, USA
[1]Corresponding author: E-mail: gerken@email.arizona.edu

## Contents

## Abstract

Rational models of human perception and cognition have allowed researchers new ways to look at learning and the ability to make inferences from data. But how good are

95

such models at accounting for developmental change? In this chapter, we address this question in the domain of language development, focusing on the speed with which developmental change takes place, and classifying different types of language development as either *fast* or *slow*. From the pattern of fast and slow development observed, we hypothesize that rational learning processes are generally well suited for handling fast processes over small amounts of input data. In contrast, we suggest that associative learning processes are generally better suited to slow development, in which learners accumulate information about what is typical of their language over time. Finally, although one system may be dominant for a particular component of language learning, we speculate that both systems frequently interact, with the associative system providing a source of emergent hypotheses to be evaluated by the rational system and the rational system serving to highlight which aspects of the learner's input need to be processed in greater depth by the associative system.

## 1. INTRODUCTION

All theories of language development, indeed all theories of cognitive development more generally, seek a balance between what knowledge about the likely structure of the world needs to come with the learner (i.e. must be innate) and the computational power of the learning mechanism needed to encode and analyze the learner's experiences. Until the last decade, theories of language development were essentially of two sorts, which we might view as having extreme values on the innate knowledge and on the mechanistic complexity scales.

On the one hand, *triggering* accounts posit that linguistic structure is innate, with some aspects of structure shared by all languages and other aspects varying parametrically across languages (Chomsky, 1957; Chomsky & Lasnik, 1993). This view assumes a very simple learning mechanism in which the child can determine which of a set of parameterized linguistic structures is valid for her language by encountering a single, specific input example or *trigger*. A similar mechanism is thought to be a work in ducklings and goslings that follow the first moving object they see after hatching (Lorenz, 1935).

On the other hand, *associative* accounts, often instantiated in connectionist network models (e.g. Rumelhart & McClelland, 1987) posit little in the way of innate knowledge, except for separate encoding of information arising from the different sensory systems. However, these accounts assume that learners can store large amounts of information over which a variety of statistical trends, relating any number of input dimensions, can be induced. An example of a statistical trend might be that the majority of words in English begin with a stressed syllable (e.g. Cutler & Carter, 1987; Jusczyk, Cutler, & Redanz, 1993).

In addition to differing in the amount of innate knowledge and computational capacity they assume of learners, triggering and associationist accounts differ as to the basis on which learners generalize from previously encountered stimuli to new stimuli. Triggering accounts assume that generalization occurs in an all-or-none fashion, via a model of the language system, or *grammar*, whereas associationist accounts assume that generalization occurs in a gradient fashion via a measure of similarity which is induced from statistical patterns in the data. The two accounts are at opposite extremes in terms of the explicitness of the representations they posit. While triggering accounts take the mental representation of grammar to be a set of discrete rules, associationist accounts reject the notion of an identifiable representation of grammar, supposing that what appears to the linguist to be a grammar is really just a collection of statistical relationships.

Both triggering and associationist accounts fail to comport with certain aspects of language development data. We explore these failures in more detail in the subsequent sections; however, we can briefly identify two types of problems that undermine both approaches. The first concerns the nature of generalization. Triggering accounts predict that once the learner encounters the relevant data (the trigger) that indicates the correct setting for a particular aspect of the child's grammar, that aspect of the grammar should have been learned. Furthermore, once a generalization is made, it should not be changed. These predictions are contradicted by the fact that mature language abilities develop over time with errors gradually decreasing (e.g. Elman, 2003; Freudenthal, Pine, Aguado-Orea, & Gobet, 2007) and by data showing that children flexibly change the generalizations they make (e.g. Gerken, 2010). At the other extreme, associationist accounts predict that large quantities of data should be required for generalization. In several cases, however, children learn from just a few examples (one of the observations that motivated triggering-style accounts in the first place, e.g. Gerken & Bollt, 2008).

The second class of problem concerns the nature of the input that is required for generalization to take place. Several recent studies have found that infants can learn patterns that are linguistically unnatural, which is at odds with triggering (e.g. Cristià, Seidl, & Gerken, 2011; Gerken & Bollt, 2008). On the other hand, children appear to generalize very little from input that contains many tokens from a single type, but given an equal number of tokens overall distributed over several types, they generalize well (Xu & Tenenbaum, 2007a). Connectionist accounts often make the incorrect prediction that repeated exposure to a single type will result in overlearning of the properties of that one category and will swamp learning about other categories that had taken place previously.

In recent years, a middle way, which at least partially addresses all these problems, has emerged between the two extremes (e.g. Frank & Tenenbaum, 2011; Gerken & Dawson, in press; Perfors, Tenenbaum, & Regier, 2006; Xu, 2007). This middle way is rational statistical inference, which, like triggering accounts, assumes that generalization from old experiences to new ones occurs via a grammar. Unlike triggering, however, rational inference does not assume that a highly constrained set of possible grammars needs to be innate. Rather, a learner can select the most probable grammar, given a set of data, by asking for each grammar under consideration: If the real grammar is $G_n$ how likely is the set of data that I have observed so far? Thus, like associationist approaches, rational inference assumes that learners keep track of statistical patterns in their input. However, once an appropriate hypothesis space is specified, the amount of input data needed to converge on a probable grammar is considerably smaller than in associationist accounts (e.g. Ng & Jordan, 2002).

The goal of this chapter is to ask how well rational statistical inference can explain a set of language abilities for which we have some knowledge of the developmental time course and of the nature of the input that is required for development. The set we have selected appears in Table 4.1. Our plan is to describe what is known about each ability, analyze how well it is explained by rational inference, and where relevant, discuss what triggering and associationist accounts have to say about the ability. To foreshadow, our analysis will reveal that rational statistical inference performs well for most developing language abilities. However, fast rational inference performs less well for abilities that entail knowledge of the statistical distribution of forms at various levels, with the distribution being largely governed by diachronic forces on the language (e.g. which syllable onsets are most frequent, which stress patterns are most frequent, etc.).

We will conclude that what is needed to account for a full theory of language development is a model that involves both rational inference and associationist elements, as well as two important kinds of interaction between them. On the one hand, we suggest that the rational system might use the representations generated by the associative system to structure and constrain its space of hypotheses. At the same time, the data encountered by the rational system may be judged as unlikely under *any* hypothesis currently under consideration, which could serve as a signal that new hypotheses, perhaps depending on new representations, are needed. This "surprise

**Table 4.1** Types of linguistic abilities reviewed, speed of acquisition (see text), and sample references

| What is learned? | Fast or slow? | Sample studies |
|---|---|---|
| Which phonetic features are distinctive in the native language | Slow | Werker and Tees (1984); Polka and Werker (1994) |
| Typical sound patterns of native language words | Slow | Jusczyk et al. (1993); Jusczyk et al. (1994) |
| Phonological rules | Fast | Gerken and Bollt (2008); Cristià et al. (2011); Chambers et al. (2003) |
| Ordering of adjacent words | Fast | Gervain et al. (2008; Gómez and Gerken (1999); Marcus et al. (1999) |
| Ordering of nonadjacent words | Slow | Gómez and Maye (2005); Santelmann and Jusczyk (1998) |
| Word meanings | Fast | Carey and Bartlett (1978); Xu and Tenenbaum (2007a); Medina et al. (2011) |
| Likely referent properties involved in word meaning | Slow | Smith et al. (2002) |

signal" could serve to induce greater activity in the associative system, leading it to more readily form new connections and representations. This interplay between surprise and the search for new explanations with the potential to reduce surprise was discussed by the philosopher Charles Sanders Peirce (1935). Conversely, statistical patterns which are *explained away* by hypotheses currently entertained by the rational system, patterns which might otherwise spur new associations, can be safely ignored by the associative system, as they have little to offer in the way of new statistical information. The process of statistical explaining away is an important feature of rational inference (Dawson, 2011; Pearl, 1988).

## 1.1. A Few Words about the Set of Language Abilities We Have Chosen

All the language abilities that we have chosen have been documented in experiments with infants and young children to the age of approximately 4 years, with an emphasis on the earlier ages in the range. We have chosen these earlier developing abilities for two reasons. First we characterize linguistic skills by how much time it takes to acquire them. Therefore, we are most interested in abilities for which there is reasonable agreement about the time course of learning, either because the studies involve learning in the laboratory or because infants of different ages reliably show different abilities with their native language.

Second, also because of our interest in establishing time course, we have chosen abilities that have been explored using experimental techniques in which learners do not need to follow instructions any more elaborate than "show me the X" (where X is an actual or nonce word) or "what is this?" (where "this" can be given a single word label). Most of the experiments do not entail giving learners any instructions at all but rather depend on behavioral measures of interest (mostly looking). Some of the experiments focus on knowledge of the learners' native language as measured by behavioral techniques in the laboratory. Others entail exposing infants to novel words or linguistic structures and testing what they were able to learn about these stimuli in a brief laboratory visit.

The abilities represent a range of linguistic components, including phonetics, phonology, syntax involving word order, and lexical semantics. Most obviously missing are studies in which children are asked to interpret or produce more complex syntax. The reason for this gap is largely that, in our view, this is an area where there is considerable disagreement about when children demonstrate knowledge of linguistic structure (e.g. Fisher, 2002; Tomasello, 2000; Tomasello & Abbot-Smith, 2002).

Finally, let us comment on the division of learning speed into the obviously too gross measure of "fast" versus "slow." We chose these categories to see if any pattern emerged if we used them. We will attempt to provide a somewhat more nuanced discussion of learning speed under each ability under consideration in turn. We have applied these labels using the following (admittedly rough) criteria: If a linguistic ability can be shown to be acquired in a laboratory visit, and there is evidence that learners of different ages perform similarly, we assign the label "fast." In contrast, if the ability is differentially present in learners of different ages, we conclude that there is a longer time course required for learning, and we assign the label "slow."

## 2. RATIONAL VERSUS ASSOCIATIVE INFERENCE

Before turning to the developing linguistic abilities shown in Table 4.1, let us provide some background on rational and associative learning models and how they might interact. We use the term "rational statistical inference" to describe model-based probabilistic inference, wherein each member of a (possibly infinite) set of hypotheses about the structure of language specifies how likely any particular pattern of data should be. Linguistic input is used to determine how likely each hypothesis is a posteriori (we have Bayesian inference in mind here, though this is not the only possible form of model-based probabilistic inference). In this way, rational inference combines top-down and bottom-up information. In contrast, an associative learning mechanism does not rely on structured representations and instead tracks a wide variety of statistics, possibly allowing new structure to emerge, which can then be leveraged in rational learning.

We suggest that, once a sufficiently constrained set of hypotheses is formed, conclusions can be drawn rather quickly, without necessarily requiring huge quantities of data. On the other hand, in less structured, associative learning, associations and statistical trends may be present within and between a wide variety of environmental sources. We discuss some potential examples of each type of learning in the next section; first, we will discuss some key features of the manifestations of rational and associative learning that currently enjoy dominance in cognitive science: Bayesian inference and connectionism, respectively.

## 2.1. The Fruits of Knowledge and Vice Versa

Consider a simple nonlinguistic example. Suppose you are stranded on an uninhabited island, and you are looking for some tasty fruit to eat. After some wandering, you come across a tree with some bright orange fruit. You pick one and take a bite. It is sweet and juicy. What do you expect of the next bite? It is possible part of the fruit is rotten, and the next bite will taste terrible. With only one data point so far, you do not have much raw statistical evidence to make generalizations. What will happen if the next bite is delicious as well? Probably you will be more confident that the third bite will be delicious than you were prior to taking the second bite.

Suppose you have finished your piece of fruit, but you still feel hungry. Consider three options: (1) you could reach for another piece from the same tree, (2) you could take a piece from a tree a few yards away with similar-looking fruit, or (3) you could reach for the tree immediately next to the original tree that bears some deep purple berries. Which options are most likely to reproduce your previous delicious experiences? Likely your intuition is that the chances of deliciousness are greatest in (1) and lowest in (3).

Why is (1) better than (2)? An obvious answer is that the new experience would share more features with the old ones. But why is (2) better than (3)? After all, the purple berry tree is physically closer to the original tree, so if deliciousness is related to location (perhaps the soil is especially nutrient rich at that spot), you might expect that eating a purple berry from the nearby tree would be better than eating an orange fruit from a tree farther away.

Most of us would be fairly confident that the second bite from the original piece of fruit will taste like the first, even though we can entertain the possibility that only part of the fruit could be rotten. Similarly, almost no one will doubt that the orange fruit from the far away tree is a better bet than the purple berry from the nearby one, provided the former appears sufficiently similar to be judged a member of the same type as the one already eaten. As sophisticated, worldly intellectuals, we have biological knowledge that tells us that there is usually little variability among parts of an individual piece of fruit and that taste usually depends more on the type of fruit than the location of the tree it came from. When we bring the full force of this knowledge to bear, we can generalize confidently with very little data.

Imagine you did not have that fancy university education and thus were completely ignorant about the ontology of fruit and fruit trees. Now the second bite (as well as the third) would be more of an adventure. Later, while you might still prefer option (1) to option (2), you would have a more difficult time choosing between (2) and (3). You would need to gather more data. If you had tried both and found that, indeed, the other orange fruit was delicious, but that the purple berry was sour, then perhaps you would begin to believe that appearance matters more than location. Even more so if you tried another purple berry near the second orange-fruit tree, and it was also sour. You still only have two data points from each type, and two from each location, but if you come to the problem predisposed to attend to appearance and location (as opposed to, say, whether it was 4:03 PM vs. 4:11 PM), you do not need much data to begin to feel at least somewhat confident that the former is an important predictor of flavor and the latter much less so. You may even make an even more sophisticated leap and conclude that various pieces of the orange fruit might share properties in addition to tastiness as do various instances of the purple berries.

The learner who begins with a predisposition (whether from some innate bias or from other previous experience) to treat appearance and location as potentially informative, might entertain some vague notion that fruit is divided into categories, with a vague prior distribution on tastiness, appearance, and location given category. The means and variances for each dimension, along with the correlations between them, could then be inferred from data. Data of the sort described above, in which two pieces of tasty orange fruit and two sour purple berries were eaten, one of each from each of two locations, would be likely if the orange fruit came from one category and the purple fruit from another and unlikely if the fruit were grouped by location. Moreover, the a posteriori correlation would be relatively high between tastiness and appearance but low between tastiness and location. In contrast, a classical connectionist network which incrementally updates its weights could learn very little from four data points. The structure of the rational learner's representation constrains the learning problem enough that (what turns out to be) the correct hypothesis (that the orange fruit belong together) is already considerably better supported than the alternatives.

## 2.2. Types and Tokens

A key aspect of the structure possessed by the rational model which differentiates it from the associative learner is the partitioning of variability into multiple hierarchical levels. Consider what the two systems would learn as they continued to gather data from that first piece of orange fruit. After one bite, neither system is very confident about what to expect on subsequent tastes. After the second bite, the rational system gets a big boost to its confidence as it now has evidence of low variability in tastiness among bites from the same piece of fruit. The associative system gets a boost as well, but it is small. Over the next several bites, the rational system confirms its impression that intra-fruit variability is low, but since it already expected this, the returns diminish quickly. Moreover, since it separates intra- and inter-fruit variability, it learns almost nothing beyond the first few bites that helps it predict what the next piece of fruit will taste like as the relevant measure of evidence for inferences about inter-fruit variability within a type is the number of distinct fruit tokens of that type observed and not the total number of observations. If the membership of the particular piece of fruit to a type is in question initially, then the effective number of tokens observed may be less than one. As such, additional observations can provide information about inter-token/intratype variability by increasing that number toward one; however, as membership becomes near-certain, no more information which is relevant for generalization can be gained from that piece.

Contrast this behavior with that of the connectionist learner. As this learner continues to take bites from that first orange fruit, it gets more and more confident that not only this piece of fruit but also other things like it (whether the similarity is in appearance, location, or any of a variety of other features) will taste good. Without an ontology to carve its experience into types and tokens, it will have an increasing tendency to predict that orange objects taste good. Its estimate of the correlation between tastiness and orangeness, as well as of the correlation between tastiness and location, keeps rising, as it keeps receiving evidence which is consistent on all three dimensions.

In the long run, as plentiful and diverse evidence is gathered, both systems will make the correct inferences, but the rational system learns a lot early (provided it represents the problem in a useful way) and then requires new varieties of experience to continue learning, whereas the associative system makes less commitment to the structure of the problem and learns gradually and steadily from even repeated experience.

## 2.3. The Bias–Variance Trade-off

The trade-off between representational commitment and learning speed is encountered in statistics and machine learning problems under the name of the "bias–variance trade-off." In a formal statistical problem, one looks for an appropriate *estimator* of some latent quantity. Naturally, with finite data, perfect estimation is impossible, and so every estimator comes with some degree of error. Error arises from two sources. The *bias* of an estimator is the extent to which it deviates *on average* from the true quantity (where the average is taken over the true distribution of the data). The *variance* of the estimator is the extent to which its value is sensitive to the particular data encountered. When the variance is large but the bias is small, the error associated with any given set of input tends to be large, but because errors occur in different directions, the average value is close to truth.

As the amount of input increases, the variance of an estimator decreases. Estimators for which the variance is low at a given sample size are called *efficient*. Estimators in another desirable class (called *consistent* estimators) may contain bias for any given amount of input, but the bias vanishes in the limit of infinite data.

In the context of the present discussion, rational and associative learners have opposing advantages: associative learning is *consistent*, but rational learning is *efficient*. Rational learning is consistent as well when it is able to entertain the correct structure, though even here it may be biased in the short term (the short-term bias here comes from quantitative, as opposed to structural, prior information).

## 2.4. A Rational–Associative Synergy

We envision a learning system which employs both associative and rational components in interaction. The associative component mines statistical relationships from a wide variety of sources, slowly winnowing the number of interdomain connections that it considers, as many do not produce any stable associations. As subspaces become sufficiently "modular," rational learning proceeds to construct and test manageable sets of hypotheses. In the other direction, as certain high-level hypotheses are sufficiently well supported by rational inference, the predictions they make serve to constrain associative learning, at the lower levels, *explaining away* some statistical patterns, thereby rendering them relatively uninformative in subsequent associative learning. Conversely, patterns that are particularly poorly predicted by existing hypotheses are ripe targets for additional data mining by the associative system.

# 3. A SELECTIVE REVIEW OF EARLY LANGUAGE ABILITIES AND THEIR SPEED OF ACQUISITION

In this section, we review the early language abilities shown in Table 4.1, above. As in the table, we characterize each ability as having been acquired quickly or slowly. We suggest that, in general, abilities that are acquired slowly reflect the gradual accumulation of data by the associative system. In contrast, abilities that can be acquired quickly and that generally do not show a difference in the age of acquisition reflect the rational system.

## 3.1. Learning Which Phonetic Features Are Distinctive in the Native Language

A well-documented phenomenon in language development is that infants begin their lives with the ability to discriminate most of the sound contrasts used in the world's languages but lose this ability some time during the first year of life (e.g. Polka & Werker, 1994; Werker & Tees, 1984). For example, while nearly all the 6- to 8-month olds and about half of the 8- to 10-month olds tested by Werker and Tees (1984) could discriminate two nonnative consonant contrasts, only about 20% of the 10- to 12-month olds could do so. One possible mechanism that has been suggested to explain infants' growing focus on native speech sounds and their decreasing focus on nonnative sounds requires learners to track the distribution of phonetic features in their input. Features that occur in a bimodal distribution (e.g. voice onset time in English) are treated as phonemic (distinctive for marking meaning differences in words), while features that occur in a unimodal distribution (e.g. aspiration in English) are treated as allophonic variants of a single phoneme (Maye, Weiss, & Aslin, 2008; Maye, Werker, & Gerken, 2002). One might imagine that tracking the distributions for dozens of phonetic features (and, indeed, determining which phonetic features to process more deeply, perhaps using a rational model) might take several months, thereby explaining the developmental time course of this aspect of language development. This conjecture is further supported by the observation that there are fewer phonetic features involved in distinguishing vowels than consonants and that infants lose their ability to discriminate nonnative vowels sooner than nonnative consonants.

Although collecting enough input data to determine whether a particular phonetic feature is unimodally or bimodally distributed requires time, the inference from a stable bimodal distribution to two distinct sound categories appears to be a relatively fast process. In laboratory studies examining this process, infants are presented for a brief time with nonce words in which a single phonetic feature is manipulated to create either a unimodal or a bimodal distribution. Infants who are presented with a bimodal distribution are more likely to discriminate new word tokens that vary on the critical feature than infants who are presented with a unimodal distribution (Maye et al., 2002, 2008). By isolating for infants the relevant phonetic feature while keeping other features constant, these studies allow infants to rapidly change the way in which they perceive the feature in question.

It appears that what takes developmental time in the studies of Werker and others is accumulating enough data from the multidimensional acoustic space to identify dimensions on which stable clusters emerge. In a hypothesis space which is constrained only by basic innate biases (not least the limits of perceptual hardware and the physical connectivity of the sensory system), any perceivable dimension may be related to any other, provided only that the neural representations have the capacity to communicate. Hence, the probability of spurious clusters which are the products of mere coincidence is high, and the presence of any given correlation is insufficient for the rational learner to posit with confidence that there is any "there" there.

However, as the associative system gradually alters the learner's representations, reducing the number of dimensions under consideration and moving from low-level "primitive" dimensions to more abstract "functional" dimensions[1], a more constrained rational learner can find meaningful structure.

## 3.2. Learning the Typical Sound Properties of Native Language Words

Another aspect of language that appears to take several months to develop is the sensitivity to frequent sound properties of native language words. Two of these properties are typical stress patterns and typical phoneme sequences, which we will refer to as phonotactic patterns. With respect to typical stress patterns, the ground-breaking work of Peter Jusczyk demonstrated that while English-learning 6-month olds fail to show a listening preference for the typical strong–weak stress pattern of English words over a weak–strong pattern, 9-month olds show a robust preference for the typical pattern (Jusczyk, Cutler, et al., 1993). Subsequent research demonstrated that 7.5-month olds are able to use their expectation about the frequency of strong–weak lexical stress to segment words with this pattern from running speech, while it is not until 3 months later that they are able to segment weak–strong words (Jusczyk, Houston, & Newsome, 1999).

Other studies generally support these early findings concerning typical word stress patterns in both English and other languages in which stress is important (e.g. Morgan & Saffran, 1995; Skoruppa et al., 2009). However, one study has shown that German 6-month olds (but not 4-month olds) prefer strong–weak over weak–strong consonant–vowel–consonant–vowel (CVCV) nonce words (Höhle, Bijeljac-Babic, Herold, Weissenborn, & Nazzi, 2009). The authors offer two explanations for these findings. First, German has proportionally fewer monosyllabic words than English, which might give German infants more experience with bisyllabic, strong–weak words. A second explanation concerns the fact that infants in the study by

---

[1] The idea here is that relevant structure is often defined not in terms of raw perceptual primitives but in terms of the relationships between those primitives, as well as quantities that are derived by combining primitives. This process is analogous to dimensionality reduction techniques in machine learning such as principal components analysis and factor analysis. Finding relationships and combinations that in some sense maximize the signal-to-noise ratio is likely a result of the associative system operating alongside some innate biases.

Höhle et al. (2009) were presented with the same CVCV nonce words, just with different stress patterns (e.g. /gába/ vs. /gabá/).

The latter explanation is consistent with the finding by Maye and colleagues described in the previous section, in which infants were able to rapidly discern unimodal versus bimodal feature distributions when only a single phonetic feature was allowed to vary. In parallel fashion, the infants in the studies by Höhle et al. may have been better able to recognize the more frequent stress pattern of German when segmental (consonant and vowel) variation was minimized. Again, it appears that the statistical machinery required by the associative learner is in place quite early, but what takes time in real language learning is applying that machinery to a very large dimensional space that needs to be winnowed down to the relevant dimensions. During the winnowing process, the learner's ability to access the relevant dimensions is not very robust; however, access can be improved if the dimension space is reduced by the experimenter.

Turning to infants' learning of typical phonotactic patterns of the words in their language, early work by Jusczyk and colleagues demonstrated that, like for typical word stress patterns, 9-month-old English learners, but not their 6-month-old counterparts, prefer lists of nonce words that exhibit more frequent phonotactic patterns over less frequent patterns (Jusczyk, Luce, & Charles-Luce, 1994). Furthermore, as in the case of typical stress patterns, 9-month olds can use typical phonotactic patterns to segment words from fluent speech (Mattys, Jusczyk, Luce, & Morgan, 1999). And as in the case of typical stress patterns, the data from English learners is corroborated by studies of children learning other languages (e.g. Jusczyk, Friederici, Wessels, Svenkerud, & Jusczyk, 1993; Sebastián-Gallés & Bosch, 2002).

In addition, the work on phonotactic pattern learning further supports the view that accumulating data on what is statistically typical of one's language is a slow process that can be used robustly throughout development. For example, in one study (Archer & Curtin, 2011), both 6- and 9-month-old infants discriminated legal onset clusters (probability in English > 0, e.g. /bl/) from illegal clusters (probability in English = 0, e.g. /dl/). However, only the 9-month olds discriminated onset clusters according to their type frequency. For example, clusters such as /pr/, which occurs as the onset of many English words, were distinguished from clusters such as /bl/, which does not begin many English words. Interestingly, neither the 6- nor 9-month olds discriminated onset clusters based on token frequency (i.e. the overall frequency in English without regard to how many words the cluster occurred in).

The ability to distinguish these different sources of variability (among words vs. among tokens of a single word) is a defining characteristic of model-based probabilistic inference. The fact that even 9-month olds appear to keep track of how often a phonotactic pattern occurs in particular words is evidence that the ability to track types versus tokens is one that is present very early in life. Whereas the type-token distinction is characteristic of a rational inference system in general, employing this distinction in the course of the slow accumulation of input statistics may reflect the influence of the rational system on the associative system.

## 3.3. Learning Phonological Rules

In contrast to the apparently slow accumulation of data regarding the typical word stress and phonotactic patterns of the native language, learning rule-like generalizations about stress and phonotactics appears to occur very rapidly in the laboratory. Beginning with stress pattern learning, Gerken (2004) exposed 9-month olds to three- to five-syllable words in which the pattern of strong and weak syllables was governed by a set of ranked (optimality theory) principles. At test, infants were able to distinguish new words with new stress patterns that confirmed to the previously encountered principles from those that did not. One of the principles for stress assignment in the Gerken's (2004) study was that syllables ending in a consonant should be stressed. Gerken and Bollt (2008) demonstrated that 9-month olds could learn that principle if they encountered three different syllable types ending in a consonant, but not if they encountered multiple tokens of only a single type. This finding is consistent with a growing body of evidence that infants and young children learn to generalize over linguistic types and not tokens, an important component of rational, but not associative, accounts of language development (Archer & Curtin, 2011; Xu & Tenenbaum, 2007b).

One finding from the study by Gerken and Bollt (2008) described above illustrates how the slow accumulation of data about what is typical in the native language interacts with the faster generalization based on rule-like structure that is a hallmark of rational inference. In one experiment, Gerken and Bollt presented 7- and 9-month olds with words whose stress patterns reflected a principle that does not occur in human language: "stress syllables that begin in /t/." The younger infants learned this principle, distinguishing a new stress pattern in which the principle interacted predictably with other ranked principles from one in which it did not. However, 9-month olds, who were able to learn the principle that syllables ending in a consonant are stressed, were not able to learn the unnatural rule that syllables starting with /t/ are stressed. A likely explanation for this developmental change is that although both groups of infants were able to make the types of rational inference required for rule learning, the older infants did not view syllable onsets as having a likely effect of word stress.

Why might this be? One possibility is related to the relation of syllable content and stress in English. At first glance, a learner might perceive a correlation between syllables starting with /t/ and stressed syllables since /t/ is the sixth most frequent onset of stressed syllables in one- and two-syllable words. In other words, based on the sheer frequency of occurrence and co-occurrence, a plausible generalization is that syllables starting in /t/ are stressed. However, a learner who was able to accumulate additional statistics of what is typical of English would find that /t/ is no more likely to be an onset of stressed than of unstressed syllables. Put another way, the frequent co-occurrence of /t/ onsets and stress can be *explained away* in English once the statistics of stressed and unstressed syllables are known. However, discovering this fact would require knowing enough words that start with an unstressed syllable to detect that proportionally no fewer of these start in /t/ than of words starting with a stressed syllable.

We have already noted that English-learning infants at 7 months have difficulty segmenting words with a weak–strong stress pattern from the speech stream, perhaps, because they have focused their word-form-learning efforts on the most frequent word forms in the language (Jusczyk et al., 1999). Quite possibly 7-month olds would not have sufficient data accumulated about the onsets of weak–strong words to view onsets as unlikely to affect word stress. In contrast, 9-month olds may have begun to accumulate sufficient data to weight syllable endings as more likely to affect stress assignment than syllable onsets. This explanation of the difference in learning between 7- and 9-month olds requires the accumulation of data about the language input over developmental time.

Although a greater knowledge of the statistics of English reveals that a relation of stress and syllable onsets is spurious, a relation between stress and syllable codas should continue to be viable with more data. Not only are final consonants very frequent on stressed syllables, conditional probabilities (Prob (coda|stress)) also support the relation in English. Therefore, there is no basis for 9-month olds to explain away the principle that syllables ending in codas are stressed in an artificial language, even though that principle is not absolutely upheld in English. In short, the data suggest that the developmental change seen in infants' ability to learn a principle about word stress assignment involves an interaction of fast rational inference and slower accumulation about the statistics of English.

Turning to infants' ability to learn about phonotactics quickly in the lab, several of studies provide parallel results to those discussed for stress patterns. Chambers, Onishi, and Fisher (2003) familiarized 16.5-month-old infants with CVC syllables in which particular consonants were artificially restricted to either initial or final position (e.g. /bæp/ not /pæb/). During test, infants listened significantly longer to new syllables that violated the familiarized positional constraints than to new syllables that obeyed them. In this study, infants could have responded based on familiar segment-by-syllable position correlations (e.g. /b/ first, /p/ last).

A similar study by Saffran and Thiessen (2003) suggests that infants are rapidly able to consider patterns that embody more abstract featural relations. They familiarized 9-month olds with words with a consistent word-shape template. For example, in one condition of their second experiment, infants were familiarized with CVCCVC words which had the pattern +V, −V, +V, −V (in which +V = voiced and −V = voiceless) on the four consonants (e.g. /gutbap/). Infants were then tested to determine if they were able to segment from fluent speech new words that fit versus did not fit the familiarized pattern. The familiarization and test words were designed so that no particular sequence of consonants occurred in both familiarization and test (e.g. g_tb_p occurred in familiarization but not in test and g_kb_p occurred in test but not in familiarization). Therefore, the influence of the familiarization phase on infants' preference during test was presumably due to word templates specified in terms of features, not specific phonemes.

In an interesting parallel to the work of Gerken and Bollt (2008), Cristià and colleagues (Cristià & Seidl, 2008; Cristià, Seidl, & Gerken, 2011) tested both 7- and 4-month olds' ability to learn phonotactic patterns that involve natural and unnatural sound classes. Infants were exposed to CVC nonce words in which the onset position was either filled by stops and nasals (which form the natural sound class of minus–consintuant) or the unnatural class of stops and fricatives. During test, infants were exposed to new words with different onsets that were either consistent or inconsistent with the grouping the infant was familiarized with (stops and nasals or stops and fricatives). While 4-month olds showed evidence of learning both natural and unnatural groupings, 7-month olds only learned the natural groupings. In keeping with the discussion of developmental change in infants' willingness to entertain natural and unnatural stress assignment principles, we suggest that the slowly accumulating statistics of English phonotactics is responsible for the 7-month olds studied by Cristià et al. (2011) rejecting the grouping of stops and fricatives as a possible generalization. One possible statistical pattern of English that might be responsible is that both stops and nasals can occur after /s/, while most fricatives do not (for further discussion, see Cristià & Seidl, 2008). However, not all stops can occur after /s/, and glides and liquids can also occur after /s/. Because glides and liquids are not part of the same putative natural class as stops and nasals, further research is needed to determine if the same developmental pattern seen for stops and nasals applies to these other sounds as well.

In summary, both stress principles and phonotactic restrictions can be learned rapidly in the laboratory by infants as young as 4 months. However, the rapid learning we see for such generalizations appears to be influenced by the slow accumulation of statistics about typical stress patterns and typical phonotactic patterns of the infant's native language.

## 3.4. Learning the Order of Adjacent Words

A number of studies have demonstrated that infants know about the word order or the general word-order properties of their native language. For example, Shady, Gerken, and Jusczyk (1995) presented 10.5-month olds with normal English sentences as well as sentences in which determiners and nouns were reversed, resulting in phrases like *kitten the*. The stimuli were recorded using a speech synthesizer to avoid disruptions in prosody that are likely to occur when a human talker produces ungrammatical sentences. Infants listened longer to the unmodified sentences, suggesting that they were able to tell the difference between the two types of stimuli. More recently, a group of researchers asked whether Italian and Japanese 8-month olds differently parsed a string of nonce syllables with an AXBY format as beginning or ending with more frequently produced A/B elements (Gervain, Nespor, Mazuka, Horie, & Mehler, 2008). Japanese is a language in which the most frequently occurring words (functors) occur sentence-finally, whereas the comparable elements in Italian occur sentence-initially. Consistent with the abstract word-order properties of their language, Japanese-learning infants listened longer to word strings that ended in frequent A and B syllables, whereas Italian-learning infants showed the opposite preference.

Other studies demonstrate that infants as young as 4 months can learn the order of word-like units in short syllable strings (Dawson & Gerken, 2012; Gómez & Gerken, 1999), as well as learning the more abstract patterns of repeated or alternating syllables (Gerken, 2006, 2010; Gómez & Gerken, 1999; Marcus, Vijayan, Rao, & Vishton, 1999). For example, several studies have shown that 7- and 9-month olds can learn an AAB pattern (first two syllables are the same) or an ABA pattern (first and third syllables are the same) easily with minimal input (Gerken, 2006, 2010; Marcus et al., 1999). Dawson and Gerken (in preparation) found that even 4-month olds were able to learn such a pattern. Interestingly, although 7- and 9-month olds can learn the AAB versus ABA pattern instantiated in syllables, they cannot learn the same patterns instantiated in musical notes or chords. In contrast, 4-month olds can learn the pattern in both media (Dawson & Gerken, 2009). Dawson and Gerken explain this developmental difference by noting that repeated notes are very frequent and therefore highly predictable, once you know the structure of Western tonal music. Research suggests that only older infants know about this structure (e.g. Saffran, 2003), and therefore, only they can explain away musical repetition as the result of general properties of musical structure and not as a local "grammatical" feature. In contrast, repetition of words in English is very rare and requires a separate explanation at all the ages tested.

All the studies cited in this section suggest that learning the order of particular words in a string, as well as more abstract patterns of frequent or repeating words, occurs quickly and shows no consistent developmental change (i.e. the long-term changes that have been observed appear as both gains and losses in capacity, presumably reflecting changes in broader knowledge, and not the gradual acquisition of the specific linguistic skills being tested).

## 3.5. Learning the Order of Nonadjacent Words

Often in natural language, the presence of a particular word or morpheme is dependent not on the word immediately preceding, but to preceding nonadjacent word. For example, in the sentence "Granny is buttering your toast," the inflection "-ing" depends not on "butter" but on "is." Santelmann and Jusczyk (1998) found that 18-month olds, but not 15-month olds listened longer to sentences like "Granny is buttering your toast" than ungrammatical versions like "Granny can buttering your toast." Taken alone, this result might either suggest that younger infants either had not accumulated enough input data to reliably learn longer distance dependencies or that they do not have the computational inclination or ability to consider dependencies between nonadjacent elements.

The latter explanation is supported by work in which a similar developmental effect for nonadjacent dependencies was observed for learning of an artificial grammar in the laboratory (Gómez, 2002; Gómez & Maye, 2005). In these studies, infants of different ages were exposed during a 2-min familiarization period to three-element strings (e.g. *pel-kicey-jic*) in which the third word depended on the first word. The middle word was not relevant to word order, and there were 3, 12, or 24 middle words, depending on the condition in which the infant participated. Across several studies, infants were only able to learn the dependency between the first and third word when the set size of the middle element was 24. Gómez (2002) argued that it is only when the set size of the middle element is large enough (as it is in natural language) to force infants to abandon their preferred pattern-finding strategy of looking for correlations between adjacent elements.

Interestingly, 17- and 18-month olds indicated that they learned the dependency by demonstrating a novelty preference at test, that is, listening longer to strings that violated the pattern that they had heard during the preceding familiarization period. In contrast, 15-month olds demonstrated that they learned the dependency but demonstrated a familiarity preference, which Gómez and Maye (2005) take to indicate that they had learned the dependency less well than the older infants. In contrast, 12-month olds failed to learn the dependency at all. The set of findings described in this section suggests that younger infants are unlikely to even look for dependencies among nonadjacent elements, while older infants (and adults) will look for such dependencies, provided their normal strategy of looking for adjacent relations is made sufficiently difficult.

One possible explanation for the developmental change observed in these studies is that infants are developing a representation of the grammar of their language using the rational inference system. This grammar can include dependencies among elements contained within a syntactic constituent. The associative system then accumulates data about dependencies in the learner's native language, and in English, the data demonstrate that "is" but not "can" predicts "-ing." Although this proposal is clearly speculative at this point, it suggests a way in which the rational and associative systems might interact over the course of development.

## 3.6. Learning Word Meanings

A well-documented phenomenon in early childhood is children's ability to learn the meaning of a word in a single exposure and to remember the word over time. This ability, often termed *fast mapping* was reported by Carey and Barlett (1978) and has been observed by numerous researchers since (e.g. Medina, Snedeker, Trueswell, & Gleitman, 2011). Recent research by Xu and Tenenbaum (2007a, 2007b) has explored fast mapping from a rational statistical inference perspective (Bayesian modeling). In particular, they examined the course of learning when a label was applied to more than a single referent. Xu and Tenenbaum (2007b) showed 3- to 4-year-olds either a single Dalmatian or three different Dalmatians and labeled each example *fep*. They then asked children to give them another *fep* from a set of toys that included Dalmatians, non-Dalmatian dogs, and other animals. Children always treated a Dalmatian as the most likely extension of *fep*. That is, even in when presented with a fast-mapping, one-referent one-label, situation, children behaved as expected. However, when the label was applied to three different Dalmatians, children (and adults) were less likely to select a dog that was not a Dalmatian than when the label was applied to a single Dalmatian. That is, word learners seem to increase their confidence in the appropriate label-referent pairing, but they achieve near-perfect performance very quickly. Importantly, Xu and Tenenbaum (2007b) compared a Bayesian model to an associative (Hebbian) learning model, which did not distinguish between types (different Dalmatians) and tokens (the same Dalmatian seen three times). The Bayesian model better matched the behavioral data.

Despite the general agreement that children are able to learn word-referent mappings relatively quickly, there is some debate about just how much exposure is needed. Xu and Tenenbaum (2007b) found that children picked the subordinate category (e.g. Dalmatian) significantly more when given three input types than when given a single input type. However, a study employing more naturalistic scenes and asking adults and preschoolers to guess the meaning of a word uttered in that scene suggested that if a particular scene was informative, no additional scenes in which the same word was used improved participants' performance (Medina et al., 2011). Medina and colleagues suggest that their results support a view in which a single hypothesis is entertained about the meaning of a word, although the hypothesis might be rejected wholesale if it is subsequently disconfirmed. A number of features differ between the study by Medina et al. (2011) and other studies, including the complexity of the scenes and importantly, whether the speaker intended to teach the participant a word (Xu and Tenenbaum—yes, Medina et al.—no), and whether a set of alternative referents was provided at test (Xu and Tenenbaum—yes, Medina et al.—no). Although providing alternative referents may be less reflective of word learning "in the wild," expecting very young learners to hear a word form and guess its meaning in a free field may also be unusual. Therefore, until additional evidence comes to light that word learning is not a form of hypothesis testing, we will view this domain as generally consistent with rational inference.

## 3.7. Learning Likely Referent Properties Involved in Word Meaning

As noted, the findings in the previous section suggest that learning the meanings of words can occur quite quickly, which we take to be generally consistent with rational statistical inference in the form of Bayesian models (though see Yu & Smith, 2012). However, it is important to note that the children in the study by Xu and Tenenbaum (2007b) were relatively experienced word learners. Other work with younger learners suggests that determining which features of word referents are likely to be important in assigning word meaning is a slower process (Smith, Jones, Landau, Gershkoff-Stowe, & Samuelson, 2002).

If learning the appropriate semantic extension of category labels is the first level of word learning, then learning to prioritize some features over others when extending category labels to novel exemplars can be thought as a form of second-order learning as it requires the child to abstract across multiple object categories and extract similarities in their featural organization. Some authors argue for an associative approach to learning at this level, suggesting that learners must first master several first-order cases before moving up the abstraction ladder to form the higher order generalization. Samuelson (2002) as well as Colunga and Smith (2005) propose connectionist models of the "shape bias" documented by Smith et al. (2002), which leverage input statistics (e.g. that labels for solid objects tend to be preceded by "a" and "the" and appear in both singular and plural forms, whereas labels for materials have only one form and can appear without a determiner or with the determiner "some") to arrive at a taxonomy in which solid object categories and substance categories occupy different regions in semantic space, and hence, labels of the former should generalize along a shape dimension but not along a color dimension, whereas the reverse is true for labels of materials.

Due to the wide variety of potentially relevant input statistics, and due to its tendency to build abstractions from the bottom-up, the associative learner requires a lot of input to acquire second-order generalizations like the (selective) shape bias. Along the way, they overextend the shape bias beyond the appropriate ontological kind, reflecting the empirical behavior of children.

There have been attempts to account for higher order learning of this sort using rational probabilistic models as well. Kemp, Perfors, and Tenenbaum (2007) frame knowledge about which feature dimensions to use in generalization as arising from the learner's representation of variability within categories along each such feature. Low variability for a particular feature reflects high consistency, and hence, novel exemplars are more likely to share this feature with those previously experienced. Kemp et al. present a hierarchical Bayesian model (HBM) which begins with the assumption that objects are divided into kinds (but does not know how many there are) and that kinds are divided into categories and learns from experience with labeled objects that solid and nonsolid categories are organized along different features.

An interesting feature about the HBM approach taken by Kemp et al. (2007) is that, under some conditions, lower order generalizations are learned before higher order ones, and under others, learning occurs in the opposite order. In the case of the shape bias, depending on the statistical distributions in the input, it is possible to learn the general tendency for labeled object categories to be organized by shape with very little data from any particular category. This is a result of the representational distinction made between types and tokens: If the learner encounters two tokens from each of several different types, and within types, the pairs always have the same shape, then the model will be very confident that categories are shape homogeneous and can confidently predict the properties of a new category from a single instance.

The case of reference may lie at the intersection of the associative and rational systems. A rational learner like the one exhibited by Kemp et al. (2007) is able to learn at multiple levels of abstraction simultaneously, provided it is looking for the right kind of ontology, namely one in which a certain class of linguistic constituent (somewhere between a noun and a noun phrase) is assumed to refer to an object and where nouns are organized into broad classes, each of which has different semantic organizing principles. With relatively few properties to focus on, learning proceeds quickly, and the model discovers the distinction between categories which are organized by shape and categories which are organized by material

Before such a rational learner can proceed, however, the child would need sufficient statistical evidence that there is more than one type of noun to begin with. In the model by Kemp et al., the fact that a different set of variability parameters should be inferred for each of a number of ontological kinds was given at the start. That is, the model's representation is structured in such a way that the color distribution of a particular object category is taken to be informative about only one ontological kind, even though it is unknown which one. This is analogous to the type–token representational distinction, at a higher level in the hierarchy. Unlike the Bayesian model, the children in Smith et al. (2002) overgeneralize their shape bias to mass–noun categories, suggesting that they do not yet have this clean representational distinction. It seems plausible that some slow, associative data mining is needed to reach the point where nouns can come in distinct ontological kinds, after which point a rational learner can take over.

## 4. DISCUSSION

In this chapter, we have reviewed empirical evidence pertaining to a variety of linguistic domains. For each domain, we have attempted to roughly classify it as "fast" if it can be learned in a short laboratory visit by learners of different ages or "slow" if the ability is differentially present in learners of different ages.

One way to characterize the pattern of fast- and slow-developing abilities that we have described is as follows: Fast learning appears to involve either domains in which the pattern observed in the input can be described as generated by a rule or in which a word-referent pairing is established (particularly by experienced word learners). Slow learning seems to share two properties. One is that it involves domains in which the learner needs to establish detailed distributions of features in the input. Examples of this type of slow learning from Table 4.1 are learning which phonetic features are distinctive in the native language, learning the typical sound patterns of native language words, and learning the likely referent properties involved in word meaning. The other example of slow learning shown in Table 4.1 is learning the ordering of nonadjacent words. Here we argue that what might take developmental time is not only accumulating data about what words and morphemes co-occur (e.g. "is" and "-ing") but knowing to look for co-occurrences among nonadjacent elements in the first place. The combinatorial explosion involved in looking for all potential co-occurrences without restricting oneself to a bounded domain is computationally prohibitive. Therefore, it appears that learners must first appropriately represent the syntactic constituents in their language, such as sentences and phrases, before they can make significant progress in finding meaningful nonadjacent relationships. Once they have made such a determination, restricting the search for co-occurrences within constituents can proceed.

To summarize, we have characterized language learning as involving two distinct but interacting inference systems. The first is a rational system (of the sort that occurs in Bayesian probabilistic inference) that is able to learn quickly, provided it begins with the appropriate hypothesis space. The second is an associative system (of the sort modeled by Hebbian associative networks) that learns more slowly, but also more flexibly, than the rational system. We have suggested two principal ways in which each system takes advantage of the "output" of the other: First, the associative system alters and simplifies the representations employed by the learner, allowing the rational system to test a better constrained set of hypotheses. In turn, the rational system provides a grammatical framework, including prospective units of analysis (e.g. syntactic constituents, word types instead of tokens), that guides the data accumulation of associative system and also allows what would otherwise be "suspicious" coincidences to be explained away, preventing overlearning of spurious associations.

## 4.1. Why Is One System Insufficient?

Occam's razor dictates that one should only propose two entities when one cannot adequately account for the data. We have outlined some strengths and weaknesses of each of the two systems and described how the weaknesses of each are compensated for by the strengths of the other in a hybrid system. But it is certainly worth considering whether a single system could reasonably account for the empirical data, even if it does not have all the advantages of a dual system. We conclude that a "pure" learner of either stripe will encounter some major difficulties when faced with the complex challenge of acquiring all the linguistic abilities that adults seem to possess. We consider these difficulties in turn for associative and rational inference.

### 4.1.1. Logical and Empirical Challenges for a Purely Associative Theory

A purely associative account of learning faces problems both in principle and in its ability to account for observed experimental data. The most obvious logical challenge was pointed out by Chomsky and others: without representational constraints, the number of correlations and generalizations that are possible from any finite data set is prohibitively enormous. In the specific context of a neurally inspired model, there is a problem of combinatorics: it is physically impossible for everything to connect to everything else. Admittedly, this is a straw argument: the most die-hard connectionist purist makes some representational assumptions, and biases are built into the way the network is arranged.

The principal empirical evidence against a purely associative account, as we see it, is twofold. First, associative accounts predict slow, gradual learning, which is at odds with data from many areas of language learning such as word learning (Xu & Tenenbaum, 2007a, 2007b), phonological categorization (Maye et al., 2002), and syntactic acquisition (Gerken, 2010). Second, and perhaps most directly in support of a need for a rational component, infants represent variability at multiple levels, treating types and tokens differently (Archer & Curtin, 2011; Xu and Tenenbaum, 2007b), which an associative account would not predict.

### 4.1.2. Challenges for a Purely Rational Theory

The chief logical problem with a pure "hypothesis-testing" theory of language learning is determining where the hypotheses come from. Triggering theories rely on a fairly detailed innate hypothesis space, but their proponents arrive at this conclusion indirectly, by arguing that language learning is impossible, and not by direct empirical evidence. It would be more satisfying, as a scientific matter, to assume as little as possible in the way of innate knowledge and develop an account of a learner that could acquire the right kinds of biases from input.

Empirically, purely rational accounts have a difficult time predicting the time course of linguistic development. While they tend to do well at accounting for patterns of behavior within the laboratory, Bayesian models rely on a precise characterization of the input in order to make specific predictions, which is not generally available for longer time courses. This is the opposite of the problem faced by connectionist models, which rely on "asymptotic" results.

### 4.1.3. Solutions Offered by a Hybrid Model

We have discussed some ways in which rational and associative inference have complementary strengths and weaknesses. One area we have focused on is learning speed. Some aspects of language development, especially those studies in brief laboratory visits, appear to occur very quickly, while others appear to proceed more slowly. The hybrid model that we are proposing arose largely as a framework for understanding these different developmental time scales.

In addition, we believe that the hybrid model offers a solution to the problem of the explosion of units and statistics that either an unconstrained associative learner or an unconstrained rational learner would face on its own. Each time that the rational inference system adds something to the grammar, the associative learner is newly constrained in terms of the units over which it keeps statistics. Although we have not dealt specifically with the different possible statistics that an associative learner might track, all of our examples rely on tracking only frequency distributions, forward conditional probabilities, adjacent dependencies, and nonadjacent dependencies within the bounds of syntactic constituents. Conversely, the associative learner may limit the set of hypotheses considered by the rational learner.

Finally, the hybrid model has the potential to harness the hypothesis-testing power of the rational system, while leveraging the "creative" power of the associative system to generate hypotheses in the first place. Peirce (1935) described "inference to the best explanation," also known as abductive inference, as follows:

**(1)** The surprising fact, C, is observed.

**(2)** But if A were true, C would be a matter of course.

**(3)** Hence, there is reason to suspect that A is true.

*—Charles Sanders Peirce (1935)*

Once the set of possible explanations is determined, a rational inference system can proceed in this manner, settling on the explanation that makes the data the least surprising. However, the associative system is needed to construct a pool of potential representations out of the sound and fury, some of which the rational system can explain away as truly signifying nothing.

We close this chapter by remarking that the hybrid framework we have outlined here is clearly not yet a fully formed theory of language learning. We have roughly divided linguistic capacities into two categories and attempted to fit these categories into the mold of either rational Bayesian inference or associative Hebbian learning, and we have attempted to describe ways in which these two systems might interact. It will likely be possible to expand upon our conception of either rational or associative so as to expand its territory beyond the blurry boundary lines we have drawn, but while the precise limits are flexible, we are hopeful that the conceptual distinctions we have made here will prove fruitful in future discussions of the nature of language learning.

## ACKNOWLEDGMENTS

This research was supported by NICHD #R01 HD042170 and NSF 0950601 to LAG.

## REFERENCES

Archer, S. L., & Curtin, S. (2011). Perceiving onset clusters in infancy. *Infant Behavior and Development, 34*(4), 534–540.
Carey, S., & Bartlett, E. (1978). Acquiring a single new word. *Papers and Reports on Child Language Development, 15,* 17–29.
Chambers, K. E., Onishi, K. H., & Fisher, C. L. (2003). Infants learn phonotactic regularities from brief auditory experience. *Cognition, 87,* B69–B77.
Chomsky, N. (1957). *Syntactic structures.* The Hague: Mouton.
Chomsky, N., & Lasnik, H. (1993). *Principles and parameters theory in syntax.* Berlin: de Gruyter.
Colunga, E., & Smith, L. B. (2005). From the lexicon to expectations about kinds: a role for associative learning. *Psychological Review, 112*(2), 347–382.
Cristià, A., & Seidl, A. (2008). Is infants' learning of sound patterns constrained by phonological features? *Language Learning and Development, 4*(3), 203–227.
Cristià, A., Seidl, A., & Gerken, L. A. (2011). Young infants learn sound patterns involving unnatural sound classes. *University of Pennsylvania Working Papers in Linguistics, 17*(1). Article 9.
Cutler, A., & Carter, D. (1987). The predominance of strong initial syllables in the English vocabulary. *Computer Speech and Language, 2,* 133–142.
Dawson, C. (2011). *"Explaining-away" effects in rule-learning: evidence for generative probabilistic inference in infants and adults.* Doctoral thesis. Tucson, AZ: The University of Arizona.
Dawson, C., & Gerken, L. A. (2009). Learning to learn differently: the emergence of domain-sensitive generalization in the second six months of life. *Cognition, 111,* 378–382.
Dawson, C., & Gerken, L. A. (2012). *Stimulus complexity affects generalization: A developmental finding.* Manuscript in preparation.
Elman, J. (2003). Development: it's about time. *Developmental Science, 6,* 430–443.
Fisher, C. (2002). The role of abstract syntactic knowledge in language acquisition: a reply to Tomasello (2000). *Cognition, 82*(3), 259–278.
Frank, M. C., & Tenenbaum, J. B. (2011). Three ideal observer models for rule learning in simple languages. *Cognition, 120*(3), 360–371.
Freudenthal, D., Pine, J. M., Aguado-Orea, J., & Gobet, F. (2007). Modeling the developmental patterning of finiteness marking in English, Dutch, German, and Spanish using MOSAIC. *Cognitive Science: A Multidisciplinary Journal, 31*(2), 311–341.
Gerken, L. A. (2004). Nine-month-olds extract structural principles required for natural language. *Cognition, 93,* B89–B96.
Gerken, L. A. (2006). Decisions, decisions: infant language learning when multiple generalizations are possible. *Cognition, 98,* B67–B74.
Gerken, L. A. (2010). Infants use rational decision criteria for choosing among models of their input. *Cognition, 115*(2), 362–366.
Gerken, L. A., & Bollt, A. (2008). Three exemplars allow at least some linguistic generalizations: implications for generalization mechanisms and constraints. *Language Learning and Development, 4*(3), 228–248.
Gerken, L. A., & Dawson, C. (in press). Grammar learning as model building. In T. Mintz (Ed.), *Statistical approaches to language.* The Hague: Taylor Francis.
Gervain, J., Nespor, M., Mazuka, R., Horie, R., & Mehler, J. (2008). Bootstrapping word order in prelexical infants: a Japanese Italian cross-linguistic study. *Cognitive Psychology, 57*(1), 56–74.

Gómez, R. L. (2002). Variability and detection of invariant structure. *Psychological Science, 13*(5), 431–436.

Gómez, R. L., & Gerken, L. A. (1999). Artificial grammar learning by 1-year-olds leads to specific and abstract knowledge. *Cognition, 70*(2), 109–135.

Gómez, R. L., & Maye, J. (2005). The developmental trajectory of nonadjacent dependency. *Infancy, 7*(2), 183–206.

Höhle, B., Bijeljac-Babic, R., Herold, B., Weissenborn, J., & Nazzi, T. (2009). Language specific prosodic preferences during the first half year of life: evidence from German and French infants. *Infant Behavior & Development, 32*(3), 262–274.

Jusczyk, P. W., Cutler, A., & Redanz, N. J. (1993). Infants' preference for the predominant stress patterns of English words. *Child Development, 64*(3), 675–687.

Jusczyk, P. W., Friederici, A. D., Wessels, J. M., Svenkerud, V. Y., & Jusczyk, A. M. (1993). Infants' sensitivity to the sound patterns of native language words. *Journal of Memory & Language, 32*(3), 402–420.

Jusczyk, P. W., Houston, D. M., & Newsome, M. (1999). The beginnings of word segmentation in English-learning infants. *Cognitive Psychology, 39*(3–4), 159–207.

Jusczyk, P. W., Luce, P. A., & Charles-Luce, J. (1994). Infants' sensitivity to phonotactic patterns in the native language. *Journal of Memory & Language, 33*(5), 630–645.

Kemp, C., Perfors, A., & Tenenbaum, J. B. (2007). Learning overhypotheses with hierarchical Bayesian models. *Developmental Science, 10*(3), 307–321.

Lorenz, K. (1935). Der Kumpan in der Umwelt des Vogels. *Journal of Ornithology, 83*, 137–413.

Marcus, G. F., Vijayan, S., Rao, S. B., & Vishton, P. M. (1999). Rule learning by seven-month-old infants. *Science, 283*, 77–80.

Mattys, S. L., Jusczyk, P. W., Luce, P. A., & Morgan, J. L. (1999). Phonotactic and prosodic effects on word segmentation in infants. *Cognitive Psychology, 38*(4), 465–494.

Maye, J., Weiss, D. J., & Aslin, R. N. (2008). Statistical phonetic learning in infants: facilitation and feature generalization. *Developmental Science, 11*, 122–134.

Maye, J., Werker, J. F., & Gerken, L. A. (2002). Infant sensitivity to distributional information can affect phonetic discrimination. *Cognition, 82*(3), B101–B111.

Medina, T. N., Snedeker, J., Trueswell, J. C., & Gleitman, L. R. (2011). How words can and cannot be learned by observation. *Proceedings of the National Academy of Sciences of the United States of America, 108*(22), 9014–9019.

Morgan, J. L., & Saffran, J. R. (1995). Emerging integration of sequential and suprasegmental information in preverbal speech segmentation. *Child Development, 66*(4), 911–936.

Ng, A. Y., & Jordan, M. (2002). On discriminative vs. generative classifiers: A comparison of logistic regression. In T. G. Dietterich, S. Becker, & Z. Ghahramani (Eds.), *Advances in Neural Information Processing Systems* (pp. 841–848). Cambridge, MA: MIT Press.

Pearl, J. (1988). *Probabilistic reasoning in intelligent systems: Networks of plausible inference*. San Francisco, CA: Morgan Kaufmann.

Peirce, C. S. (1935). Pragmatism and abduction. In C. Hartshorne (Ed.), *Collected papers of Charles Sanders Peirce* (pp. 112–135). Cambridge, MA: Harvard University Press.

Perfors, A., Tenenbaum, J. B., & Regier, T. (2006). *Poverty of the stimulus? A rational approach*. Paper presented at the 28th Annual Conference of the Cognitive Science Society, Vancouver, British Columbia, Canada.

Polka, L., & Werker, J. F. (1994). Developmental changes in perception of nonnative vowel contrasts. *Journal of Experimental Psychology: Human Perception and Performance, 20*, 421–435.

Rumelhart, D., & McClelland, J. (1987). Learning the past tenses of English verbs: implicit rules or parallel distributed processing? In B. MacWhinney (Ed.), *Mechanisms of language acquisition* (pp. 195–248). Mahwah, NJ: Lawrence Erlbaum Associates

Saffran, J. R. (2003). Absolute pitch in infancy and adulthood: the role of tonal structure. *Developmental Science, 6*(1), 35–43.

Saffran, J. R., & Thiessen, E. D. (2003). Pattern induction by infant language learners. *Developmental Psychology, 39*, 484–494.

Samuelson, L. K. (2002). Statistical regularities in vocabulary guide language acquisition in connectionist models and 15-20-month-olds. *Developmental Psychology, 38*(6), 1016–1037.

Santelmann, L. M., & Jusczyk, P. W. (1998). Sensitivity to discontinuous dependencies in language learners: evidence for limitations in processing space. *Cognition, 69*(2), 105–134.

Sebastián-Gallés, N., & Bosch, L. (2002). Building phonotactic knowledge in bilinguals: role of early exposure. *Journal of Experimental Psychology: Human Perception and Performance, 28*(4), 974–989.

Shady, M. E., Gerken, L. A., & Jusczyk, P. W. (1995). Some evidence of sensitivity to prosody and word order in ten-month-olds. In MacLaughlin, D, & McEwan, S. (Eds.), *Proceedings of the 19th Boston University Conference on Language Development*, Vol. 2. Sommerville, MA: Cascadilla Press.

Skoruppa, K., Pons, F., Christophe, A., Bosch, L., Dupoux, E., Núria Sebastián-Gallés, N., et al. (2009). Language-specific stress perception by 9-month-old French and Spanish infants. *Developmental Science, 12*(6), 914–919.

Smith, L. B., Jones, S. S., Landau, B., Gershkoff-Stowe, L., & Samuelson, L. (2002). Object name learning provides on-the-job training for attention. *Psychological Science, 13*, 13–19.

Tomasello, M. (2000). Do young children have adult syntactic competence? *Cognition, 74*(3), 209–253.

Tomasello, M., & Abbot-Smith, K. (2002). A tale of two theories: response to Fisher. *Cognition, 83*(2), 207–214.

Werker, J. F., & Tees, R. C. (1984). Cross-language speech perception: evidence for perceptual reorganization during the first year of life. *Infant Behavior and Development, 7*, 49–63.

Xu, F. (2007). Rational statistical inference and cognitive development. In P. Carruthers, S. Laurence, & S. Stich (Eds.), *The innate mind: Foundations and the future* (pp. 199–215). Oxford, UK: Oxford University Press.

Xu, F., & Tenenbaum, J. B. (2007a). Sensitivity to sampling in Bayesian word learning. *Developmental Science, 10*, 288–297.

Xu, F., & Tenenbaum, J. B. (2007b). Word learning as Bayesian inference. *Psychological Review, 114*, 245–272.

Yu, C., & Smith, L. B. (2012). Modeling cross-situational word–referent learning: prior questions. *Psychological Review, 119*(1), 21–39.

# CHAPTER FIVE

# Learning about Causes from People and about People as Causes: Probabilistic Models and Social Causal Reasoning

**Daphna Buchsbaum, Elizabeth Seiver, Sophie Bridgers, and Alison Gopnik[1]**

Institute of Human Development, Department of Psychology, University of California at Berkeley, Tolman Hall, Berkeley, CA 94720, USA
[1]Corresponding author: E-mail: gopnik@berkeley.edu

## Contents

## Abstract

A major challenge children face is uncovering the causal structure of the world around them. Previous research on children's causal inference has demonstrated their ability to learn about causal relationships in the physical environment using probabilistic evidence. However, children must also learn about causal relationships in the social environment, including discovering the causes of other people's behavior, and understanding the causal relationships between others' goal-directed actions and the outcomes of those actions. In this chapter, we argue that social reasoning and causal reasoning are deeply linked, both in the real world and in children's minds. Children use both types of information together and in fact reason about both physical and social causation in fundamentally similar ways. We suggest that children jointly construct and update causal theories about their social and physical environment and that this process is best captured by probabilistic models of cognition. We first present studies

*Advances in Child Development and Behavior*, Volume 43
ISSN 0065-2407,
http://dx.doi.org/10.1016/B978-0-12-397919-3.00005-8

showing that adults are able to jointly infer causal structure and human action structure from videos of unsegmented human motion. Next, we describe how children use social information to make inferences about physical causes. We show that the pedagogical nature of a demonstrator influences children's choices of which actions to imitate from within a causal sequence and that this social information interacts with statistical causal evidence. We then discuss how children combine evidence from an informant's testimony and expressed confidence with evidence from their own causal observations to infer the efficacy of different potential causes. We also discuss how children use these same causal observations to make inferences about the knowledge state of the social informant. Finally, we suggest that psychological causation and attribution are part of the same causal system as physical causation. We present evidence that just as children use covariation between physical causes and their effects to learn physical causal relationships, they also use covariation between people's actions and the environment to make inferences about the causes of human behavior.

# 1. INTRODUCTION

In the past 10 years, the probabilistic models approach to cognitive development, also known as rational constructivism, has begun to be applied to many aspects of children's development, particularly their causal inference and learning. In the first wave of this research, however, the focus was squarely on physical knowledge, such as the relation between blickets and blicket detectors (or the workings of other physical machines). In these types of studies, for example, an experimenter may place a series of blocks on top of a machine. Some blocks are "blickets" and make the machine produce an effect (e.g., lighting up and playing music), while other blocks do not. Children are then asked to make causal inferences from the evidence they see, such as which block was a blicket or which new block should make the machine go. In this vein, work from our lab and others has demonstrated that children possess sophisticated causal reasoning abilities, including making rational inferences from probabilistic input (e.g., Gopnik et al., 2004; Kushnir & Gopnik, 2005, 2007; Schulz, Bonawitz, & Griffiths, 2007; Schulz, Gopnik, & Glymour, 2007; Sobel & Kirkham, 2006; Sobel, Tenenbaum, & Gopnik, 2004).

These initial studies were generally limited to investigating how children learn by observing causal relationships in their physical environment and did not take the child's social environment into account. From an early age, children are exquisitely sensitive social beings and their causal learning takes place in a rich social context. A natural question is therefore how social interaction informs and influences children's causal learning and how causal reasoning influences children's social inferences.

Data about "purely physical" causes does not exist in a vacuum – blickets are not putting *themselves* on the machine, after all. There is a social and psychological component to the causal learning that results from our interactions with other people. Even in the relatively simple context of a blicket detector experiment, the child not only must consider the physical evidence of the machine's activation but also must make inferences about the experimenter's actions and mental states. Did she put the blicket on the machine in the right way? She says she knows what makes the machine go, but does she? Is she just trying to make the machine go or does she also want to teach me how it works? Children can use the physical blicket evidence to make social inferences (the block did not work, so she must not know what she is doing) or use the experimenter's testimony and actions to make inferences about the blickets (since she says she knows what she is doing, she must be teaching me about which blickets I should use, so I will pick the same one).

In general, social and physical causation will be inextricably linked in most real-life causal learning, especially since the goal-directed actions of others lead to many of the causal outcomes children observe. In fact, even infants and toddlers seem to expect that the causally relevant events they observe in the world will have been produced by the actions of social agents (Bonawitz et al., 2010; Meltzoff, Waismeyer, & Gopnik, in press; Saxe, Tenenbaum, & Carey, 2005; Saxe, Tzelnic, & Carey, 2007).

We argue that children jointly construct theories about both the physical and the social world, which in turn generate higher-order theories that shape children's interpretation of future events. This natural learning process parallels the scientific method, and thus, we can characterize children's learning with the metaphor of children as intuitive scientists.

This metaphor might suggest that children just learn on their own, but neither children nor scientists are solitary learners. Both scientists and children learn extensively from the actions, reports, and tuition of others.

Teachers serve a particularly important function in this regard, both formally in the classroom and informally in the world. Recent work on "natural pedagogy" (Csibra & Gergely, 2006, 2009; Gergely, Egyed, & Király, 2007) and children's understanding of testimony (e.g., Corriveau, Meints, & Harris, 2009; Jaswal, Croft, Setia, & Cole, 2010; Koenig & Harris, 2005; Pasquini, Corriveau, Koenig, & Harris, 2007) has demonstrated that infants and young children are sensitively tuned to others and can learn from them in complex and subtle ways. The pedagogical intent of a social demonstrator can influence everything from children's exploration of a novel toy (Bonawitz et al., 2011) to their generalizations about objects' functional properties (Butler & Markman, in press). The expertise (e.g., Koenig & Jaswal, 2011; Kushnir, Vredenburgh, & Schneider, under review; Sobel & Corriveau, 2010) and past accuracy (e.g., Birch, Vauthier, & Bloom, 2008; Corriveau et al., 2009) of a social informant affects what children learn from this informant in the future.

At the same time that children learn from others, they also learn *about* others. In the past 10 years, "theory of mind" research has found not only more and more sophisticated psychological understanding at younger ages but also a strikingly consistent rational pattern of advances in that understanding as children get older (Wellman & Liu, 2004). More recently, there has been a renewed interest in children's social cognition and their understanding of social concepts such as in-groups and out-groups (Dunham, Baron, & Banaji, 2008; Kinzler, Dupoux, & Spelke, 2007; Rhodes & Gelman, 2008) and personality traits (Liu, Gelman, & Wellman, 2007). We suggest that the outcomes of other people's actions are not only informative about the causal systems they act on but also socially informative about the actors themselves. Furthermore, we argue that children's inferences about psychological causes of behavior such as traits are fundamentally causal inferences, relying on the same probabilistic learning mechanisms as their inferences about physical systems such as blicket detectors.

Other recent results further support the notion that we can apply probabilistic models to both the social context of causal understanding and the causal context of the social world. Schulz and Gopnik (2004) found that children inferred psychological causal relationships from covariation in much the same way that they inferred physical and biological relationships. Kushnir, Xu, and Wellman (2010) and Ma and Xu (2011) found that infants as young as 14 months old showed some capacity to infer an underlying desire from a person's pattern of nonrandom sampling behavior. Additionally, Kushnir, Wellman, and Gelman (2008) and Sobel, Sommerville, Travers, Blumenthal, and Stoddard (2009) found that children's causal inferences are sensitive to the social environment. On the computational side, Shafto and colleagues (Bonawitz et al., 2011; Shafto & Goodman, 2008; Shafto, Goodman, Gerstle, & Ladusaw, 2010) have modeled how pedagogical information may be used differently than nonpedagogical information in solving inductive problems.

How children learn from social sources of causal information becomes an especially interesting question when we move beyond artificial laboratory tasks such as blicket detectors. Much of the real-world causal evidence children receive involves complex statistical patterns of both actions and outcomes. Consider the case of learning which actions are necessary to open a door. Children might notice that people almost always grasp and then turn a doorknob before the door opens, but sometimes they pull a handle instead. They frequently insert a key into a lock and then turn it before trying the doorknob, but not always. Sometimes the sequence of actions must be repeated a couple of times (for instance, in the case of a jammed lock); other times, the sequence fails and is not followed by the door opening at all. Often, other actions precede the door opening as well – putting down groceries, fumbling around in a purse, ringing a doorbell, sliding a bolt – which of these are causally necessary and which are incidental? Does the order they were performed in matter? Finally, in addition to these observations, children might receive direct testimony about the door. For instance, someone who lived in the house might say that jiggling the key almost always works or someone unfamiliar with the door might guess that this is the case. How might children combine these statements with other sources of causal evidence?

In just this simple example of opening a door, we can see that there are not only many potential types of causal information available but also many different sources of statistical variation and ambiguity. There is variation in the physical data – actions (and other causes) may not always bring about their effects or may only lead to the desired outcome in certain combinations. There is variation in the action sequence – repeated demonstrations of bringing about the same outcome may include different actions. There is variation in people's behavior – some individuals might succeed at opening the door while others fail or might be successful with one door while failing to open another. There is even variation in direct testimony – people may express differing levels of certainty and causal knowledge, and the testimony of multiple people may even conflict. Finally, children must also take into account their own prior knowledge and expectations about not only the causal system in question but also the intentions, knowledgeability, and helpfulness of their social informant, all of which could vary widely across situations.

On the other hand, while all this ambiguity can make the causal inference problem children face more challenging, there are times when the presence of statistical variation can actually be quite illuminating and aid inference. Actions that do not consistently precede outcomes are less likely to be causally necessary. Actions that reliably appear together and, in fact, predict each other, are more likely to be coherent units, corresponding to intentional, goal-directed action. Variations in the certainty and accuracy of a social informant can facilitate our judgments of the trustworthiness of the information they provide. Variation in the success and failure of individuals might help us infer situational or psychological causes for their behavior such as personality traits.

Formal modeling can be extremely helpful in disentangling these complex inferences. First, formal models give us a way of precisely characterizing hypotheses about what the child thinks and knows. Rational constructivism, and probabilistic computational models in particular, is a natural way to approach understanding how social information, along with other evidence, contributes to children's causal reasoning, because they allow us to systematically represent both beliefs and evidence. Intuitively, this can be seen as a formal version of the approach developmental psychologists have used historically. The method is to hypothesize that children have particular beliefs or conceptions of the world and to assume that children's answers and actions follow rationally from those beliefs. For example, if children initially have a non-representational theory of mind, we would expect them to rationally infer in a false-belief task that a person will immediately search for an object in the location where it actually resides rather than where she last saw it. The classic developmental methodology, then, is to work backward and infer children's current theories from their answers and actions, by assuming that they are operating under the theory that is most consistent with their behavior.

Describing the child's current conception of the world as a particular rational model gives us a more exact way of both characterizing the child's beliefs and working out the predictions that should rationally follow from those beliefs. It also lets us make predictions about how children should rationally update those beliefs with new evidence. By specifying a model, we make explicit our hypotheses about the prior biases and information children bring to a problem and how these biases should be combined with new information in order to update beliefs or even potentially change models or theories. Conversely, we can compare different possible models of the children's beliefs and see which models are most congruent with children's behavior. This approach allows us to give a more precise justification for attributing particular theories to the children, theories that may or may not be like adult theories.

Second, probabilistic models give us a way of more precisely combining and weighting how different factors interact in the child's mind to bring about a particular response. It is common in developmental psychology to see children make different judgments in different contexts. This inconsistency has sometimes been taken to mean that all children's cognition is variable and context dependent and that there is no coherent conceptual structure to be found (e.g., Greeno, 1998; Lave & Wenger, 1991; Thelen & Smith, 1994). At other times, it has led to unresolved debates, for example, about whether early imitation is rational or not. As we will see, probabilistic models allow one to precisely show how multiple sources of evidence, reflecting different contexts, can be rationally combined and integrated to lead to a particular response.

In this chapter, we report two lines of research that apply the ideas of probabilistic modeling to social cognition and explore the complex and interdependent relationship between social and causal learning. In the first set of studies, we examine how the social context, in the form of both demonstrations and testimony, influences children's causal learning. We also examine how causal learning can influence the understanding and segmentation of action and how observed statistical structure in human action can affect causal inferences. In the second set of studies, we examine how children might use covariation in human behavior to infer and attribute mental traits to others, in the same way that they use covariation in cause and effect data to infer physical causal structure. Both lines of research extend probabilistic models from reasoning about purely physical causes to include children's social cognitive development, while also characterizing the distinctive aspects of psychological and physical causal reasoning.

## 2. THE SOCIAL CONTEXT OF CAUSAL REASONING

### 2.1. Jointly Inferring Causal Structure and Action Structure

As we discussed in the introduction, many if not most of the causal outcomes children witness are the result of intentional human action. Children must be able to distinguish the unique actions they see other people performing and recognize their effects in order to understand the reasons behind others' behavior and in order to potentially bring about those effects themselves. But before we can interpret actions, we first must parse a continuous stream of motion into meaningful behavior (Byrne, 2003). What cues do we use to do this? How might infants and young children begin to break into the behavior stream in order to identify intentional, goal-directed actions?

Could the causal relationships between actions and their outcomes in the world help children understand action structure itself? How might children identify reaching, grasping, and turning and then group them into the action "opening the door"?

One way that infants might be able to segment actions is by using statistical regularities in human motion. There is now a lot of evidence that both infants and adults use statistical patterns in spoken language to help solve the related problem of segmenting words from continuous speech (e.g., Aslin, Saffran, & Newport, 1998; Pelucchi, Hay, & Saffran, 2009; Saffran, Aslin, & Newport, 1996; Saffran, Newport, & Aslin, 1996). In these experiments, infants (and adults) listen to an artificial language constructed of made-up words, usually created from English syllables (e.g., dutaba, patubi, pidabu). The words are assembled into a continuous speech stream (e.g., dutabapatubipidabu…), with other potential segmentation cues such as intonation and pauses removed. In these experiments, as in many words in real languages, syllables within a word have higher transitional probabilities than syllables between words – you are more likely to hear ta followed by ba (as in dutaba) than to hear bi followed by pi (as in patubi pidabu). Both infants and adults are able to use these transitional probabilities in order to distinguish words in these artificial languages (dutaba, patubi, pidabu), from part-words – combinations of syllables that cross a word boundary (e.g., tabapa, tubipi), and from nonwords, combinations of syllables that do not appear in the artificial language at all (e.g., dupapi, babibu). Infants have also been shown to succeed at statistical language segmentation even when more naturalistic language stimuli are used (Pelucchi et al., 2009).

More recently, a similar sensitivity to statistical regularities has been shown to play a role in action segmentation in both adults (Baldwin, Andersson, Saffran, & Meyer, 2008) and infants (Roseberry, Richie, Hirsh-Pasek, Golinkoff, & Shipley, 2011). Intriguingly, there is also evidence that children can successfully map words learned through this type of segmentation to meanings (Estes, Evans, Alibali, & Saffran, 2007) and, conversely, can use words they already know to help find segment boundaries and discover new words (Bortfeld, Morgan, Golinkoff, & Rathbun, 2005). Similarly, a recent study shows that, in the visual domain, children use statistical patterns to infer the boundaries between objects and then use that information to make further predictions about how objects will behave (Wu, Gopnik, Richardson, & Kirkham, 2011). So children do not just detect the statistics and then segment the streams accordingly. They actually treat those statistical units as if they were meaningful.

In the same way that words have meanings, intentional actions usually lead to causal outcomes. This suggests that just as identifying words assists in mapping them to meanings, segmenting human action may bootstrap learning about causation and vice versa. Recent work has demonstrated that adults can segment videos of common everyday behaviors into coherent actions (Baldwin et al., 2008; Hard, Tversky, & Lang, 2006; Meyer, Decamp, Hard, Baldwin, & Roy, 2010; Newtson, Engquist, & Bois, 1977; Zacks & Tversky, 2001; Zacks, Speer, Swallow, & Maley, 2010) and that both children and adults can infer causal relationships from conditional probabilities (Cheng, 1997; Gopnik et al., 2004; Griffiths, Sobel, Tenenbaum, & Gopnik, in press; Griffiths & Tenenbaum, 2009). However, researchers have not yet explored whether action parsing and causal structure can be learned jointly.

In our work (Buchsbaum, Griffiths, Gopnik, & Baldwin, 2009, 2012), we adapted a Bayesian word segmentation model (Goldwater, Griffiths, & Johnson, 2009), with actions composed of individual small motion elements (SMEs) taking the place of words composed of phonemes or syllables, and extended this model to incorporate causal information. The key intuition behind this model is that action segmentation and causal structure are jointly learned, taking advantage of statistical evidence in both domains. In the model, sequences of motion that correspond to known actions are considered more likely to be causes, and sequences of motion that appear to be causal (they predict outcomes in the world) are considered more likely to be actions. The inferred action boundaries help determine the inferred causal structure and vice versa. This corresponds to our hypothesis that people believe intentional actions and causal effects go hand in hand. If statistical action structure is a cue to causal relationships then, like our model, people should think statistically grouped actions are more likely to be potential causes than other equivalent sequences. Additionally, if people believe that causal sequences of motion are also likely to be actions, then adults should find causal sequences to be more meaningful and coherent than other sequences with equivalent statistical regularities. Finally, if action segmentation and causal relationships are truly jointly learned, then we should see cue combination and cue conflict effects emerge, as in other cases of joint perceptual inference (Ernst & Banks, 2002).

We tested all these predictions in a set of experiments using "artificial action grammars" as in Baldwin et al. (2008). Just as a sentence is composed of words, which are in turn composed of phonemes or syllables, here an action sequence is composed of actions, which are themselves composed of SMEs. Similar to Baldwin et al., we used video clips of object-directed motions to create three-motion actions, which we then combined to create continuous videos of a person manipulating an object.

Just as people can recognize words from an artificial language, and distinguish them from nonwords and part-words, we also know that they can recognize artificial actions grouped only by statistical relationships and can distinguish these sequences from nonactions (motions that never appeared together) and part-actions (motion sequences that cross an action boundary) (Baldwin et al., 2008). We wanted to see whether people think these statistically defined actions are meaningful sequences that can help them understand and interpret others' behavior and whether they believe that these actions are likely to be causal.

In the first experiment, after watching a video, adult participants rated actions, part-actions, and nonactions on how coherent the sequences seemed to be. They were given the example of removing a pen cap and then writing with the pen as motions "going together" and of removing a pen cap and then tying your shoes as motions "not going together." Participants also rated sequences on how likely they thought those motions were to be causal. In this case, we gave participants a cover story. They were told that some of the sequences of motion they were observing would make the manipulated object play music, but there was no sound in the video, so they would just have to guess how likely each sequence was to cause music.

Adults rated the sequences corresponding to actions as both more coherent and more likely to be causal than the nonactions and part-actions. In fact, after the experiment, some of the participants commented on how much more "sense" some of the action sequences made, often coming up with post hoc intentional explanations for the actor's behaviors ("she shook it to see if anything was inside, then emptied it, then looked inside to check"). This is striking because the "nonactions" of one video were in fact the "actions" of another, meaning that people found the very same sequences of motion to be more meaningful based purely on how frequently they appeared together and how well the component motions predicted each other.

These results show that people's sensitivity to statistical patterns in action is not just an artifact of the impoverished stimuli but plays a real role in their understanding of the structure of observed human behavior. The fact that people found the statistically grouped actions to be more coherent suggests that they do not experience the sequences they segment out as arbitrary but assume that they are meaningful groupings that play some (possibly intentional) role. This is further supported by the fact that, even without being presented with overt causal structure, people believe that the statistically grouped actions are more likely to be causally effective, suggesting that inference of action structure and causal structure really are linked.

People seem to use statistical action structure to infer causal relationships but can they use causal relationships to identify meaningful actions? We hypothesized that when statistical cues to action segmentation are unavailable, adults will be able to use causal structure to identify coherent units of action. In a second experiment, we had adults watch specially constructed videos where all possible combinations of three motions appeared equally often together, so that joint and transitional probabilities could not be used to identify groupings. However, one particular sequence of three motions was chosen to be causal and was always followed by the manipulated object playing music, and this time the sound in the video was on. Adults easily identified the correct set of causal motions from within the longer sequence, one of the first demonstrations of causal variable discovery from a continuous stream of events. Additionally, even though there were no statistically grouped actions in this experiment, participants perceived the causal sequence as being more meaningful (going together better) than the other sequences, suggesting that they had nonetheless segmented it out as a coherent action based on its causal efficacy.

In a third experiment, we looked at the inferences people make when both types of cues – statistical action structure and causal relationships – are present. Can people combine information from both these sources of evidence, even when they conflict? This type of cue integration is often used as evidence of true joint inference, for instance, when visual and haptic information about the same stimuli are combined in inferences about an object's size (Ernst & Banks, 2002). As in our first experiment, we showed adults videos of statistically grouped actions, but now we selected a part-action (a set of motions crossing an action boundary) as the causal sequence that leads to music. Adults appeared to take both the causal relationships and the statistical structure into account, correctly identifying the part-action as the most likely cause, but continuing to rate actions as more likely to also be causal when compared to other part-actions and nonactions. Similarly, they judged the causal part-action to be very cohesive, even though it violated the statistical regularities of the action sequence, suggesting that its causal properties led to it being considered a coherent unit of human action.

Together, these three studies demonstrate that adults, at least, can combine statistical regularities and causal structure to divide observed human behavior into meaningful actions. They can also use this inferred segmentation to help them identify likely causal actions. Additionally, the parallels between people's word segmentation and action segmentation abilities support the possibility of a more general statistical learning mechanism. These results also provide a demonstration that causal and social information can be jointly used to infer goal structures. In the following section, we will look at whether young children make similar types of inferences. Can children identify causal subsequences of action from within a longer action sequence when deciding which actions to imitate?

## 2.2. Causal Imitation from Social Demonstrations

Imitation is a characteristic and pervasive behavior of human children and so it seems like a natural mechanism for identifying and learning causal actions. How do children choose what to imitate from all the actions they see performed around them? When they see a sequence of behaviors preceding an interesting outcome, can they choose the relevant actions? Do they imitate different portions of sequences when given different evidence about their effectiveness?

Recent studies of children's imitation have produced varying answers to the question of whether children are in fact capable of inferring causal action sequences from observed demonstrations. Children can use information about an actor's prior intentions to help them identify causally effective actions (Carpenter, Call, & Tomasello, 2002). Similarly, when children observe unsuccessful demonstrations, they reproduce the actor's intended goals rather than the unsuccessful actions themselves (Hamlin, Hallinan, & Woodward, 2008; Meltzoff, 1995). In some cases, they vary the precision and faithfulness of their imitation with apparent causal relevance (Brugger, Lariviere, Mumme, & Bushnell, 2007; Harnick, 1978; Williamson & Markman, 2006) and selectively imitate actions based on how causally effective they appear to be (Schulz, Hooppell, & Jenkins, 2008; Want & Harris, 2001; Williamson, Meltzoff, & Markman, 2008). At other times, however, children will "overimitate," reproducing apparently unnecessary parts of a causal sequence (Horner & Whiten, 2005; Lyons, Young, & Keil, 2007; Lyons, Damrosch, Lin, Macris, & Keil, 2011; McGuigan & Whiten, 2009; McGuigan, Whiten, Flynn, & Horner, 2007) or copying an actor's precise means (Meltzoff, 1988) even when this makes them less efficient at accomplishing their goal.

There are even cases where children do both in the same study. In the "rational imitation" studies by Gergely, Bekkering, and Király (2002), children saw an experimenter whose hands were either free or confined activate a machine using their forehead. Children both produced exact imitations of the actor (touching their head to the machine to make it go) and produced more obviously causally efficient actions (touching the machine with a hand), though the proportion of such actions differed in the different intentional contexts. In fact, finding a distribution of imitative responses is the norm across all these studies. Even in the most intriguing demonstrations of overimitation, it is not the case that all children blindly mimic the demonstrator's actions, and similarly, even in experiments where children show an overall appreciation for causal efficacy, some children still imitate unnecessary or ineffective actions.

We are interested in reconciling these results by suggesting that perhaps all these imitative choices are the result of rational imitation using a combination of social, physical, and statistical evidence as well as prior knowledge. In particular, evidence for which actions are causally necessary includes more than just the immediately observed demonstration. It also includes children's previous experiences with causal systems and objects, their prior observations of bringing about the same effect, and social information including the adult's knowledge state, intentions, and pedagogical stance (we know that observing a helpful teacher versus a neutral [Bonawitz et al., 2011; Brugger et al., 2007], ineffective [Schulz et al., 2008; Want & Harris, 2001; Williamson et al., 2008], or naïve [Bonawitz et al., 2011; Butler & Markman, in press] demonstrator changes children's inferences). If different imitative choices are the result of different evidence, then we should be able to manipulate these choices and get children to imitate different portions of the same action sequences by changing the combination of social and physical evidence they receive.

Moreover, in many real-world situations, the causal structure of a demonstrated sequence of actions is not fully observable, and which actions are necessary and which are superfluous may be unclear. Therefore, there is often no single "right answer" to the question of what to imitate. After all, a longer "overimitation" sequence might actually be necessary to bring about an effect, though that might initially seem unlikely. One way in which children may overcome this difficulty is by using statistical evidence provided by repeated observations of bringing about the effect. By watching someone unlock and open a door or turn on a light bulb on multiple occasions, children can detect which actions consistently predict the desired outcome and which do not.

To test this prediction, we ran an experiment that manipulated the statistical evidence children received from a series of demonstrated action sequences (Buchsbaum, Griffiths, Gopnik, & Shafto, 2011). We used a Bayesian model to help us construct demonstration sequences that normatively predict selective imitation in some cases and "overimitation" in others. If children make rational inferences from variations in the action sequences they observe, then their choice of whether to imitate only part of an action sequence versus the complete sequence should similarly vary with the evidence.

In this study, children watched a naïve informant (who claimed to have no knowledge of how the toy worked) demonstrate five sequences of three actions each on a toy (e.g., the experimenter squishing the toy, then shaking it, and then rolling it would be one sequence). Some of these sequences but not others led to the toy playing music. In the "ABC" data condition, the same three actions (e.g., knock, shake, pull) always made the toy play music, while in the "BC" data condition, the first action of the successful sequences varied while the final two actions preceding the music stayed the same (e.g., knock, shake, pull, or squish, shake, pull, or roll, shake, pull would all be followed by the toy playing music). Children either could exactly reproduce one of the three-action sequences that had caused the toy to activate or could just produce the final two actions in isolation.

Intuitively, it is more likely that all three-actions are necessary in the "ABC" condition, while perhaps only the final two-actions are necessary in the "BC" condition. However, both three-action and two-action sequences reflect potentially correct hypotheses about what caused the toy to activate in either condition. It could be that the last two-actions by themselves cause the toy to activate in the "ABC" condition and the first is superfluous or it could be that three-actions are necessary in the "BC" condition, but the first action can vary. It is just the probability of these hypotheses that changes between the two conditions. Our Bayesian model predicts just those differences in probability.

If children automatically encode the adult's successful actions as causally necessary, then they should exclusively imitate three actions in both conditions. However, if children are also using more complex statistical information, then we expect that children in the "ABC" condition should reproduce three actions more often than children in the "BC" condition and that children in the "BC" condition might imitate the two-action subsequence by itself. This is, in fact, what we found – children imitated all three actions almost exclusively in the "ABC" condition, while children in the "BC" condition imitated much more variably, with a number of them imitating the two-action subsequence, even though they had never seen it performed on its own and even though three actions would have also activated the toy. Like adults in our first set of experiments, preschool children used statistical patterns to identify causal subsequences within longer sequences of action.

The particular model parameters that best fit children's performance also tell us something about children's expectations going into this task. The model suggested that children employ a causal Occam's razor, assuming that simpler hypotheses, which require fewer unique causal sequences to explain the data, are more likely than more complex hypotheses. The model also suggested that children were biased to imitate the adult's complete action sequence (though this bias could be overcome), perhaps indicating a preexisting belief that adults usually do not perform extraneous actions.

Children might make this "rational actor" assumption because they are using information about the adult's knowledgeability (e.g., Jaswal, 2006; Kushnir et al., 2008), reliability (e.g., Koenig, Clément, & Harris, 2004; Zmyj, Buttelmann, Carpenter, & Daum, 2010), and intentional stance (Bonawitz et al., 2011; Butler & Markman, in press). For instance, children might notice that the experimenter always performs three actions and infer that the experimenter, while not knowing the exact causal sequence, knows that it must be three actions long. We explored this possibility in a next experiment, where we manipulated the intentional state of the demonstrator rather than the statistics of the demonstration.

In our original study, the experimenter acted clueless, as if she did not know anything about how the machine worked. In the next study, the experimenter became a knowledgeable teacher. She told the children that she was showing them how the machine worked – and then showed them exactly the same sequences of actions as in the original "BC" condition. Now, children were much more likely to "overimitate;" almost all of them reproduced a complete sequence of three actions. So children made different causal inferences depending on the social context. When it was their turn to bring about the effect, children chose to reproduce more of the demonstrated actions when the demonstrator was a knowledgeable teacher than when she was naïve about the workings of the toy. Intuitively, children, like our model, understood that a helpful teacher would only be demonstrating all these extra actions if they were in fact necessary to make the toy work (see, e.g., Shafto & Goodman, 2008, for more details on Bayesian models of inference from pedagogically versus non-pedagogically selected data).

These studies suggest that causal learning is informed by both social knowledge and statistical information. Children are sensitive to probabilities, knowledge state, and pedagogical intent when deciding which actions to imitate. These studies also suggest a rational account of "overimitation." In particular, imitating three actions in these studies can be thought of as a kind of overimitation, reproducing parts of a causal sequence that are not actually demonstrably necessary for the effect. These results suggest that this behavior varies depending on the statistics of the data and the probability of various hypotheses concerning them. "Overimitation" also varies depending on the social demonstrator. By explicitly representing the contributions of these different sources of evidence and using them to assign probabilities to causal hypotheses, a Bayesian model can predict these behaviors quite precisely.

Many of the studies of imitation we discussed earlier in this section did not provide the child with either clearly pedagogical or nonpedagogical demonstrators. These demonstrators may have used cues such as directed gaze and pointing (Csibra & Gergely, 2009; Gergely et al., 2007; Senju, Csibra, & Johnson, 2008), leading children to assume that they were in a teaching situation. In general, these studies also showed children only one way to bring about the desired effect and used causal systems where children's prior expectations were unclear. These differences may help explain why children's imitative choices seem so varied across studies. This work also suggests that despite appearances, such behavior is a rational response to different combinations of social, statistical, and physical information. In situations where causal structure is ambiguous, children not only take advantage of social demonstrations, they use relevant information about the demonstrators themselves to make causal inferences.

## 2.3. Causal Inference from Social Testimony

The previous experiments show that social observation influences children's causal reasoning. Children used the demonstrator's intentional state to help infer which actions were causally necessary to produce an effect. Presumably, children in these experiments were learning not only about the causal system but also about the causal demonstrator. What assumptions might children have made about the value of the demonstrator as a social informant and how might these assumptions guide children's future interactions with that person? In this section, we address these questions by investigating the influence of a different type of social information: verbal testimony. What can we learn from other people's causal statements about the world and what might the world tell us about the reliability of those statements and thus, other people?

Much of what we know about the world we learn from what other people tell us to be true. Our parents, teachers, and peers are continually providing us with information about the causal structure and mechanisms of our environment (e.g., Callanan & Oakes, 1992). However, the role of verbal testimony in causal learning is not obvious a priori. Cause and effect relationships can often be inferred from direct observation without explicit instruction. Again, a child could learn that turning a key in the lock makes a door open because someone said this is so, but a child could just as successfully learn this causal link simply by observing someone turning a key and seeing the door open. So how might children use informant testimony in the context of causal inference?

When what we hear corroborates what we observe, then testimony should facilitate children's causal understanding. However, as we discussed in the introduction, the real world is stochastic and unpredictable, and informants might be ignorant, mistaken, or even deceptive. What would happen if the testimony children receive conflicts with what they see? Would children choose one source to rely on or integrate information from each to inform their causal judgments? To use testimony effectively, we must know when it is prudent to trust others and when they are likely giving inaccurate information. What would a conflict between testimony and observation tell children about the credibility of their informant?

Young children have a strong bias to trust the testimony of others (Jaswal et al., 2010). However, children are not entirely credulous. Just as they can use patterns of evidence to make sophisticated judgments about the relative strengths of different causes (e.g., Kushnir & Gopnik, 2005), children can use patterns of past accuracy to make sophisticated judgments about the relative credibility of different informants. Preschoolers are more likely to trust future testimony from informants who have demonstrated that they tend to be knowledgeable and accurate over that of informants who have demonstrated ignorance and inaccuracy (e.g., Corriveau et al., 2009; Koenig & Harris, 2005; Pasquini et al., 2007). This phenomenon is referred to as selective trust (Koenig & Harris, 2005). Past accuracy is not the only cue children rely on, however. As we saw in our studies of children's imitation, children also take the expressed confidence of the informant into account and are more likely to trust the testimony of informants who speak with confidence than informants who indicate that they are unsure (e.g., Jaswal & Malone, 2007; Tenney, Small, Kondrad, Jaswal, & Spellman, 2011).

Informants are not only reporters about the world but also reporters of their own knowledge states. Informants may be unreliable because they hold mistaken beliefs about the world or because they hold mistaken beliefs about the extent of their own knowledge. Thus, yet another cue children might use to evaluate testimony is an informant's level of self-knowledge: how well their confidence predicts their accuracy (what Tenney et al., 2011, refer to as calibration). Research on eyewitness testimony has suggested that though children are sensitive to an informant's confidence and past accuracy, they are not sensitive to an informant's level of self-knowledge, whereas adults are attuned to all three cues (Tenney et al., 2011).

Some recent research has explored how children combine social information with their observations when making causal inferences. This research, including the studies on imitation in our lab, has found that just as children consider testimony from certain informants more informative than others based on past reliability, children find the interventions of certain causal demonstrators more informative than others based on the social information the demonstrators offer. For example, children favor the causal interventions of a demonstrator who claims to be knowledgeable about the causal system over those of a demonstrator who claims to be naïve (Kushnir et al., 2008). Children also learn more from a disambiguating intervention when the demonstrator supplies an explanation relevant to the causal problem at hand than when the demonstrator supplies an irrelevant rationale (Sobel & Sommerville, 2009). Additionally, children are better able to infer causal strength from probabilistic data when the demonstrator acts surprised by the anomalous outcomes (Sobel et al., 2009). Together this research shows that children's causal inferences are not solely determined by the statistical evidence children observe but are also mediated by the social information communicated by the demonstrator.

What happens, though, when the social information explicitly contrasts with children's observations? How might children handle a conflict between what observed statistical data show and what an informant says? Furthermore, what inferences do children make about the reliability of an informant based on the information they provide and the causal evidence children see? In the following experiment (Bridgers, Buchsbaum, Seiver, Gopnik, & Griffiths, 2011, 2012), we explored children's causal and social inferences when they were presented with a disagreement between an informant's statements and their own causal observations.

The experiment involved four between-subject conditions: the knowledgeable conflict condition, the naïve conflict condition, the knowledgeable baseline condition, and the naïve baseline condition. In the conflict conditions, we investigated how 3-, 4-, and 5-year-olds resolve a conflict between the information provided by either a knowledgeable or a naïve informant and by probabilistic causal demonstrations. In the baseline conditions, we explored preschoolers' baseline trust in a knowledgeable and a naïve informant's testimony in the absence of conflicting data. We describe the conflict conditions first.

The knowledgeable and naïve conflict conditions had two within-subject phases: the causal phase and the generalization phase. First, in the causal phase, children were introduced to two blocks (the "causal" pair) and a machine that lit up and played music when certain blocks were placed on top. An informant explained to the children that one block was better at activating the machine than the other. In the knowledgeable conflict condition, the informant claimed to really know which block was better, while in the naïve conflict condition, the informant said she was just guessing. The informant then left the room, and a second, neutral experimenter demonstrated the blocks on the machine, providing probabilistic evidence that in both conditions, challenged the informant's statement: The block endorsed by the informant was actually less causally efficacious, statistically speaking, than the unendorsed block. The endorsed block only activated the machine two out of six times, while the unendorsed block activated it two out of three times (past research has shown that children can correctly infer causal strength from this pattern of activation; see Kushnir & Gopnik, 2007). Children were then asked to choose which block they thought was better at activating the machine. Children were thus confronted with an ambiguous situation in which they had to decide whether or not the informant or perhaps their own observations were unreliable. In the generalization phase, the informant returned with two novel blocks (the "generalization" pair) and, in both conditions, claimed that she *knew* which block was better at activating the machine. Last, children were asked by the neutral experimenter to choose one of these new blocks to make the machine go.

One might expect that when provided with contradictory verbal and visual information, children would always trust what they directly see over what they hear. However, children might instead rationally combine their prior beliefs about the reliability of these types of sources with the evidence to make a joint causal and social inference. In doing so, children would also update their beliefs about the validity of both the informant's testimony and the observed causal data, which would affect their later inferences from these sources. Therefore, as in our previous experiments looking at children's causal imitation, we expected children's inferences to vary with both the social and the causal evidence.

Our results suggest just such an interaction. In the causal phase of the naïve conflict condition, children overwhelmingly trusted the data and chose the unendorsed block as better at activating the machine, while children in the knowledgeable conflict condition were torn between the two blocks. Thus, when there was strong evidence supporting the causal efficacy of each block (the knowledgeable informant's testimony for the endorsed block and the causal observations for the unendorsed block), children were at chance between inferring the endorsed or the unendorsed block as the better cause. When the testimony was weaker (because the informant was naïve), children favored the block that the causal data suggested was better. Though the causal evidence was constant across conditions, children put more confidence in the knowledgeable informant's claim than in the naïve informant's guess and so were willing to believe the informant over their own observations when she expressed certainty but not when she expressed uncertainty. As predicted and again, as demonstrated in our imitation experiments, children's causal inferences about the same pattern of causal data differed depending on the social context. These results suggest that children combine informant testimony and causal data to infer causal relations even when these cues conflict.

In the conflict conditions, the informants expressed different levels of knowledge about the causal blocks initially but both were wrong in their endorsements. Thus, in addition to different levels of claimed knowledgeability, the informants also had different levels of self-knowledge. Even though both informants made incorrect predictions about the causal blocks' relative causal strengths, the naïve informant actually demonstrated more self-knowledge because she was aware that she did not know about the blocks. The knowledgeable informant, on the other hand, was oblivious to the fact that she was mistaken in her beliefs. Therefore, when both informants later say that they "know" about the generalization blocks, it is more judicious to trust the previously naïve informant because she is more likely to actually know about the causal system when she says that she does. Would children be sensitive to this difference?

At first glance, the answer appears to be no. In the generalization phase, there was no difference in performance across the two conditions; children were equally likely to extend trust to the informant who was correctly uncertain in her prior testimony as to the informant who was incorrectly certain. In both the knowledge and the naïve conflict conditions, children were willing to trust the informant and intervened with the generalization block she endorsed more often than the unendorsed block. Children's failure to selectively trust the naïve informant in the generalization phase implies that, as earlier research has suggested, children are more sensitive to an informant's expressed knowledge level about the general world than to her level of self-knowledge (e.g., Tenney et al., 2011).

However, there may be alternative explanations for children's performance in the generalization phase that do not assume that children entirely lack a concept of self-knowledge. In the causal phase, the informant endorses one block, while the causal data "endorse" the other. However, in the generalization phase, though the informant endorses one of the new blocks, there is no evidence about the second block. Since there is no evidence directly contradicting the informant's claim, there is a relatively low cost in choosing to intervene with the endorsed generalization block over the unendorsed one. Furthermore, the conflicting data observed in the causal phase are probabilistic, suggesting that perhaps the causal data, rather than the informant, are the unreliable information source. Maybe the informant was correct about the relative efficacies of the causal blocks and the particular pattern of causal data the children observed were merely a fluke (for instance, the result of faulty wiring or battery failure) and unrepresentative of the actual causal system. Additionally, children's strong tendency to trust testimony may have further convinced them to trust the informant about the generalization blocks regardless of the conflict observed and the informant's prior knowledge state. In summary, given children's bias to believe testimony, their beliefs about the reliability of stochastic data, and the low cost of intervening with the endorsed generalization block, children could be sensitive to self-knowledge and still rationally trust both informants more or less equally.

To help us better understand children's performance in the generalization phase of the conflict conditions, we need to consider the level of trust that children place in a knowledgeable and a naïve informant's causal testimony when no conflicting causal data are present. In the knowledgeable and naïve baseline conditions, children were told by either a knowledgeable or a naïve informant, respectively, that one block was better than another at making a machine go, without seeing any causal demonstrations of either one. These two conditions are identical in structure to the generalization phase of the two conflict conditions, but since there is no preceding causal phase, children only have the informant's current testimony to guide their intervention choice. We predicted that in general across both baseline conditions, children would trust the informant but would be more likely to do so when the informant expressed certainty than when she expressed uncertainty. And that is basically what we found: A majority of children chose to intervene with the endorsed block across both conditions though slightly fewer did so when the informant was naïve.

We can compare children's performance at baseline to their performance in the generalization phase of the conflict conditions. In both situations, children are presented with informant testimony endorsing one of two blocks but are not given a chance to observe the blocks on the machine. However, in the baseline conditions, children have no prior experience with the informants, while in the generalization phase of the conflict conditions, children have witnessed a disagreement between the informants' earlier statements and the causal data. If children's trust in the informants is influenced by this conflict, we would expect children to be less trusting of the informants in the generalization phase of the conflict conditions than in the baseline conditions. When we make this comparison, we find that overall, more children intervened with the endorsed block in the baseline conditions than in the generalization phase of the conflict conditions, suggesting that children were in fact more willing to trust the informants before observing a conflict between their testimony and the causal data than afterward. Moreover, there was a greater decline in children's trust in the knowledgeable informant than in the naïve one. This may indeed suggest that children are potentially sensitive to self-knowledge though further research is necessary to test this claim.

This experiment confirms that children's causal judgments are informed by both social knowledge (in this case, testimony) and statistical data. Additionally, these experiments provide us with further insight into how children combine information from these sources. They demonstrate that children do not entirely discount one source and privilege another when the information from each conflicts. Rather children are evaluating, weighting, and integrating information from both social and physical cues to guide their inferences about both the causal system and the informant.

This situation lends itself particularly well to Bayesian modeling since children are being asked to combine information from two probabilistic sources and the disagreement between the two only adds to the complexity and ambiguity of the information each source provides. We are developing just such a model (Buchsbaum et al., in press) to better understand how children might be relating testimony and direct observation in their social and causal inferences (for a related model, see Eaves & Shafto, this volume).

## 3. USING CAUSAL INFERENCE TO LEARN ABOUT PEOPLE

The studies described in the preceding sections demonstrate how the social domain can inform our inferences about physical causation and how the causal outcomes of people's actions can be used to make inferences about both the causal structure of the physical world and the intentions, knowledge, and reliability of the social demonstrator or informant. But as adults, we not only make causal inferences about physical systems, we also make extensive inferences about the causes of people's behavior, a process termed "attribution." How do children reason about these psychological causes? Does their reasoning about the causes of human behavior proceed along the same lines as their reasoning about physical causation?

Even in the earliest years of life, babies are already making attributions about other people and figuring out the causes of their behavior. For example, even infants expect there to be different sources of movement for physical objects and people (Saxe et al., 2005; Schult & Wellman, 1997; Woodward, Phillips, & Spelke, 1993). In other studies, infants are capable of even more sophisticated reasoning about others' behavior; for example, they expect that agents who help others reach their goal will be treated differently than agents who hinder others' progress and they also treat helpers and hinderers differently themselves (Hamlin, Wynn, & Bloom, 2007; Kuhlmeier, Wynn, & Bloom, 2003).

As children grow older, they show increasingly sophisticated understanding of such social constructs as in-groups and out-groups. Some more sophisticated aspects of social cognition, however, do not seem to emerge until much later in children's development, in some cases not until the school-age period (Rholes & Ruble, 1984; Ruble & Dweck, 1995). This includes the propensity to causally explain human behavior in terms of personality traits.

In particular, people explain the causes of human actions in different ways. First, they may attribute a person's actions to internal, individual, and enduring characteristics (i.e., traits). An internal attribution places the cause of behavior in the mind of the acting agent. To revisit the case of interpreting the opening of a door, we might see someone open a door and think she did it because she is the kind of curious person who enjoys opening doors. Second, people may attribute actions to external situations, circumstances, or other objects in the environment. An external attribution for opening the door might be that it was a hot day outside or that the cat needs

to be let in. These different styles of attribution have far-reaching consequences; social psychologists have found that a preference for one type of
causal explanation and attribution affects other kinds of social cognition and
behavior, such as motivation, achievement, blame, mental health, and
general emotional well-being (e.g., Levy & Dweck, 1998), even in children
(Levy & Dweck, 1999; Patrick, Skinner, & Connell, 1993). Especially in
Western cultures, many adults have a bias to attribute the actions of others to
individual enduring traits of the person rather than to external situations
(Jones & Harris, 1967; Ross, 1977). Some researchers have suggested that
this is because these adults have developed an intuitive theory that explains
action in terms of such traits (Molden, Plaks, & Dweck, 2006; Morris &
Peng, 1994; Rosati et al., 2001). That theory might then bias the observer's
interpretation of behavioral evidence toward favoring internal causes.

   Where do these attributions come from? It is unclear when and why
children begin to explain action in terms of internal, individual, and
enduring traits. Even very young children explain action in terms of
internal mental states (Flavell, Flavell, Green, & Moses, 1990). However,
trait explanations include two additional factors beyond mental states
themselves – traits are specific to particular individual people, and they are
constant over time and across situations. Many researchers have demonstrated that children do not spontaneously explain actions in terms of traits
or endorse trait explanations for a single instance of behavior until middle
childhood (Alvarez, Ruble, & Bolger, 2001; Peevers & Secord, 1973;
Rholes & Ruble, 1984; Shimizu, 2000). However, other studies show that
when preschoolers are given trait labels or behavioral frequency information, they can use that information to make inferences about future
behavior and that they can infer the right trait label from frequent
behaviors (Boseovski & Lee, 2006; Ferguson, Olthof, Luiten, & Rule,
1984; Heyman & Gelman, 1999; Liu et al., 2007; Matsunaga, 2002). On
the other hand, these preschoolers still did not spontaneously construct trait
explanations; rather they simply matched the frequency of behaviors to
trait labels that were provided for them. This suggests that the failure to
attribute traits more broadly is not simply a problem with word comprehension or conceptual development.

   More significantly, we do not know the learning mechanisms that
underlie the course of attribution in childhood and beyond. Kelley was one
of the first psychologists to suggest that person and situation covariation
evidence might play an important role in internal versus external attributions
(Kelley, 1967; Plaks, Grant, & Dweck, 2005). Empirical studies confirm that

adults use statistical information tracking multiple people in multiple situations to make behavioral attributions (Cheng & Novick, 1990; Hewstone & Jaspars, 1987; Morris & Larrick, 1995; Orvis, Cunningham, & Kelley, 1975; Sutton & McClure, 2001). However, adults already have intuitive theories of action they can apply to the covariation data to interpret and predict behavior. Could covariation play a role in the development of trait attribution itself?

As we discussed earlier in this chapter, Bayesian causal learning theories, in particular, suggest that children make new rational inferences by systematically combining prior knowledge and current covariation evidence to arrive at the right causal hypothesis. This suggests a potential mechanism for the development of attribution. Children may begin by observing person and situation covariation evidence that confirms a particular type of hypothesis, particularly the hypothesis that internal traits cause actions. Once that theory has been highly confirmed, it will be more difficult to overturn in the future, though it might still be overturned with sufficient evidence. Eventually, in adulthood, this may result in a consistent "trait bias" that is difficult and thus requires a larger amount of contrary evidence to overcome.

In a series of studies, we examined the developmental origins of Kelley's social schemas. We integrated research on the development of causal inference and trait attribution to see if the same domain-general machinery children used to learn about physical causation in our experiments on causal imitation and causal testimony might also underlie their reasoning about psychological causation.

## 3.1. Reasoning about Psychological Causes

First, Seiver, Gopnik, and Goodman (in press) conducted a study where 4- and 6-year-old children observed a scenario of two dolls playing on two activities (chosen from a bicycle, trampoline, and diving board). Children were either in the doll condition (where the two doll characters acted consistently on the two activities and differently from each other) or in the toy condition (where both dolls played on one toy activity and did not play on the other). The children in each condition received different covariation information about the person and situation while still observing the same overall frequency of playing and not playing. At the end, we asked the children to explain the dolls' actions (e.g., "Why did Josie play on the bicycle?") and predict their behavior in a future situation.

In the doll condition, one doll always plays and the other doll never plays. This evidence suggests that something about the individual rather than the situation is responsible for their behavior. In the toy condition, the two characters never play on one toy and always play on the other, suggesting instead that the situation or the toy itself is responsible for their actions. So how would children explain the dolls' behavior in these two different conditions? Four-year-olds more closely tracked the behavioral data than 6-year-olds and offered explanations that matched the data. For example, in the doll condition, when the overall pattern of behaviors indicated that something about the person was responsible for the dolls' behavior, both 4- and 6-year-olds gave internal explanations for their behavior – explanations about the person, including physical characteristics such as age or height or mental states such as desires and beliefs. However, in the toy condition, when the data indicated that the situations were driving the dolls' actions (i.e., they both played on one activity and did not play on the other), 4-year-olds appropriately gave more external explanations – explanations involving the environment or the specific toy activity – but 6-year-olds persisted in giving internal explanations. This difference in attribution style between the two age groups in the toy condition suggests that the 4-year-olds were more sensitive to the covariation data than the 6-year-olds. Further evidence included a control condition where children were asked to explain why a single doll did or did not play on a single activity. In this case, the data are ambiguous about the possible cause of the behavior. In the control condition, 6-year-olds gave internal explanations significantly more often than chance and 4-year-olds were, correctly, at chance.

The prediction question provided additional evidence for 6-year-olds' preference for internal causes. In the doll condition, children were asked to predict whether each doll would play or not play on a new toy. Both 4- and 6-year-olds generalized from the previous pattern of data and said that the doll who had played before would play on the new toy and the doll who did not play before would continue to refrain from playing. In the toy condition, children were asked to predict whether a new doll would play or not play on the same two toys. Four-year-olds again accurately assessed the data and said she would play on the toy the other dolls played on but would not play on the one that they backed away from. Six-year-olds, on the other hand, did not predict consistent behavior in this case.

This provides further evidence for age differences in children's behavioral causal inference. Four-year-olds predicted the pattern of playing and not playing would be consistent in the future, irrespective of whether it favored internal or external attributions. Six-year-olds thought that only the behavioral data that supported internal attributions would generalize to future behavior.

This pattern of results suggests that 6-year-olds have developed a specific prior attributional theory that the internal qualities of a person, rather than the situation, drive their behavior. Six-year-olds seem to have developed expectations about the source of people's actions, so when they are asked to explain the cause of a person's behavior, 6-year-olds use both the actual evidence at hand and their prior beliefs to arrive at a conclusion. The 4-year-olds, in contrast, seem to use a more general "bottom-up" data-based strategy and only use the most immediately available data to draw conclusions.

How domain specific or how general is this higher-order bias? Would it only be applied to the case of psychological causation or would children reason similarly about internal versus external causes of physical outcomes? Studies with adults suggest that there is a relationship between cultural attributional biases and seemingly unrelated views about physical causes. Some studies have shown in adults that culturally based attributional biases affect scientific reasoning (e.g., Morris & Peng, 1994). Even though culturally based differences may be rooted in social cognition, they also cause differences in reasoning about simple Newtonian physics. Westerners, for example, who have a stronger social trait bias, are also more likely to attribute causal power to individual physical objects rather than to relationships or forces.

## 3.2. From People to Magnets

To explore potential attributional biases in understanding physical causation, we replicated the previous study with children but changed the outcome of interest to a physical rather than psychological one – "stickiness" instead of willingness to play. Without changing the task in any other way, we altered the cover story to implicate physical instead of psychological causation. Thus, rather than saying that the doll character was playing on the scooter, we would say that the doll was sticking to the scooter. The relevant explanatory question then became "Why did the Josie doll stick to the scooter?" We again divided children's responses into two categories. In "internal" responses, children talked about the properties of the doll. In "external" responses, they talked about properties of the toy.

When we made this small modification, changing the language used to describe the dolls to be physical rather than agentive, 6-year-olds lost their overall preference for internal explanations. Moreover, for predicting future sticking or not sticking, 6-year-olds now reliably extended the data pattern in both conditions. That is, they were willing to use the most recently available data to make causal inferences instead of relying on their prior beliefs.

Four-year-olds, however, still gave more accurate explanations than 6-year-olds – they continued to follow the data pattern more closely and gave more internal explanations in the doll condition and external explanations in the toy condition. Closer examination of the results suggests that once again the 6-year-olds had shifted from largely relying on the data to relying instead on a prior bias. Unlike in the original psychological case, however, the 6-year-olds gave explanations in terms of a rather different everyday causal theory – namely, magnetism. They often appealed to the scientific properties of magnetism, such as the relationship between magnets and metal, in their explanations. They also were more likely to give interactive causal explanations that implicated both the doll and the toy as causes for the outcome (e.g., "she has metal shoes and the skateboard is a magnet"). Children never produced these interactive explanations in the social case, and 4-year-olds rarely produced them in the physical case. These explanations suggest that the 6-year-old children relied on a deeper and more scientifically based causal framework about stickiness and magnetism, in particular, rather than relying on the data. Four-year-olds tended to give more vague answers such as "she has sticky stuff on her feet" and were less sophisticated in terms of appealing to physical mechanisms and magnets. However, they again tracked the data more accurately, perhaps due to this less sophisticated understanding of magnetism's interactive properties, and therefore weaker prior beliefs.

## 3.3. Cross-Cultural Studies

We are also conducting versions of these studies in Beijing, China, to compare children's beliefs about psychological causes across cultures. Research with adults shows that broadly speaking, the cultural preference for trait explanations in the United States is not present in Chinese culture (e.g., Morris & Peng, 1994). If there is truly a cultural difference in prior expectations about the causes of people's actions, then 6-year-olds in a non-trait-biased culture should not perform the same way as the American

6-year-olds; that is, 6-year-olds in China should not show a bias favoring internal explanations. Although the data collection is still ongoing, preliminary results suggest that 6-year-olds in Beijing have a similar expectation in the control condition, where the data does not support an internal or an external explanation, to American (and Chinese) 4-year-olds. They are at chance for preferring internal or external explanations. These findings suggest that by the age of 6, children's prior beliefs about others' behavior are influenced by culture and these attributional styles shape their interpretation of new behavioral information.

## 4. CONCLUSIONS

Taken together, the studies in this chapter show how the tools of probabilistic modeling and Bayesian learning can be applied to the social as well as the physical domain and how the physical and social domains can jointly inform each other. When children learn about causes from other people, whether through demonstration or testimony, they appear to integrate their prior hypotheses about pedagogy, cues to informant reliability, and the statistical evidence they observe from people's actions. Children are sensitive to the pedagogical intent of a demonstrator and can use this information to aid their decisions about which of the demonstrator's actions to imitate in order to bring about an effect. Similarly, children can use an informant's statements to help them evaluate the data produced by a causal system and likewise can use these data to evaluate the credibility of the testimony produced by an informant. They also can use covariation information to decide whether a situational or psychological cause is a better explanation for a person's behavior and take into consideration whether the event involves people or just physical objects. Together, these studies demonstrate that causal reasoning and social reasoning are linked, both in the real world and in children's minds. When children reason about physical causal systems, they are incorporating social information, and when children reason about seemingly purely social issues like personality trait attribution, they are applying the same causal reasoning that they use for physical systems.

The rational constructivist approach can help us understand how children resolve, and even benefit from, multiple sources of ambiguous and probabilistic data, and social data, in particular, in order to solve challenging causal learning problems. And because these data are often probabilistic,

Bayesian models help us describe the complex, uncertain, joint inferences about the nature of both other people and the world that underlie our ability to learn from others. At the same time, the work on attribution shows how similarly complex integrations between prior knowledge and current statistics can lead children to understand the actions of others in a new way. In fact, we can construe the information we get from people, either in the form of testimony or observable actions, as causal information. These studies suggest that children use covariation evidence to construct abstract causal schemas that they then employ to explain the behavior of both the people and the objects around them.

The studies on imitation and pedagogy, in particular, suggest that we would be wise to fully consider the social environment when looking at children's physical causal reasoning. The degree of confidence that the social demonstrator has, and the level of authority they convey to the child, might not just socially influence the child to feel pressured to respond in a certain way but also might actually change their inferences about the physical causal events they are observing. In fact, incorporating this social evidence into causal reasoning is a rational response, especially in the face of uncertainty. Therefore, to get a complete picture of how children understand the causal landscape of both the physical and the social worlds we need to understand how they use the entire rich set of data they encounter in the real world. Studies directly manipulating social information, such as how pedagogically the demonstrator is behaving and how much certainty she expresses, integrate the human element into experiments that model causal understanding.

Future research should computationally address how children develop priors about the causes and results of people's behavior and of the social information they provide. What leads children to believe that a person is an expert, and what process guides their assumptions based on that attribution? What are the components of children's pedagogical understanding, and what prior beliefs do children have about the likely causes and effects of pedagogical behavior? How do children integrate data about people's beliefs (via testimony) and actions when making attributions about people's behavior? How do children conceptualize people causing changes in other people's beliefs or actions? What are children's prior beliefs about person-to-person causes, and how would they parse these events? Furthermore, how would they integrate physical causes into those judgments?

The studies in this chapter begin to show how we can move beyond basic laboratory problems, like determining the causal structure of blicket detectors, to more complex inferences that more closely mirror the real world. The probabilistic models approach can be applied to real and ecologically significant kinds of conceptual change. It sheds new light on classic topics in cognitive development such as the nature of imitation and trait attribution. Instead of looking at how children evaluate individual or isolated events, we can more appropriately study how children *learn* in and from the complex social–physical environment that makes up the world around them.

## ACKNOWLEDGMENTS

This work is supported by National Science Foundation Graduate Research Fellowships to D.B. and E.S. and National Science Foundation Grant BCS-1023875 to A.G. and by the McDonnell Foundation Causal Learning Initiative and Grant.

## REFERENCES

Alvarez, J. M., Ruble, D. N., & Bolger, N. (2001). Trait understanding or evaluative reasoning? An analysis of children's behavioral predictions. *Child Development, 72*(5), 1409–1425.

Aslin, R. N., Saffran, J. R., & Newport, E. L. (1998). Computation of conditional probability statistics by 8-month-old infants. *Psychological Science, 9*(4), 321–324.

Baldwin, D., Andersson, A., Saffran, J., & Meyer, M. (2008). Segmenting dynamic human action via statistical structure. *Cognition, 106*(3), 1382–1407.

Birch, S. A. J., Vauthier, S. A., & Bloom, P. (2008). Three- and four-year-olds spontaneously use others' past performance to guide their learning. *Cognition, 107*(3), 1018–1034.

Bonawitz, E. B., Ferranti, D., Saxe, R., Gopnik, A., Meltzoff, A. N., Woodward, J., et al. (2010). Just do it? Investigating the gap between prediction and action in toddlers' causal inferences. *Cognition, 115*(1), 104–117.

Bonawitz, E. B., Shafto, P., Gweon, H., Goodman, N. D., Spelke, E., & Schulz, L. E. (2011). The double-edged sword of pedagogy: Instruction limits spontaneous exploration and discovery. *Cognition, 120*(3), 322–330.

Bortfeld, H., Morgan, J. L., Golinkoff, R. M., & Rathbun, K. (2005). Mommy and me: Familiar names help launch babies into speech-stream segmentation. *Psychological Science, 16*(4), 298–304.

Boseovski, J. J., & Lee, K. (2006). Children's use of frequency information for trait categorization and behavioral prediction. *Developmental Psychology, 42*(3), 500–513.

Bridgers, S., Buchsbaum, D., Seiver, E., Gopnik, A., & Griffiths, T. L. (2011). *Which block is better at making the machine go?: How children balance their trust in an informant vs. the data.* Poster presented at Biennial Meeting of the Cognitive Development Society. October.

Bridgers, S., Buchsbaum, D., Seiver, E., Gopnik, A., & Griffiths, T. L. (2012). *Which block is better at making the machine go?: How children balance their trust in an informant vs. the data.* Manuscript in preparation.

Brugger, A., Lariviere, L. A., Mumme, D. L., & Bushnell, E. W. (2007). Doing the right thing: Infants' selection of actions to imitate from observed event sequences. *Child Development, 78*(3), 806–824.

Buchsbaum, D., Bridgers, S., Whalen, A., Seiver, E., Griffiths, T. L., & Gopnik, A. (in press). Do I know that you know what you know? Modeling testimony in causal inference. In *Proceedings of the 34th Annual Cognitive Science Society.*

Buchsbaum, D., Gopnik, A., Griffiths, T. L., & Shafto, P. (2011). Children's imitation of causal action sequences is influenced by statistical and pedagogical evidence. *Cognition, 120*(3), 331–340.

Buchsbaum, D., Griffiths, T. L., Gopnik, A., & Baldwin, D. (2009). Learning from actions and their consequences: Inferring causal variables from a continuous sequence of human action. In N. A. Taatgen, & H. van Rijn (Eds.), *Proceedings of the 31st Annual Conference of the Cognitive Science Society* (pp. 2493–2498). Austin, TX: Cognitive Science Society.

Buchsbaum, D., Griffiths, T. L., Gopnik, A., & Baldwin, D. (2012). *Inferring action structure and causal relationships in continuous sequences of human action.* Manuscript in preparation.

Butler, L. P., & Markman, E. M. (in press). Preschoolers use intentional and pedagogical cues to guide inductive inferences and exploration. *Child Development.*

Byrne, R. W. (2003). Imitation as behaviour parsing. *Philosophical Transactions of the Royal Society London B, 358*(1431), 529–536.

Callanan, M. A., & Oakes, L. M. (1992). Preschoolers' questions and parents' explanations: Causal thinking in everyday activity. *Cognitive Development, 7*(2), 213–233.

Carpenter, M., Call, J., & Tomasello, M. (2002). Understanding "prior intentions" enables two-year-olds to imitatively learn a complex task. *Child Development, 73*(5), 1431–1441.

Cheng, P. W. (1997). From covariation to causation: A causal power theory. *Psychological Review, 104*(2), 367–405.

Cheng, P. W., & Novick, L. R. (1990). A probabilistic contrast model of causal induction. *Journal of Personality and Social Psychology, 58*(4), 545–567.

Corriveau, K. H., Meints, K., & Harris, P. L. (2009). Early tracking of informant accuracy and inaccuracy. *British Journal of Developmental Psychology, 27*(2), 331–342.

Csibra, G., & Gergely, G. (2006). Social learning and social cognition: The case for pedagogy. In Y. Munakata, & M. H. Johnson (Eds.), *Processes of change in brain and cognitive development. Attention and performance*, Vol. 21 (pp. 249–274). Oxford: Oxford University Press.

Csibra, G., & Gergely, G. (2009). Natural pedagogy. *Trends in Cognitive Sciences, 13*(4), 148–153.

Dunham, Y., Baron, A. S., & Banaji, M. R. (2008). The development of implicit intergroup cognition. *Trends in Cognitive Sciences, 12*(7), 248–253.

Eaves, B., & Shafto, P. (this volume). Unifying pedagogical reasoning and epistemic trust. In F. Xu & T. Kushnir (Eds.), *Advances in child development and behavior.*

Ernst, M. O., & Banks, M. S. (2002). Humans integrate visual and haptic information in a statistically optimal fashion. *Nature, 415*, 429–433.

Estes, K. G., Evans, J. L., Alibali, M. W., & Saffran, J. R. (2007). Can infants map meaning to newly segmented words? *Psychological Science, 18*(3), 254–260.

Ferguson, T. J., Olthof, T., Luiten, A., & Rule, B. G. (1984). Children's use of observed behavioral frequency versus behavioral covariation in ascribing dispositions to others. *Child Development, 55*(6), 2094–2105.

Flavell, J. H., Flavell, E. R., Green, F. L., & Moses, L. J. (1990). Young children's understanding of fact beliefs versus value beliefs. *Child Development, 61*(4), 915–928.

Gergely, G., Bekkering, H., & Király, I. (2002). Rational imitation in preverbal infants. *Nature, 415*, 755.

Gergely, G., Egyed, K., & Király, I. (2007). On pedagogy. *Developmental Science, 10*(1), 139–146.

Goldwater, S., Griffiths, T. L., & Johnson, M. (2009). A Bayesian framework for word segmentation: Exploring the effects of context. *Cognition, 112*(1), 21–54.

Gopnik, A., Glymour, C., Sobel, D. M., Schulz, L. E., Kushnir, T., & Danks, D. (2004). A theory of causal learning in children: Causal maps and Bayes nets. *Psychological Review, 111*(1), 3–32.

Greeno, J. G. (1998). The situativity of knowing, learning, and research. *American Psychologist, 53*(1), 5–26.

Griffiths, T. L., Sobel, D. M., Tenenbaum, J. B., & Gopnik, A. (in press). Bayes and blickets: Effects of knowledge on causal induction in children and adults. *Cognitive Science.*

Griffiths, T. L., & Tenenbaum, J. B. (2009). Theory-based causal induction. *Psychological Review, 116*(4), 661–716.

Hamlin, J. K., Hallinan, E. V., & Woodward, A. L. (2008). Do as I do: 7-month-old infants selectively reproduce others' goals. *Developmental Science, 11*(4), 487–494.

Hamlin, J. K., Wynn, K., & Bloom, P. (2007). Social evaluation by preverbal infants. *Nature, 450,* 557–559.

Hard, B. M., Tversky, B., & Lang, D. S. (2006). Making sense of abstract events: Building event schemas. *Memory and Cognition, 34*(6), 1221–1235.

Harnick, F. S. (1978). The relationship between ability level and task difficulty in producing imitation in infants. *Child Development, 49*(1), 209–212.

Hewstone, M., & Jaspars, J. (1987). Covariation and causal attribution: A Logical model of the intuitive analysis of variance. *Journal of Personality and Social Psychology, 53*(4), 663–672.

Heyman, G. D., & Gelman, S. A. (1999). The use of trait labels in making psychological inferences. *Child Development, 70*(3), 604–619.

Horner, V., & Whiten, A. (2005). Causal knowledge and imitation/emulation switching in chimpanzees (Pan troglodytes) and children (Homo sapiens). *Animal Cognition, 8*(3), 164–181.

Jaswal, V. K. (2006). Preschoolers favor the creator's label when reasoning about an artifact's function. *Cognition, 99*(3), B83–B92.

Jaswal, V. K., Croft, A. C., Setia, A. R., & Cole, C. A. (2010). Young children have a specific, highly robust bias to trust testimony. *Psychological Science, 21*(10), 1541–1547.

Jaswal, V. K., & Malone, L. S. (2007). Turning believers into skeptics: 3-year-olds' sensitivity to cues to speaker credibility. *Journal of Cognition and Development, 8*(3), 263–283.

Jones, E. E., & Harris, V. A. (1967). The attribution of attitudes. *Journal of Experimental Social Psychology, 3*(1), 1–24.

Kelley, H. H. (1967). Attribution theory in social psychology. In D. Levine (Ed.), *Nebraska symposium on motivation,* Vol. 15 (pp. 192–238). Lincoln: University of Nebraska Press.

Kinzler, K. D., Dupoux, E., & Spelke, E. S. (2007). The native language of social cognition. *Proceedings of the National Academy of Sciences of the United States of America, 104*(30), 12577–12580.

Koenig, M. A., Clément, F., & Harris, P. L. (2004). Trust in testimony: Children's use of true and false statements. *Psychological Science, 15*(10), 694–698.

Koenig, M. A., & Harris, P. L. (2005). Preschoolers mistrust ignorant and inaccurate speakers. *Child Development, 76*(6), 1261–1277.

Koenig, M. A., & Jaswal, V. K. (2011). Characterizing children's expectations about expertise and incompetence: Halo or pitchfork effects? *Child Development, 82*(5), 1634–1647.

Kuhlmeier, V., Wynn, K., & Bloom, P. (2003). Attribution of dispositional states by 12-month-olds. *Psychological Science, 14*(5), 402–408.

Kushnir, T., & Gopnik, A. (2005). Young children infer causal strength from probabilities and interventions. *Psychological Science, 16*(9), 678–683.

Kushnir, T., & Gopnik, A. (2007). Conditional probability versus spatial contiguity in causal learning: Preschoolers use new contingency evidence to overcome prior spatial assumptions. *Developmental Psychology, 43*(1), 186–196.

Kushnir, T. et al. "Who can help me fix this toy?:" The distinction between causal knowledge and word knowledge guides preschoolers' selective requests for information. *Developmental Psychology.*

Kushnir, T., Wellman, H. M., & Gelman, S. A. (2008). The role of preschoolers' social understanding in evaluating the informativeness of causal interventions. *Cognition, 107*(3), 1084–1092.

Kushnir, T., Xu, F., & Wellman, H. M. (2010). Young children use statistical sampling to infer the preferences of other people. *Psychological Science, 21*(8), 1134–1140.

Lave, J., & Wenger, E. (1991). *Situated learning: Legitimate peripheral participation.* Cambridge: Cambridge University Press.

Levy, S. R., & Dweck, C. S. (1998). Trait-versus process-focused social judgment. *Social Cognition, 16*(1), 151–172.

Levy, S. R., & Dweck, C. S. (1999). The impact of children's static versus dynamic conceptions of people on stereotype formation. *Child Development, 70*(5), 1163–1180.

Liu, D., Gelman, S. A., & Wellman, H. M. (2007). Components of young children's trait understanding: Behavior-to-trait inferences and trait-to-behavior predictions. *Child Development, 78*(5), 1543–1558.

Lyons, D. E., Damrosch, D. H., Lin, J. K., Macris, D. M., & Keil, F. C. (2011). The scope and limits of overimitation in the transmission of artefact culture. *Philosophical Transactions of the Royal Society of London B, 366*(1567), 1158–1167.

Lyons, D. E., Young, A. G., & Keil, F. C. (2007). The hidden structure of overimitation. *Proceedings of the National Academy of Sciences of the United States of America, 104*(50), 19751–19756.

Ma, L., & Xu, F. (2011). Young children's use of statistical sampling evidence to infer the subjectivity of preferences. *Cognition, 120*(3), 403–411.

Matsunaga, A. (2002). Preschool children's inferences about personality traits. *Japanese Journal of Developmental Psychology, 13*, 168–177.

McGuigan, N., & Whiten, A. (2009). Emulation and "overemulation" in the social learning of causally opaque versus causally transparent tool use by 23- and 30-month-olds. *Journal of Experimental Child Psychology, 104*(4), 367–381.

McGuigan, N., Whiten, A., Flynn, E., & Horner, V. (2007). Imitation of causally opaque versus causally transparent tool use by 3- and 5-year-old children. *Cognitive Development, 22*(3), 353–364.

Meltzoff, A. N. (1988). Infant imitation after a 1-week delay: Long-term memory for novel acts and multiple stimuli. *Developmental Psychology, 24*(4), 470–476.

Meltzoff, A. N. (1995). Understanding the intentions of others: Re-enactment of intended acts by 18-month-old children. *Developmental Psychology, 31*(5), 838–850.

Meltzoff, A. N., Waismeyer, A. S., & Gopnik, A. (in press). Learning about causes from people: Observational causal learning in 24-month old infants. *Developmental Psychology.*

Meyer, M., Decamp, P., Hard, B., Baldwin, D., & Roy, D. (2010). Assessing behavioral and computational approaches to naturalistic action segmentation. In S. Ohlsson, & R. Catrambone (Eds.), *Proceedings of the 32nd Annual Cognitive Science Society* (pp. 2710–2715). Austin, TX: Cognitive Science Society.

Molden, D. C., Plaks, J. E., & Dweck, C. S. (2006). "Meaningful" social inferences: Effects of implicit theories on inferential processes. *Journal of Experimental Social Psychology, 42*(6), 738–752.

Morris, M. W., & Larrick, R. P. (1995). When one cause casts doubt on another: A normative analysis of discounting in causal attribution. *Psychological Review, 102*(2), 331–355.

Morris, M. W., & Peng, K. (1994). Culture and cause: American and Chinese attributions for social and physical events. *Journal of Personality and Social Psychology, 67*(6), 949–971.

Newtson, D., Engquist, G., & Bois, J. (1977). The objective basis of behavior units. *Journal of Personality and Social Psychology, 35*(12), 847–862.

Orvis, B. R., Cunningham, J. D., & Kelley, H. H. (1975). A closer examination of causal inference: The roles of consensus, distinctiveness, and consistency information. *Journal of Personality and Social Psychology, 32*(4), 605–616.

Pasquini, E. S., Corriveau, K. H., Koenig, M., & Harris, P. L. (2007). Preschoolers monitor the relative accuracy of informants. *Developmental Psychology, 43*(5), 1216–1226.

Patrick, B. C., Skinner, E. A., & Connell, J. P. (1993). What motivates children's behavior and emotion? Joint effects of perceived control and autonomy in the academic domain. *Journal of Personality and Social Psychology, 65*(4), 781–791.

Peevers, B. H., & Secord, P. F. (1973). Developmental changes in attribution of descriptive concepts to persons. *Journal of Personality and Social Psychology, 27*(1), 120–128.

Pelucchi, B., Hay, J. F., & Saffran, J. R. (2009). Statistical learning in a natural language by 8-month-old infants. *Child Development, 80*(3), 674–685.

Plaks, J. E., Grant, H., & Dweck, C. S. (2005). Violations of implicit theories and the sense of prediction and control: Implications for motivated person perception. *Journal of Personality and Social Psychology, 88*(2), 245–262.

Rhodes, M., & Gelman, S. A. (2008). Categories influence predictions about individual consistency. *Child Development, 79*(5), 1270–1287.

Rholes, W. S., & Ruble, D. N. (1984). Children's understanding of dispositional characteristics of others. *Child Development, 55*(2), 550–560.

Rosati, A. D., Knowles, E. D., Kalish, C. W., Gopnik, A., Ames, D. R., & Morris, M. W. (2001). The rocky road from acts to dispositions: Insights for attribution theory from developmental research on theories of mind. In B. F. Malle, L. J. Moses, & D. A. Baldwin (Eds.), *Intentions and intentionality: Foundations of social cognition* (pp. 287–303). Cambridge, MA: The MIT Press.

Roseberry, S., Richie, R., Hirsh-Pasek, K., Golinkoff, R. M., & Shipley, T. F. (2011). Babies catch a break: 7- to 9-month-olds track statistical probabilities in continuous dynamic events. *Psychological Science, 22*(11), 1422–1424.

Ross, L. (1977). The intuitive psychologist and his shortcomings: Distortions in the attribution process. In L. Berkowitz (Ed.), *Advances in experimental social psychology*, Vol. 10 (pp. 173–220). New York: Academic Press.

Ruble, D. N., & Dweck, C. S. (1995). Self-perceptions, person conceptions, and their development. In N. Eisenberg (Ed.), *Social development: Review of personality and social psychology*, Vol. 15 (pp. 109–139). Thousand Oaks, CA: Sage Publications.

Saffran, J. R., Aslin, R. N., & Newport, E. L. (1996). Statistical learning by 8-month-old infants. *Science, 274*(5294), 1926–1928.

Saffran, J. R., Newport, E. L., & Aslin, R. N. (1996). Word segmentation: The role of distributional cues. *Journal of Memory and Language, 35*(4), 606–621.

Saxe, R., Tenenbaum, J. B., & Carey, S. (2005). Secret agents: Inferences about hidden causes by 10- and 12-month-old infants. *Psychological Science, 16*(12), 995–1001.

Saxe, R., Tzelnic, T., & Carey, S. (2007). Knowing who dunnit: Infants identify the causal agent in an unseen causal interaction. *Developmental Psychology, 43*(1), 149–158.

Schult, C. A., & Wellman, H. M. (1997). Explaining human movements and actions: Children's understanding of the limits of psychological explanation. *Cognition, 62*(3), 291–324.

Schulz, L. E., Bonawitz, E. B., & Griffiths, T. L. (2007). Can being scared cause tummy aches? Naive theories, ambiguous evidence, and preschoolers' causal inferences. *Developmental Psychology, 43*(5), 1124–1139.

Schulz, L. E., & Gopnik, A. (2004). Causal learning across domains. *Developmental Psychology, 40*(2), 162–176.

Schulz, L. E., Gopnik, A., & Glymour, C. (2007). Preschool children learn about causal structure from conditional interventions. *Developmental Science, 10*(3), 322–332.

Schulz, L. E., Hooppell, C., & Jenkins, A. C. (2008). Judicious imitation: Children differentially imitate deterministically and probabilistically effective actions. *Child Development, 79*(2), 395–410.

Seiver, E., Gopnik, A., & Goodman, N. D. (in press). Did she jump because she was the big sister or because the trampoline was safe? Causal inference and the development of social attribution. *Child Development*

Senju, A., Csibra, G., & Johnson, M. H. (2008). Understanding the referential nature of looking: Infants' preference for object-directed gaze. *Cognition, 108*(2), 303–319.

Shafto, P., & Goodman, N. D. (2008). Teaching games: Statistical sampling assumptions for learning in pedagogical situations. In B. C. Love, K. McRae, & V. M. Sloutsky (Eds.), *Proceedings of the 30th Annual Conference of the Cognitive Science Society* (pp. 1632–1637). Austin, TX: Cognitive Science Society.

Shafto, P., Goodman, N. D., Gerstle, B., & Ladusaw, F. (2010). Prior expectations in pedagogical situations. In S. Ohlsson, & R. Catrambone (Eds.), *Proceedings of the 32nd Annual Cognitive Science Society* (pp. 2182–2187). Austin, TX: Cognitive Science Society.

Shimizu, Y. (2000). Development of trait inference: Do young children understand the causal relation of trait, motive, and behavior? *Japanese Journal of Educational Psychology, 48*(3), 255–266.

Sobel, D. M., & Corriveau, K. H. (2010). Children monitor individuals' expertise for word learning. *Child Development, 81*(2), 669–679.

Sobel, D. M., & Kirkham, N. Z. (2006). Blickets and babies: The development of causal reasoning in toddlers and infants. *Developmental Psychology, 42*(6), 1103–1115.

Sobel, D. M., & Sommerville, J. A. (2009). Rationales in children's causal learning from others' actions. *Cognitive Development, 24*(1), 70–79.

Sobel, D. M., Sommerville, J. A., Travers, L. V., Blumenthal, E. J., & Stoddard, E. (2009). The role of probability and intentionality in preschoolers' causal generalizations. *Journal of Cognition and Development, 10*(4), 262–284.

Sobel, D. M., Tenenbaum, J. B., & Gopnik, A. (2004). Children's causal inferences from indirect evidence: Backwards blocking and Bayesian reasoning in preschoolers. *Cognitive Science, 28*(3), 303–333.

Sutton, R. M., & McClure, J. (2001). Covariational influences on goal-based explanation: An integrative model. *Journal of Personality and Social Psychology, 80*(2), 222–236.

Tenney, E. R., Small, J. E., Kondrad, R. L., Jaswal, V. K., & Spellman, B. A. (2011). Accuracy, confidence, and calibration: How young children and adults assess credibility. *Developmental Psychology, 47*(4), 1065–1077.

Thelen, E., & Smith, L. B. (1994). *A dynamic systems approach to the development of cognition and action.* Cambridge, MA: The MIT Press.

Want, S. C., & Harris, P. L. (2001). Learning from other people's mistakes: Causal understanding in learning to use a tool. *Child Development, 72*(2), 431–443.

Wellman, H. M., & Liu, D. (2004). Scaling of Theory-of-Mind tasks. *Child Development, 75*(2), 523–541.

Williamson, R. A., & Markman, E. M. (2006). Precision of imitation as a function of preschoolers' understanding of the goal of the demonstration. *Developmental Psychology, 42*(4), 723–731.

Williamson, R. A., Meltzoff, A. N., & Markman, E. M. (2008). Prior experiences and perceived efficacy influence 3-year-olds' imitation. *Developmental Psychology, 44*(1), 275–285.

Woodward, A. L., Phillips, A. T., & Spelke, E. S. (1993). Infants' expectations about the motion of animate versus inanimate objects. In *Proceedings of the 15th Annual Conference of the Cognitive Science Society* (pp. 1087–1091). Hillsdale, NJ: Lawrence Erlbaum Associates.

Wu, R., Gopnik, A., Richardson, D. C., & Kirkham, N. Z. (2011). Infants learn about objects from statistics and people. *Developmental Psychology, 47*(5), 1220–1229.

Zacks, J. M., Speer, N. K., Swallow, K. M., & Maley, C. J. (2010). The brain's cutting-room floor: Segmentation of narrative cinema. *Frontiers in Human Neuroscience, 4*(168), 1–15.

Zacks, J. M., & Tversky, B. (2001). Event structure in perception and conception. *Psychological Bulletin, 127*(1), 3–21.

Zmyj, N., Buttelmann, D., Carpenter, M., & Daum, M. M. (2010). The reliability of a model influences 14-month-olds' imitation. *Journal of Experimental Child Psychology, 106*(4), 208–220.

# CHAPTER SIX

# Rational Randomness: The Role of Sampling in an Algorithmic Account of Preschooler's Causal Learning

## E. Bonawitz, A. Gopnik, S. Denison, and T. L. Griffiths[1]

Department of Psychology, University of California at Berkeley, Berkeley, California, USA
[1]Corresponding author: E-mail: tom_griffiths@berkeley.edu

## Contents

## Abstract

Probabilistic models of cognitive development indicate the ideal solutions to computational problems that children face as they try to make sense of their environment. Under this approach, children's beliefs change as the result of a single process: observing new data and drawing the appropriate conclusions from those data via Bayesian inference. However, such models typically leave open the question of what cognitive mechanisms might allow the finite minds of human children to perform the complex computations required by Bayesian inference. In this chapter, we highlight one potential mechanism: sampling from probability distributions. We introduce the idea of approximating Bayesian inference via Monte Carlo methods, outline the key

*Advances in Child Development and Behavior*, Volume 43
ISSN 0065-2407,
http://dx.doi.org/10.1016/B978-0-12-397919-3.00006-X

ideas behind such methods, and review the evidence that human children have the cognitive prerequisites for using these methods. As a result, we identify a second factor that should be taken into account in explaining human cognitive development—the nature of the mechanisms that are used in belief revision.

# 1. RATIONAL RANDOMNESS

Over the past 10 years, probabilistic approaches to cognitive development have become increasingly prevalent and powerful. These approaches can be seen as a computational extension of the "theory theory"—the idea that children's learning is similar to learning in science. In both cognitive development and science, learners begin with beliefs about the world that are gradually, but rationally, revised in the light of new evidence. Probabilistic models provide a way of characterizing both these beliefs—as structured models of the world—and the process of belief revision.

In this chapter, we will describe recent work that addresses two problems with the probabilistic approach. One is what we will call the "algorithm problem." Probabilistic approaches to cognitive development, like rational models in general, began with a computational level analysis. Researchers have shown that, given particular patterns of evidence, children draw rationally normative conclusions. However, this raises the question of exactly what computations or algorithms children's minds might perform to yield those answers. This problem is particularly important because some of the most obvious possible procedures, such as enumerating each possible hypothesis and checking it against the evidence, are clearly computationally intractable.

The other problem is what we will call the "variability problem." When we ask a group of children a question, typically they will produce a variety of answers. When we say that 4-year-olds get the rationally "right" answer, what we really mean is that more of them produce the correct answer than we would expect by chance. Moreover, individual children characteristically will give different answers to the same question on different occasions. They show lots of variability in their individual behavior; their explanations often appear to randomly jump from one idea to the next rather than linearly converging on the correct beliefs (Piaget, 1983; Siegler, 1996). We can witness this same kind of apparently random variability in children's play and informal experimentation. Rather than systematically acting to test one hypothesis at a time, children appear to veer at random from one kind of test to another (Chen & Klahr, 1999; Inhelder & Piaget, 1958).

This variability was one of the factors that originally led Piaget to describe young children's behavior as irrational. Indeed, such findings have led some researchers to suggest that children's behavior is always intrinsically variable and context dependent (e.g., Greeno, 1998; Lave & Wenger, 1991; Thelen & Smith, 1994). This would seem to make children's learning very different from the kind of systematic and rational hypothesis testing we expect from science.

In this chapter, we will argue that the solutions to these two problems, the algorithm problem and the variability problem, are related. Sampling from a probability distribution, rather than exhaustively enumerating possibilities, is a common strategy in algorithms for Bayesian inference used in computer science and statistics. There are many different sampling algorithms, but all of them have the feature that only a few hypotheses are, or even a single randomly selected hypothesis is, tested at a time. It can be shown that in the long run, an algorithmic process of this kind will approximate the ideal Bayesian solution to the search problem.

First, we will argue that the idea of sampling, in general, helps make sense of children's variability. We will argue that the way children act *is* consistent with a rational account of belief revision and only seems irrational because our intuitions about what an ideal learner should look like do not take into account the complexity of the inferences that children need to make and the algorithmic procedures they use to make them. In particular, systematic variability is a hallmark of sampling processes. By thinking about how children might use effective algorithmic strategies for making such inferences, we come to see these apparently irrational behaviors in a different light. We are starting to show empirically that children's variability is, in fact, systematic in just the way we would predict if they were using a sampling-based algorithm.

Second, we will describe two particular psychologically plausible sampling algorithms that can approximate ideal Bayesian inference—the Win-Stay, Lose-Shift (WSLS) procedure, and a variant of the Markov Chain Monte Carlo (MCMC) algorithm. We will show empirically that, in different contexts, children may use something like these algorithms to make inferences about the causal structure of the world.

## 2. THE ALGORITHM PROBLEM AND MARR'S LEVELS OF ANALYSIS

Marr (1982) identified three distinct levels at which an information-processing system can be analyzed: the *computational*, *algorithmic*, and *implementational* levels. We will focus on the computational and algorithmic levels here. (The implementational level, which answers the question of how the system is physically realized—e.g., what neural structures and activities implement the learning processes described at the algorithmic level—warrants focus in future work.) We will first give a brief overview of the computational and algorithmic levels and then delve more deeply into the specific algorithms young learners may be using.

## 2.1. Computational Level

Marr's computational level focuses on the computational problems that learners face and the ideal solutions to those problems. For example, Bayesian inference provides a computational-level account of the inferences people make when solving inductive problems, focusing on the form of the computational problem and its ideal solution. Bayesian models are useful because they provide a formal account of how a learner should combine prior beliefs and new evidence to change her beliefs.

In Bayesian inference, a learner considers how to update her beliefs (or hypotheses, *h*) given some observed evidence (or data, *d*). Assume that the learner has different degrees of belief in the truth of these hypotheses before observing the evidence and that these degrees of belief are reflected in a probability distribution $p(h)$, known as the *prior*. Then, the degrees of belief the learner should assign to each hypothesis after observing data *d* are given by the *posterior* probability distribution $p(h|d)$ obtained by applying Bayes' rule:

$$p(h|d) = \frac{p(d|h)p(h)}{\sum_{h' \in H} p(d|h')p(h')},$$ [6.1]

where $p(d|h)$ indicates the probability of observing *d* if *h* were true and is known as the *likelihood*.

An important feature of Bayesian inference is that it does not just yield a single deterministically correct hypothesis given the evidence. Instead, Bayesian inference provides an assessment of the probability of all the possible hypotheses. The "prior" distribution initially tells you the probability of all the possible hypotheses. Each possible hypothesis can then be assessed against the evidence using Bayes rule. This produces a new distribution of less likely and more likely hypotheses. Bayesian inference proceeds by adjusting the probabilities of all the hypotheses, the distribution, in the face of new data. It transforms the "prior" distribution you started with—your degrees of belief in all the possible hypotheses—into a new "posterior" distribution. So, in principle, Bayesian inference not only determines which hypothesis you think is most likely but also changes your assessment of all the other less likely hypotheses.

The idea that inductive inference can be captured by Bayes' rule has been applied to a number of different aspects of cognition, demonstrating that people's inferences are consistent with Bayesian inference in a wide range of settings (e.g., Goodman, Tenenbaum, Feldman, & Griffiths, 2008; Griffiths & Tenenbaum, 2009; Kording & Wolpert, 2004; Weiss, Simoncelli, & Adelson, 2002; Xu & Tenenbaum, 2007). People do seem to update their beliefs given evidence in the way that specific Bayesian models predict.

Bayesian models have proved especially helpful in understanding how children might develop intuitive theories of the world. We can think of intuitive theories as hypotheses about the structure of the world, particularly its causal structure. Causal graphical models (Pearl, 2000; Spirtes, Glymour, & Schienes, 1993) and more recently hierarchical Bayesian models (Tenenbaum, Griffiths, & Kemp, 2006) provide particularly perspicuous representations of such hypotheses. In particular, by making explicit and systematically relating the structure of hypotheses to probabilistic patterns of evidence, Bayesian causal models can establish the probability of particular patterns of data given particular hypotheses. This means that Bayesian inference can then be used to combine prior beliefs and the likelihood of newly observed evidence given various hypotheses to update the probability of hypotheses—making some beliefs more and others less likely.

In fact, there is now extensive evidence that this computational approach provides a good explanatory account of how children infer hypotheses about causal structure from evidence. We can manipulate the evidence children see about a causal system as well as their beliefs about the prior probability of various hypotheses about that structure and see how this influences their inferences about that system. Quite typically children choose the hypotheses with the greatest posterior probability in Bayesian terms (Bonawitz, Fischer, & Schulz, in press; Bonawitz, et al., 2012; Goodman et al., 2008; Gopnik, Sobel, Schulz, & Glymour, 2001; Gopnik et al., 2004; Kushnir & Gopnik, 2005, 2007; Lucas, Gopnik, & Griffiths, 2010; Schulz, Bonawitz et al, 2007; Schulz, Gopnik et al, 2007; Sobel, Tenenbaum, & Gopnik, 2004).

However, the finding that the average of children's responses looks like the posterior distributions predicted by these rational models does not necessarily imply that learners are actually carrying out the calculation instantiated in Bayes' rule at the *algorithmic* level. Indeed, given the computational complexity of exact Bayesian inference, this would be impossible. So, it becomes interesting to ask *how* learners might be behaving in a way that is consistent with Bayesian inference.

## 2.2. Algorithmic Level

Marr's algorithmic level asks how an information-processing system does what it does; for example, what cognitive processes do children use to propose, evaluate, and revise beliefs? The computational level has provided an important perspective on children's behavior, affording interesting, and testable qualitative and quantitative predictions that have been borne out empirically. But it is just the starting point for exploring learning in early childhood. Indeed, considering other levels of analysis can help to address significant challenges for Bayesian models of cognitive development.

In particular, most computational-level accounts do not address the problem of *search*. For most problems, the learner cannot actually consider every possible hypothesis, as it would be extremely time-consuming to enumerate and test every hypothesis in succession. Researchers in artificial intelligence (AI) and statistics have raised this concern, showing that given complex problems and the time constraints of real-world inference, full Bayesian inference quickly becomes computationally intractable (e.g., Russell & Norvig, 2003). Thus, rational models raise questions about how a learner might search through a (potentially infinite) space of hypotheses: If the learner simply maximized, picking out only the most likely hypothesis to test, she might miss out on hypotheses that are initially less likely but actually provide a better fit to the data. This problem might appear to be particularly challenging for young children who, in at least some respects, have more restricted memory and information-processing capacities than adults (German & Nichols, 2003; Gerstadt, Hong, & Diamond, 1994).

Applications of Bayesian inference in computer science and statistics often try to solve the computational problem of enumeration and evaluation of the hypothesis space by sampling a few hypotheses rather than exhaustively considering all possibilities. These approximate probabilistic calculations use what are called "Monte Carlo" methods. A system that uses this sort of sampling will be variable—it will entertain different hypotheses apparently at random. But this variability will be *systematically related* to the probability of the hypotheses—more probable hypotheses will be sampled more frequently than less probable ones. The success of Monte Carlo algorithms for approximating Bayesian inference in computer science and statistics suggests an exciting hypothesis for cognitive development. The algorithms children use to perform inductive inference might be similarly based on sampling from the appropriate probability distributions. We explore this *"Sampling Hypothesis"* in detail in the remainder of the chapter.

The Sampling Hypothesis provides a way to reconcile rational reasoning with variable responding, and it has the potential to address both the algorithmic and the search problem. It also establishes an empirical research program in which we look for the signatures of sampling in general and of specific sampling algorithms in particular in children's behavior.

## 3. APPROXIMATING BAYESIAN INFERENCE WITH MONTE CARLO METHODS

Monte Carlo algorithms include a large class of methods that share the same general pattern. They first define the distribution that samples will come from, then randomly generate the samples, and finally aggregate the results. The goal is usually to approximate an expectation of a function over a probability distribution (e.g., the mean of the distribution or the probability that a sample from the distribution has a particular property); that is, an approximation of the distribution is given by summing over all the different individual samples generated during the MCMC process.

The simplest Monte Carlo methods directly generate samples from the probability distribution in question. For example, if you wanted to know the mean of the distribution that assigns equal probability to the numbers 1 through 6, you could calculate the exact mean by averaging over each probability for each value (1 through 6). Monte Carlo methods provide an alternative to numerically computing the mean: instead, you could imagine rolling a fair die to generate samples from this distribution, tracking the results of each roll, and then averaging the results together. This process would let you uncover an important fact about the distribution without having to numerically calculate the probability of each possible outcome individually. Although in this example, it would be relatively trivial to numerically compute the exact mean, Monte Carlo sampling provides an alternative approach that can be used when the distributions become harder to evaluate, such as considering the product of multiple dice rolls. When the probability distributions we want to sample from get even more complex, more sophisticated methods need to be used to generate samples. In particular, it can quickly become computationally intractable to take samples directly from the posterior distribution itself, so various Monte Carlo algorithms have been developed to best approximate these different kinds of complexity.

Monte Carlo algorithms for approximating Bayesian inference are thus methods for obtaining the equivalent of samples from the posterior distribution without computing the posterior distribution itself. One class of methods, based on a principle known as *importance sampling*, generate hypotheses from a distribution other than the posterior distribution and then assigns weights to those samples (akin to increasing or decreasing their frequency) in order to correct for the bias produced by using a different distribution to generate hypotheses (see Neal, 1993, for details).

The strategy of sampling from other known distributions and then updating the sample to correct for bias can also be used to develop algorithms for probabilistically updating beliefs over time. For example, in a particle filter (see Doucet, de Frietas, & Gordon, 2001, for details), hypotheses are generated based on a learner's current beliefs and then reweighted to reflect the evidence provided by new observations. This provides a way to approximate Bayesian inference that unfolds gradually over time, with only a relatively small number of hypotheses being considered at any one instant.

Another class of Monte Carlo methods makes use of the properties of Markov chains. These Markov chain Monte Carlo algorithms, such as the Metropolis Hastings algorithm, explore a posterior probability distribution in a way that requires only a single hypothesis to be considered at a time (see Gilks, Richardson, & Spiegelhalter, 1996, for details). In these algorithms, a learner generates a hypothesis by sampling a variant on his or her current hypothesis from a "proposal" distribution. The proposed variant is compared to the current hypothesis, and the learner stochastically selects one of the two hypotheses. This process is then repeated, and the learner gradually explores the space of hypotheses in such a way that each hypothesis will be considered for an amount of time that is proportional to the posterior probability of that hypothesis.

Overall, Monte Carlo methods have met with much success in exploring posterior distributions that are otherwise too computationally demanding to evaluate (see Robert & Casella, 2004, for a review). Recent work by Griffiths and Colleagues has explored how Monte Carlo methods can be used to develop psychological models that incorporate the cognitive-computational limitations that adult learners face. Some empirically generated psychological process models turn out to correspond to the application of Monte Carlo methods. For example, Shi, Feldman, and Griffiths (2008) showed that importance sampling corresponds to exemplar models, a traditional process-level model that has been applied in a variety of domains. Sanborn, Griffiths, and Navarro (2010) used particle filters to approximate rational statistical inferences for categorization. Bonawitz and Griffiths (2010) show that importance sampling can be used as a framework for analyzing the contributions of generating and then evaluating hypotheses.

Other research supports the idea that adults may be approximating ideal solutions through a process of sampling. For example, adults, like children, often generate multiple answers to a question. If you ask adults how many beans are in a large jar, they will provide a range of responses. A classic result shows that the averaged result of many such responses converges on the right answer, even though any individual guess may be very far from the correct mean ("The Wisdom of Crowds"; Galton, 1907; Surowiecki, 2004). The same effect holds even when a single person makes multiple guesses, supporting the idea that (adult) individuals are not simply providing their best guess but rather are sampling from a distribution (Vul & Pashler, 2008). Related work suggests that people often base their decisions on just a few samples (Goodman et al., 2008; Mozer, Pashler, & Homaei, 2008), and in many cases, an optimal solution is to take only one sample (Vul, Goodman, Griffiths, & Tenenbaum, 2009). These results suggest that adults may be approximating probabilistic inference through psychological processes that are *equivalent* to sampling from the posterior. That is, the learner need not compute the full posterior distribution in order to sample responses that still lead to an approximation of the posterior. Here, we use "sampling from the posterior" to entail any sampling processes that produce equivalent samples, without necessarily requiring the learner to compute the full posterior.

These processes that approximate the full posterior are consistent with what we have termed the Sampling Hypothesis. The signature of sampling-based inferences is the fact that apparently random guesses actually reflect the probability of the hypotheses they embody. Each person may produce a different hypothesis about the outcome of two dice rolls on a different occasion, but hypotheses that are closer to correct—that is those that have a higher probability in the posterior distribution—will be more likely to be produced than those that are less likely. If two fair dice are rolled, the most likely outcome is 7; however, people generate a range of guesses with varying probability. Guesses of 6 or 8 will be five times more likely to be true than guesses of 2 or 12. The Sampling Hypothesis predicts that human beings are also five times more likely to produce those guesses; indeed, it predicts that the probability that an individual will guess any particular outcome will match the probability of generating that outcome under the true distribution.

## 4. THE SAMPLING HYPOTHESIS AND CHILDREN'S INFERENCES

Might children's inferences be consistent with the Sampling Hypothesis? The first step in exploring this claim is to see whether children produce responses that are consistent with Bayesian inference in general. The second step is to see whether children produce behaviors that are consistent with sampling in particular. In order to demonstrate that children's responding is consistent with Bayesian inference, we must demonstrate that children are sensitive both to their prior beliefs and to the evidence they observe. As we described above, many studies show that children choose the probabilistically most likely hypothesis, but to truly test the prediction that children are sensitive to *posterior* distributions, then children's responses should change when both their prior beliefs and the probability of the evidence are independently manipulated. We highlight a few studies that suggest children produce responses consistent with Bayesian inference. We then briefly discuss alternatives to the sampling hypothesis. Finally, we turn to more detailed empirical evidence supporting the claim that children sample responses.

### 4.1. Preschoolers Producing Responses Consistent with Bayesian Inference

Before we are able to identify whether children sample responses in a way that approximates a posterior distribution, we must first demonstrate that children's responses are consistent with those distributions. Schulz, Bonawitz, et al. (2007) presented preschoolers with stories pitting their existing theories against statistical evidence. Each child heard two stories in which two candidate causes co-occurred with an effect. Evidence was presented in the form: AB → E, AC → E, AD → E, etc. In one story, all variables came from the same domain; in the other, the recurring candidate cause, A, came from a different domain (A was a psychological cause of a biological effect). After receiving this statistical evidence, children were asked to identify the cause of the effect on a new trial. Consistent with the predictions of the Bayesian framework, both prior beliefs and evidence played a role in children's causal predictions. Four-year-olds were more likely to identify "A" as the cause after observing the evidence than at Baseline. Results also revealed a role of theories in guiding children's predictions. All children were more likely to identify A as the cause within domains than across domains.

A particularly interesting empirical feature of this study is that because Schulz *et al.* had a measure of children's prior beliefs at baseline, they could demonstrate that proportionally the children's responses (after having observed the evidence) were consistent with posterior distributions predicted by Bayesian models. That is, after observing the evidence, some children endorsed hypothesis "A" and others endorsed the other hypothesis. The proportion of children who favored "A" was the probability of "A" being the actual cause, given the prior beliefs of the children and the evidence observed. For example, when the posterior predicted 80% probability for hypothesis "A," then results revealed about 80% of the children choosing "A".

Other studies reveal children producing graded responses to evidence reflecting Bayesian posteriors (Bonawitz & Lombrozo, in press; Kushnir & Gopnik, 2005, 2007; Sobel et al., 2004). For example, Bonawitz and Lombrozo (in press) investigated whether young children prefer explanations that are simple, where simplicity is quantified as the number of causes invoked in an explanation, and how this preference is reconciled with probability information. Preschool-aged children were asked to explain an event that could be generated by one or two causes, where the probabilities of the causes varied across several conditions. Children preferred explanations involving one cause over two but were also sensitive to the probability of competing explanations. That is, as evidence gradually increased favoring the complex explanation, the proportion of children favoring the complex explanation also increased. These data provide support for a more nuanced sensitivity to evidence. When evaluating competing causal explanations, preschoolers are able to integrate evidence with their prior beliefs (in this case employing a principle of parsimony like Occam's razor as an inductive constraint). However, because children's prior beliefs were not independently evaluated, it is difficult to say whether the proportion of responses generated by children in these studies matched a true posterior distribution predicted by a Bayesian model.

## 4.2. Alternatives to Sampling

The studies above suggest that children are sensitive to evidence in ways predicted by Bayesian inference; at least, a proportion of children select the hypothesis that is best supported by the evidence and their prior beliefs. There is also variability in children's responses—the proportion of times that they select a hypotheses increases as the hypothesis receives more support, but they will still sometimes produce an alternative hypothesis. But does that mean that children are sampling their responses from a posterior distribution? It might instead be that the variability in the children's responses is simply the effect of noise—in fact, this is the most common, if generally implicit, assumption in most developmental studies. This noise could be the result of cognitive load, context effects, or methodological flaws that lead children to stochastically produce errors. For example, in the Schulz, Bonawitz, et al. (2007) study, all the children might indeed be choosing the most likely hypothesis on each trial, always preferring the within-domain or cross-domain answer. But they might fail to express that hypothesis correctly because of memory or information-processing or communication problems. We call this alternative the *Noisy Maximizing* alternative to the sampling hypothesis.

Another alternative is that children's behavior does reflect the probability of hypotheses but does so through the result of a simpler process than sampling from the posterior. Consider a similar though simpler phenomenon that can be found in a much older literature. Children, like adults and even nonhuman animals, frequently produce a pattern called probability matching in reinforcement learning (e.g., Jones & Liverant, 1960). If children are rewarded 80% of the time for response "A" but 20% of the time for response "B," they are likely to produce "A" 80% of the time and "B" 20% of the time. If these responses reflect an implicit hypothesis about the causal power of the action ("A" will cause the reward), this probability matching looks a lot like the behavior in the more explicitly cognitive causal learning tasks. It might, however, simply be the result of a strategy we will call "Naïve Frequency Matching." Children using this strategy would simply match the frequency of their responses to the frequency of the rewards.

The idea that the variability of children's responses could result from sampling is related to probability matching in that it predicts that the learner's responses on aggregate will match the posterior. Thus, probability matching following reinforcement is consistent with the Sampling

Hypothesis, but it is also consistent with the Naïve Frequency Matching account. These two accounts differ in that sampling implies a level of sophistication that goes beyond what is typically assumed when the term "probability matching" is used. Rather than simply matching the frequency of rewarded responses, sampling predicts that children's responding matches the posterior probabilities of different hypotheses.

Moreover, there is still something puzzling about probability matching from the point of view of simple reinforcement theory. Why would children use a naïve frequency matching strategy? Why do not all the children select the more probable hypothesis? This is the strategy, after all, that is most likely to yield a right answer and so enable the children to be rewarded. Why are 20% of children choosing the *less* likely hypothesis? If children are *sampling* responses from the posterior distribution, this could explain this result. On this view, the variability in children's responses may actually itself be rational, at least sometimes. In particular, it may reflect a strategy children use to select which hypotheses could explain the data they have observed.

There is little work exploring probability matching in children beyond simple reinforcement learning. What there is suggests that children do not, in fact, probability match when they are considering more cognitive hypotheses—particularly linguistic hypotheses (Hudson Kam & Newport, 2005, 2009). In what follows, we present a set of studies that present the first test of the Sampling Hypothesis with children, distinguishing sampling from both the Naïve Frequency Matching and the Noisy Maximizing alternatives.

## 4.3. Empirical Support for Children's Sampling

In a first set of experiments, we explored the degree to which children match posterior probabilities in a causal inference task, set up as a game about a toy that activates when particular colored chips are placed inside a bin (Denison, Bonawitz, Gopnik, & Griffiths, 2010). The toy allowed us to precisely determine the probability of different hypotheses about which chip had fallen into the bin. Earlier studies have showed that even young infants are sensitive to probability in these contexts—6-month-olds assume that the more frequent color chip will be more likely to be selected from the bag (Denison, Reed, & Xu, in press). In the first experiment, we tested two key predictions of the sampling hypothesis: probability matching and an effect of the dependency between responses.

These are both known consequences of sampling behavior (Vul & Pashler, 2008).

Children were introduced to a toy—a large box with an activator bin and an attached smaller toy that could light up and play music. The experimenter demonstrated that placing red chips or blue chips into the activator bin caused the toy to activate. Then, a distribution of 20 red and 5 blue chips were placed into a transparent container and transferred into a rigid opaque bag. The experimenter placed the bag on top of the toy and "accidentally" knocked it over away from the child and toward the activator bin and the toy activated. The child was asked what color chip they thought fell into the bin to activate the toy (see Fig. 6.1). Children in the *short-wait* condition completed two additional trials immediately following this first trial, and children in the *long-wait* condition completed two additional trials each 1-week apart (all trials consisted of the same 80:20 distribution).

We manipulated time between guesses because (following results with adults from Vul and Pashler, 2008), we suspected that there would be greater dependence among guesses if they were spaced close together. As described previously, one of the requirements of producing a "good" approximation to the posterior is independence between samples (although, there are a few special cases in which some dependency between responses can still yield accurate approximations—a point we will return to later). In general, however, the sampling hypothesis predicts different patterns of response when there is more dependence between hypotheses. Thus, we predicted that the *long-wait* condition should have produced more independence between the hypotheses (e.g., the children may not have remembered what they had just said) and so produce a better approximation to the posterior.

Results indicated that, collapsed across conditions, children's guesses on Trial 1 were in line with the signature of sampling: probability matching. Children guessed the red chip (i.e., the more probable chip) on 70% of trials and the blue chip on 30% of trials, not significantly different from the predicted distribution of 80% and 20%, respectively, but significantly different from chance (50%). Children's responses were also in agreement with the dependency results found with adults; children in both conditions showed some dependencies between guesses, but the dependencies were greater in the *short-wait* than in the *long-wait* conditions. As the sampling hypothesis would predict, because there was less dependence, there was also a better fit to the actual probabilities in the *long-wait* condition.

**Figure 6.1** Stimuli and procedure used for testing the Sampling Hypothesis in children. For color version of this figure, the reader is referred to the online version of this book.

Although the results of this first experiment suggest that children's responses reflected probability matching, they are also congruent with the Noisy Maximizing prediction. That is, children may have attempted to provide maximally accurate "best guesses" but simply failed to do so at ceiling levels due to factors such as task demands or cognitive load. In a second experiment, we tested the probability matching prediction more directly by systematically manipulating the distributions of chips children saw across three conditions. In a 95:5 condition, children counted 19 red and 1 blue chips; in a 75:25 condition, they counted 15 red and 5 blue chips; and in a 50:50 condition, they counted 10 red and 10 blue chips. As predicted, children's responses reflected probability matching. Children's tendency to guess the red chip increased linearly as the proportion of red to blue chips increased from 50:50 to 75:25 to 95:5 (see Fig. 6.2). This result is congruent with probability matching but not noisy maximizing, as noisy maximizing would have resulted in similar performance between the 75:25 and 95:5 conditions.

In a third experiment, we tested the probability matching prediction with a different more complex set of hypotheses. Do children continue to produce guesses that reflect probability matching when more than two alternative hypotheses are available? In this experiment, children in two conditions were given distributions that included three different colors of chips: red, blue, and green. The procedure unfolded as it did in the first two experiments. As in the second experiment, the distributions were systematically manipulated across conditions. Children in the *82:9:9 Condition* saw distributions of 18 red, 2 blue, and 2 green chips and children in the *64:18:18 Condition* saw 14 red, 4 blue, and 4 green chips. In this experiment, children in both conditions guessed that the red chip had activated the machine more often than would be expected by chance but again they also did not choose the red chip at ceiling levels. Children's responses reflected

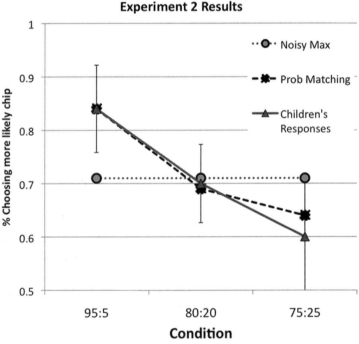

**Figure 6.2** Results of children's predictions in Experiment 2 and the 80:20 first predictions from Experiment 1 as compared to predictions of the *Noisy Max* and the Probability Matching models.

probability matching in that children in the *82:9:9 Condition* guessed the red chip 72% of the time, significantly more often than children in the *64:18:18 Condition*, who guessed the red chip 53% of the time. The proportion of children choosing the red chip in the *82:9:9 Condition* was not different from the predicted distribution of 82% and the proportion of children who did so in the *64:18:18 Condition* was not different from the predicted distribution of 64%.

Children in the second and third experiments produced guesses that are consistent with the probability matching prediction of the sampling hypothesis. However, as we mentioned previously, children in a variety of reinforcement learning paradigms have demonstrated probability matching to the frequencies of reinforced responses. The current studies did not involve any reinforcement, and children responded to the number of chips in the container rather than to frequency of effects, so they could not simply be explained in terms of reinforcement learning. However, these results are still consistent with a variation of the Naïve Frequency Matching account. Although responses were not reinforced, children in these experiments may have matched their responses to the overall frequency of the chips—they said "red" more often simply because they saw more red chips. We conducted a fourth experiment to test the prediction that children's responses will match the *posterior distribution* of hypotheses and not simply match the frequencies of the different colored chips encountered in the experimental session.

The frequencies of chips can be separated from the probability of selecting each color by introducing a constraint on the generative process. In a variant of the procedure used in the first three experiments, children counted two separate distributions of chips with the experimenter: one distribution of 14 red and 6 blue chips and a second distribution of 0 red and 2 blue chips. The experimenter placed the separate distributions into two identical bags, mixed the placement of the bags around out of the child's view, and then randomly chose one of the bags to place on the machine and knock over. In this case, if children are solely concerned with the frequencies of each color of chip, they should guess a red chip on 64% of the trials and a blue chip on 36% of the trials. If they are instead producing guesses based on the probability of either color chip falling from the randomly chosen bag, they should guess the red chip 35% of the time and the blue chip 65% of the time [P(blue chip) = (1/2 × 6/20 + 1/2 × 2/2)]. Children guessed the red chip on 32% of the trials, different from chance (50%) and the frequency matching prediction (64%) but not different from the posterior probability matching prediction (35%).

In sum, results from these four experiments suggest that children's responses in a simple causal inference task were in agreement with the sampling hypothesis. First, children showed dependencies between guesses on three consecutive trials and this dependency decreased as a function of time between guesses and more independence led to greater probability matching. Second, children provided responses that, on aggregate, reflected the posterior distribution of hypotheses when making guesses involving either two possible hypotheses or three possible hypotheses, ruling out the possibility that children were noisily maximizing. Finally, children's guesses matched the posterior distribution of hypotheses rather than the simple frequencies of observed colors of chips. They rationally integrated the probability of randomly selecting one of the two distributions with the frequency of the chips within the distributions.

## 5. EXPLORING SPECIFIC SAMPLING ALGORITHMS IN CHILDREN'S CAUSAL INFERENCES

The experiments discussed in the previous section provide preliminary support for the Sampling Hypothesis, suggesting that children are doing something that looks like sampling as opposed to noisily maximizing and that children are going beyond making simple frequency tabulations in causal learning tasks. While these results suggest that learners sample responses from posterior distributions, these studies were not designed to explore specific algorithms a learner might be using to select a hypothesis as she encounters new data, and they do not propose a specific mechanism for search through a hypothesis space.

There are myriad ways in which a learner could move through the space of hypotheses consistent with sampling algorithms. Learners may resample a best guess from the full posterior every time a new piece of data is observed. Learners may sample a hypothesis and stick with it until there is impetus to reevaluate (e.g., maybe data reach some threshold of "unlikeliness" to have been generated by the current hypothesis). The way in which a learner chooses to reevaluate hypotheses may also differ: she may make subtle changes to the hypothesis she's currently entertaining; she may go back and resample completely from the full posterior distribution; or she may choose a best guess from some surrogate distribution (an approximation to the posterior distribution). Learners could sample and simultaneously consider a few hypotheses or just one. These ideas about specific sampling and search algorithms have analogs in computer science and machine learning. We present two different studies designed to test whether children might be using variants of two types of search algorithms—a WSLS algorithm and a MCMC algorithm.

In order to explore the win-stay, lose-shift (WSLS) and Markov chain Monte Carlo (MCMC) algorithms, we presented children with more complex causal learning tasks that unfolded over time. Children received new evidence at several stages, and at each stage, we asked them to provide a new guess about what was going on. The pattern of responses that children produced and particularly the dependencies among those responses, helped allow us to discriminate which specific algorithms they employed.

## 5.1. WSLS Algorithms

To explore the algorithms children use in updating their beliefs, we designed both deterministic and probabilistic causal tasks. In the deterministic task, data necessarily "rule out" a set of possible hypotheses; in the probabilistic task, the data are consistent with all hypotheses but statistically may favor certain hypotheses over others. The task proceeds as follows: We let children take an initial guess, before seeing any evidence; we then show children some evidence and ask them about their hypotheses after the evidence; we then show children more evidence and ask them again about their hypotheses, and so forth and so on. Thus, children observed a sequence of data, and we could use the responses of an individual child as he or she moved through the hypothesis space following each piece of evidence to help us tease apart different specific algorithms.

In particular, we were interested in algorithms based on the WSLS principle. These algorithms entertain a single hypothesis at a time, staying with that hypothesis as long as it adequately explains the observed data and shifting to a new hypothesis when that is no longer the case. The WSLS principle has a long history in computer science, where it is used in reinforcement learning and game theory (Nowak & Sigmund, 1993; Robbins, 1952), and psychology, where it has served as an account of human concept learning (Restle, 1962). Bonawitz, Denison, Chen, Gopnik, and Griffiths (2011) provided a mathematical proof that demonstrates how specific algorithms using the WSLS principle can be used to sample from posterior distributions. The result is a set of surprisingly simple sequential algorithms for performing Bayesian inference.

The deterministic case of WSLS means that data necessarily rule out a set of hypotheses. The algorithm simply involves a process where the learner stays with a hypothesis when data are consistent and shifts to a new hypothesis when data are inconsistent. The probabilistic case presents a more interesting and ecologically plausible test of WSLS, so we focus on the probabilistic studies here.

In the probabilistic causal task, we introduced children to a machine that could be activated with different kinds of blocks. An experimenter demonstrated that three kinds of blocks activate the machine with different probabilities: red blocks activated the machine on five out of six trials, the green blocks on three out of six trials, and the blue blocks just once out of six trials. We then introduced children to a new block that had "lost its color" and told children we needed their help guessing what color the block should be: red, blue, or green. We then asked children what happened each time the mystery block was placed on the machine (either the machine activated or did not); after each observation, we asked children what color they thought the block was now.

One specific WSLS algorithm proceeds on the problem of inferring the identity of the mystery block given probabilistic data as follows. The learner starts out by sampling a hypothesis from the prior distribution before seeing any data about the mystery block. Let us say that she happens to choose red by sampling it randomly from her prior; all that means is that she rolls a weighted die such that the weights of the colors on the die are proportional to her beliefs about how likely the block is to be each color before seeing the evidence. In this case, for example, the prior evidence provides an equal probability for each block initially, so she might be equally likely to guess red, blue, or green. In another case, she might have reason to think that red blocks were more common, so that she would weight the internal throw of the die more heavily toward red, though blue or green might also turn up. Let us say this learner happens to roll red. Then, the mystery block is set on the machine and it turns out that it activates the toy. The learner now must decide whether to stay with red or shift to another hypothesis. In this simple WSLS algorithm, the decision to stay or shift is made based purely on the likelihood for the observed data. As seen in the demonstration phase, the red block activates the machine five out of six times and so the likelihood of seeing the toy light if the block really is red is simply 5/6. So, to make the choice to stay, we can imagine a coin with 5/6 probability of landing on stay and 1/6 probability landing on shift. That is, although the evidence is consistent with the red block hypothesis, there is still a (small) chance that the coin will come up shift, and the learner will return to the updated posterior (which includes all the evidence observed so far) to sample their next guess. Each time the learner observes a new piece of data, she makes the choice whether to stay or shift, in this way, based only on the most recent data she has observed.

When applying this WSLS algorithm, an individual learner may look like she is randomly veering from one hypothesis to the next, sometimes abandoning a likely hypothesis or sampling an unlikely one, sometimes being too strongly influenced by a piece of data and sometimes ignoring data that is unlikely under her current hypothesis. However, looking across a population of learners reveals a surprising property of this algorithm: Aggregating all the hypotheses selected by all the learners returns the Bayesian predicted posterior distribution (or at least a sample-based approximation thereof). Thus, the WSLS algorithm provides a more efficient way to do Bayesian inference. The learner can maintain just a single hypothesis in her working memory and need only recompute and resample from the posterior on occasion. Nevertheless, the responding of participants on aggregate still act like a sample from the posterior distribution.

We can contrast this WSLS algorithm with *independent* sampling in which a learner simply samples a new hypothesis from the posterior distribution each time a response is required. In other words, on each trial, the learner will choose red, blue, or green in proportion to the probability that the block is that particular color given the accumulated evidence. The WSLS algorithm shares with independent sampling the property that responses on aggregate will match the posterior probability, but the algorithms differ in terms of the dependencies between responses. Because the learner resamples a hypothesis after each new observation of data in the independent sampling algorithm, there is no dependency between an individual's successive guesses. In contrast, the WSLS algorithm predicts dependencies between responses: if the data are consistent with the current hypothesis, then the learner is likely to retain that hypothesis. This specific instantiation of WSLS is thus one of the special cases where the algorithm approximates the correct distribution even though there are dependencies between subsequent guesses. This establishes some clear empirical predictions: Both algorithms will produce a pattern of responses consistent with Bayesian inference on any given trial, but they differ in the predictions that they make about the relationship between responses on successive trials.

The first thing we can examine is simply whether children's responses approximate the posterior distribution produced by Bayesian inference in aggregate; indeed, children's predictions on aggregate correlated highly with Bayesian posteriors (Fig. 6.3). Next, we can examine the dependencies between responses for the individual learners to investigate whether WSLS or independent sampling provide a better fit to children's responses. To compare children's responses to the WSLS and independent sampling algorithms, we first calculated the "shift probabilities" under each model. Calculating shift probabilities for independent sampling is relatively easy: because each sample is independently drawn from the posterior, the shift probability is simply calculated from the posterior probability of each hypothesis after observing each piece of evidence. Shift probabilities for WSLS were calculated such that resampling is based only on the likelihood associated with the current observation, given the current hypothesis. That is, with probability equal to this likelihood, the learner resamples from the full posterior. We also computed the log-likelihood scores for both models—the probability that we would observe the pattern of responses from the children given each model. Children's responses highly correlated with and had higher log-likelihood scores from the WSLS algorithm. This suggests that the pattern of dependencies between children's responses is better captured by the WSLS algorithm than by an algorithm such as independent sampling.

## 5.2. MCMC Algorithms

The results of the WSLS experiments suggest one algorithm that learners might use to sample and evaluate hypotheses. In the experiments, we have considered so far, the space of possible hypotheses was relatively limited. Children only had to consider whether a red blue or green chip or block activated the machine. However, the question of how a learner *searches* through a space of hypotheses remains an important issue for cases when the space of hypotheses is much larger. Constructing an intuitive theory based on observing the world often confronts learners with a more complex space of possibilities.

In particular, in the examples we discussed so far, the causal categories the children saw (red, blue, and green blocks) and the causal laws (chips activate the machine) were both well defined—they did not have to be learned. In other cases, children have been shown to use probabilistic inference to uncover even relatively complex and abstract causal laws (e.g., the difference between a causal chain and a common cause structure, Schulz, Gopnik, et al., 2007, or between a disjunctive or conjunctive causal principle, Lucas

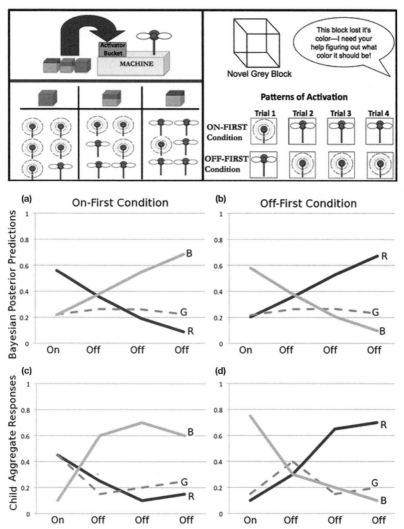

**Figure 6.3** Method for WSLS and Bayesian posterior probability and children's data from WSLS experiment for each block, red (R), green (B), and blue (B) after observing each new instance of evidence using parameters estimated from fitting the Bayesian model to the data. For interpretation of the references to color in this figure legend, the reader is referred to the online version of this book.

et al., 2010). Schulz, Goodman, Tenenbaum, and Jenkins (2008) and Seiver, Gopnik, and Gooman (in press) also showed that children can uncover new causal categories and concepts. In more realistic cases of theory change, learners, however, might face the "chicken-and-egg" problem: the laws can only be expressed in terms of the theory's core concepts, but these concepts are only meaningful in terms of the role they play in the theory's laws. How is a learner to discover the appropriate concepts and laws simultaneously, knowing neither to begin with? How could a learner search through this potentially infinite space of possibilities?

Recent ongoing work by Bonawitz, Ullman, Gopnik, and Tenenbaum has the goal of studying empirically how children's beliefs evolve through such a process of theory discovery, and understanding computationally how learners can converge quickly on a novel but veridical system of concepts and causal laws. Goodman et al. (2008) and Ullman, Goodman, and Tenenbaum (2010) describe a sampling method using a grammar-based Metropolis Hastings MCMC algorithm. The grammar generates the prior probabilities for the theories and the MCMC algorithm can be used to evaluate these theories given evidence. Specifically, the grammar is a broad language for defining theories, which is able to build a potentially infinite space of possibilities (see also Ullman et al., 2010). This grammar produces the space of possible hypotheses and even provides a measure of the prob- ability of each hypothesis: this prior probability of each hypothesis is the probability that each hypothesis is generated by the grammar. The algorithm begins with a specific theory, $t$, and then uses the grammar to propose random changes to the currently held theory. This new proposed theory is probabilistically accepted or rejected, depending on how well it explains the data compared to the current theory as well as how much simpler or more complex it is.

Ullman et al. (2010) suggested that this method can explain how human learners, including young children, can rationally approximate an ideal Bayesian analysis. This method allows a practical learner to search over a potentially infinite space of theories, holding on to one theory at a time and discarding it probabilistically as new potentially better alternatives are considered.

Bonawitz and colleagues have begun to explore how well this MCMC approach captures children's inferences about magnetic objects. Magnetism provides an interesting domain in which to conduct this investigation, because the space of possible kinds of causal interactions, the number of possible groups of objects, and the specific sorting of objects into those groups is very large. In particular, we can consider the search problem at multiple stages. First, given no evidence, we can consider which theories are a priori most likely. Second, given informative but still ambiguous data, we can see how the probability of various theories will change. Third, given disambig- uating data, we can see if the system converges on the correct answer.

Observing unlabeled but potentially magnetic objects, like unlabeled blocks, interacting with two labeled instances of objects from causally meaningful categories (i.e., blocks that are labeled with north and south polarities) provides a particularly interesting test. No matter how many observations are provided between the unlabeled and labeled blocks, ambiguity remains: an ideal learner would not be able to infer whether the actual law is that like attracts like and opposites repel or whether the law is that likes repel and opposites attract. Bonawitz, Ullman, Gopnik, and Tenenbaum implemented a grammar-based Metropolis Hastings algorithm of magnetism discovery following this ambiguous evidence. Their model discovered these two possible alternative theories and these two theories scored highest in the search. Given that both these theories were consistent with the observed data and were intuitively simple, this shows that stochastic search is an algorithm that can indeed be used to find reasonable theories. After providing disambiguating evidence, the model was also able to pick out the single most likely theory.

These modeling results and those of Ullman et al. (2010), which inspired this investigation, demonstrate that in practice, the MCMC algorithm can use relatively minimal data to effectively search through an infinite space of possibilities, discovering likely candidate theories and sorting of objects into classes.

Bonawitz, Ullman, Gopnik, and Tenenbaum are also empirically examining children's reasoning about magnets to see whether children search through and evaluate hypotheses in a way consistent with the model predictions. In their ongoing studies, children are asked about their beliefs at different phases of the experiment: before they observe any evidence, after they observe some ambiguous (but still informative) evidence, and after they observe disambiguating evidence. They have found that prior to observing the evidence, children entertain a broad space of possible causal theories about the possible groupings and inter-actions between the magnets. These hypotheses reflect the prior proba-bilities over theories generated by the grammar. Following the ambiguous evidence, children rationally respond by favoring the two "best" theories (that likes attract and opposites repel and that likes repel and opposites attract), as predicted by the results of the search algorithm. When the children see a single disambiguating intervention (e.g., when two objects sorted into the same group interact and either attract or repel), they converge on the correct theory—even when this means abandoning the theory they just held.

Strikingly, neither the initially ambiguous evidence nor the single disambiguating trial are sufficient to infer the correct theory. Nevertheless, children are able to make an inductive leap during the experiment. They simultaneously integrate the partially informative (but still ambiguous) evidence given by the initial observed interactions with the final disambiguating trial between two unlabeled blocks. Thus, even in the course of a short experiment, preschool-aged children are able to solve a simple version of the chicken-and-egg problem in a basically rational way. They search through a space of possible hypotheses and integrate multiple pieces of evidence across different phases of the experiment.

MCMC algorithms provide an account of how a learner could move through a potentially infinite space of possible hypotheses and still produce behavior consistent with exact Bayesian inference. There are several directions in which this line of research can be extended. One important step is to understand and characterize the "building blocks" for intuitive theories. Following from this, it will be interesting to investigate how it might be computationally plausible for a system to learn to use simple algorithms to construct complex theories from these building blocks (Kemp, Goodman, & Tenenbaum, 2010). A second extension is to apply these models to "common sense" domains such as physics, psychology, and biology and to the "real-world" theories that children actually learn. Developmental learning mechanisms for this kind of abstract knowledge are currently poorly understood.

## 6. DISCUSSION

We began this chapter with two problems for the idea that probabilistic models can capture how children learn intuitive theories—the algorithm problem and the variability problem. We have suggested that the Sampling Hypothesis may provide an answer to both these problems. In the first experiment, we showed that children's causal inferences have some of the key signatures of sampling—particularly a pattern of probability matching that goes beyond naïve frequency matching.

We then introduced specific sampling algorithms that approximate Bayesian inference. First, we found that preschoolers' responses on a causal learning task were better captured by a WSLS algorithm than by independent sampling. An attractive property of the WSLS algorithm is that it does not require the learner to compute and resample from the full posterior distribution after each observation. These results suggest that even responses that sometimes appear nonoptimal may in fact represent an approximation to a rational process and provide an account of how Bayesian inference could be approximated by learners with limited cognitive capacity.

We also presented an account of how a learner might search through a potentially infinite hypothesis space, inspired by computational models, which include MCMC searches over logical grammars (Ullman et al., 2010). These searches include randomly proposed changes to a currently held theory, which are probabilistically accepted, dependent on the degree to which the new theory better accounts for the data. These same search and inference capacities may help to drive theory change in the normal course of children's cognitive development. At the least, Bonawitz et al.'s current experiments suggest that preschool-aged children are able to discover a correct theory from a space of many possible theories. Children search through a large space of possible hypotheses and are able to integrate multiple pieces of evidence across different phases of the experiment to evaluate the best theory.

## 6.1. Open Questions

We have suggested that a learner could search through a hypothesis space in a number of ways, dependent perhaps on the task demands, developmental change, or even individual preference. Which algorithm a learner uses may also depend on the efficiency of the algorithm. However, how we define efficiency may depend on how difficult it is to compute posterior probabilities, and then how difficult it is to generate one or a few samples from the posterior. Efficiency may require considering how many samples must be observed before the correct posterior is approximated and the cost of each observation. Thus, which algorithms are most efficient may depend on the nature of the problem being solved and on the capacities of the learner. So, we do not have good answers to when specific algorithms may be favored over others and in which contexts, but it is an important line for future research.

We can also ask whether sampling behavior is rational. A casual answer is "yes"—because we show how a "rational" or "computational" level analysis can be approximated at the algorithmic level. However, again assessing rationality depends on the goals of the learner. In some circumstances, a learner may want to quickly converge on the most likely answer. In other circumstances, however, the learner may want to explore more of the possibilities. These "exploit" or "explore" strategies might lead a learner to use different kinds of algorithms. Sampling and searching through a space of hypotheses may be a particularly useful learning mechanism for exploratory learning. It allows a learner the possibility of discovering an unlikely hypothesis that may prove correct later (after observing additional data). Were a learner to simply maximize, always choosing the most likely hypothesis, he might miss out on such a discovery.

One of the most promising implications of examining learning at the algorithmic level is that other aspects of development (e.g., memory limitations, changes in inhibition, changes in executive function) can be connected more explicitly to rational models of inference. For example, a particle filter approximates the probability distribution over hypotheses at each point in time with a set of samples (or "particles") and provides a scheme for updating this set to reflect the information provided by new evidence. The behavior of the algorithm depends on the number of particles. With a very large number of particles, each particle is similar to a sample from the posterior. With a small number of particles, there can be strong sequential dependencies in the representation of the posterior distribution. Developmental changes in cognitive capacity might correspond to changes in the number of particles, with consequences that are empirically testable.

Finally, we suggested that moving forward also involves connecting the algorithms that children might be using to carry out learning with ways in which the algorithms could be implemented in the brain. Ma, Beck, Latham, and Pouget (2006) suggest that cortical circuits may carry out sample-based approximations, reflecting the variability in the environment. Probabilistic sampling algorithms can also capture ways in which inputs should be combined (e.g., across time, sensory modalities, etc.) taking the reliability of the input into account and recent research on neural variability demonstrates this in the brain (Beck et al., 2008; Fetsch, Pouget, DeAngelis, & Angelaki, in press). Other work may examine the implication of how growing dense connections between brain regions connect to particular algorithms and how those algorithms are affected as regions are pruned (as in later adolescence).

# 7. CONCLUSIONS

In the course of development, children change their beliefs, moving from a less to more accurate picture of the world. How do they do this given the vast space of possible beliefs? And how can we reconcile children's cognitive progress with the apparent irrationality of many of their explanations and predictions? The solution we have proposed is that children may form their beliefs by randomly sampling from a probability distribution. This Sampling Hypothesis suggests a way of efficiently searching a space of possibilities in a way that is consistent with probabilistic inference and it leads to predictions about cognitive development. The studies presented here suggest that preschoolers are approximating a rational solution to the problem of probabilistic inference via a process that can be analyzed as sampling and that the samples that children generate are affected by evidence. By thinking about the computational problems that children face and the algorithms they might use to solve those problems, we can approach the variability of children's responses in a new way. Children may not just be effective learners despite the variability and randomness of their behavior. That variability, instead, may itself contribute to children's extraordinary learning abilities.

## REFERENCES

Beck, J., Ma, W. J., Kiani, R., Hanks, T. D., Churchland, A. K., Roitman, J. D., et al. (2008). Bayesian decision making with probabilistic population codes. *Neuron, 60,* 1142–1152.

Bonawitz, E., Denison, S., Chen, A., Gopnik, A., & Griffiths, T. L. (2011). A simple sequential algorithm for approximating Bayesian inference. *Proceedings of the 33rd Annual Conference of the Cognitive Science Society.*

Bonawitz, E.B., Fischer, A., & Schulz, L. (in press). Teaching three-and-a-half year olds to reason about ambiguous evidence. *Journal of Cognition and Development.*

Bonawitz, E. B., & Griffiths, T. L. (2010). Deconfounding hypothesis generation and evaluation in Bayesian models. *Proceedings of the 32nd annual conference of the cognitive science society.*

Bonawitz, E.B., & Lombrozo, T. (in press). Occam's rattle: children's use of simplicity and probability to constrain inference. *Developmental Psychology.*

Bonawitz, E. B., van Schijndel, T., Friel, D., & Schulz, L. (2012). Balancing theories and evidence in children's exploration, explanations, and learning. *Cognitive Psychology, 64,* 215–234.

Chen, Z., & Klahr, D. (1999). All other things being equal: acquisition and transfer of the control of variables strategy. *Child Development, 70*(5), 1098–1120.

Denison, S., Bonawitz, E. B., Gopnik, A., & Griffiths, T. L. (2010). Preschoolers sample from probability distributions. *Proceedings of the 32nd annual conference of the cognitive science society.*

Denison, S., Reed, C., & Xu, F. (in press). The emergence of probabilistic reasoning in very young infants: evidence from 4.5- and 6-month-old infants. *Developmental Psychology.*

Doucet, A., de Freitas, N., & Gordon, N. J. (Eds.). (2001). *Sequential Monte Carlo methods in practice.* Berlin: Springer-Verlag.

Fetsch, C.R., A. Pouget, A., DeAngelis, G.C., & Angelaki, D.E. (in press). Neural correlates of reliability-based cue weighting during multisensory integration. *Nature Neuroscience.*

Galton, F. (1907). Vox populi. *Nature, 75.* 450–445.

German, T. P., & Nichols, S. (2003). Children's inferences about long and short causal chains. *Developmental Science, 6,* 514–523.

Gerstadt, C. L., Hong, Y. J., & Diamond, A. (1994). The relationship between cognition and action: performance of children 31/2–7 years old on a stroop-like day–night test. *Cognition, 53,* 129–153.

Gilks, W. R., Richardson, S., & Spiegelhalter, D. J. (1996). *Markov Chain Monte Carlo in practice.* Boca Raton, FL: Chapman and Hall/CRC.

Goodman, N. D., Tenenbaum, J. B., Feldman, J., & Griffiths, T. L. (2008). A rational analysis of rule-based concept learning. *Cognitive Science, 32,* 108–154.

Gopnik, A., Glymour, C., Sobel, D., Schulz, L., Kushnir, T., & Danks, D. (2004). A theory of causal learning in children: causal maps and Bayes nets. *Psychological Review, 111,* 1–31.

Gopnik, A., Sobel, D. M., Schulz, L. E., & Glymour, C. (2001). Causal learning mechanisms in very young children: two-, three-, and four-year-olds infer causal relations from patters of variation and covariation. *Developmental Psychology, 37*(5), 620–629.

Greeno, J. (1998). The situativity of knowing, learning, and research. *American Psychologist, 53,* 5–26.

Griffiths, T. L., & Tenenbaum, J. B. (2009). Theory-based causal induction. *Psychological Review, 116,* 661–716.

Hudson Kam, C. L., & Newport, E. L. (2005). Regularizing unpredictable variation: the roles of adult and child learners in language formation and change. *Language Learning and Development, 1*(2), 151–195.

Hudson Kam, C. L., & Newport, E. L. (2009). Getting it right by getting it wrong: when learners change languages. *Cognitive Psychology, 59*(1), 30–66.

Inhelder, B., & Piaget, J. (1958). *The growth of logical thinking from childhood to adolescence.* New York: Basic Books.

Jones, M. H., & Liverant, S. (1960). Effects of age differences on choice behavior. *Child Development, 31*(4), 673–680.

Kemp, C., Goodman, N., & Tenenbaum, J. (2010). Learning to learn causal models. *Cognitive Science, 34*(7), 1185–1243.

Kording, K., & Wolpert, D. M. (2004). Bayesian integration in sensorimotor learning. *Nature, 427,* 244–247.

Kushnir, T., & Gopnik, A. (2005). Children infer causal strength from probabilities and interventions. *Psychological Science, 16,* 678–683.

Kushnir, T., & Gopnik, A. (2007). Conditional probability versus spatial contiguity in causal learning: preschoolers use new contingency evidence to overcome prior spatial assumptions. *Developmental Psychology, 44,* 186–196.

Lave, J., & Wenger, E. (1991). *Situated learning: Legitimate peripheral participation.* New York: Cambridge University Press.

Lucas, C. G., Gopnik, A., & Griffiths, T. L. (2010). Developmental differences in learning the forms of causal relationships. *Proceedings of the 32nd annual conference of the cognitive science society.*

Ma, W. J., Beck, J. M., Latham, P. E., & Pouget, A. (2006). Bayesian inference with probabilistic population codes. *Nature Neuroscience, 9,* 1432–1438.

Marr, D. (1982). *Vision.* San Francisco: Freeman Publishers.

Mozer, M., Pashler, H., & Homaei, H. (2008). Optimal predictions in everyday cognition: the wisdom of individuals or crowds? *Cognitive Science, 32,* 1133–1147.

Neal, R. M. (1993). *Probabilistic inference using Markov chain Monte Carlo methods. Technical report CRG-TR-93-1.* Department of Computer Science, University of Toronto.

Nowak, M., & Sigmund, K. (1993). A strategy of win-stay, lose-shift that outperforms tit-for-tat in the prisoner's dilemma game. *Nature, 364,* 56–58.

Pearl, J. (2000). *Causality: Models, reasoning and inference.* Cambridge, UK: Cambridge University Press.

Piaget, J. (1983). Piaget's theory. In Mussen P. (Ed.), *Handbook of child psychology* (4th ed., Vol. 1). New York: Wiley.

Restle, F. (1962). The selection of strategies in cue learning. *Psychological Review, 69,* 329–343.

Robbins, H. (1952). Some aspects of the sequential design of experiments. *Bulletin of the American Mathematical Society, 58,* 527–535.

Robert, C., & Casella, G. (2004). *Monte Carlo statistical methods* (2nd ed. New York: Springer.

Russell, S. J., & Norvig, P. (2003). *Artificial intelligence: A modern approach* (2nd ed. Upper Saddle River, NJ: Prentice Hall.

Sanborn, A. N., Griffiths, T. L., & Navarro, D. J. (2010). Rational approximations to rational models: alternative algorithms for category learning. *Psychological Review, 117*(4), 1144–1167.

Schulz, L. E., Bonawitz, E. B., & Griffiths, T. L. (2007). Can being scared make your tummy ache? Naive theories, ambiguous evidence and preschoolers' causal inferences. *Developmental Psychology, 43,* 1124–1139.

Schulz, L. E., Goodman, N. D., Tenenbaum, J. B., & Jenkins, C. A. (2008). Going beyond the evidence: abstract laws and preschoolers' responses to anomalous data. *Cognition, 109*(2), 211–223.

Schulz, L. E., Gopnik, A., & Glymour, C. (2007). Preschool children learn about causal structure from conditional interventions. *Developmental Science, 10*(3), 322–332.

Seiver, E., Goodman, N.D., Gopnik, A. (in press). Did she jump because she was the big sister or because the trampoline was safe? Causal inference and the development of social attribution. *Child Development.*

Shi, L., Feldman, N. H., & Griffiths, T. L. (2008). Performing Bayesian inference with exemplar models. *Proceedings of the 30th annual conference of the cognitive science society.*

Siegler, R. S. (1996). *Emerging minds: The process of change in children's thinking.* New York: Oxford University Press.

Sobel, D. M., Tenenbaum, J. M., & Gopnik, A. (2004). Children's causal inferences from indirect evidence: backwards blocking and Bayesian reasoning in preschoolers. *Cognitive Science, 28*(3), 303–333.

Spirtes, P., Glymour, C., & Schienes, R. (1993). *Causation prediction and search.* New York: Springer-Verlag.

Surowiecki, J. (2004). *The wisdom of crowds: Why the many are smarter than the few and how collective wisdom shapes business, economies, societies and nations.* New York: Little, brown.

Tenenbaum, J. B., Griffiths, T. L., & Kemp, C. (2006). Theory-based Bayesian models of inductive learning and reasoning. *Trends in Cognitive Science, 10,* 309–318.

Thelen, E., & Smith, L. B. (1994). *A dynamics systems approach to the development of perception and action.* Cambridge, MA: MIT Press.

Ullman, T., Goodman, N., & Tenenbaum, J. (2010). Theory acquisition as stochastic search. In S. Ohlsson, & R. Catrambone (Eds.), *Proceedings of the 32nd annual conference of the cognitive science society* (pp. 2840–2845). Austin, TX: Cognitive Science Society.

Vul, E., Goodman, N. D., Griffiths, T. L., & Tenenbaum, J. B. (2009). One and done? Optimal decisions from very few samples. *Proceedings of the 31st annual conference of the cognitive science society.*

Vul, E., & Pashler, H. (2008). Measuring the crowd within: probabilistic representations within individuals. *Psychological Science, 19*(7), 645–647.

Weiss, Y., Simoncelli, E. P., & Adelson, E. H. (2002). Motion illusions as optimal percepts. *Nature Neuroscience, 5*(6), 598–604.

Xu, F., & Tenenbaum, J. B. (2007). Word learning as Bayesian inference. *Psychological Review, 114*(2), 245–272.

CHAPTER SEVEN

# Developing a Concept of Choice

## Tamar Kushnir

Department of Human Development, Cornell University, Ithaca, NY 14853,
E-mail: tk397@cornell.edu

## Contents

## Abstract

Our adult concept of *choice* is not a simple idea, but rather a complex set of beliefs about the causes of actions. These beliefs are situation-, individual- and culture-dependent, and are thus likely constructed through social learning. This chapter takes a rational constructivist approach to examining the development of a concept of choice in young children. Initially, infants' combine assumptions of rational agency with their capacity for statistical inference to reason about alternative possibilities for, and constraints on, action. Preschoolers' build on this basic understanding by integrating domain-specific causal knowledge of physical, biological, and psychological possibility into their appraisal of their own and others' ability to choose. However, preschoolers continue to view both psychological and social motivations as constraints on choice – for example, stating that one cannot choose to harm another, or to act against personal desires. It is not until later that children share the adult belief that choice mediates between conflicting motivations for action. The chapter concludes by suggesting avenues for future research – to better characterize conceptual changes in beliefs about choice, and to understand how such beliefs arise from children's everyday experiences.

*Advances in Child Development and Behavior*, Volume 43
ISSN 0065-2407,
http://dx.doi.org/10.1016/B978-0-12-397919-3.00007-1

# 1. INTRODUCTION

As adults, we share the intuition that many of our everyday actions are choices. Our concept of choice guides our explanations of behavior (Gilbert & Malone, 1995; Ross & Nisbett, 1991), our understanding of causal agency (Blakemore & Frith, 2003; Haggard & Tsakiris, 2009; Wegner, 2002) and intentionality (Guglielmo, Monroe, & Malle, 2009), and our intuitions about morality and social responsibility (Nichols & Knobe, 2007; Pizarro & Helzer, 2010; Vohs & Schooler, 2008). We see choices in everyday acts of no consequence—what we put on our sandwich, whether we say hello to a stranger passing on the street. We also see choice in actions with major consequences—who we marry, what we study in college. Given the centrality of the concept of choice in adult reasoning, it is surprising that we know relatively little about its developmental origins. That is, while it has long been acknowledged that *having* choices is important to healthy cognitive and social development (e.g. Leotti, Iyengar, & Ochsner, 2010; Ryan & Deci, 2000), we know almost nothing about when young children first understand of actions *as* choices or about how a concept of choice is initially acquired through early experience.

Well, this is not completely true. We know something. We know that parents, teachers, and other adults talk to children about choices (Killen & Smetana, 1999; Nucci & Weber, 1995). We know that through development, with increasing conviction, children think of themselves as free and autonomous (Helwig, 2006; Ryan & Lynch, 1989). We know that even in adults, the idea of choice is different for different individuals and for different cultural groups (Kitayama, Snibbe, Markus, & Suzuki, 2004; Pöhlmann, Carranza, Hannover, & Iyengar, 2007; Savani et al., 2010). We also know (well, at least we believe) that children do not start out life with a concept of choice, at least not one that looks like ours. So, we know that somehow this concept of choice must be learned.

What we don't know is exactly *how* it is learned. This is where rational constructivism can help. It can serve as a guiding principle to ask the necessary questions about learning and speculate on the answers: What prior assumptions form the basis for children's concept of choice? How and when does the concept change? What sort of experiences might provide the right sort of evidence for change? This technique has been applied successfully in other conceptual domains, and many of the chapters in this volume are proof of its success. Applying this framework here will hopefully yield some answers and spark new questions to drive further research.

## 2. REPRESENTATION AND REALITY

Before addressing the developmental question, a few caveats are in order. The first is an acknowledgment of the complexity of the concept; choice is a simple word but not a simple idea. Instead, it captures a set of related concepts and intuitions, all of which are central to how we understand the causes of our own and others actions. Our concept is both local—influencing "construals" of specific situations as affording/not affording choice—and global—influencing our "worldviews" of free will, autonomy, and moral responsibility. There are aspects of our concept of choice that are culturally universal, and other aspects that are highly culturally variable. In the words of Iyengar (2010): "Though all humans share a basic need and desire for choice, we do not all see choice in the same places or to the same extent". The individual, situational, and cultural differences in beliefs about choice strongly suggest that learning—and in particular social learning—plays a critical role in how this concept is constructed over development.

The second caveat concerns the relationship between beliefs about choice and actuality. I take the view, shared by many who research similar intuitions in adults, that our belief in choice is part of our general understanding of the psychological world (Baumeister, Mele, & Vohs, 2010; Guglielmo et al., 2009). So, I will leave aside questions about actuality—how we *actually make* choices (human decision making) and whether we *actually have* choices (the so-called "problem of free will")—for others to ponder. Choice lives in the mind of the beholder; it relates to reality but is not wholly explained by it. For example, we sometimes feel we made a choice even when the evidence suggests that we did not (Wegner, 2002). Also, we sometimes feel as if we were led by circumstance to act in a particular way, even when those circumstances do not technically force our actions. Moreover, as mentioned above, the very same acts may count as choices for one individual but not for another (Paulhus & Carey, 2011) or by many individuals in one cultural group and not another (Kitayama et al., 2004; Miller & Chakravarthy, 2011; Savani et al., 2010). As a final complication, our appraisals of the same choice behaviors sometimes vary depending on whether we are attributing responsibility to other individuals or to ourselves (Norenzayan & Nisbett, 2000; Pronin & Kugler, 2010; Ross & Nisbett, 1991).

One final point concerns the relationship between the concept of choice and the experience of agency. It is tempting to conclude, based on intuition alone, that our concept of choice arises directly from our experience of our own actions as "freely willed." Even infants experience agency, so if that is the only basis for our concept, there is not much of a developmental story to be told. This seems to be the position of some neuroscientists and philosophers (e.g. Holton, 2010), and it has empirical support: Experimental investigations of the varieties of agentic experience show that when such experience is enhanced or disrupted, our beliefs about choice can be enhanced or disrupted accordingly (Blakemore & Frith, 2003; Haggard & Tsakiris, 2009; Wegner, 2002). The opposite causal story—that our concept of choice is the first and foremost product of social cognition, arising from our interactions with and observations of other people, and only later gets applied to our own agentic experience—is perhaps less intuitive. It too, however, has empirical support: directly manipulating beliefs in free choice and autonomy can profoundly influence our experience of agency (Aarts & Van den Bos, 2011; Pronin, Wegner, McCarthy, & Rodriguez, 2006). Thus, we are left with a chicken-and-egg problem—which comes first, the experience of agency or the concept of choice? An interesting answer may reveal itself in developmental data, in particular if developmental changes are in any way related to children's emerging ability to guide and control their actions.

In short, choice is a theory—a social cognitive theory and a theory about our own experience. The development of these ideas is informed by evidence but does not reduce to a mere "empirical generalization" (Gopnik & Melzoff, 1997; Gopnik & Wellman, 1992) from evidence. This is precisely what makes the question of how we learn to view actions in this way so interesting and important.

## 3. RATIONAL STARTING STATES: POSSIBILITY AND CONSTRAINT

Central to our concept of choice is the ability to entertain alternative possibilities for action: If an action is a choice, it could have been otherwise. On the other hand, if an action is not a choice, it had to occur exactly as it did—it could not have been otherwise. This implies that our understanding of choice is inseparable from our understanding of *constraints*—internal and external factors that limit choices by limiting alternative courses of action. Examples range from the properties of the external environment (you can't choose a rainy day, you can't choose to order Mexican food at a Thai restaurant), the limits of physical possibility (you can't choose to fly or have super-human strength), and the limits of epistemic possibility (you can't chose to know what the Mona Lisa looks like if you have never seen her, you can't choose to understand theoretical physics if you haven't studied it). The extent to which we can understand and imagine the alternatives (in general or in any given situation) determines whether we view an action as a choice. When there are no alternative possibilities or where the possibilities are limited, then there is, respectively, no choice or limited choice.

It has been suggested that the ability to imagine alternative possibilities for actions—and thus to construe actions as choices—emerges toward the end of the preschool years, alongside or after the ability to engage in explicit counterfactual reasoning (Harris, German, & Mills, 1996; Nichols, 2004; Sobel, 2004). While there are certainly important developments in children's concept of choice around this age (which I will return to later), it is not the earliest that we see evidence of an understanding of possibility and constraint. Rather, this understanding originates in infancy and is based on two related assumptions that infants make about psychologically caused actions, both of which are rational.

## 3.1. Rational Agency, Freedom, and Constraint

The first of the two is the assumption of rational agency—the belief that psychological agents will act in the most efficient manner to achieve their goals (Gergely & Csibra, 2003; Gergely & Jacobs, this volume). In a classic demonstration of this assumption, Gergely, Bekkering, and Király (2002) allowed 14-month-old infants to observe an actor pressing a panel with her head to turn on a light. The actor was either free to use her hands (they were placed on the table in front of her) or her hands were occupied (she used them to wrap herself in a blanket). After this demonstration, infants were given the panel themselves. In the "hands free" condition, infants pressed the panel with their heads, imitating the means as well as the goal of the action. Critically, however, in the "hands occupied" condition, infants imitated the action using the more efficient means—that is, they pressed the panel with their own free hands. Thus, infants show, through their selective imitation, that they distinguish between the free, intentional actions and the constrained, unintentional ones.

Even younger infants show through their looking behavior that they expect rational agency and thus expect differences in actions in the presence or absence of constraints. For example, after being habituated to an agent traversing a barrier, 9-month-olds recognize that it will try more efficient means of achieving an outcome if a barrier is removed (Csibra, Gergely, Bíró, Koós, & Brockbank, 1999). By 10 months, infants understand how physical constraints can lead to failure to achieve a goal. Brandone and Wellman (2009) showed 10- and 12-month-old infants an actor reaching over a barrier for a ball but failing to get it. Infants later expected the actor to behave completely differently—they expect him to reach directly for *and* to get the ball—when the barrier was absent.

Infants robustly distinguish free from constrained actions in many situations, even when the differences between the actions are not physically apparent. For example, infants selectively imitate the same acts when they are linguistically marked as intentional ("there!") versus accidental ("oops!" e.g. Carpenter, Aktar, & Tomasello, 1998). Similarly, they behave differently toward actors who "teasingly" show an unwillingness to share or help than to actors who demonstrate good intentions but genuine inability (Behne, Carpenter, Call, & Tomasello, 2005; Dunfield & Kuhlmeier, 2010; Hamlin, Wynne, & Bloom, 2008). Moreover, a number of studies have found that 15- to 18-month-old infants understand how lack of information will determine subsequent actions—an epistemic, rather than a physical constraint (Buttelmann, Carpenter, & Tomasello, 2009; Kovács, Téglás, & Endress, 2010; Onishi & Baillargeon, 2005; Southgate, Senju, & Csibra, 2007). Thus, infants do not necessarily have to see a constraint to reason that an action was not intentionally (freely) performed.

## 3.2. The Statistics of Alternative Possibility

One advantage of assuming agents will rationally act to achieve goals is that it leads to inferences about alternative possibilities—at least for constrained actions. However, one of the hallmarks of understanding choice is the ability to entertain alternative possibilities for *free* actions as well. This type of inference does not automatically follow from the assumption of rational agency. In fact, it is quite the opposite: free (unconstrained) actions that are efficient should occur exactly as they did, not otherwise. Thus, rational agent assumptions alone would lead infants to consider *one* possibility for free actions, not multiple possibilities—which would restrict their ability to reason about choice.

The ability to understand multiple alternative possibilities for free action comes from another assumption infants make about psychological agents: when acting in accordance with their own intentions, goals, and desires, agents can (and consistently do) violate statistical probabilities. Put another way, psychologically caused actions are not only efficient but also nonrandom. Thus, to learn that free actions are choices, infants must rely on another rational, early-emerging ability—that of statistical inference.

Consider an action that an observer would expect to be statistically random—a person taking toys out of a toy box with his or her eyes closed. Not only adults but also preschoolers (Denison, Konopczynski, Garcia, & Xu, 2006) and even infants (Téglás, Girotto, Gonzalez, & Bonatti, 2007; Xu & Garcia, 2008) expect randomly drawn samples to be representative of underlying populations and vice versa. For example, Xu and colleagues (Xu and Garcia; 2008; Xu & Denison 2009, and Denison & Xu this volume) showed 8- and 11-month-old infants a person taking four red balls and one white ball out of a box with her eyes closed. When the contents of the box were revealed, infants looked longer at an unexpected population (a box full of mostly white balls with some red balls) than at an expected population (mostly red balls and some white balls). However, when 11-month-old infants saw a person with an explicitly expressed preference draw the sample intentionally (i.e. with her eyes open and looking in the box), Xu and Denison (2009) found that these infants did not form expectations about the contents of the box. This is, in fact, a special case of infants' assumption of rational agency: infants made random sampling assumptions about the constrained actions (eyes closed) but not the intentional ones (eyes open). Coupled with the fact that infants were familiarized with the actor's preference in advance, this demonstration leaves unclear whether infants imagined alternative possibilities for the nonrandom, eyes-open action.

One way to find out is to contrast two types of free actions—one that violates random sampling assumptions and one that does not. Imagine a person intentionally taking several toys of one type (say, five rubber frogs) out of a toy box full of two types of toys (rubber frogs and rubber ducks) and playing happily with them. If most or all of the toys in the box are frogs, the statistical information is in keeping with random draws from the box; thus, this situation would provide no evidence that the person chose rubber frogs over rubber ducks. If, however, the box is full of rubber ducks with very few rubber frogs in it, then the sample of five frogs is not likely to have been drawn by chance. More likely, the person chose to take only frogs and so is displaying a greater *preference* for frogs than for ducks. Generally, determining preferences requires attending to the relation between choices made and alternative options *not* chosen—in this case, the other toys in the box. Thus, if infants can use the violation of random sampling to learn about a person's preference in this manner, it suggests that they are attending to alternative possibilities for free action—in other words, it shows that they view the action as a choice.

Kushnir, Xu, and Wellman (2010) showed random groups of 20-month-old infants this exact scenario. Infants saw a female experimenter select five toys of one type (e.g. frogs) out of a box containing a minority of that type (e.g. 18% frogs to 82% ducks) or a majority of that type (e.g. 82% frogs to 18% ducks). Social and affective cues signaling both intention and desire to play with the toys were constant and positive across conditions. Later on, a bowl of ducks and a bowl of frogs were placed in front of the child and the experimenter asked for a toy. Infants were more likely to give her the frogs when they were in the minority of items in the box previously. When they were previously in the majority, the infants handed her both frogs and ducks equally (in fact, in the majority condition, they were slightly more likely to hand her ducks, perhaps assuming she would prefer something new to play with). Thus, even though her actions were unconstrained and intentional in both conditions, infants inferred that she made a choice—acted based on her preference for frogs and not based on some other causal factor—only when the alternatives were mostly ducks—that is, when the sample was nonrandom.

In a similar study, Ma and Xu (2011) found that infants as young as 16 months use violations of random sampling to infer that others' preferences are different from their own. More recently, using modified violation-of-expectation paradigm, we found that younger (10-month-old) infants make action predictions based on the same statistical relations, inferring that an actor will reach for another instance of a toy that she had originally chosen from a minority of toys in the box but not when that same toy when it was haphazardly removed from the majority (Wellman, Kushnir, & Xu, submitted for publication).

Note that if there were *no* alternative objects in the box and the only available objects were of the type chosen, then infants could have based their inference on the situational constraint that no other option was available, rather than on the statistical likelihood that the action occurred randomly. Thus, we made sure that infants knew about both types of toys in the box in two ways—we allowed them to play with the box contents before the experimenter sampled items and we labeled each type of object in both conditions ("Look! Ducks and Frogs!"). In this way, we ensured that their inferences were based on evaluating the statistical relation between the sample and the alternative possibilities in the population.

As further evidence that this is indeed a statistical inference, we showed that 3- and 4-year-olds children infer the strength of agent's preference from the *degree* of nonrandomness of the sample. We varied the proportion of toys in the box across three groups of preschoolers. In the first group, 18% of the toys were of the selected type (e.g. red foam circles) and 82% were of an alternative type (e.g. blue foam flowers). In the second group, 50% were of the selected type. In the final group, 100% were of the selected type. After they saw the selection, children were asked to give the agent (a puppet named Squirrel) "the toy that he likes" out of the three possible choices: the selected type (red circles), the alternative type (blue flowers), or a novel type (yellow cylinders). The results showed that preschoolers inferences were a function of the strength of the statistical evidence for nonrandom sampling—they were most likely to infer a preference for the selected object when it was in the minority of objects in the box (18% condition), slightly less likely when the proportions were equal (50% condition), and least likely when it was the only object in the box (100% condition).

The ability to engage in statistical inference about samples and populations ensures that children not only watch what choices people make but they also watch the choices they avoid. Both might be critical aspects of learning about the specific inner motivations—the likes and dislikes—of other people.

## 4. FILLING IN THE DETAILS

So far I have tried to show how the earliest concept of choice—the understanding of alternative possibilities for action and constraints on possibility—could be based on combining assumptions about rational agency with a capacity for statistical inference. Together, these assumptions support further learning about situations that do or do not afford choice in early childhood.

### 4.1. Acquiring New Domain-Specific Knowledge

The assumption of rational agency ensures that children, like adults, will consider constraints when reasoning about whether a situation affords choice. Though this may be an early and fundamental general principle, there is still a lot that infants and children have to learn about the specific situational constraints. Large physical obstacles, such as the barriers in the studies above, are understood to be constraints quite early. Understanding other constraints may require infants to accumulate some relevant experience first. For example, infants can reason that a blindfold imposes a constraint only after they have tried one on themselves (Meltzoff & Brooks, 2008; Senju, Southgate, Snape, Leonard, & Csibra, 2011). Also, when achieving a goal involves a sequence of complicated steps, infants can reason about the exact actions required to do so efficiently only after themselves exploring the relations between actions and outcomes (Sommerville, Woodward, & Needham, 2005). Some constraints, then, might only be understood as such only after personal experience (see Sommerville, this volume; also Paulus, Hunnius, Vissers, & Bekkering, 2011).

By the time children are in preschool, the sorts of constraints they are able to consider are more sophisticated, reflecting their more sophisticated conceptual knowledge of physical, biological, and psychological phenomena (Gelman, 2003; Gelman & Wellman, 1991; Inagaki & Hatano, 1993; Schult & Wellman, 1997). They learn these constraints as part of their intuitive theories of these and other conceptual domains. For example, after children learn that the flu will make you tired and weak, they can understand why a child with the flu cannot choose to run fast and play with her friends. This knowledge does not constitute a conceptual shift in understanding choice—the general framework of possibility and constraint is the same—but it marks a significant change in the details of what children consider as a choice.

In order to see how domain-specific knowledge about constraint inform children's early concept of choice, we asked preschool children both counterfactual and hypothetical questions about possibility and constraint. We expect that their responses should reflect their early understanding of alternative possibilities for free actions and limitations of possibility for constrained actions.

Kushnir, Chernyak, and Wellman (2009) told 4-year-olds stories adapted from Schult and Wellman's (1997) study of children's psychological, biological, and physical explanations for human actions. In some stories, a character desired to perform a *possible* action (e.g. stepping off a stool and going to the ground) and in others a character desired to perform an *impossible action* (e.g. stepping off a stool and floating in the air). Across stories, the final outcome was the matched—the character, regardless of her initial desire, ended up performing the same action (e.g. stepping off of the stool on to the ground). After seeing the outcome, children were asked whether the character could have done otherwise. This question appealed to either a *possible choice* to do something different than the initial desired actions (e.g. "Did she have to do that, or could she have stayed on the stool?") or an *impossible choice* in line with the impossible desired action (e.g. "Did she have to do that, or could she have just floated in the air?"). Children correctly said that the character could make a possible, but not an impossible, choice. This demonstrated that children's responses depended on the nature of the action (whether it was possible or impossible) not on character's initial desire or on the final outcome.

In another study (Chernyak, Kushnir, Sullivan, & Wang, 2011), we asked children to reason about possible and impossible choices in the future. Children heard three stories about characters that habitually performed one activity, but one day wanted to try another. In one story, the alternative action was possible (e.g. wanting to drinking milk instead of juice). In another, it was physically constrained (e.g. wanting to walking through a brick wall instead of around it). In the third story, the action was epistemically constrained (e.g. wanting to draw a monkey without knowing what one looks like). We asked children two questions about each story—a Choice Question ("Can he do that?") and an Action Prediction Question ("Will he do that?"). As before, the results showed that children distinguish between possible and impossible choices. That is, children endorsed the characters choice and ability to act on his new stated desire when it was possible but not when it was physically or epistemically constrained.

## 4.2. Imagining Possible Alternatives

If all of the alternate possibilities for action were available to see—like toys in a toy box—then children would always have clear evidence for choice. But, unfortunately, this is almost never the case. Do children need concrete evidence of alternate possibilities in order to figure out what others choose? Theoretical analyses suggest that even without concrete alternatives, infants may infer that all intentional actions are nonrandom samples, and they may even imagine (at least skeletally) the population of actions they might be drawing from (Gweon, Tenenbaum, & Schulz, 2010; Lucas, Griffiths, Xu, & Fawcett, 2009; Xu & Tenenbaum, 2007). This may explain why children do not need multiple instances of the same action (i.e. a large sample) to think of that action as a choice—why, for example, after reaching for one single frog in the presence of a single duck, infants expect others' actions to be preferentially directed at that frog in the future (Sommerville & Woodward, in press; Woodward, 1998).

This also sets the stage for further developments. Preschoolers are characteristically different from infants in their ability to imagine, to pretend, and to describe alternative worlds—both realistic and fantastical—where numerous possibilities for action exist (Harris, 1993; Lillard, 1993; Woolley, 1997). This could consequently lead to changes in understanding choice by expanding the population of actions children consider as alternatives. Do individual children judgments of the same action (choice/not choice) depend on their ability to generate alternatives? Can inducing children to imagine more (or fewer) alternatives in advance alter their conceptions of others' actions as choices? More generally, is there a relationship between imagination and choice, and is it systematic? Rational? I think that all of these questions warrant further exploration.

## 5. CHOICE AND AGENCY

Infants are creatures with limited agency, they spend most of their time being carried around, put down, cared for, and fussed over by others. What opportunities do infants have, then, to experience choice for themselves? Initially, there are probably none. However, quickly through the first few months of life, infants begin to gain control of their bodies and move voluntarily—this includes the ability to direct eye gaze and, relatedly, to turn their heads toward interesting sights and sounds (Aslin, 2012). The ability to move the rest of the body voluntarily follows shortly after. It is remarkable, and highly suggestive of some rudimentary understanding of agency, that infants will use their limited capacity for free action whenever they can, for example, working to exert control over interesting effects in the environment (Watson & Ramey, 1972).

Given these early tendencies to capitalize on every opportunity to exert agency, it is unsurprising to find that young children's beliefs about their own agency are often overblown. Illusions of agency and control are found in adults as well, but some studies suggest that are perhaps greater in childhood. For example, when outcomes are weakly associated with their own actions, preschool children consistently misjudge them as strongly associated (Kushnir, Wellman, & Gelman, 2009; Kushnir & Gopnik, 2005). Older children also show overconfidence in their own agency: In a study, Metcalfe, Eich, and Castel (2010) investigated beliefs about agentic control in children (ages 8–10) and adults using a computer game in which participants were asked to click on X's and avoid O's. The game at times included random distortions that decreased control, time delays between clicks and effects ("lag"), and spatial gaps between clicks and effects ("magic") that increased the radius of accuracy and therefore improved performance. Metcalfe et al. (2010) asked participants to judge how "in control" they felt as well as to rate their accuracy. While both children and adults correctly judged their lack of control when their clicks were distorted, children were more likely than adults to incorrectly judge themselves to be fully responsible, especially for favorable outcomes. This metacognitive error is consistent with similar findings showing that children tend to conflate their contribution to collaborative activities (Foley & Ratner, 1998; Sommerville & Hammond, 2007).

How might these illusions of agency affect children's understanding of their own choices? Perhaps children feel overconfident that *all* of their voluntary acts are choices, and they are impervious to constraints on their own actions. This idea is supported by studies showing that children often incorrectly state an intention to do what they did ("I meant to" or "I tried to") even when their actions are purely accidental (Shultz & Wells, 1985) or physically forced (Montgomery & Lightner, 2004). Do children similarly believe that they "choose to" act in accordance with constraints—that, under constrained conditions, their actions could have been otherwise?

We investigated this question by giving children the experience of free or constrained agency and then asking them to reflect on whether their actions could have been otherwise (Kushnir et al., 2009). Children (ages 4 and 5) were asked to draw a series of shapes, thus they could experience their actions and also see the effects of their actions (the drawings). Each child drew two pictures. In the *Free Drawing* trial, children were asked to draw a dot. In the *Physically Constrained Drawing* trial, children were asked to draw a line, but the experimenter held their hand preventing its movement across the page, resulting in a dot. Thus, the outcome in each trial was the same (a dot), but the acts that produced that outcome were different (free vs. constrained). We asked children the same question after each trial: "could you have drawn the line?" and asked them to explain their response. Children appropriately attributed their ability to do otherwise when their actions were free and not when they were physically constrained; most also appropriately explained the events that constrained them (e.g. "because you were holding my hand" or "because I couldn't move").

These results suggest that preschoolers are not overconfident that their own actions are always choices. One potential problem with this conclusion, however, is that the physical constraint—forcing the child's hand to stay in one place—also changed their physical experience of agency. It may be that

4-year-olds are still overconfident that their actions are choices when their experience of agency is unrestricted.

To investigate this further, we designed a different type of constraint, one that did not limit the physical experience of agency. This experiment (Chernyak, Kushnir, & Wellman, 2010) had the same basic set-up as the previous one; there were two trials counterbalanced within subjects, *Free Drawing* and *Constrained Drawing*. This time, however, we did not physically control the outcome across trials, we simply told children to "draw something different" from the experimenter. Critically, this meant that children had the same experience of agency across both Free and Constrained trials. Indeed, each drawing made by the child was truly their own creation—some were simple shapes, some were faces, houses, etc. On each trial, the experimenter also drew a picture. In the Free Drawing trial, children could see what she drew. In the Constrained Drawing trial, the experimenter kept her picture hidden from the child behind an occluder and revealed it only after the child had completed his/her own drawing (before asking the choice question). Then, children were asked if they could have drawn the same shape as the experimenter (i.e. "could you have drawn the line?"), given that there was/was not previously an occluder present. The results showed that their understanding of this epistemic constraint was not distorted by their experience of agency. In the Free Drawing trial, children said that they were free to draw the experimenter's picture. But in the Constrained Drawing trial, they appropriately said that they were *not* free (and some even explained why—e.g. "because I couldn't see it").

Combined, these studies indicate that children are responsive to situational constraints when reflecting on their own choices. The experience of action may still play a role in their understanding, but it is mediated by other considerations.

This brings up another related question: In the stream of everyday activity, which actions stand out to young children as choices, and which do not? We have begun to address this question using a preschool-friendly adaptation of Savani et al.'s (2011) choice memory task for adults. In this task, children are given the opportunity to make six choices: two for personal gain (choosing a toy to play with and a sticker to take home), two that are prosocial (choosing to share with a puppet and to avoid harming/harm another puppet), and two neutral (choosing a color note card and a crayon to write their names). After engaging in a short unrelated building task, children are asked "can you tell me what *choices* you made here today?" Preliminary results from 28 four-year-old children show that most children listed one or more of the six events and no other incidental events, indicating that they understood the appropriate use of the word "choice." Interestingly, there were systematic differences between the items—children were most likely to list the personal gain events and least likely to list the neutral and prosocial events as choices. Further probes showed that this was not a difficulty with memory for the events or salience. These data are preliminary but offer a tantalizing possibility that preschool children apply the word "choice" to their own actions quite narrowly, mainly when referring to events that lead to personally beneficial outcomes.

## 6. SOCIAL CONSTRAINTS

So far I have made three claims about our early concept of choice. First, that it begins with a rational understanding of possibility and constraint. Second, that the details of what is/isn't as a choice can change as children develop more knowledge about different domain-specific constraints on action and greater ability to imagine different possibilities for action. Finally, young children reason about their own choices in a similar way—recognizing that sometimes they are free to choose and sometimes they are constrained.

These beliefs are certainly foundational, but they are far from the whole story. For one thing, we adults usually take the role of choice in these simple scenarios for granted. When we reflect on choice at all, it is mostly when faced with situations that make choice difficult, not easy, and constraints that make some actions unfavorable, not impossible. Many of these difficulties arise from conflict between choice and moral considerations, rule following, or social obligations to other people.

It is not surprising that these difficult circumstances give rise to the most individual and cultural variability in adult concepts of choice. It is also not surprising that our sense of autonomy and independence from social influences continues to develop well beyond the preschool years. Relevant to concepts of choice are several findings about school-age children: it is not until age 8 that children (at least Western children) begin to predict that people will act on personal preferences over social rules (Kalish & Shiverick, 2004). It is also not until late elementary school that Western (American) children begin to diverge from Eastern (Indian) children in the prevalence of psychological, rather than situational, explanations for actions (Miller, 1984). Parallel age-related and cultural differences can be seen in children's motivation to act under conditions of choice or social constraint (Leotti et al., 2010).

It seems likely, then, that developmental changes in children's understanding of choice in these difficult circumstances continues to change over the elementary school years and varies across cultures. In a study, we surveyed 4- to 11-year-old children in two cultures—the USA and Nepal—about their understanding of choice in the face of social constraints (Chernyak et al., 2011). Each child heard a series of stories about characters who desire to perform simple, unconstrained actions (e.g. drinking milk instead of juice), physically and epistemically constrained actions (e.g. floating in the air instead of falling after a jump, doing something you do not know how to do), and socially constrained actions. We included a broad range of social constraints—from moral acts to social and artifact conventions, capturing the range of social, moral, and obligatory understandings that are present as early as the preschool years (Rakoczy, Warneken, & Tomasello, 2008; Smetana, 1981; Turiel, 1983).

For the "simple" items, all children across ages and cultures endorsed freedom of choice to perform simple acts but recognized that acts that violate physical and mental laws (such as gravity, object solidity, or knowledge limitations) were constrained. This result is unsurprising, given that prior work does not suggest cultural differences in what counts as a constraint in either physical or psychological domains (Morris & Peng, 1994; Wellman, Fang, Liu, Zhu, & Liu, 2006).

Critically, however, the results showed developmental and cultural differences in children's views on "difficult" items that involved social constraints. These differences immerged over time: Young children (ages 4– 7) in both cultures viewed moral and social obligations as constraints on action equally often—and only slightly less often than physical and epistemic constraints. That is, they often said that the story characters *could not* act on his/her desires in the face of social constraints. Divergence in responses began around age 8 and continued to age 11. Americans 8- to 11-year-olds were increasingly likely to say that characters could act freely on their desires even if they go against social constraints. Nepalese 8- to 11-year-olds, on the other hand, continued to say that social obligations would constrain choice. These results nicely parallel age-related and culture-specific changes in other aspects of children's social cognition, such as causal attribution, self-concept, moral reasoning, and autobiographical memory (Kalish, 2002; Kalish & Shiverick, 2004; Miller, 1984; Schweder, Mahapatra, & Miller, 1987; Wang, 2004).

It seems that young children in both cultures, and older Nepali children, construe social events as situational constraints, similar to physical and epistemic limitations on actions. I would, however, caution against saying that there are *no* developmental changes in Nepalese children—it is highly unlikely that they have a consistent view on social obligation as a constraint on choice throughout life. For adults, social obligations complicate choice regardless of culture. In support of this idea, current theories explain cultural differences not by positing radically different concepts of choice but rather by detailing where individuals (or cultures) place the act of choice with respect to both internal desires and external social obligations. For some theorists, culture shapes our desires themselves, and working for the benefit of others becomes desirable (Miller, Das, & Chakravarthy, 2011). For others, the sense of self (who is doing the "choosing") may be confined to the individual or may include group considerations (Kitayama et al., 2004). There are surely developmental changes in both cultures, and our initial measures are not sensitive enough to detect them fully.

## 7. CHOICE AS AN INTERNAL MENTAL ACTIVITY

Can it really be that the only changes that need to be explained regarding developing concepts of choice are changes in the details of constraint? I think not. From infancy into the preschool years, there seems to be some continuity in children's concepts of choice, namely that they view choice as a necessary behavioral outcome of an internal motivation, such as desire or preference. But we as adults do not see choice as necessarily determined by desires. To us, choice is a mental activity, separate from other mental activities, not always predicted by our apparent goals and desires. We feel (and believe) that choice plays a causal role in determining action on it is own accord, separate from other internal and external causal forces (though of course interacting with them). Examples of this separation are easily found by intuition: I understand that I can like one activity, but choose to do another; I believe that though I follow a rule, I could choose to break it. Thus, choice is something possessed by an agent; is separate from the agent's desires, goals, and beliefs; and allows agents the power to break from moral or social obligation. This is precisely what it means to have an intuitive notion of "free will." And this intuition is present in all of us—part of the human experience—regardless of culture or circumstance (e.g. Sarkissian et al., 2010).

Perhaps, the biggest developmental puzzle is how children make this conceptual leap. That is, how does choice become an internal mental, rather than external behavioral, idea? How do children learn that choice is not just something people *do*, but also something people *have*?

We are far from understanding how these changes happen. We can only speculate crudely on the sorts of experiences children have that might be relevant: experience acting in accordance with social obligation or personal choice, observations of others complying with or violating social constraints, the role of language in framing, and explaining actions. The critical next step seems to be to specify more fully what evidence might be leading children to change their beliefs about choice and investigate whether different concepts emerge from different patterns of evidence. I think there are at least two important sources of evidence that require further exploration—social evidence from language and agentic evidence from having to navigate difficult choices.

## 7.1. Social Evidence: The Language of Choice

Language can have profound effects on early conceptual learning, even before children are producing much of it themselves. Moreover, all concepts that are socially constructed (in whole or in part) engage linguistic evidence to some extent (Harris & Koenig, 1996). What kind of language might inform children's understanding choice and constraint? The following three seem important, though there are surely more:

1. *Modal verbs.* Modal verbs surely play a critical role in how children reason about situational constraints on action; contrast between words such as *can* and *can't*, *must* and *may* can be understood as the amount of choice or obligation in the acts described. The earliest understandings of modality fall into two categories of meaning, which are usually lumped together as root (or "agent-oriented") modalities (Papafragou, 1998a, 1998b; Wells, 1979). This includes dynamic modality—which primarily includes descriptions of possibility ("I can play the piano") and constraint ("I can't see what's over there")—and deontic modality, which refers to obligation ("You should eat your peas," "you must take off your shoes in the house"). There is some controversy surrounding the early meanings of root modal verbs—in particular whether possibility ("can" and "will") is understood earlier than impossibility ("can't and won't"). One area for new research is to examine how children's developing understanding of such words and their understanding of choice and constraint are bi-directionally linked.

For example, applying the word "can" in new situations might give children ideas about possibility that they did not have before. On the other hand, new understandings of possibility and constraint might lead children to apply modal verbs accordingly and in new ways.

2. *Forced choice desire statements.* Children (at least, middle-class Western children) are often given choice in simple situations, such as what they would like to eat or to wear. Sometimes parents offer choices in an open-ended way (e.g. "what would you like for breakfast today?"). Other times, especially when children are very young, parents restrict their choices to only two or three items (e.g. "would you like cereal or toast for breakfast today?"). In fact, parents in our "more choice is better" culture (Swartz, 2010) may feel these "two-item forced choice desire statements" are a useful way to get children to comply with their wishes. For example, when trying to get a child to go to bed: "do you want to brush your teeth first or put on your pajamas first?" works better than "time for bed, go brush your teeth!" Parents may inadvertently, through these statements, be sending children the message that every action is a choice between two possibilities. An intriguing idea, then, is that we might well find individual differences in choice concepts based on how parents, caregivers, and others verbally structure their statements about choice to young children.

3. *The words "choice" and "choose."* There is no research systematically documenting when children use the words "choice" and "choose" in everyday conversation and certainly no understanding of the semantic development of these words at the level of detail of other mentalistic terms such as *want, know, think, believe* (Bartsch & Wellman, 1995; Papafragou, 2001). In everyday observations of behavior, mental state verbs—choice included—are not directly observable but actions are (Papafragou, Cassidy, & Gleitman, 2007). This fact makes actions much more salient and leads to the question of how children might learn mental verbs in context without some help. Studies by Papafragou et al. (2007) showed that syntactic cues and observational evidence combine for ideal learning of verbs like *think* and *know*. The syntactic cues come from complement structures ("She thinks that he wants a cookie") and the observational evidence comes from situations where thoughts (or knowledge states) are in conflict with reality. It would be interesting to investigate whether (and how) this works for choice as well. For example, could observations of nonrandom sampling in lead children (or even adults for that matter) to label those actions with the word "choice"?

These semantic developments generate interesting questions related to developing concepts of choice: How frequent are they in input to children? In what situations do the most often emerge? Are there developmental and cultural (cross-linguistic) differences, and do these relate systematically to understandings of choice? How does language interact with statistical evidence from observing actions, with conceptual knowledge about constraints, and with agentic experience?

## 7.2. Agentic Evidence: Learning from Difficult Choices

As adults, our view on choice is that it acts as a mental "mediator"—the activity that is responsible for initiating action and, when necessary, resolving conflicts between all of the various internal and external factors that influence us. It is when reasoning about constraints that make choices difficult, rather than impossible, that we sense this conflict occurring. As discussed, social obligations create such difficulty. Do we, after a long tiring day, take the last seat on the bus or offer it to an elderly passenger? In offering the seat, we believe that we have chosen another's comfort over our own. Another difficulty, coming from our internal rather than external circumstances, arises from conflicting desires. For example, to successfully lose weight, dieters must believe that they can choose to eat healthy food (even if they do not like it) and also that they can resist the temptation to eat unhealthy foods (even their favorite ones). Success at dieting rests critically on the belief that we can, in a sense, separate choice from desire.

Ongoing investigations give us reason to suspect that preschool children do not fully make this separation. The above-mentioned studies on social constraint suggest that young children do not view kindness to others as a choice; in reasoning both about past and future actions, they say that they could not have done (and cannot do) otherwise in situations that pose harm others, violate social rules, or put self-interest above the needs of others (Chernyak et al., 2010, 2011). Also, preliminary results show that 4-year-olds consistently deny that other people (or themselves) can choose to do something they *don't* want to do or choose *not* to do something they do want to do. It is not until age 6 that they endorse the ability to act against or inhibit desires. This belief is shared by both American and Chinese children, thus may be culturally universal (Gopnik, personal communication).

What these studies suggest is that it takes time to grasp the fact that difficulties are not hard-and-fast constraints. One way that children might arrive at this idea is through experiencing and navigating internal conflict when making difficult choices themselves. For example, young children have trouble inhibiting their own desires, but they want to follow the rules of the adults (parents, teachers, etc.) that encourage them to do so. It is not hard to imagine that this may be one conflict that is a regular occurrence in children's daily lives. Another conflict may arise when actions that benefit the self-harm another; children's natural empathic and prosocial tendencies may make such choices difficult without any need for external (adult) intervention.

Resolving these situations on their own might give children a sense that something other than desire, obligation, or empathy are in control and thus would lead them to posit another mental variable. Choice is the natural fit, in particular if they are already imagining the various different possibilities for action caused by these conflicting mental states. Thus, through their own internal struggle with conflicting personal and prosocial desires, children might invoke a placeholder (the "mediator" choice), which develops into the adult intuition of free will.

## REFERENCES

Aarts, H., & Van Den Bos, K. (2011). On the foundations of beliefs in free will: Intentional binding and unconscious priming in self-agency. *Psychological Science, 22*, 532–537.

Aslin, R. N. (2012). Infant eyes: A window on cognitive development. *Infancy, 17*(1), 126–140.

Bandura, A. (2008). Reconstrual of "free will" from the agentic perspective of social cognitive theory. In J. Baer, J. C. Kaufman, & R. F. Baumeister (Eds.), *Are we free? Psychology and free will* (pp. 86–127). Oxford, UK: Oxford University Press.

Bartsch, K., & Wellman, H. M. (1995). *Children talk about the mind*. New York: Oxford University Press.

Behne, T., Carpenter, M., Call, J., & Tomasello, M. (2005). Unwilling versus unable: Infants' understanding of intentional action. *Developmental Psychology, 41*, 328–37.

Brandone, A. C., & Wellman, H. M. (2009). You can't always get what you want: infants understand failed goal-directed actions. *Psychological Science, 20*(1), 85–91.

Buttelmann, D., Carpenter, M., & Tomasello, M. (2009). 18-Month-old infants show false-belief understanding in an active helping paradigm. *Cognition, 112*, 337–342.

Blakemore, S., & Frith, C. (2003). Self-awareness and action. *Current Opinion in Neurobiology, 13*, 219–224.

Baumeister, R. F., Mele, A. R., & Vohs, K. D. (2010). *Free will and consciousness: How might they work?* New York: Oxford University Press.

Carpenter, M., Akhtar, N., & Tomasello, M. (1998). Fourteen- to 18-month-old infants differentially imitate intentional and accidental actions. *Infant Behavior and Development, 21*, 315–330.

Carruthers, P. (2009). Mindreading underlies metacognition. *Behavioral and Brain Sciences, 32*, 164–182.

Chernyak, N., Kushnir, T., Sullivan, K. M., & Wang, Q. (2011). A comparison of American and Nepalese children's concepts of free will. *Proceedings of the 33rd Annual Meeting of the Cognitive Science Society*.

Chernyak, N., Kushnir, T., & Wellman, H. M. (2010). Developing notions of free will: Preschoolers understanding of how intangible constraints bind their freedom of choice. *Proceedings of the 32nd Annual Meeting of the Cognitive Science Society.*

Csibra, G., Gergely, G., Bíró, S., Koós, O., & Brockbank, M. (1999). Goal attribution without agency cues: The perception of 'pure reason' in infancy. *Cognition, 72,* 237–267.

Denison, S., Konopczynski, K., Garcia, V., & Xu, F. (2006). Probabilistic reasoning in preschoolers: Random sampling and base rate. In R. Sun, & N. Miyake (Eds.), *Proceedings of the 28th Annual Conference of the Cognitive Science Society* (pp. 1216–1221). Florence, KY: Psychology Press.

Dennett, D. C. (2003). *Freedom evolves.* New York: Penguin Books.

Dunfield, K. A., & Kuhlmeier, V. A. (2010). Intention-mediated selective helping in infancy. *Psychological Science, 21,* 523–527.

Foley, M. A., & Ratner, H. H. (1998). Children's recoding in memory for collaboration: A way of learning from others. *Cognitive Development, 13,* 91–108.

Gelman, S. A. (2003). *The essential child.* New York, NY: Oxford University Press.

Gelman, S. A., & Wellman, H. M. (1991). Insides and essences: Early understandings of the non-obvious. *Cognition, 38,* 213–244.

Gergely, G., Bekkering, H., & Király, I. (2002). Rational imitation in preverbal infants. *Nature, 415*(6873).

Gergely, G., & Csibra, G. (2003). Teleological reasoning in infancy: The naive theory of rational action. *Trends in Cognitive Sciences, 7,* 287–292.

Gilbert, D. T., & Malone, P. S. (1995). The correspondence bias. *Psychological Bulletin, 117,* 21–38.

Gopnik, A., Glymour, C., Sobel, D. M., Schulz, L. E., Kushnir, T., & Danks, D. (2004). A theory of causal learning in children: Causal maps and Bayes nets. *Psychological Review, 111,* 1–30.

Gopnik, A., & Melzoff, A. N. (1997). *Words, thoughts, and theories.* Cambridge, MA: MIT Press.

Gopnik, A., & Wellman, H. M. (1992). Why the child's theory of mind really is a theory. *Mind and Language, 7*(1–2), 145–171.

Guglielmo, S., Monroe, A. E., & Malle, B. F. (2009). At the heart of morality lies folk psychology. *Inquiry, 52,* 449–466.

Gweon, H., Tenenbaum, J. B., & Schulz, L. E. (2010). Infants consider both the sample and the sampling process in inductive generalization. *Proceedings of the National Academy of Sciences of the United States of America, 107*(20), 9066–9071.

Haggard, P., & Tsakiris, M. (2009). The experience of agency: Feeling, judgment and responsibility. *Current Directions in Psychological Science, 18,* 242–246.

Hamlin, J. K., Wynn, K., & Bloom, P. (2008). Social evaluation by preverbal infants. *Nature, 450,* 557–559.

Harris, P. L. (1993). Thinking about what is not the case. *International Journal Of Psychology, 28*(5), 693–707.

Harris, P. L., & Koenig, M. A. (2006). Trust in testimony: How children learn about science and religion. *Child Development, 77,* 505–524.

Harris, P. L., German, T. P., & Mills, P. E. (1996). Children's use of counterfactual thinking in causal reasoning. *Cognition, 61,* 233–259.

Helwig, C. C. (2006). The development of personal autonomy throughout cultures. *Cognitive Development, 21*(4), 458–473.

Heyman, G., & Gelman, S. (2000). Beliefs about the origins of human psychological traits. *Developmental Psychology, 36,* 663–678.

Holton, R. (2010). Disentangling the will. In R. F. Baumeister, A. R. Mele, & K. D. Vohs (Eds.), *Free will and consciousness: How might they work?* (pp. 82–100). New York: Oxford University Press.

Inagaki, K., & Hatano, G. (1993). Young children's understanding of the mind-body distinction. *Child Development, 64*, 1534–1549.

Inagaki, K., & Hatano, G. (1999). Children's understanding of mind-body relationships. In M. Siegal, & C. C. Peterson (Eds.), *Children's understanding of biology and health*. New York: Cambridge University Press.

Iyengar, S. (2010, July). Sheena Iyengar on the art of choosing [Video file]. Retrieved from http://www.ted.com/talks/sheena_iyengar_on_the_art_of_choosing.html

Kalish, C. W. (1998). Reasons and causes: Children's understanding of conformity to social rules and physical laws. *Child Development, 69*, 706–720.

Kalish, C. (2002). Children's predictions of consistency in people's actions. *Cognition, 84*, 237–265.

Kalish, C. W., & Shiverick, S. M. (2004). Children's reasoning about norms and traits as motives for behavior. *Cognitive Development, 19*(3), 401–416.

Killen, M., & Smetana, J. (1999). Social interactions in preschool classrooms and the development of young children's conceptions of the personal. *Child Development, 70*, 486–501.

Kitayama, S., Snibbe, A., Markus, H., & Suzuki, T. (2004). Is there any 'free' choice? Self and dissonance in two cultures. *Psychological Science, 15*(8), 527–533.

Kirkham, N., Slemmer, J., & Johnson, S. (2002). Visual statistical learning in infancy: Evidence for a domain general learning mechanism. *Cognition, 83*, B35–B42.

Koenig, M. A., & Harris, P. L. (2005). Preschoolers mistrust ignorant and inaccurate speakers. *Child Development, 76*, 1261–1277.

Kohlberg, L. (1963). The development of children's orientation toward a moral order. *Vita Humana, 6*, 11–33.

Kovács, A. M., Téglás, E., & Endress, A. D. (2010). The social sense: Susceptibility to others' beliefs in human infants and adults. *Science, 330*, 1830–1834.

Kushnir, T., & Gopnik, A. (2005). Children infer causal strength from probabilities and interventions. *Psychological Science, 16*, 678–683.

Kushnir, T., Chernyak, N., & Wellman, H. M. (2009). Preschoolers' understanding of freedom of choice. In N. Taatgen, & H. van Rijn (Eds.). *Proceedings of the 31st annual meeting of the Cognitive Science Society* 87–92.

Kushnir, T., Wellman, H. M., & Gelman, S. A. (2009). A self-agency bias in children's causal inferences. *Developmental Psychology, 45*, 597–603.

Kushnir, T., Xu, F., & Wellman, H. M. (2010). Young children use statistical sampling to infer the preferences of others. *Psychological Science, 21*, 1134–1140.

Leotti, L. A., Iyengar, S. S., & Ochsner, K. N. (2010). Born to choose: Biological bases for the need for control. *Trends in Cognitive Science, 14*(10), 457–463.

Lillard, A. S. (1993). Pretend play skills and the child's theory of mind. *Child Development, 64*(2), 348–371.

Lucas, C., Griffiths, T. L., Xu, F., & Fawcett, C. (2009). A rational model of preference learning and choice prediction by children. *Advances in Neural Information Processing Systems (NIPS), 21*.

Ma, L., & Xu, F. (2011). Young children's use of statistical sampling evidence to infer the subjectivity of preferences. *Cognition, 120*, 403–411.

Markus, H. R., & Kitayama, S. (1991). Culture and the self: Implications for cognition, emotion, and motivation. *Psychological Review, 98*, 224–253.

Meltzoff, A. N., & Brooks, R. (2008). Self-experience as a mechanism for learning about others: A training study in social cognition. *Developmental Psychology, 44*, 1257–1265.

Metcalfe, J., Eich, T. S., & Castel, A. D. (2010). Metacognition of agency across the lifespan. *Cognition, 116*(2), 267–282.

Miller, J. G. (1984). Culture and the development of everyday social explanation. *Journal of Personality and Social Psychology, 46*, 961–978.

Miller, J. G., Das, R., & Chakravarthy, S. (2011). Culture and the role of choice in agency. *Journal of Personality and Social Psychology, 101*, 46–61.

Montgomery, D. E., & Lightner, M. (2004). Children's developing understanding of the differences between their own action and passive movement. *British Journal of Developmental Psychology, 22*, 417–438.

Morris, M. W., & Peng, K. (1994). Culture and cause: American and Chinese attributions for social and physical events. *Journal of Personality and Social Psychology, 67*, 949–971.

Nichols, S. (2004). The folk psychology of free will: Fits and starts. *Mind & Language, 19*, 473–502.

Nichols, S., & Knobe, J. (2007). Moral responsibility and determinism: The Cognitive Science of Folk Intuitions. *Noûs, 41*, 663–685.

Norenzayan, A., & Nisbett, R. E. (2000). Culture and causal cognition. *Current Directions In Psychological Science, 9*(4), 132–135.

Nucci, L. (1981). Conceptions of personal issues: A domain distinct from moral or societal concepts. *Child Development, 52*, 114–121.

Nucci, L. P., & Weber, E. K. (1995). Social interactions in the home and the development of young children's conceptions of the personal. *Child Development, 66*, 1438–1452.

Oakes, L., & Madole, K. (2000). The future of infant categorization research: A process-oriented approach. *Child Development, 71*, 119–126.

Onishi, K., & Baillargeon, R. (2005). Do 15-month-old infants understand false beliefs? *Science, 308*, 255–258.

Papafragou, A. (2001). Mindreading and verbal communication. *Mind and Language, 17*, 55–67.

Papafragou, A. (2002). Modality and theory of mind: Perspectives from language development and autism. In S. Barbiers, F. Beukema, & W. van der Wurff (Eds.), *Modality and its Interaction With the Verbal System* (pp. 185–204). Amsterdam: Benjamins.

Papafragou, A., Cassidy, K., & Gleitman, L. (2007). When we think about thinking: The acquisition of belief verbs. *Cognition, 105*, 125–165.

Paulhus, D. L., & Carey, J. M. (2011). The FAD-Plus: Measuring lay beliefs regarding free will and related constructs. *Journal Of Personality Assessment, 93*(1), 96–104.

Paulus, M., Hunnius, S., Vissers, M., & Bekkering, H. (2011). Bridging the gap between the other and me: The functional role of motor resonance and action effects in infants' imitation. *Developmental Science, 14*(4).

Phillips, A., & Wellman, H. (2005). Infants' understanding of object-directed action. *Cognition, 98*, 137–155.

Piaget, J. (1932). *The moral judgment of the child*. London, UK: Routledge & Kegan Paul.

Piaget, J. (1969). *The psychology of the child*. New York: Basic Books. [Originally published in 1966].

Pizarro, D. A., & Helzer, E. (2010). Freedom of the will and stubborn moralism. In R. F. Baumeister, A. R. Mele, & K. D. Vohs (Eds.), *Free will and consciousness: how might they work?*. New York: Oxford University Press.

Pöhlmann, C., Carranza, E., Hannover, B., & Iyengar, S. S. (2007). Repercussions of self-construal for self-relevant and other-relevant choice. *Social Cognition, 25*(2), 284–305.

Pronin, E., & Kugler, M. B. (2010). People believe they have more free will than others. *Proceedings of the National Academy of Sciences of the United States of America, 107*(52), 22469–22474.

Pronin, E., Wegner, D. M., McCarthy, K., & Rodriguez, S. (2006). Everyday magical powers: The role of apparent mental causation in the overestimation of personal influence. *Journal of Personality and Social Psychology, 91*, 218–231.

Rakoczy, H., Warneken, F., & Tomasello, M. (2008). The sources of normativity: Young children's awareness of the normative structure of games. *Developmental Psychology, 44*, 875–881.

Repacholi, B., & Gopnik, A. (1997). Early reasoning about desires: Evidence from 14- and 18-month-olds. *Developmental Psychology, 33*, 12–21.

Robinson, E. J., & Whitcombe, E. L. (2003). Children's suggestibility in relation to their understanding about sources of knowledge. *Child Development, 74*, 48–62.

Ross, L., & Nisbett, R. E. (1991). *The person and the situation: Perspectives of social psychology.* New York: McGraw-Hill.

Ryan, R. L., & Deci, E. L. (2000). Self-determination theory and the facilitation of intrinsic motivation, social development, and well-being. *American Psychologist, 55*, 68–78.

Ryan, R. M., & Lynch, J. H. (1989). Emotional autonomy versus detachment: Revisiting the vicissitudes of adolescence and young adulthood. *Child Development, 60*(2), 340–356.

Saffran, J., Aslin, R., & Newport, E. (1996). Statistical learning by 8-month-old infants. *Science, 274*, 1926–1928.

Sarkissian, H., Chatterjee, A., De Brigard, F., Knobe, J., Nichols, S., & Sirker, S. (2010). Is belief in free will a cultural universal? *Mind & Language, 25*(3), 346–358.

Savani, K., Morris, M. W., Naidu, N. V. R., Kumar, S., & Berlia, N. (2011). Cultural conditioning: Understanding interpersonal accommodation in India and the U.S. in terms of the modal characteristics of interpersonal influence situations. *Journal of Personality and Social Psychology, 100*, 84–102.

Schulz, L., Bonawitz, E., & Griffiths, T. (2007). Can being scared cause tummy aches? Naive theories, ambiguous evidence, and preschoolers' causal inferences. *Developmental Psychology, 43*, 1124–1139.

Schult, C. A., & Wellman, H. M. (1997). Explaining human movements and actions: Children's understanding of the limits of psychological explanation. *Cognition, 62*, 291–324.

Shultz, T. R., & Wells, D. (1985). Judging the intentionality of action-outcomes. *Developmental Psychology, 21*, 83–89.

Schwartz, B. (2004). *The paradox of choice: Why more is less.* New York: Ecco.

Schweder, R. A., Mahapatra, M., & Miller, J. G. (1987). Culture and moral development. In J. Kagan, & S. Lamb (Eds.), *The emergence of morality in young children* (pp. 1–79). Chicago, IL: The University of Chicago Press.

Senju, A., Southgate, V., Snape, C., Leonard, M., & Csibra, G. (2011). Do 18-month-olds really attribute mental states to others? A critical test. *Psychological Science, 22*(7), 878–880.

Smetana, J. G. (1981). Preschoolers' understanding of moral and social rules. *Child Development, 52*, 1333–1336.

Sobel, D. M. (2004). Exploring the coherence of young children's explanatory abilities: Evidence from generating counterfactuals. *British Journal of Developmental Psychology, 22*, 37–58.

Sommerville, J. A., & Crane, C. C. (2009). Ten-month-old infants use prior information to identify an actor's goal. *Developmental Science, 12*, 314–325.

Sommerville, J. A., & Hammond, A. J. (2007). Treating another's actions as one's own: Children's memory of and learning from joint activity. *Developmental Psychology, 43*, 1003–1018.

Sommerville, J. A., Woodward, A. L., & Needham, A. (2005). Action experience alters 3-month-old infants' perception of others' actions. *Cognition, 96*, B1–B11.

Southgate, V., Senju, A., & Csibra, G. (2007). Action anticipation through attribution of false belief. *Psychological Science, 18*, 587–592.

Spelke, E. S., Breinlinger, K., Macomber, J., & Jacobson, K. (1992). Origins of knowledge. *Psychological Review, 99*, 605–632.

Swartz, B. (2004). The paradox of choice: Why more is less. NY: Harper Collins.

Téglás, E., Girotto, V., Gonzalez, M., & Bonatti, L. L. (2007). Intuitions of probabilities shape expectations about the future at 12 months and beyond. *Proceedings of the National Academy of Sciences, USA, 104*, 19156–19159.

Tomasello, M., & Haberl, K. (2003). Understanding attention: 12- and 18-month-olds know what's new for other persons. *Developmental Psychology, 39*, 906–912.

Turiel, E. (1983). *The development of social knowledge.* New York: Cambridge University Press.

Vohs, K. D., & Schooler, J. W. (2008). The value of believing in free will: Encouraging a belief in determinism increases cheating. *Psychological Science, 19*, 49–54.

Wang, Q. (2004). The emergence of cultural self-construct: Autobiographical memory and self-description in American and Chinese children. *Developmental Psychology, 4*(1), 3–15.

Watson, J. S., & Ramey, C. T. (1972). Reactions to response-contingent stimulation in early infancy. *Merill-Palmer Quarterly, 18*, 219–227.

Wegner, D. (2002). *The illusion of conscious will.* Cambridge, MA: MIT Press.

Wellman, H. M. (1990). *The child's theory of mind.* Cambridge, MA: MIT Press.

Wellman, H. M., Cross, D., & Watson, J. (2001). Meta-analysis of theory of mind development: The truth about false belief. *Child Development, 72*, 655–684.

Wellman, H., Phillips, A., Dunphy-Lelii, S., & LaLonde, N. (2004). Infant social attention predicts preschool social cognition. *Developmental Science, 7*, 283–288.

Wellman, H. M., Fang, F., Liu, D., Zhu, L., & Liu, G. (2006). Scaling of theory of mind understanding in Chinese children. *Psychological Science, 17*, 1075–1081.

Wellman, Kushnir, & Xu, in preparation. Infants Use Statistical Sampling to Understand the Psychological World.

Wellman, H. M., & Liu, D. (2004). Scaling of theory of mind tasks. *Child Development, 75*, 523–541.

Wellman, H. M., & Miller, J. G. (2006). Developing conceptions of responsive intentional agents. *Journal of Cognition and Culture, 6*, 27–55.

Wells, G. (1979). Learning and using the auxiliary verb in English. In V. Lee (Ed.), *Language development.* Beckenham: Croom Helm.

Woodward, A. (1998). Infants selectively encode the goal object of an actor's reach. *Cognition, 69*, 1–34.

Woodward, A. (2009). Infants' grasp of others' intentions. *Current Directions in Psychological Science, 18*, 53–57.

Woodward, A. L., Sommerville, J. A., & Guajardo, J. J. (2001). How infants make sense of intentional action. In B. Malle, L. Moses, & D. Baldwin (Eds.), *Intentions and intentionality: Foundations of Social Cognition* (pp. 149–169). Cambridge, MA: MIT Press.

Woolley, J. D. (1997). Thinking about fantasy: Are children fundamentally different thinkers and believers from adults? *Child Development, 68*(6), 991–1011.

Xu, F., & Denison, S. (2009). Statistical inference and sensitivity to sampling in 11-month-old infants. *Cognition, 112*, 97–104.

Xu, F., & Garcia, V. (2008). Intuitive statistics by 8-month-old infants. *Proceedings of the National Academy of Sciences of the United States of America, 105*, 5012–5015.

Xu, F., & Tenenbaum, J. B. (2007). Word learning as Bayesian inference. *Psychological Review, 114*(2), 245–272.

CHAPTER EIGHT

# When Children Ignore Evidence in Category-Based Induction
## Irrational Inferences?

## Marjorie Rhodes
Department of Psychology, New York University, New York, NY 10003,
E-mail: marjorie.rhodes@nyu.edu

## Contents

## Abstract

The process of induction—generalizing information obtained from limited samples to inform broader understandings—plays a critical role in learning across the life span. Previous research on the development of induction has found important developmental changes in one critical component of induction—how children and adults evaluate whether a sample of evidence is informative about a broader category. In particular, when acquiring knowledge about biological kinds, adults view samples that provide diverse representation of a category (e.g. an eagle, a penguin, and a robin, for the category *birds*) as more informative than a less diverse sample (e.g. three robins) for drawing inferences about the kind. In contrast, children younger than 8 years often neglect this feature of sample composition, viewing both types of samples as equivalently informative. Is this a case of children making irrational inferences? This chapter examines how these findings can be reconciled with rational constructivist approaches to cognitive development, focusing on (1) the role of the sampling context in determining how learners incorporate information about sample composition into inductive inferences and (2) how developmental differences in learners' intuitive theories influence how they make sense of new evidence. This chapter highlights how strong tests of rational approaches come from incidences where children's performance appears to be quite nonnormative.

*Advances in Child Development and Behavior*, Volume 43
ISSN 0065-2407,
http://dx.doi.org/10.1016/B978-0-12-397919-3.00008-3

219

## 1. INTRODUCTION

The theme of this volume is that children are rational constructivists, that is, they actively try to make sense of their environment (the constructivist part) and they do so by integrating new evidence with their prior beliefs via a process that approximates probabilistic statistical inference (the rational part; Xu, 2007). As shown by the numerous chapters in this volume, as well as by the breadth of topics they cover, this perspective has led to advances in our understanding of cognitive development across a wide range of questions. A rational constructivist account of cognitive development is compelling because it describes how domain-general learning mechanisms can give rise to domain-specific knowledge, applies across a wide range of learning tasks, and moves beyond old arguments between nativism and empiricism to describe a learning process that both accounts for prior knowledge and allows for change (Gopnik & Wellman, in press).

A central question in developmental psychology is whether the mechanisms by which we acquire knowledge are similar across development or undergo fundamental change. The answer to this question from the perspective of rational constructivism is clear: Although there may be substantial changes in children's knowledge and theories across development, the learning process—how beliefs are updated in response to new evidence—relies on similar mechanisms from early infancy (Denison, Reed, & Xu, in press; Dewar & Xu, 2010) to childhood (Schulz, Bonawitz, & Griffiths, 2007; Xu & Tenenbaum, 2007a, 2007b) through adulthood (Kemp & Tenenbaum, 2009; Tenenbaum, Kemp, & Shafto, 2007). This perspective challenges us to think critically about instances when children's responses to evidence are quite different from adult responses, and in particular, instances where children's inferences appear—at least at first, second, and even third glance—to be irrational.

In this chapter, I examine an instance of apparent irrationality, focusing on how children acquire generic knowledge about biological kinds. Generic knowledge is generalizable knowledge about abstract kinds. For example, generic knowledge about dogs includes that they bark, have four legs, and have fur. Generic knowledge is not tied to specific individuals and need not apply to every individual category member. Yet, because kinds cannot be directly observed, much generic knowledge is acquired via induction from individual instances (Rips, 1975). For example, upon learning that a particular dog barks, a child might infer that dogs, in general, bark. This facilitates use of generic knowledge to make predictions about new instances. For example, upon learning that a single bird has hollow bones, we can assume that other birds will also have them; upon experiencing that a birthday party involves bringing presents and eating cake, we can predict what will take place at other parties in the future; upon learning that one girl likes sparkly stickers, we might expect other girls to like sparkly stickers as well. As demonstrated by these examples, these inferences are probabilistic and not always accurate. Yet, the underlying mechanisms reflected here—categorizing individuals as fundamentally alike and using these categories to generalize knowledge—are fundamental means by which we make sense of, predict, and interact with the environment. Although the acquisition of generic knowledge via induction is an important process across many domains, here I focus on these issues particularly for biological kinds. This focus follows much previous work on induction and is of particular interest because of the rich, hierarchical structure of the biological world (Atran, 1990).

## 2. THE PROBLEM OF INDUCTION AND A RATIONAL SOLUTION

Imagine that a child encounters a dog for the first time (perhaps, her friend's golden retriever) and learns that he is friendly and likes to be petted. How far should she generalize this knowledge? Certainly, it seems reasonable to generalize this knowledge to other encounters with this particular dog. Thus, if she encounters the dog again the next day, she can confidently go right up and pet him. But, how much farther should she generalize this knowledge? Should she now assume that other golden retrievers are friendly too, so that she can confidently approach and pet other golden retrievers that she meets? What about other dogs more generally? Or other four-legged furry animals? Clearly, some generalization beyond the individual is warranted—assuming that other golden retrievers will be friendly is a pretty good bet. But, generalizing too far could get the child into trouble; if she generalizes to all dogs, she could find herself in a dangerous situation if she encounters a vicious pit bull, and if she generalizes to all four-legged furry animals, even more so if she encounters a mountain lion.

Determining how far to generalize information is a basic problem of all inductive inference. Rational constructivist approaches suggest one perspective on how such inferences might be constrained. For example,

Xu and Tenenbaum (2007a, 2007b) demonstrated that children are attentive to the composition of evidence within a sample, can infer the population that particular samples represent, and then restrict their generalizations to the represented population. They examined these processes in a word-learning context, another key inductive challenge of childhood. On their task, children were shown an array of different kinds of dogs, for example, including a range of subtypes (golden retrievers, basset hounds, Dalmatians, etc.) and were shown a sample of three of these dogs labeled as "blickets." On this task, children attended closely to the sample composition to determine how far to extend the word *blicket* on subsequent test items. If children were shown three golden retrievers labeled as blickets, they extended the term only to other golden retrievers. In contrast, if they were shown three dogs of different subtypes, they extended the word to the basic level.

From a rational perspective, children's performance in this task can be understood as follows. First, when shown the very first piece of evidence, children might consider multiple hypotheses: (1) that blicket is the name of the subtype "golden retriever" or (2) that blicket is the name of the basic-level category "dog." Perhaps they consider these two hypotheses to be approximately equally likely, before they are exposed to further evidence. Second, after they are exposed to further evidence (e.g. two more golden retrievers or two different dogs), they evaluate the likelihood that they would have seen each set of evidence, under each of the initial hypotheses. Whereas both sets of evidence are consistent with the hypothesis that blicket refers to "dog," the observation of a sample of all golden retrievers under this hypothesis is unlikely. Xu and Tenenbaum suggested that children would view this sample as a "suspicious coincidence." In other words, the likelihood of the obtained sample is higher under the hypothesis that blicket refers to golden retriever than the hypothesis that blicket refers to dog, leading children to favor the narrower hypothesis in this case.

The extension from this word-learning example to the acquisition of generic knowledge ought to be straightforward. For example, if the child observed that three golden retrievers are friendly and like to be petted, she should feel confident that the property "is friendly" applies to golden retrievers, but less sure that it applies to dogs generally. In contrast, if she observed that three dogs of different subtypes are friendly and like to be petted, she should extend the property to the basic level. Extensive prior work suggests, however, that in just these types of contexts, children's inferences often appear to neglect these dimensions of sample composition.

Instead, children have been found to generalize to basic-level categories equally often based on less representative evidence (the three golden retrievers, hereafter, the "nondiverse sample") and more representative samples (the three different dogs, hereafter, the "diverse sample"), as reviewed below. Does this neglect of sample composition in children's reasoning reflect irrationality? Does this indicate, for example, that they fail to update the probabilities of their initial hypotheses following differing samples of evidence? To begin to address these questions, I first review the evidence that children often fail to consider sample composition when acquiring generic knowledge about biological kinds via induction.

## 3. EVIDENCE THAT CHILDREN HAVE DIFFICULTY BEING RATIONAL

Extensive prior work shows that adults' are very sensitive to sample composition for induction involving biological kinds. In particular, adults view samples that provide diverse representation of a category (as in the three dogs of different subtypes above) as supporting conclusions about the kind (dogs), but samples that provide less diverse representation of a category (as in the three golden retriever sample above) as supporting narrower inferences. For example, as reviewed below, adults view a diverse sample (e.g. a penguin, an owl, and a robin) as more informative than a nondiverse sample (e.g. three robins) for drawing inferences about abstract categories (e.g. birds). These effects have been termed "diversity effects" and are a primary feature of adult inductive inference that models of induction have aimed to explain (Heit, 2000).

Adults robustly consider sample diversity when evaluating samples of evidence. Osherson, Smith, Wilkie, Lopez, & Shafir (1990) found that adults rated inductive arguments that built on diverse premises as stronger than inductive arguments that built on less diverse premises. For example, an argument supporting a general conclusion (e.g. "all mammals have four-chamber hearts") was rated as stronger when it built on premises that included a diverse sample of mammals (e.g. "dogs and whales have four-chamber hearts") rather than a less diverse sample of mammals (e.g. "dogs and wolves have four-chamber hearts"). Also, evidence selection tasks show that adults seek out diverse evidence. For example, to test if a property is true of mammals, adults prefer to examine diverse over nondiverse samples of mammals (Kim & Keil, 2003; Lopez, 1995; Lopez, Atran, Coley, Medin,

& Smith, 1997; Rhodes, Brickman, & Gelman, 2008; Rhodes, Gelman, & Brickman, 2008). Sample diversity is not the only criterion that adults use to evaluate evidence—they can also rely on causal knowledge, for example, or other specific background knowledge that is relevant to the question at hand (Medin, Coley, Storms, & Hayes, 2003). Yet, sample diversity is an important factor that adults consider across many different types of experimental tasks (Heit, 2000; Lopez et al., 1997). Critically, basing broader inferences on diverse samples is consistent with computational accounts of rational statistical inference (Heit, 2000; Tenenbaum et al., 2007).

Yet, in contrast to adults' robust consideration of sample diversity, young children have been found to neglect sample diversity across many inductive reasoning tasks. In many previous studies, children younger than 9 years have treated diverse and nondiverse samples as equivalently informative for inferences about kinds. For example, children between the ages of 5 and 8 years are just as likely to infer that "all birds have hollow bones" after learning that three nondiverse birds have hollow bones (e.g. three robins) as learning that three diverse birds have hollow bones (e.g. an eagle, an owl, and a robin; Gutheil & Gelman, 1997; Lopez, Gelman, Gutheil, & Smith, 1992; see also Li, Bihau, Li, Li, & Deak, 2009). Younger children also do not consider sample diversity when selecting evidence; for example, 6-year-olds are just as likely to select a nondiverse sample (e.g. two Dalmatians) as a diverse sample (e.g. a Dalmatian and a pit bull) to find out if something is true of a category (e.g. dogs; Rhodes, Brickman, et al. 2008; Rhodes, Gelman, et al., 2008). In these studies, diversity effects have been found to emerge around ages 8–9 and to become more robust by ages 10–11.

Children's failure to recognize the informative value of diverse evidence does not relate to difficulty with the task demands in these experiments or to general problems noticing or processing information about sample diversity. For example, Rhodes, Gelman, et al. (2008) showed that although 6-year-olds could reliably distinguish diverse from nondiverse sets, they still did not prefer to base generalizations on information obtained from diverse samples. Also, Rhodes, Brickman et al. (2008) showed that 6-year-olds do apply some systematic strategies to selecting between samples on the types of questions used in these experiments. For example, 6-year-olds preferred to base inferences on samples containing typical, over atypical, exemplars. Yet, although children showed some systematic criteria for evaluating samples, they once again did not factor sample diversity into these judgments.

More generally, Heit & Hahn (2001) and Shipley & Shepperson (2006) provided evidence that children can distinguish diverse from nondiverse samples and reason about them systematically. For example, Heit and Hahn presented 5-year-olds with two samples of dolls, including three diverse dolls belonging to one character and three nondiverse dolls belonging to another character. Participants were then shown a different doll and were asked to predict to whom the doll belonged. On these questions, children reliably responded that the target toy belonged to the character that owned the diverse set of toys. These findings demonstrate that young children can recognize sample diversity and sort based on diversity. They do not, however, indicate that young children view diverse samples as a stronger basis for induction. Instead, children may solve these problems by recognizing that diverse items better match diverse (rather than nondiverse) sets of evidence. Similarly, Shipley & Shepperson (2006) reported that preschool children prefer to test toys from two subclasses (e.g. one blue whistle and one red whistle) in order to determine if whistles "make good party favors." Although this task also reveals that young children recognize and reason about sample diversity, because participants were not asked to make an inference about a larger set (e.g. whistles not included in either specific subclass), this study also does not provide evidence that young children use sample diversity to determine whether a sample provides a good basis for broader generalizations (i.e. about a larger category or unobserved instance).

Thus, children's failure to consider sample composition when evaluating samples of evidence does not relate to task demands, difficulty noticing or processing diversity, or more general difficulty making decisions based on sample diversity. As shown in the work by Xu and Tenenbaum (2007a, 2007b) discussed above, as well as other recent works, it is also clear that children's failure to consider sample diversity does not relate to general problems in statistical reasoning or, in particular, reasoning about how samples represent populations. Xu and colleagues have shown that quite sophisticated abilities reasoning about the relation between samples and populations emerge early in infancy. For example, infants expect a sample drawn from a bowl containing equal proportions of blue and yellow balls to contain equal proportions of blue and yellow and are surprised if the obtained sample is all blue (Xu & Denison, 2009; Xu & Garcia, 2008). Infants are not applying a simple matching strategy to solve these tasks; their expectations break down if they know the sampler has a preference for blue, for example, suggesting that they only expect samples to accurately represent populations if they are drawn randomly.

Given these statistical abilities for reasoning about the relation of samples to populations, it is surprising that children do not consider sample composition when acquiring new generic knowledge via inductive reasoning. Children ought to realize, for example, that a diverse sample of dogs provides better representation of the category dogs than a nondiverse sample. Why do children fail to consider sample composition during category-based induction? Does this failure indicate that the mechanisms that support the acquisition of generic knowledge in childhood are somehow less rational than those that do so in adulthood? To tackle this issue and consider its implications for cognitive development, I next consider two factors that may enable children to consider sample composition in a rational manner, toward the aim of better understanding the circumstances when they do not.

## 4. TWO FACTORS THAT (MAY) INFLUENCE RATIONALITY

### 4.1. The Learning Context

A critical difference between the category-based induction studies reviewed above and Xu and Tenenbaum (2007a, 2007b) is the *purpose* of the sample being presented. In Xu and Tenenbaum, an intentional adult selects the samples in order to show the child a new concept. Thus, the goal of the sample is information *communication*—the adult has some information (e.g. the meaning of the word *blicket*) that the child does not have, and the adult selects a sample to demonstrate the concept. In a broad sense, this interaction represents a pedagogical exchange. From this perspective, pedagogical learning does not require a formal teacher, but instead is defined by the epistemic gap between the teacher and the learner, as well as the intent of the teacher to communicate information to the learner. In contrast, in the induction experiments summarized above, children were not taught properties on purposefully presented samples; rather they were asked to *discover* new information via induction. Thus, one possibility is that sample composition plays different conceptual roles in the *discovery* versus *communication* of new knowledge.

During information communication (teaching), efficient teachers purposefully select evidence to create samples that clearly and unambiguously represent concepts of interest (referred to as *pedagogical sampling*, Shafto & Goodman, 2008). For example, if a teacher wants to teach about a property of birds, it seems more effective to present a sample containing three different kinds of birds (e.g. a canary, a peacock, and an eagle) than a sample containing only one kind of bird (e.g. three canaries). The latter sample is ambiguous regarding whether the property applies to all birds or only to canaries, whereas the diverse sample more efficiently communicates that the property applies to all birds. Shafto and Goodman (2008) showed that adults assigned to teaching roles readily engage in this kind of effective sampling—without explicit instruction to do so—picking samples that will most unambiguously and efficiently communicate the underlying distribution to the learner. Furthermore, adults assigned to learner roles assumed that teachers would provide informative samples, and this assumption helped them learn more efficiently.

During information communication, sample composition provides a window into the communicative goal of the teacher. For example, a learner may assume, "The teacher is trying to teach me something. She had all these dogs to choose from, but she chose three of the same kind. That decision was purposeful and intended to help me learn. She must be trying to tell me that this is about just that kind of dog." Thus, children's early emerging abilities to reason about sample composition in pedagogical contexts may stem from an intuitive sense of how sampling behavior reflects communicative goals. In this manner, the "suspicious coincidence" noticed by the children in Xu and Tenenbaum (2007a, 2007b) is suspicious with respect to the adult's intent (e.g. "if she were trying to teach me about all dogs, it would be odd for her to pick this narrow sample") not to the state of the world (e.g. *not* "if this were true of all dogs, it would be odd that I've only encountered this narrow sample).

In contrast, when learning involves knowledge *discovery* instead of *communication*, sample composition is relevant to testing hypothesis about the world. A diverse sample of dogs provides a strong test of a hypothesis about dogs as a kind, for example, whereas a nondiverse sample of dogs provides a weak test (Heit, Hahn, & Feeney, 2005). Thus, one possibility is that children recognize sample composition as a window into the communicative intent of a teacher—and thus consider sample composition in a rational manner in these cases—but not as an indicator of how informative a sample is for the process of information discovery.

Rhodes, Gelman, and Brickman (2010) directly tested this hypothesis, using a method similar to Xu & Tenenbaum (2007a). In this work, 5-year-old children and adults were exposed to an array of animals from a basic-level category (e.g. an array of dogs). Participants were shown samples to help them learn a new fact about the animal category (e.g. to find out which animals have an epithelium inside). Across condition, samples were presented either by an animal expert who knew a great deal about the animals or by a novice who did not know anything about them (see Kushnir, Wellman, & Gelman, 2008). In the Expert condition, across items, the expert either presented a diverse sample of dogs (a basset hound, Dalmatian, and golden retriever) or a nondiverse sample of dogs (three basset hounds), with the clearly stated intention of teaching "which animals have an epithelium inside." In the Novice condition, across items, the puppet checked various animals (the same exemplars as were shown by the Expert) to discover if they had an epithelium and reported the results to the child. Because the novice did not know which animals had the property ahead of time, it should have been clear to children that they were not selected with particular communicative intent. The aim of the Expert condition (from the child's perspective) was information communication, whereas the aim of the Novice condition was to discover the information along with the puppet. Across conditions, children were exposed to identical evidence presented by a puppet; the conditions varied only in whether the sample was systematically selected by a knowledgeable teacher to communicate information or by a novice aiming to discover information.

Indeed, in the Expert condition, preschool-age children inferred that the property applied only to the subordinate category (e.g. only to Dalmatians) when they were shown a nondiverse sample, but to the basic-level kind when they were shown a diverse sample. In contrast, in the Novice condition, 5-year-olds extended the property to the basic level following both types of samples. Adults, in contrast, showed the same pattern across both conditions—they reliably extended to the subordinate following the nondiverse sample and to the basic level following diverse samples, regardless of who presented the sample. These data suggest that preschoolers consider sample composition during learning events where the learning goal involves information *communication*, but not information *discovery*. In contrast, adults consider sample composition in both types of learning contexts.

In a follow-up study, Rhodes et al. further compared 5-year-olds understanding of sample composition for knowledge *communication* versus *discovery* by placing the children themselves either in the position of "teacher" or "scientist." Here, children were asked to select samples either to *teach* someone else that a basic-level category contains a novel property (e.g. that all dogs have an epithelium inside) or to *discover whether* a basic-level category contains a novel property (e.g. whether all dogs have an epithelium inside). Children were offered a choice between diverse and nondiverse samples of dogs. In the teacher condition, children indeed reliably selected the sample that provided diverse representation of the category, whereas in the scientist condition, children responded at chance. These data provide further evidence that children recognize the role of sample composition in effectively communicating information, but not as an indicator of the strength of samples for hypothesis testing.

These studies help to resolve the apparent discrepancy between Xu and Tenenbaum and studies of category-based induction, by suggesting that children recognize the role of sample composition in information communication prior to information discovery. Yet, they do not address why children fail to consider sample composition during information discovery on these tasks. Although showing that children engage in rational inference in pedagogical contexts in an important step to characterizing how children acquire generic knowledge, much knowledge acquisition occurs in the absence of knowledgeable teachers who purposefully select samples for children. Thus, it is critical to examine why children fail to consider sample composition when they discover samples of evidence on their own, with an aim of resolving this pattern with the general rational constructivist framework.

## 4.2. Intuitive Theories

To consider why children fail to overlook sample composition when selecting their own samples to discover new generic knowledge, it is useful to consider their intuitive theories of the biological world, which ought to shape the types of evidence they view as relevant to these problems. Toward this aim, Rhodes and Brickman (2010) proposed that children have abstract expectations that biological kinds are highly homogenous (see Atran, 1990) and that these expectations lead them to treat diverse and nondiverse samples from a category as interchangeable.

Expectations of category homogeneity entail the extent to which people assume that—despite superficial differences—all members of a category are fundamentally alike. There is abundant indirect evidence that young children expect some categories to be more homogenous than adults do. For example, young children (aged 4–7 years) have strong expectations that the members of natural kind categories will demonstrate category-typical properties—even in the face of contrasting individuating information—whereas older children (aged 10 years) and adults allow for more individual variation (Berndt & Heller, 1986; Taylor, 1996; Taylor, Rhodes, & Gelman, 2009). Also, preschool-age children are more likely than adults to believe that categories are objective and coherent (Kalish, 1998; Rhodes & Gelman, 2009) and to infer that a property observed in one individual will be found in other members of a kind (Gelman, 1988; Rhodes & Gelman, 2008). Young children also often neglect subtypes within basic-level categories (e.g. they fail to recognize basset hounds and Dalmatians as meaningfully different kinds of dogs, Waxman, Lynch, Casey, & Baer, 1997), perhaps because they view basic-level categories as highly coherent.

Gelman (2003) has argued that cognitive biases to assume that basic-level categories are homogenous play a powerful role in early conceptual development and propel knowledge acquisition by allowing children to overlook superficial differences and focus on underlying regularities (e.g. in order to learn the conceptual category *dog*, children must overlook superficial difference in size and color and focus on the properties that all dogs share). Yet, focusing on similarities may also lead children to overlook meaningful and important variation (Gelman & Kalish, 1993). From this perspective, an important component of conceptual change across childhood entails increased consideration of within-category variability.

How might developmental differences in expectations about within-category homogeneity and variability influence how children and adults evaluate samples during inductive reasoning? Rhodes and Brickman (2010) proposed that children's strong expectations that biological categories are homogenous lead them to be less discriminating about whether a given sample of evidence is informative (e.g. because children assume that all dogs are fundamentally alike, it does not matter to them which particular dogs are observed to support an inference about the category as a whole; Rhodes, Brickman, et al., 2008a, 2010).

To test this hypothesis, Rhodes and Brickman (2010) showed 7-year-olds and adults a set of perceptually and taxonomically diverse birds. Children assigned to a Variability condition were prompted to consider differences among birds (e.g. that some fly and some do not fly, some hunt for food and some dig for food, etc.). Children assigned to a Similarity condition saw the same visual stimuli but were prompted to consider similarities (e.g. that all birds have feathers, all birds feed their babies mashed up foods, etc.). Children assigned to a Control condition were shown the same visual stimuli, but were not prompted to think about any properties. Following the primes, children completed measures of their consideration of sample diversity in evaluating samples of evidence. For example, they were asked to select between examining diverse samples (e.g. a robin and a blue jay) or nondiverse samples (e.g. two robins) to test whether a novel property is true of a category (e.g. "to find out if birds have gizzards inside"). Children in the Variability condition reliably chose diverse samples, whereas children in the Similarity and Control conditions performed at chance. Adults selected diverse samples in all conditions. This study experimentally demonstrates that increasing attention to within-category variability increases diversity-based reasoning among children.

The effect of the Variability primes was quite robust. The Variability primes improved performance on multiple measures of diversity-based reasoning and increased diversity-based reasoning for both the animal categories presented in the prime (e.g. birds) and for other animal categories (e.g. pigs, frogs). Thus, the prime appeared to function not by increasing children's specific knowledge about *birds*, but by challenging children's more generalized expectations about the homogeneity of animal categories. The effect of the Variability primes was also appropriately selective, however. A follow-up control study documented that although Variability primes increased diverse sample selections for inferences about broad categories (e.g. birds), they did not do so for inferences about specific subtypes (e.g. robins), for which picking a nondiverse sample (e.g. two robins) would be more informative. Thus, the Variability primes did not lead children to view diversity as better across the board, but rather, to engage in diversity-based reasoning in a normative manner.

The data reviewed above suggest that young children overlook sample composition when acquiring new generic knowledge about biological kinds because they have strong expectations that biological categories are homogenous. Is this neglect of sample composition irrational? Some models (Kemp & Tenenbaum, 2009; Tenenbaum et al., 2007) suggest a possible way to reconcile this finding with a rational constructivist perspective. These models indicate that domain-specific intuitive theories shape the prior probabilities that people bring to learning events. As in all rational inference, from this perspective, inferences result from the interaction between participants' prior expectations (e.g. their prior estimate of the probability that a property found in one bird will be found in all birds, for example) and the new evidence that they receive. As described by Kemp and Tenenbaum (2009), these prior expectations can stem from intuitive theories or conceptual biases. Thus, developmental differences in these prior probability estimates (with younger children having higher baseline prevalence estimates, reflecting their assumptions that all category members are fundamentally alike) could explain developmental differences in sensitivity to sample diversity.

Yet, this possibility requires direct examination. This framework suggests that developmental differences in consideration of sample composition relate to differences in initial theories (i.e. prior expectations about how properties are distributed across categories), not differences in learning mechanisms. If so, although children initially view a hypothesis that a property applies to a basic level as more likely than a hypothesis that a property applies only to a subtype, they should be able to update their beliefs in response to new evidence if that new evidence is compelling enough. Yet, direct evidence that they do so is needed.

## 5. RATIONAL IN THE END?

Mechanisms for rational statistical inference are clearly in place early in childhood. The data summarized above, as well as in other chapters of this volume, indicate that these mechanisms contribute to learning across a wide range of content domains and learning challenges. In the present context, they appear to guide how children acquire generic knowledge via communication from experts.

So, are children's responses to evidence as they acquire generic knowledge via induction rational in the end? This remains an open question. During information communication, children use sample composition to constrain their inferences, consistent with rational models. Yet, whether they do so for information discovery—when they select samples themselves, when samples are produced via procedures that lack transparency, or when samples are produced in the absence of communicative goals—remains much less clear. These issues will be important to explore in future work, both to consider how learning mechanisms vary across pedagogical and nonpedagogical settings and to determine the scope of conceptual learning that can be accounted for by a rational constructivist perspective.

Whereas much of the work on rational constructivism has focused on identifying developmental continuities, rational constructivism also provides a useful framework for considering developmental differences. This perspective prompts us to consider such differences very carefully and to determine whether differences reflect changes in the intuitive theories or in the mechanisms by which beliefs are updated in response to new evidence. The example of category-based induction discussed in this chapter illustrates that a key test of these models may lie in the cases where children's responses to evidence appear quite different from adults' responses.

The research reviewed in this chapter also has implications for the role of pedagogical cues in the acquisition of generic knowledge. Some have argued that pedagogical cues serve to signal to children that information is generic (Csibra & Gergely, 2009). From this perspective, when children realize they are being taught by a knowledgeable teacher, they assume that the demonstrated information is generalizable. Although the present studies are consistent with the broad proposal that children respond differently to information in the presence of pedagogical cues, these data suggest an alternate conclusion regarding the particular effects of these cues. The data reviewed above suggest that children assume that information is generic in the *absence* of pedagogical cues. In particular, as shown in the Novice condition of Rhodes et al. (2010), in the absence of pedagogical cues, children generalized the information to basic-level categories following both diverse and nondiverse samples. The Expert condition suggests that pedagogical cues functioned to help children properly *restrict* their inferences, not to broaden them. Similarly, Rhodes and Brickman (2010) indicated that children have strong assumptions of category homogeneity (that the members of categories share many generic features). These data are consistent with the proposal that children treat certain information as generic by default (Cimpian & Erickson, 2012). From this perspective, pedagogical cues are not necessary for children to treat information as generic, but rather to guide them to when they should apply information more narrowly. More generally, pedagogical cues may not signal either generic or specific information per se, but rather that a sample is being selected purposefully and thus that children should pay attention to sample composition and generalize appropriately. Resolving the discrepancies across these perspectives is an important area for future work.

## REFERENCES

Atran, S. (1990). *Cognitive foundations of natural history: Towards an anthropology of science.* New York: Cambridge University Press.

Berndt, T. J., & Heller, K. A. (1986). Gender stereotypes and social inferences: A developmental study. *Journal of Personality and Social Psychology, 50,* 889–898.

Cimpian, A., & Erickson, L. C. (2012). Remembering kinds: New evidence that categories are privileged in children's thinking. *Cognitive Psychology, 64,* 161–185.

Csibra, G., & Gergely, G. (2009). Natural pedagogy. *Trends in Cognitive Sciences, 13,* 148–153.

Denison, S., Reed, C., & Xu, F. (in press). The emergence of probabilistic reasoning in very young infants: Evidence from 4.5- and 6-month-old infants. *Developmental Psychology.*

Dewar, S., & Xu, F. (2010). Induction, over hypothesis, and the origins of abstract knowledge: Evidence from 9-month-old infants. *Psychological Science, 21,* 1871–1877.

Gelman, S. A. (1988). The development of induction within natural kind and artifact categories. *Cognitive Psychology, 20,* 65–96.

Gelman, S. A. (2003). *The essential child: Origins of essentialism in everyday life*. New York: Oxford University Press.

Gelman, S. A., & Kalish, C. W. (1993). Categories and causality. In R. Pasnak, & M. L. Howe (Eds.), *Emerging themes in cognitive development* (pp. 3–32). New York: Springer-Verlag.

Gopnik, A., & Wellman, H.M. (in press). Reconstructing constructivism: Causal models, Bayesian learning mechanisms and the theory theory. *Psychological Bulletin*.

Gutheil, G., & Gelman, S. A. (1997). Children's use of sample size and diversity information within basic-level categories. *Journal of Experimental Child Psychology, 64*, 159–174.

Heit, E. (2000). Properties of inductive reasoning. *Psychonomic Bulletin & Review, 7*, 569–592.

Heit, E., & Hahn, U. (2001). Diversity-based reasoning in children. *Cognitive Psychology, 43*, 243–273.

Heit, E., Hahn, U., & Feeney, A. (2005). Defending diversity. In W. Ahn, R. L. Goldstone, B. C. Love, A. B. Markman, & P. Wolfi (Eds.), *Categorization inside and outside the lab: Festschrift in honor of Douglas L. Medin* (pp. 87–99). Washington, DC: American Psychological Association.

Kalish, C. W. (1998). Natural and artificial kinds: Are children realists or relativists about categories? *Developmental Psychology, 34*, 376–391.

Kemp, C., & Tenenbaum, J. (2009). Structured statistical models of inductive reasoning. *Psychological Review, 116*, 20–58.

Kim, N. S., & Keil, F. C. (2003). From symptoms to causes: Diversity effects in diagnostic reasoning. *Memory and Cognition, 31*, 155–165.

Kushnir, T., Wellman, H. M., & Gelman, S. A. (2008). The role of preschoolers' social understanding in evaluating the informativeness of causal interventions. *Cognition, 107*, 1084–1092.

Li, F., Bihua, C., Li, Y., Li, H., & Deak, G. (2009). The law of large numbers in children's diversity-based reasoning. *Thinking & Reasoning, 15*, 388–404.

Lopez, A. (1995). The diversity principle in the testing of arguments. *Memory and Cognition, 23*, 374–382.

Lopez, A., Atran, S., Coley, J. D., Medin, D. L., & Smith, E. E. (1997). The tree of life: Universal and cultural features of folkbiological taxonomies and inductions. *Cognitive Psychology, 32*, 251–295.

Lopez, A., Gelman, S. A., Gutheil, G., & Smith, E. E. (1992). The development of category-based induction. *Child Development, 63*, 1070–1090.

Medin, D. L., Coley, J. D., Storms, G., & Hayes, B. L. (2003). A relevance theory of induction. *Psychonomic Bulletin & Review, 3*, 317–332.

Osherson, D. N., Smith, E. E., Wilkie, O., Lopez, A., & Shafir, E. (1990). Category-based induction. *Psychological Review, 97*, 185–200.

Rips, L. J. (1975). Inductive judgments about natural categories. *Journal of Verbal Learning and Verbal Behavior, 14*, 665–681.

Rhodes, M., & Brickman, D. (2010). The role of within-category variability in category-based induction: A developmental study. *Cognitive Science, 34*, 1561–1573.

Rhodes, M., Brickman, D., & Gelman, S. A. (2008). Sample diversity and premise typicality in inductive reasoning: Evidence for developmental change. *Cognition, 108*, 543–556.

Rhodes, M., & Gelman, S. A. (2008). Categories influence predictions about individual consistency. *Child Development, 79*, 1271–1288.

Rhodes, M., & Gelman, S. A. (2009). A developmental examination of the conceptual structure of animal, artifact, and human social categories across two cultural contexts. *Cognitive Psychology, 59*. 294–274.

Rhodes, M., Gelman, S. A., & Brickman, D. (2008). Developmental changes in the consideration of sample diversity in inductive reasoning. *Journal of Cognition and Development, 9*, 112–143.

Rhodes, M., Gelman, S. A., & Brickman, D. (2010). Children's attention to sample composition in learning, teaching, and discovery. *Developmental Science, 13*, 421–429.

Schulz, L., Bonawitz, E., & Griffiths, T. (2007). Can being scared make your tummy ache? Naïve theories, ambiguous evidence, and preschoolers' causal inferences. *Developmental Psychology, 43*, 1124–1139.

Shafto, P., & Goodman, N. (2008). Teaching games: Statistical sampling assumptions for learning in pedagogical situations. In V. Sloutsky, B. Love, & K. McRae (Eds.), *Proceedings of the 30th Annual Cognitive Science Society*. Austin, TX: Cognitive Science Society.

Shipley, E. F., & Shepperson, B. (2006). Test sample selection by preschool children: Honoring diversity. *Memory and Cognition, 34*, 1444–1451.

Taylor, M. (1996). The development of children's beliefs about social and biological aspects of gender differences. *Child Development, 67*, 1555–1571.

Taylor, M. G., Rhodes, M., & Gelman, S. A. (2009). Boys will be boys, cows will be cows: Children's essentialist reasoning about human gender and animal development. *Child Development, 79*, 1270–1287.

Tenenbaum, J., Kemp, C., & Shafto, P. (2007). Theory-based Bayesian models of inductive reasoning. In A. Feeney, & E. Heit (Eds.), *Inductive reasoning: Experimental, developmental, and computational approaches.*. New York: Cambridge University Press.

Waxman, S., Lynch, E., Casey, L., & Baer, L. (1997). Setters and Samoyeds: The emergence of subordinate level categories as a basis for inductive inference. *Developmental Psychology, 33*, 1074–1090.

Xu, F. (2007). Rational statistical inference and cognitive development. In P. Carruthers, S. Laurence, & S. Stich (Eds.), *The Innate mind: Foundations and future*, Vol. 3. Oxford University Press.

Xu, F., & Denison, S. (2009). Statistical inference and sensitivity to sampling in 11-month-old infants. *Cognition, 112*, 97–104.

Xu, F., & Garcia, V. (2008). Intuitive statistics by 8-month-old infants. *Proceedings of the National Academy of Sciences of the United States of America, 105*, 5012–5015.

Xu, F., & Tenenbaum, J. B. (2007a). Word learning as Bayesian inference. *Psychological Review, 114*, 245–272.

Xu, F., & Tenenbaum, J. B. (2007b). Sensitivity to sampling in Bayesian word learning. *Developmental Science, 10*, 288–297.

# CHAPTER NINE

# A Number of Options: Rationalist, Constructivist, and Bayesian Insights into the Development of Exact-Number Concepts[1]

## Barbara W. Sarnecka* and James Negen
Department of Cognitive Sciences, University of California, Irvine, CA 92697-5100
*E-mail: sarnecka@uci.edu

## Contents

## Abstract

The question of how human beings acquire exact-number concepts has interested cognitive developmentalists since the time of Piaget. The answer will owe something to both the rationalist and constructivist traditions. On the one hand, some aspects of

[1] This work was supported by NSF grant DRL-0953521 to the first author.

*Advances in Child Development and Behavior*, Volume 43
ISSN 0065-2407,
http://dx.doi.org/10.1016/B978-0-12-397919-3.00009-5

numerical cognition (e.g. approximate number estimation and the ability to track small sets of one to four individuals) are innate or early-developing and are shared widely among species. On the other hand, only humans create representations of exact, large numbers such as 42, as distinct from both 41 and 43. These representations seem to be constructed slowly, over a period of months or years during early childhood. The task for researchers is to distinguish the innate representational resources from those that are constructed, and to characterize the construction process. Bayesian approaches can be useful to this project in at least three ways: (1) As a way to analyze data, which may have distinct advantages over more traditional methods (e.g. making it possible to find support for a null hypothesis); (2) as a way of modeling children's performance on specific tasks: Peculiarities of the task are captured as a prior; the child's knowledge is captured in the way the prior is updated; and behavior is captured as a posterior distribution; and (3) as a way of modeling learning itself, by providing a formal account of how learners might choose among alternative hypotheses.

# 1. THE PROBLEM

## 1.1. Exact-Number Concepts

This chapter is concerned with how children learn concepts for exact numbers, especially numbers above four. Other writing on this topic has used the terms "natural numbers" or "positive integers," both of which are also correct. The natural numbers are the "counting numbers"—one, two, three, . . . and so on. They are a subset of the whole numbers (which are comprised of the natural numbers and zero), which in turn are a subset of the integers (the whole numbers plus negative numbers, excluding fractions and decimals), which are a subset of the rational numbers (i.e. anything that can be expressed as a ratio of two integers), which are a subset of the real numbers (i.e. anything that can be plotted a number line, including all rational numbers, plus nonterminating, nonrepeating decimals such as $\pi$ and the square root of 2).

We use the term "exact numbers" for a few reasons. First, the term "natural number" is occasionally (and mistakenly) taken to mean that these concepts are "natural" in the sense of being innate, unlearned, or shared with other species. Not so. Exact numbers such as 42 (and even those as low as five and six) are not "natural" in that sense. They are constructed during childhood, based on cultural input. And as far as we know, they are unique to humans (really large number concepts, such as the concept 2014, certainly seem unique to humans).

The terms "natural number" and "positive integer" may also leave some readers confused about what, exactly, we think children know. Adults with some mathematical training may have an explicit concept "natural number," which includes beliefs such as, "The natural numbers start at one and go on forever; there is no highest natural number" or, "Adding or multiplying any two natural numbers together produces another natural number." But we want to be clear in this chapter that we are *not* claiming that children have such explicit knowledge about "natural numbers" or, "positive integers" as mathematical objects.

Instead, we are interested in children's ability to represent exact numerical quantities of five or more. How can a child represent the information that there are, for example, 8 blocks in a tower, 12 friends on the playground, or 24 cookies in the oven? That is, how are the words "eight," "twelve" and "twenty-four" understood by the child?

Children do represent and reason about numbers long before they understand the formal properties of the natural numbers or the positive integers in an explicit, mathematical sense. Consider the following quotations, both from the same child (the first author's 6-year-old son, JS). The first quotation demonstrates that JS represents at least some natural numbers. The second demonstrates his confusion about countable infinity, which is a property of the natural numbers.

**(1)** JS (age 5 years, 11 months): "If you have a thousand dollars and you lose a hundred, that's the same as if you have ten dollars and you lose one."

**(2)** JS (age 6 years, 6 months): "Luca said that a googolplex is the highest number, but he was wrong. There is no highest number."
BWS: "Yes, because you can always add one to any number and get a higher one."
JS: "Until infinity."
BWS: "Yes."
JS: "And after infinity, it starts from the highest negative number, and counts back."
BWS: "It does what?"
JS: "It counts all the way back to zero. It's a big loop. And infinity and zero are the ends."

As these examples show, a child can represent natural-number concepts without explicitly representing the formal properties of the natural numbers as a set. To avoid giving the impression that we are talking about the latter, meta-numerical type of knowledge, this chapter uses the terms exact numbers and "exact-number concepts" for the mental representations of exact numerical quantities such as five, six, seven, eight, and higher natural numbers.

## 1.2. What Makes the Acquisition of Exact-Number Concepts Interesting?

Are numbers a cultural invention? It seems indisputable that at least some are. Take the number $\pi$, for example. No one knows anything about $\pi$ until they hear about it from someone else, and there are plenty of people in the world who never acquire a concept of $\pi$ at all. (Of course, whoever originally formulated the concept $\pi$ was an exception to this statement, but it is true for all the rest of us.)

On the other hand, research over the past 40 years has shown that other types of numerical concepts are not cultural inventions, but are the outputs of cognitive systems that have evolved through natural selection. Most obviously, the approximate number system (often abbreviated *ANS*) allows humans and other animals to represent approximate numerical quantities of at least up to several hundred.

Separately from the ANS, humans and other animals also have the ability to create mental models for small sets of up to three or four individuals. This ability is sometimes called parallel individuation. As that name suggests, this is not a number system, but a system for identifying and tracking individuals (which may be objects, noises, actions, etc.) It is not a number system because it does not include any symbol for the *number* of objects in the set. Instead, it maintains a separate symbol for each individual being tracked. Number is represented only implicitly.

What makes exact-number concepts interesting is that a number like 42 cannot be represented by either of these innate systems. The ANS is only approximate, and parallel individuation only works for up to three or four items. So, how can numbers like "exactly 42" be represented? The answer is that the representational system supporting the concept "exactly 42" is constructed over a period of months or years during early childhood.

This is why any plausible account of the origins of exact, large number concepts must be both rationalist and constructivist. It must be rationalist in specifying the role played by those innate systems that represent some numerical content, and it must be constructivist in explaining how we go beyond those innate systems. Following Carey (2009), we will argue that exact-number concepts are a cultural invention, which must be redis-covered/reconstructed by each individual child during development, based on cultural input. The exact-number system, once acquired, has vastly more representational power than the innate systems, and forms the basis for all later-acquired number concepts (e.g. negative numbers, rational numbers, real numbers, etc.).

Finally, we take up the question of how Bayesian inference can be useful to this project, and we discuss three ways that it has already been used (Table 9.1). First, Bayesian methods can be used to analyze data. Depending on the data set and the question being addressed, these methods may have advantages over more traditional, frequentist methods. In the example we discuss, Bayesian inference makes it possible to find positive support for the null hypothesis, rather than simply rejecting or failing to reject the null. This can sometimes be a distinct advantage. Second, Bayesian methods can be used to model subjects' performance on specific tasks. In this case, peculiarities of the task are captured as a prior; the subject's knowledge is captured in the way the prior is updated; and the subject's observed behavior is captured in the posterior distribution. Third, Bayesian methods can be used to model learning itself. In this case, Bayes provides a formal account of how learners might choose among alternative hypotheses.

**Table 9.1** Three ways of using Bayesian inference in this research

| Application | Prior | Evidence | Posterior |
|---|---|---|---|
| Bayesian data analysis (to understand data) | Prior belief about population parameters (means, standard deviations, etc.) | Data collected in an experiment | Updated belief about what the population parameters are likely to be |
| Bayesian task modeling (to understand a task) | Contaminant influences on the child's behavior: task demands, pragmatics, order effects, etc. | The child's knowledge and/ or perceptions | Probabilistic description of how a child will behave in the task with a given state of knowledge and/or perceptions |
| Bayesian concept-creation modeling (to understand how a concept could be acquired) | Prior preferences in a space of possible truths about the world | Typical input that a child would receive | Inferences about the world that the child is likely to make (i.e. knowledge that the child develops) |

## 2. WHY ANY REASONABLE ACCOUNT OF THESE PHENOMENA MUST BE RATIONALIST

### 2.1. The Innate, Approximate Number System

Any effort to understand human numerical cognition must begin with the ANS. Readers who are already familiar with the ANS should feel free to skip the following section, which provides a brief description of the ANS in nonhuman animals, human infants, and adults.

The ANS is cognitive system that yields a mental representation of the approximate number of individuals in a set (e.g. Feigenson, Dehaene, & Spelke, 2004). Number is represented by a physical magnitude in the brain, and this magnitude is proportional to the actual number of individuals perceived. For example, if a person sees sets of 20 and 40 items, the neural magnitude for the set of 40 will be about twice as large as the neural magnitude for the set of 20 (e.g. Nieder & Miller, 2003). For this reason, representations of number in the ANS are often called "analog-magnitude" representations.

A key signature of the ANS (across development and across species) is that the discriminability of any two set sizes is a function of the ratio between them (for review, see Carey, 2009). It is equally as difficult to tell 8 from 16 items as it is to tell 16 from 32 items, or 50 from 100, or 80 from 160, because all of these cases compare sets with a ratio of 1:2.

Note that the discriminability of set sizes is not determined by their absolute difference. The comparison 8 versus 16 has a ratio of 1:2 and an absolute difference of 8. This is of the same difficulty as the comparison 80 versus 160, because the ratio in the latter case is still 1:2, even though the absolute difference (80) is ten times greater. On the other hand, discriminating 8 versus 16 is much easier than discriminating 152 versus 160. In this case, the absolute differences are both 8, but the ratio in the second comparison is much smaller (approximately 1:1.05).

This property of ratio dependence gives rise to two effects often mentioned in the literature. The first is the magnitude effect, which says that if the absolute difference between two set sizes is held constant, lower numbers are easier to discriminate than higher ones. For example, 5 and 10 are easier to tell apart than 105 and 110. The second is the distance effect, which says that if you are comparing two numbers to the same target, the one that is farther away from the target should be easier to discriminate from it. For example, it is easier to tell the difference between 10 and 15 than between 10 and 11. Both of these effects reflect the fact that discriminability in the ANS is a function of ratio.

## 2.1.1. Approximate Number Representation in Nonhuman Animals

The mental representation of approximate numbers is widespread among species. In a landmark study by Platt and Johnson (1971), rats were trained to press a bar some number of times in order to receive a food reward. After the rat had pressed the bar the required number of times, a food pellet would appear in the feeder. The rat had to leave the bar and run over to the feeder to find out whether the food was there. If the rat stopped pressing too soon, no reward would be in the feeder. If the rat pressed the bar more than the required number of times, the reward would be there, but the rat would have wasted some effort by pushing the bar more times than necessary. In this way, rats were motivated to press the bar just the number of times needed to get the food.

Different groups of rats were trained on different numbers. For example, one group was trained to press the bar 4 times, another group was trained to press it 8 times, and still other groups of rats were trained on the numbers 16 and 24. The results were clear. Each group of rats learned to press the bar as many times as needed. The mean number of presses in each group was actually one to two presses higher than the number trained, reflecting the fact that the rats were a little bit conservative. (Better to press the bar an extra time or two than to risk an empty feeder.)

In Platt and Johnson's (1971) study, number was correlated with other variables. Other studies deconfounded those variables and showed that rats do actually represent the *number* of presses and not just the total amount of energy expended in pressing the bar, or the total time spent pressing the bar. In a creative and early example, Mechner and Guevrekian (1962) showed that depriving rats of water makes them respond faster and with greater energy, but does not make them change the number of presses. To do this, the rat must represent number separately from duration and energy expenditure (see Meck & Church, 1983, for a related finding).

Note that rats do not perform perfectly. They do not press the bar *exactly* the right number of times on every trial. And the distribution of their errors is an important clue that the system they are using is the same ANS found in humans and other animals. The errors reveal scalar variability—a key signature of the ANS. Formally, scalar variability means that the ratio of the standard deviation of the subject's estimates to the mean of those estimates is a constant. In the case of the ANS, the mean estimate is equal to the target number (i.e., the number that the subject is trying to guess), so the spread of errors around each target number is a fixed proportion of the target number itself (see Fig. 9.1). This proportion differs for different subjects. The smaller it is, the more accurate the subject's estimation ability.

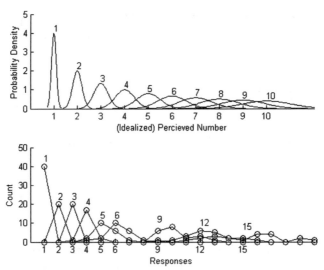

**Figure 9.1** On top is an idealized set of distributions with scalar variability. The line with the "1" above it is the distribution of perceptions when a participant is shown 1 item, the line with a "2" is a response curve to 2 items, and so on. Note that the mean is equal to the correct number and the standard deviation increases linearly with the mean. On the bottom are some actual responses taken from adults (Negen & Sarnecka, under review). Participants were asked to tap a space bar 1, 2, 3, 4, 5, 6, 9, 12, and 15 times. Again, the lines are labeled with the correct responses. Though the real data are much noisier, one can still see the mean approximately matches the correct number and the standard deviation increases with the mean.

Looking at Fig. 9.1, we can see that errors on ANS estimation tasks follow a predictable pattern: The mean of guesses for every target number is the same as the target number itself because errors fall symmetrically above and below the target. In the case of Platt and Johnson's (1971), rats, the mean fell slightly above the target because task incentivized conservative behavior, as mentioned above. But in studies without such a reward structure, the mean of estimates is typically equal to the target. Also, errors close to the target are more frequent than errors far away from it. For example, if the target number is 32, then 31 will be a more common error than 21.

These signatures—the symmetrical distributions of estimates, the mean of estimates for each target being the same as the target itself, and the scalar variability in the estimates—are characteristic of the ANS. These same signatures, have been found in the numerical cognition of a variety of other species including crows, pigeons, monkeys, apes, and dolphins (Dehaene, 1997; Gallistel, 1990).

## 2.1.2. Approximate Number Representation in Human Infants

Given that this very useful cognitive system is widely shared among verte-brate species, it is not surprising that humans also have it. Researchers from several different laboratories have shown that preverbal human infants represent approximate numerical quantities using the ANS system (e.g., Brannon, Abbot, & Lutz, 2004; McCrink & Wynn, 2004; Xu & Spelke, 2000).

Rather than making infants press bars for food rewards, these studies rely on infants' tendency to get bored, or "habituate" when they see the same thing over and over again. In these studies, infants are shown different sets of a particular number, over and over until they get bored. The infants' boredom is measured by how long they look at the display. For example, many studies use a criterion of half the initial looking time. This means that if the infant initially looks at the display for 6 seconds, the researchers keep showing the same display until the infant only looks at it for 3 seconds (or less). At that point, the test trials are begun. If the infant looks at the new (test) display significantly longer than 3 s, the researchers conclude that the infant noticed some difference between the old, habituation displays and the new, test display.

In one important study of infant number representation, Xu and Spelke (2000) habituated one group of 6-month-old infants to displays containing 8 dots and another group of infants to displays containing 16 dots. Xu and Spelke made sure to test infants' representation of number rather than other correlated variables (e.g. the sizes of individual dots, the total area covered by each display, the total summed perimeter length of the dots, etc.).

Results showed that infants do represent number. Those who were habituated to the 8-dot displays recovered interest when they were shown a 16-dot display; those who were habituated to the 16-dot displays recovered interest when they were shown an 8-dot display. Later studies showed that 6-month-old infants also discriminate 16 from 32 dots and 4 from 8 dots (Xu, 2003; Xu, Spelke, & Goddard, 2005; see also Lipton & Spelke, 2004).

Supporting the idea that infants were using the ANS, infants' success was a function of the ratio between the two set sizes. Six-month-old infants succeed at a 1:2 ratio (4 vs. 8, 8 vs. 16, or 16 vs. 32 dots), but they fail at a ratio of 2:3 (4 vs. 6, 8 vs. 12, or 16 vs. 24 dots). By 9 months of age, infants succeed at the 2:3 ratios but fail at 3:4 (e.g. they fail to discriminate 6 vs. 8, 12 vs. 16, or 24 vs. 32 dots). Thus, human infants form analog representations of approximate numbers long before they learn anything about counting or number words.

### 2.1.3. Exact-Number Concepts are Connected to the Approximate Number System

The fact that approximate number representation is innate in humans does not necessarily mean that it underlies the acquisition of exact-number concepts. But there is evidence from both adults and children to suggest that exact-number concepts, once they are acquired, are mapped onto analog representations in the ANS.

For example, many studies (e.g. Moyer & Landauer, 1967) have shown adults pairs of written Arabic numerals (e.g. 7 and 9) and asked them to indicate which was numerically greater. Participants' responses show both distance and magnitude effects in terms of reaction times (and sometimes in terms of error rates, though performance is often at ceiling in terms of accuracy). In other words, it takes people longer to judge that $8 > 7$ than that $7 > 6$ (magnitude effect). It also takes people longer to judge that $7 > 6$ than that $8 > 6$ (distance effect).

Recent studies have tried to specify the kinds of mappings that exist between ANS representations and exact-number words in adults (Izard & Dehaene, 2008; Sullivan & Barner, 2010). In one such study, Jessica Sullivan and David Barner asked adult participants to estimate (by saying a number word) the number of dots in an array. The arrays were too large for parallel individuation and were shown too fast for verbal counting, forcing participants to rely on the ANS. Results suggested that for relatively low number words (up to 30 or so), adults seemed to have a direct, individual ANS mapping for each number word. (That is, people have an ANS-based estimate of how many "twelve" is, how many "twenty-one" is, and so on, up to about 30.) This was indicated by the fact that estimates for numbers below 30 were not biased when participants were given misleading information about the range of set sizes used in the experiment. On the other hand, estimates for larger numbers were biased by this type of information. For example, if participants were told to expect arrays of up to 750 dots, when in fact the most numerous array shown had only 350, participants' estimates of numerosity were systematically biased upward, but only for arrays of more than about 30 dots. This suggests that words for numbers higher than about 30 are mapped to the ANS, but they are mapped in terms of an overall structure. That is, people know the order of the number words, and they expect later numbers to be mapped onto larger ANS magnitudes, but they don't maintain a separate representation of the magnitude of each individual number.

Recent evidence suggests that an ANS-to-number-word mapping emerges soon after children have learned the first few exact numbers. We (Negen & Sarnecka, under review) showed 3- and 4-year-old children cards with pictures of one to four items. The children's task was to say how many pictures were on the card. (These children did not yet understand how to use counting to solve the problem.) Using Bayesian methods of data analysis (discussed in more detail in Section 5), we found evidence that children's answers were drawn from an underlying distribution in which variability was scalar. In other words, we found evidence for a mapping between ANS representations and the number words "one" through "four". Later (about 6 months after acquiring all of the counting principles), children learn to extend this mapping out to all of the number words they know (Le Corre & Carey, 2007). By around 5 to 6 years old, children map number words to ANS magnitudes much as adults do.

Thus, in both adults and children, exact-number concepts are mapped to magnitude representations in the ANS. For this reason, any plausible theory of how exact-number concepts are acquired must be somewhat rationalist. It must at least recognize that exact numbers are mapped to the ANS ideally, it would offer an account of how and when ANS representations (which are, by definition, approximate) become connected to representations of exact numbers.

## 2.2. Another Innate System Relevant to Exact-Number Concepts

Infants also create and maintain working-memory models of small sets of individuals (objects, sounds, or events). Up to three individuals at a time can be represented this way. For example, when infants are habituated to displays of two objects, they recover attention when shown one or three (Antell & Keating, 1983; Bijeljac-Babic, Bertoncini, & Mehler, 1991; Feigenson, 2005; Starkey & Cooper, 1980; Wood & Spelke, 2005; Wynn, 1992a, 1996). Unlike the ANS, this is not a system that represents number *per se*. It is a system that represents individuals. The system does not include any symbols for "two" or "three," but instead maintains a separate symbol for each individual. Other information about the individual (such as its type and properties) can also be bound to these symbols. Thus, whereas the ANS system could represent the content "approximately 10," the parallel individuation system could represent the content, "big duck, little car, little doll."

Because it maintains a separate symbol for each individual, only a limited number of individuals can be represented at any one time. For infants, constraints on attention and working memory seem to place this limit at three (e.g. Feigenson, Carey, & Hauser, 2002). That is, up to three individuals can be tracked at once. If four or more individuals are presented, the infant is not able to track them. When this constraint is exceeded, performance falls to chance in many tasks. For example, Feigenson et al. (2002) found that children could correctly discriminate that $2 < 3$ but not $2 < 4$. This is especially odd because if they simply failed to represent the fourth item in the set of 4, the $2 < 4$ problem would reduce to $2 < 3$, which they pass. Presenting more than three items seems to make the system simply "shut off" and fail to produce any useful output.

Although it does not include any symbols for numbers, this parallel individuation system is relevant to exact-number concepts for several reasons. First, exact-number concepts require some notion of *individual* or *one*, and this notion comes from the attention and memory mechanisms that identify and track individuals. (No representation of *exactly one* exists in the ANS, where number is always approximate.)

Second, the parallel individuation system supports judgments of numerical identity: Is this object or sound or event *the same one*, or *a different one* than the object/sound/event that came before it? Number concepts require that different individuals can be identified as such because number is a property of sets, which are comprised of separate individuals. Without criteria for individuation and some representation of the separateness of different individuals (i.e. some criteria for determining numerical identity), no numerical content could be represented at all.

Finally, parallel individuation supports at least some rudimentary "chunking" of individuals into sets. As described above, infants generally fail to track sets of more than three items. For example, if an infant sees one, two, or three toy cars placed inside a box and is allowed to reach inside the box to retrieve the toys, the infant's search behavior shows that the infant remembers whether there are one, two, or three items in the box. However, if four items (e.g. four cars) are placed in the box, the infant searches no longer than if only one car had been placed there, indicating that the infant can represent the information "car, car, car" but fails to represent "car, car, car, car." This is the set-size limit of three individuals, described above.

However, recent work by Feigenson and Halberda (2008) shows that if infants are shown two shoes and two cars going into the box, they will search for all four items—something about having two different types of item helps the infants to create two representations of two individuals each, rather than directly representing all four items. These abilities—to identify and track individuals, and to create higher-order, "chunked" representations of sets of individuals—are required for the representation of exact, large numbers.

## 3. CAREY'S RATIONALIST, CONSTRUCTIVIST ACCOUNT OF HOW EXACT-NUMBER CONCEPTS ARE ACQUIRED

### 3.1. Why Any Reasonable Account of these Phenomena must be Constructivist

Given these innate capacities, the reader might wonder whether it makes sense to talk about the "construction" of exact-number concepts at all. Is it likely that exact-number concepts themselves are innate? The answer is no, it is not likely, for the simple reason that none of the innate capacities are up to the job of representing exact, large numbers.

The system of exact numbers has enormous representational power. Using exact numbers, we can represent very large numbers, very precisely. On the day of this writing, J.S. (the 6-year-old mentioned in the anecdotes above) was heard complaining that, "The American flag is super hard to draw," because it has 50 stars, 13 stripes *"and the blue!"* He added in an irate tone that this totaled *"64 things to draw!"* and went on to express his sincere admiration for the Japanese flag.

The concepts of exactly 50, exactly 13, and exactly 64 simply cannot be formulated over ANS representations, which have approximate, real-number values, rather than exact, natural-number values. In other words, there is no way to represent "64 things" as distinct from 63.9 things, or 64.5 things, in the ANS. On the other hand, the parallel individuation system has no explicit representation of number at all. Number is represented only implicitly because there is a symbol maintained for each individual in the set. Because more attentional resources are required to represent each additional individual, the number of individuals that can be represented is strictly limited to three or four. Thus, parallel individuation cannot, on its own, support the representation of exact large numbers. This is why a theory of the construction of exact-number concepts is needed.

## 3.2. Conceptual-Role Bootstrapping

Carey has put forward an in-depth proposal for how exact-number concepts could be constructed, through a uniquely human kind of learning called conceptual-role bootstrapping (Carey, 2009; see also Block, 1986; Quine, 1960). Conceptual-role bootstrapping is not to be confused with semantic bootstrapping or syntactic bootstrapping, both of which are ways of solving mapping problems in the domain of word learning.

Conceptual-role bootstrapping is a way of solving a different problem—the problem of how to construct a representational system (for a given domain of knowledge) that is discontinuous with the representational system that the learner had before. "Discontinuous" means that the content of the new conceptual system cannot be formulated over the vocabulary of the old conceptual system. In practice, this may happen for either of two reasons: (1) The new system is incommensurable with the old one, in the sense that most or all of the old conceptual framework must be discarded to make way for the new one, or (2) The new system has massively greater representational power than the old one. Exact-number concepts fall into this second category; they are not incommensurable with the antecedent representations of the ANS and parallel individuation, but they have massively greater (not just incrementally greater) representational power.

## 3.3. Bootstrapping Exact-Number Concepts

Episodes of conceptual-role bootstrapping happen as follows. The learner first acquires a placeholder structure—a set of symbols that are structured (i.e. they have some fixed relation to each other) but are not initially defined in terms of the learner's existing vocabulary of concepts. In this case, the set of placeholder symbols is the list of counting words and the order of the list is its structure. Importantly, the words are not (and cannot be) initially defined in terms of the learner's existing vocabulary of number concepts, which include only approximate representations of number from the ANS. (Recall that the parallel individuation system contains no explicit representation of number at all.) Thus, the first step in bootstrapping exact-number concepts is to learn the placeholder structure—the list of number words and the pointing gestures that are deployed along with it. But these words and gestures are initially just placeholders, devoid of exact-number content.

Over a period of many months (often more than a year), the child gradually fills in these placeholder symbols (the counting words and gestures) with meaning. For example, children must learn that number words are about *quantity* (Sarnecka & Gelman, 2004); that they are specifically about *discontinuous* quantity (i.e. discrete individuals such as blocks, rather than continuous substances such as water, Slusser, Ditta, & Sarnecka, under review; Slusser & Sarnecka, 2011a); and that numerosity (as opposed to, e.g. total spatial extent) is the relevant quantitative dimension (Slusser & Sarnecka, 2011b).

Of course, children must also learn the exact meaning of each number word, and how they do this is very interesting. Recall that parallel individuation supports mental models of one to three individuals and that children can under some circumstances "chunk" individuals into nested representations. In order to learn the meaning of the word "one," the child must create a summary symbol for states of the nervous system when exactly one individual is being tracked (Le Corre & Carey, 2007).

The role of the ANS in this process is a matter of some debate. On the one hand, the ANS contains no representation (not even an implicit representation) of exactly 1. On the other hand, the ANS does contain summary symbols for numerosities, and 1 is discriminable from 2 in this system, even if the representations of 1 and 2 are real-number approximations rather than natural numbers. Furthermore, recent evidence suggests that even those children who know only a few number words (e.g. "one," and "two") do have ANS representations defined for those number words (Negen & Sarnecka, under review). All of which suggests that ANS representations are somehow recruited even in the early stages of exact-number-concept construction.

Children take a long time to learn the meanings of number words. Their progression is most clearly illustrated by the changes in their performance on the Give-N task (Wynn, 1992b). In this task, the child is given a set of objects (e.g. a bowl of 15 small plastic bananas) and is asked to give a certain number of them to a puppet. For example, the child might be asked to "Give *five* bananas to the lion." The somewhat surprising finding is that many young children who count perfectly well (i.e., they recite the counting list correctly while pointing to one object at a time) are unable to give the right number of bananas to the lion. Instead of counting to determine the right set size, they just grab one banana, or a handful, or they give the lion all the bananas. Even when children are explicitly told to count the items, they do not use their counting to create a set of the requested size (Le Corre, Van de Walle, Brannon, & Carey, 2006).

Studies using the Give-N task have shown that children move through a predictable series of performance levels, often called number-knower levels (e.g. Condry & Spelke, 2008; Le Corre & Carey, 2007; Le Corre et al., 2006; Lee & Sarnecka 2010, 2011; Negen & Sarnecka, in press; Sarnecka & Gelman, 2004; Sarnecka & Lee, 2009; Slusser & Sarnecka, 2011a, 2011b; Wynn, 1990). These number-knower levels are found not only in child speakers of English but also in Japanese and Russian (Sarnecka et al., 2007).

The number-knower levels are as follows. At the earliest (i.e. the "pre-number-knower") level, the child makes no distinctions among the meanings of different number words. On the Give-N task, pre-number knowers might always give one object or might always give a handful, but the number given is unrelated to the number requested. At the next level (called the "one-knower" level), the child knows that "one" means 1. On the Give-N task, this child gives exactly 1 object when asked for one and gives 2 or more objects when asked for any other number. After this comes the "two-knower" level, when the child knows that "two" means 2. Two knowers give 1 object when asked for "one" and 2 objects when asked for "two," but they do not reliably produce the right answers for any higher number words. The two-knower level is followed by a "three-knower" and then a "four-knower" level.

After the "four-knower" level, however, it is no longer possible to learn the meanings of larger number words (five, six, seven, etc.) in the same way as the small numbers have been learned. This is because the innate systems of number representation do not support the mental representation of 5 in the way that they support the representation of 1 through 4. Specifically, parallel individuation does not allow for the tracking of five individuals at a time, and the difference between 5 and 6 is not easily discriminable by young children via the ANS.

Thus, the meaning of "five" must be learned differently from how the meanings of "one" through "four" were learned. Carey's proposal is that children learn the meanings "five" and all higher numbers when they induce the cardinal principle of counting (Gelman & Gallistel, 1978; Schaeffer, Eggleston, & Scott, 1974). The cardinal principle of counting makes the cardinal meaning of every number word dependent on its ordinal position in the counting list. (In other words, the cardinal principle guarantees that for every list of counting symbols, the fifth symbol must mean 5, 13th symbol must mean 13, the 64th symbol must mean 64, etc.) At this point the meaning of the ordered list of placeholder symbols (i.e. the counting words) becomes clear.

To understand the cardinal principle, is to understand the logic of exact numbers. This requires an implicit understanding of succession (the idea that each number is formed by adding one to the number before it) and of equinumerosity (the idea that every set of numerosity N can be put into one-to-one correspondence with any other set of numerosity N; Izard, Pica, Spelke, & Dehaene, 2008). Supporting this idea, recent empirical studies find that children who understand the cardinal principle of counting (as measured by the Give-N task) do indeed show an implicit understanding of succession and equinumerosity as well. Only cardinal-principle knowers know that adding one item to a set means moving one word forward in the counting list; whereas adding two items to a set means moving two words forward in the list (Sarnecka & Carey, 2008). Similarly, only cardinal-principle knowers show a robust understanding that two sets with perfect 1-to-1 correspondence *must* be labeled by the same number word, whereas two sets *without* 1-to-1 correspondence must be labeled by different number words (Sarnecka & Wright, in press).

## 4. THREE WAYS THAT BAYES CAN HELP WITH THIS PROJECT

Research exploring the development of exact-number concepts can make use of Bayesian inference in different ways. Here, we discuss three of them: Bayesian data analysis, Bayesian task modeling, and Bayesian concept-creation modeling. What all of these Bayesian approaches have in common is that they involve some sort of prior information, which is weighted against some form of evidence to form a posterior distribution. The approaches differ in the kinds of information captured by the prior, the evidence, and the posterior.

### 4.1. Using Bayes to Analyze Data (Agnostic Bayesianism)

The first approach is *Bayesian data analysis*. Of the three, this is the one supported by the largest statistical literature (e.g. Gelman, Carlin, Stern, & Rubin, 1995; 2003). It requires no theoretical commitments about the developing mind, because Bayesian methods are used only to analyze data. This is sometimes called *Agnostic Bayes* (e.g. Jones & Love, 2011) because it does not require any commitment to the idea that the mind itself makes inferences in a Bayesian way.

In Bayesian data analysis, priors are formulated over things that researchers want to estimate in a data set, such as the rate of correct responses to a question or the effect size of a given between-group difference. The evidence is the set of sample observations. The posterior is an updated belief about the population.

For example, imagine that we have a sample of 24 children, and we ask each of them the same question about whales: Is a whale a mammal, or a fish? We will accept only two possible responses—"mammal" (the correct answer) or "fish" (the incorrect answer). In this group of children, 22 answer "mammal" and the other 2 answer "fish". We want to estimate how many children in the population of interest will say that whales are mammals. To do this, we first set a prior, saying that the set of responses can equally be anything from 0% correct to 100% correct. This distribution is known as a flat prior or Beta(1,1).

Our data are the 22 "mammal" and 2 "fish" responses that we collected from the children. These data combine with the prior to form the posterior, Beta(23,3). This posterior is a probability distribution for the rate of "whales-are-mammals" responses in the population of interest, given our data and the prior, and assuming that our sample was randomly drawn from that population. This posterior distribution is shown in Fig. 9.2.

This posterior allows us to interpret the data without calculating a p-value. The probability density around a 50% correct-response rate in the population (i.e. the probability that the children in the population have no knowledge of what whales are, and that they children in our sample

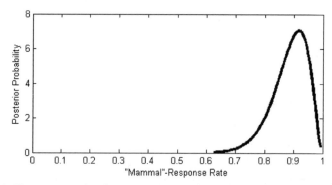

**Figure 9.2** The posterior distribution over rates of "whales-are-mammals" responses in the population, given a flat prior and 22/24 "yes" answers in our data set. Intuitively, it should make sense that the highest probability is at 22/24 and very little probability exists below about 70% correct.

answered randomly) is extremely low (less than 0.001) compared to the peak. From this, it is already reasonable to infer that the data do not reflect chance responding. Furthermore, a 95% credible interval stretches from about 74% to 97% on this posterior distribution, meaning that we can conclude with 95% certainty that somewhere between 74% and 97% of children in the population of interest actually will say that whales are mammals. Further reinforcing this, we can calculate a Bayes factor, which is an expression of preference for one hypothesis over another. In this case, the alternative hypothesis (the rate could be anything from 0% to 100%) is preferred over the null (a correct-response rate of 50%, indicating chance responding) by a factor of 2431. This is considered extremely strong evidence. Space precludes a review of all of the ways that posteriors can be formed and interpreted (for review, see A. Gelman et al., 1995; 2003). But this basic approach—forming priors, calculating posteriors, looking at confidence intervals, and calculating Bayes factors—can be applied in virtually any case where researchers would otherwise use t-tests, analyses of variance (ANOVAs), regressions, and so on.

One clear advantage of this type of data analysis over more traditional methods is that the Bayesian methods make it possible to find positive support for the null hypothesis, rather than simply rejecting or failing to reject it. In classical hypothesis testing (using t-tests, ANOVAs, etc.), a null hypothesis can be rejected if enough evidence is found against it, but evidence can never be found *for* the null.

With a Bayesian approach, it is actually possible to use a prior as the alternative hypothesis in a way that allows either hypothesis (the null or the alternative) to be preferred after the data are taken into account. This is particularly well understood in the case of t-tests, for which there even exists a simple online calculator (Rouder, Speckman, Sun, Morey, & Iverson, 2009). There is also an excel sheet available for approximating this kind of approach for ANOVAs, though it requires researchers to separately calculate sums of squares used in the usual F-tests (Masson, 2011; for technical details, see Dickey and Lientz, 1970).

We know of only one number-concept development study using this type of agnostic Bayesian method (Negen & Sarnecka, under review). The paper asks whether children who know the meanings of only a few number words (e.g. "one," "two," and "three") have already mapped those words to representations in the ANS. Operationally, the question is whether children's responses on a number-word task are drawn from an underlying distribution with scalar variability. (As mentioned above, scalar variability is a key signature of the distribution of ANS representations in the brain.)

Previous studies (e.g. Cordes, Gelman, Gallistel, & Whalen, 2001) have only been able to test for the absence of this signature. To test whether the signature could actually be inferred from the data, we calculated a Bayes factor. The null hypothesis (i.e. that variability was scalar) was preferred by a factor of about 14. In other words, it was 14 times more likely that the data came from an underlying distribution with scalar variability than that the data came from an underlying distribution where variability was (linearly) non-scalar. This is very strong evidence for the null hypothesis. In general, this type of analysis is useful in situations where researchers want to present evidence *for* the null hypothesis—for example, to argue that subjects *are* guessing at random, that two means *are* the same, that variables *are* unrelated, and so on.

Because Bayesian data analysis tends to result in the calculation of Bayes factors, it is also useful when several models are being compared frequently. A current example is the debate over logarithmic and linear performance in bounded number-line tasks (e.g. Siegler, Thompson, & Opfer, 2009). Most studies to date have compared linear and logarithmic models by (1) calculating the median response for each child, (2) finding the best fit for the linear and logarithmic models, and (3) counting the number of children fit better by each model.

If one considers only the relatively simple log and linear models, this method seems adequate. However, it would be more formally rigorous to use a Bayes factor. This would also allow for the strength-of-preference to be calculated for each individual child, which may be useful. Finally, a Bayes factor naturally punishes models that make over-broad predictions, so it would allow for rigorous comparisons between the simple log and linear models and also models that have more parameters in them (e.g. Barth, Slusser, Cohen, & Paladino, 2011; Cohen & Blanc-Goldhammer, 2011; Slusser, Santiago & Barth, under review).

At the moment, the use of Bayesian data analysis is not widespread among developmental scientists. We see at least three reasons why this is so. First, there is very little training available in how to use these methods, although some progress has been made on this front with a few authors posting free, online training books (e.g. Wagenmaker & Lee, in preparation).

Second, because the methods are relatively unfamiliar to reviewers, authors are required to explain the analysis at much greater length than would be needed for traditional, frequentist methods; they must explain both how the analysis was done and why they used Bayesian methods instead of frequentist ones. This turns every paper into something of a statistics tutorial—even when the authors are not interested in convincing anyone else to use Bayesian methods but simply want to present their empirical work. This problem would presumably decrease over time, if the methods were used more widely.

Third, virtually nothing exists in the way of "friendly" software (GUI-based, standardized, professionally supported) to help with the analysis in any but the simplest of cases. (E.g., there is no Bayesian equivalent of SPSS.) This problem does not even seem to be recognized as a problem; most statistical software is still being developed and released in R, which is text based and largely decentralized.

## 4.2. Using Bayes to Model Subjects' Behavior on a Task

A second way to adopt a Bayesian approach to studying number-concept development is to use *Bayesian task modeling*. This method allows us to separately model the demands of a task and the knowledge state of the subject and to think about how those combine to create the observed behavior.

This method has been used to model children's behavior on the Give-N task (Lee & Sarnecka, 2010, 2011). In this task, the child is asked to produce sets of a certain number (e.g. "Please put *three* bananas on the lion's plate."). The prior captures the base rate of responses for each task. This is roughly how children would respond in the absence of any numerical information. For example, if you could somehow ask for "banana(s)" in a way that did not provide any singular/plural or other cues about how many bananas were wanted.

Lee and Sarnecka (2011) inferred their prior from a large set of Give-N data, by aggregating across all the wrong guesses that children made. The resulting prior is shown in Fig. 9.3 (left panel). Children have a high probability of giving just 1 item, a somewhat lower probability of giving 2, still lower and approximately equal probabilities of giving 3–5, and significantly lower probabilities of giving any number larger than that. However, there is a bump up at 15.

This distribution is intuitively sensible. If children understand that they should give something from the bowl but have no information about how many things they should give, it seems reasonable that they should give one item or a handful of items (each object is about 2 cm in diameter, so children can typically grab two to five objects at once). Nor does it seem surprising (to

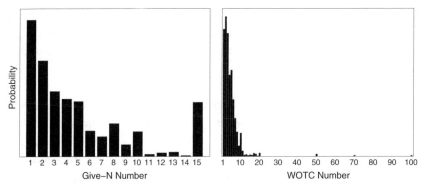

**Figure 9.3** Inferred base rates (i.e. priors) for the Give-N task and What's-On-This-Card tasks from Lee & Sarnecka, 2011

anyone who has spent time with preschoolers) that it is relatively common for children to give the entire set of 15 items, either by dumping them all onto the lion's plate at once or by placing one item at a time on the plate until there are none left.

If the child knows the exact meanings of any exact number words (e.g. *one*, *two*, and *three*), this information changes the base rate for that child. A three-knower will usually give the correct number of items when asked for "one," "two," or "three" and will very rarely produce those set sizes when asked for any other number. The intuitive operation of the model is illustrated in Fig. 9.4. The child depicted is a three-knower, reflected by the fact that the numbers 1, 2 and 3 are underlined in the first thought bubble, representing the prior. The prior probability of any given set size being produced (as shown in Fig. 9.3) is represented here by the size of each numeral, with numerals for higher-probability set sizes appearing in larger type.

If the child hears the request, "Give me *two*," the posterior probability (illustrated in the thought bubble on the upper right) is very high for 2 and very low (too small to be pictured) for any other number. In other words, this simplified model predicts that children who are three-knowers will *always* give 2 objects when asked for two.

If the request is, "Give me *five*," then the probabilities for 1, 2, and 3 immediately drop to very near zero. (In the figure, these numerals do not appear in the lower-right thought bubble.) This reflects the fact that the child is a three-knower, and three-knowers know that whatever "five" means, it cannot mean 1, 2, or 3 (Wynn, 1992b). What remains are all the other numbers of objects the child could give, each of which has the same probability (relative to all the alternatives) as it did in the prior. Chances are

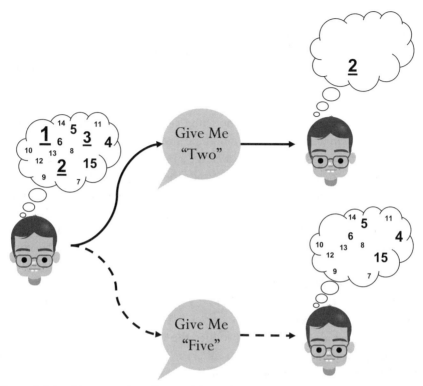

**Figure 9.4** Intuitive operation of Lee and Sarnecka's (2011) model, showing a child who is a three-knower responding to instructions to "give two" or to "give five" (Lee & Sarnecka, 2011). For color version of this figure, the reader is referred to the online version of this book.

that the child will produce a set of 4, 5, or 15 in response to this request. Other set sizes are less likely to be produced, as reflected by their smaller numerals.

The key point here is that the base rate has a large impact on the observed performance. It answers the question, for example, why might a child give four items instead of six for a given request, if that child does not know what either "four" or "six" mean? The answer is, because the prior (base-rate) probability of giving four items is higher.

Note that this kind of modeling does not commit the user to the idea that children make any of the calculations involved, either explicitly or implicitly. Formally, this is a computational model (a model of how cognitive parameters and task demands lead to observed behavior) rather than an algorithmic model (a model of exactly how the various cognitive processes are implemented). A Bayesian operation takes a base rate of responding (the prior) and updates it using the child's knowledge (the data) to produce an actual, observed rate of responding (the posterior). This does not imply that the child represents any of these concepts. It is simply a description of how task demands and different states of knowledge combine to form different patterns of behavior in the task.

One way that Bayesian task modeling can be very useful is in allowing researchers to investigate the "psychological reality" of theoretical constructs across tasks. Using this type of modeling, we can assess children on multiple tasks that are believed to tap the same underlying knowledge and then compare performance across tasks, even if the task demands and resulting performance data are very different.

To continue with the earlier example, Lee and Sarnecka (2011) tested children on two tasks, both of which are supposed to reveal the child's number-knower level. One was the Give-N task mentioned above; the other was the What's-On-This-Card task (Gelman, 1993; Le Corre & Carey, 2007; Le Corre et al., 2006). The Give-N task asks children to produce the set corresponding to a given a number word; the What's-On-This-Card task asks children to produce the number word for a given set.

The priors for each task were different because the kinds of behavior possible on each task were different. For example, the What's-On-This-Card prior (Figure 9.3, right panel) did not have a bump up at 15 because the bump up at 15 was an artifact of the Give-N task. It reflected the fact that there were 15 items in the bowl set before the child and that children often dumped out and handed over all the items. On the other hand, any number word a child could think of was a possible response on the What's-On-This-Card task, whereas on the Give-N task, the only possible responses were the numbers 1–15.

Number-knower levels are most often assessed using the Give-N task. But if they are a psychologically "real" phenomenon (rather than an artifact of Give-N task demands), then the number-word knowledge inferred for children on the Give-N and What's-On-This-Card tasks should be the same, despite the different task demands. And indeed, this is what Lee and Sarnecka found for most children. Furthermore, by combining information from the two different tasks, Lee and Sarnecka's (2011) model was able to diagnose the knower levels of many children with a much higher degree of certainty than was possible using the data from either task alone.

In practice, it is often the case that researchers who use Bayesian task modeling will also want to use Bayesian data analysis. Some authors have argued that this is necessary to realize the full potential of the approach (e.g. Kruschke, 2010; Lee, 2010, 2011a, 2011b). Estimating the parameters of a model like the one described above is actually a very hard problem. A widely accepted alternative is to sample from the posterior (rather than attempting to fully describe it) and then examine the samples. This process, known as Markov-Chain Monte-Carlo, is well studied and is implemented in several free software packages (e.g. WinBUGS; Thomas, 1994).

## 4.3. Using Bayes to Model Learning Itself

The third way to adopt a Bayesian approach in this research is to use *Bayesian concept-creation modeling*, where Bayesian methods are used to model the creation of a new concept. Here, the prior is some set of beliefs in a model learner's virtual mind—some set of bets or preferences about what is probably true in the world. If the model is to be cognitively plausible, these prior beliefs should be ones that could plausibly be attributed to human learners at the outset of the learning episode. In the case of exact-number concept creation, for example, priors should reflect the known limits of the ANS and/or parallel individuation system.

The evidence is the input received by the learner. Here, the requirement for a cognitively plausible model is that the input must match real-world experiences that children actually have. For example, researchers trying to model word learning might base the input on transcripts of natural, child-directed speech.

The posterior is a distribution over various inferences a child could make. The explanatory value of the model depends on this posterior distribution giving most of its mass to inferences that children actually do make. In other words, at the end of the learning episode, the model learner must represent the knowledge in question. For example, a model learner acquiring English count/mass syntax should agree that number words cannot quantify over mass nouns (e.g. *the three furniture*). That is, any rule that accepts *the three furniture* should have low posterior probability.

This approach is particularly helpful for addressing arguments over learnability. Philosophers have famously argued that any set of data can be fit equally well by an infinite space of hypotheses. For instance, the English language could be a subject-verb-object language up until January 1, 2025, and then suddenly switch to being a verb-subject-object language. All the data available at the time of this writing are equally consistent with this 2025-change hypothesis and the alternative, no-change hypothesis. The intuition that this 2025-change hypothesis is silly, counterproductive, needlessly complex, and/or confusing is met with the counterargument that (1) these objections just reflect a bias toward what we already somehow know and (2) there is no formal way to measure complexity.

Rips, Asmuth, and Bloomfield (2006, 2008) have put forward such an argument about the development of exact-number concepts. Specifically, researchers are challenged to explain how young children (who know only some exact numbers) could infer that numbers keep going in a linear progression, rather than following a modular principle, such that at some arbitrary number (e.g. 10), the numbers stop counting up and start over again at 1. (Rips and colleagues point out that some notational systems, such as days of the week, months of the year, and hours of the day, do have a modular structure—so modular systems must in principle be learnable by children.) In other words, the numbers the child knows are like all the years in which English has been a subject-verb-object language. No matter how many there have been, the next one could be different.

Recent work by Piantadosi, Tenenbaum, and Goodman (in press) has shown that a Bayesian model learner can overcome this hurdle and construct exact-number concepts with a linear progression, even when the evidence is theoretically consistent with either a modular or a linear system. The model works by describing various systems for matching number words with meanings as lambda calculi. An example of a one-knower might be

$$\lambda\, S \,.\, (\text{if (singleton? } S)\ \text{``one''}\ \text{``two''}),$$

which outputs "one" if given a set $S$ with 1 item and otherwise outputs "two". The prior favors calculi that (a) are short, (b) use fewer elements of recursion, and (c) re-use primitives. In many ways, this formally captures the intuition of certain systems being "simpler".

Piantadosi and colleagues address the question of how children could infer a linear number system, given the available evidence, rather than a modular number system. The answer is that the model's prior prefers systems that can be described in a shorter calculus, with fewer primitives. (Note that this is a formal definition of "simpler," undermining the claim that there is no way to measure complexity.)

By this definition, linear systems are less complex than modular systems, which require all the machinery of a linear system in order to get from 1 to 10 (or whatever the highest number of the module is), and then additional machinery to tell the user to stop and start again from 1. When fed true-to-life number-word input, Piantadosi's model learner selects the correct (linear) hypothesis because it has the greatest posterior likelihood given the data and the prior, even against the infinite space of other hypotheses.

It is not that Piantadosi's model learner *cannot* learn a modular system—it is just that positive evidence for a modular system must be provided in order to overcome the simpler, linear hypothesis. When the learner is fed modular information (real-world number-word input that has been altered to reflect a modular system), a modular system is indeed what it learns. This is intuitively appealing when one considers the learning trajectories of real children: Children represent at least some exact numbers by about age 4; at that age, most of them have not yet learned the cycles of hours in a day, days in a week, or months in a year. However, they are not fundamentally incapable of learning the cyclical systems and neither is the model learner. It just takes the model longer to learn modular systems ("longer" meaning that it requires more data), which mimics the learning trajectories of real children.

One objection to Piantadosi's model might be that it simply does not consider a very rich space of hypotheses. But the same general method can be used to address a space of hypotheses of any size. For example, the model does not consider that the meaning of number words might change at some specified future date, because the model learner does not have access to date information. However, even if the model were modified to include this information, the date-change hypothesis would be doomed from the outset because it would require an expression such as "if the date is before X" and then two full models of number-word meanings (one for all dates before the change and another one for all later dates). Such a model would be much less likely under the prior (which prefers shorter descriptions with fewer primitives) and thus would not be selected. This argument holds equally true for any other alternative that would encumber the correct system with conditional variance, for which there is no negative evidence.

In very general terms, Bayesian concept-creation modeling provides a way of separately modeling prior biases and observations and for both of these to be interesting, well-specified, research-supported, necessary components of the concept-creation process. This is exciting because a similar approach has been useful in explaining human induction in other areas (e.g. Perfors, Tenenbaum, Griffiths, & Xu, 2011). Indeed, the approach seems so flexible across domains that in some cases, domain-general priors may eventually replace domain-specific constraints.

Thus, Bayesian concept-creation modeling represents a convenient way of formally describing what we know to be true about development: That the rationalists and the constructivists have always *both* been right (at least in part) because both priors and evidence matter. Even if a human infant and a puppy are raised by the same, loving human family, the baby will grow up to speak a human language and the dog will not, because of prior constraints. On the other hand, if a Japanese baby and a French baby are switched at birth, it is the baby raised in Japan who will learn to speak Japanese, and the one raised in France who will learn to speak French, because of the evidence in the environment. By creating models that take both these aspects of development seriously, Bayesian concept-creation modeling allow us to move beyond tiresome debates where each side emphasizes either prior constraints or learning, but no theory seems able to accommodate both.

Finally, it is worth mentioning that for all three types of Bayesian approaches discussed here, it would be possible to take a similarly proba-bilistic approach that retains much of the power of these models without using Bayes' rule. For instance, the model by Piantadosi and colleagues (in press) could rank hypotheses by some criterion other than posterior prob-ability. One could design a scoring system wherein hypotheses earned points for good fit and desirable calculi, and the hypothesis earning the most points would be the winner. Such a model would likely lead to very similar conclusions but would not technically be Bayesian. The appeal of Bayesian formalisms is that they are already very well studied and well described and are therefore most convenient for researchers to use.

## 5. SUMMARY

The study of early number concepts is a thriving field that provides many insights into the developing mind. As the search for the origins of numerical thought continues, the future researcher has many options. A complete theory must be somewhat rationalist, because children are genetically endowed with at least some abstract numerical concepts. A complete theory must also be somewhat constructivist, because children clearly move beyond the innate building blocks of number, eventually acquiring much more complicated mathematical constructs such as inte-gers, rational numbers, and so on. Bayesian approaches hold great promise in this area, whether as a way of analyzing data, of modeling subjects' performance on individual tasks or of modeling the creation of number concepts themselves.

## AUTHOR NOTE

This material is based upon work supported by the National Science Foundation under DRL-0953521 to the first author. Any opinions, findings, and conclusions or recommendations expressed in this material are those of the authors, and do not necessarily reflect the views of the National Science Foundation.

## REFERENCES

Antell, S. E., & Keating, D. P. (1983). Perception of numerical invariance in neonates. *Child Development, 54*, 695–701.

Barth, H., Slusser, E., Cohen, D., & Paladino, A. (2011). A sense of proportion: Commentary on Opfer, Siegler and Young. *Developmental Science, 14*(5), 1205–1206.

Bijeljac-Babic, R., Bertoncini, J., & Mehler, J. (1993). How do 4-day-old infants categorize multisyllabic utterances? *Developmental Psychology, 29*, 711–721. doi:10.1037/0012-1649.29.4.711.

Block, N. (1987). Advertisement for a Semantics for Psychology. *Midwest Studies in Philosophy, 10*, 615–678. doi:10.1111/j.1475-4975.1987.tb00558.x.

Brannon, E. M., Abbot, S., & Lutz, D. (2004). Number bias for the discrimination of large visual sets in infancy. *Cognition, 93*(2), B59–B68.

Carey, S. (2009). *The origin of concepts.* Boston: MIT Press.

Cohen, D. J., & Blanc-Goldhammer, D. (2011). Numerical bias in bounded and unbounded number line tasks. *Psychonomic Bulletin & Review, 18*, 331–338. doi:10.3758/s13423-011-0059-z.

Condry, K. F., & Spelke, E. S. (2008). The development of language and abstract concepts: The case of natural number. *Journal of Experimental Psychology: General, 137*, 22–38. doi:10.1037/0096-3445.137.1.22.

Cordes, S., Gelman, R., Gallistel, C. R., & Whalen, J. (2001). Variability signatures distinguish verbal and nonverbal counting for both large and small numbers. *Psychonomic Bulletin & Review, 8*(4), 698–707.

Dehaene, S. (1997). *The number sense.* New York: Oxford University Press.

Dickey, J. M., & Lientz, B. P. (1970). The weighted likelihood ratio, sharp hypotheses about chances, the order of a Markov chain. *The Annals of Mathematical Statistics, 42*, 204–223.

Feigenson, L. (2005). A double dissociation in infants' representation of object arrays. *Cognition, 95*, B37–B48.

Feigenson, L., Carey, S., & Hauser, M. (2002). The representations underlying infants' choice of more: Object files versus analog magnitudes. *Psychological Science, 13*(2), 150–156.

Feigenson, L., Dehaene, S., & Spelke, E. (2004). Core systems of number. *Trends in Cognitive Sciences, 8*(7), 307–314.

Feigenson, L., & Halberda, J. (2008). Conceptual knowledge increases infants' memory capacity. *Proceedings of the National Academy of Science of the United States of America, 105*, 9926–9930.

Gallistel, C. R. (1990). *The organization of learning.* Cambridge, MA: Bradford Books/MIT Press.

Gelman, R. (1993). .A rational-constructivist account of early learning about numbers and objects. In D. Medin (Ed.), *Learning and motivation, Vol. 30* (pp. 61–96). New York: Academic Press.

Gelman, A., Carlin, J. B., Stern, H. S. & Rubin, D. B. (1995; 2003). Bayesian data analysis.

Gelman, R., & Gallistel, C. R. (1978). *The child's understanding of number.* Oxford: Harvard University Press.

Izard, V., & Deheane, S. (2008). Calibrating the mental number line. *Cognition, 106*, 1221–1247.

Izard, V., Pica, P., Spelke, E. S., & Dehaene, S. (2008). Exact equality and successor function: Two key concepts on the path towards understanding exact numbers. *Philosophical Psychology, 21*, 491–505.

Jones, M., & Love, B. C. (2011). Bayesian fundamentalism or enlightenment? On the explanatory status and theoretical contributions of bayesian models of cognition. *Behavioral and Brain Sciences, 34*, 169–188.

Kruschke, J. K. (2010). Bridging levels of analysis: Comment on McClelland et al. and Griffiths, et al. *Trends in Cognitive Sciences, 14*, 344–345.

Le Corre, M., & Carey, S. (2007). One, two, three, four, nothing more: An investigation of the conceptual sources of the verbal counting principles. *Cognition, 105*, 395–438.

Le Corre, M., Van de Walle, G., Brannon, E. M., & Carey, S. (2006). Re-visiting the competence/performance debate in the acquisition of the counting principles. *Cognitive Psychology, 52*(2), 130–169.

Lee, M. D. (2010). Emergent and structured cognition in Bayesian models: Comment on Griffiths et al. and McClelland, et al. *Trends in Cognitive Sciences, 14*, 345–346.

Lee, M. D. (2011a). How cognitive modeling can benefit from hierarchical bayesian models. *Journal of Mathematical Psychology, 55*, 1–7.

Lee, M. D. (2011b). In praise of ecumenical bayes. *Behavioral and Brain Sciences, 34*(4), 206–207.

Lee, M. D., & Sarnecka, B. W. (2010). A model of knower-level behavior in number-concept development. *Cognitive Science, 34*, 51–67.

Lee, M. D., & Sarnecka, B. W. (2011). Number-knower levels in young children: Insights from Bayesian modeling. *Cognition, 120*, 391–402.

Lipton, J. S., & Spelke, E. S. (2004). Discrimination of large and small numerosities by human infants. *Infancy, 5*(3), 271–290.

MacWhinney, B. (2000). *The CHILDES Project: Tools for analyzing talk.* (3rd ed.). Mahwah, NJ: Lawrence Erlbaum Associates.

Masson, M. E. (2011). A tutorial on a practical Bayesian alternative to null-hypothesis significance testing. *Behavior Research Methods, 43*(3), 679–690.

McCrink, K., & Wynn, K. (2004). Large number addition and subtraction by 9-month-old infants. *Psychological Science, 23*(3), 776–781.

Mechner, F., & Guevrekian, K. (1962). Effects of deprivation upon counting and timing in rats. *Journal of the Experimental Analysis of Behavior, 5*, 463–466.

Meck, W. H., & Church, R. M. (1983). *Journal of Experimental Psychology: Animal Behavior Processes, 9*, 320–334. doi:10.1037/0097-7403.9.3.320.

Moyer, R. S., & Landauer, T. K. (1967). Time required for judgements of numerical inequality. *Nature, 215*, 1519–1520.

Negen, J. & Sarnecka, B.W. (in press). Number-concept acquisition and general vocabulary development. *Child Development*

Negen, J., & Sarnecka, B. W. (under review). Early number learning and the approximate number system: Re-visiting the variability argument.

Nieder, A., & Miller, E. K. (2003). Coding of cognitive magnitude: Compressed scaling of numerical information in the primate prefrontal cortex. *Neuron, 37*, 149–157.

Perfors, A., Tenenbaum, J. B., Griffiths, T. L.,, & Xu, F. (2011). A tutorial introduction to Bayesian models of cognitive development. *Cognition, 120*, 302–321.

Piantadosi, S. P., Tenenbaum, J. B., & Goodman, N. D. (in press). Bootstrapping in a language of thought: a formal model of numerical concept learning. *Cognition, 123*, 199–217. http://dx.doi.org/10.1016/j.cognition.2011.11.005

Platt, J. R., & Johnson, D. M. (1971). Localization of position within a homogenous behavior chain: Effects of error contingencies. *Learning and Motivation, 2*(4), 386–414.

Quine, W. V. O. (1960). *Word and Object.* Cambridge: MIT Press.

Rips, L. J., Asmuth, J., & Bloomfield, A. (2006). Giving the boot to the bootstrap: How not to learn the natural numbers. *Cognition, 101*, B51–B60.

Rips, L. J., Bloomfield, A., & Asmuth, J. (2008). From numerical concepts to concepts of number. *Behavioral and Brain Sciences, 31*, 623–642.

Rouder, J. N., Speckman, P. L., Sun, D., Morey, R. D., & Iverson, G. (2009). Bayesian t tests for accepting and rejecting the null hypothesis. *Psychonomic Bulletin and Review, 16*(2), 225.

Sarnecka, B. W., & Gelman, S. A. (2004). Six does not just mean a lot: Preschoolers see number words as specific. *Cognition, 92*, 329–352.

Sarnecka, B. W., & Carey, S. (2008). How counting represents number: What children must learn and when they learn it. *Cognition, 108*, 662–674. doi:10.1016/j.cognition.2008.05.007.

Sarnecka, B. W., Kamenskaya, V. G., Yamana, Y., Ogura, T., & Yudovina, Y. B. (2007). From grammatical number to exact numbers: Early meanings of 'one,' 'two,' and 'three' in English, Russian and Japanese. *Cognitive Psychology, 55*, 136–168. http://dx.doi.org/10.1016/j.cogpsych.2006.09.001.

Sarnecka, B. W., & Lee, M. D. (2009). Levels of number knowledge in early childhood. *Journal of Experimental Child Psychology, 103*, 325–337. http://dx.doi.org/10.1016/j.jecp.2009.02.007.

Sarnecka, B. W. & Wright, C. E. (in press). The exact-numbers idea: Children's understanding of cardinality and equinumerosity. *Cognitive Science*.

Schaeffer, B., Eggleston, V. H., & Scott, J. L. (1974). Number development in young children. *Cognitive Psychology, 6*, 357–379.

Siegler, R. S., Thompson, C. A., & Opfer, J. E. (2009). The logarithmic-to-linear shift: One learning sequence, many tasks, many time scales. *Mind, Brain, and Education, 3*(3), 143–150.

Slusser, E., Ditta, A., & Sarnecka, B. W. (under review). Connecting numbers to discrete quantification: A step in the child's construction of integer concepts.

Slusser, E. B., & Sarnecka, B. W. (2011a, March). Extending representations of discrete and continuous quantities to early number-word learning. Paper given as part of symposium "The development of discrete and continuous quantification from infancy to childhood" (M. Le Corre & P. Cheung, Chairs) at the biennial meeting of the Society for Research in Child Development, Montreal, Canada.

Slusser, E., & Sarnecka, B. W. (2011b). Find the picture of eight turtles: A link between children's counting and their knowledge of number-word semantics. *Journal of Experimental Child Psychology, 110*, 38–51. doi:10.1016/j.jecp.2011.03.006, PMC3105118 [Available 2012/9/1].

Starkey, P., & Cooper, R. G. (1980). Perception of numbers by human infants. *Science, 210*(4473), 1033–1035.

Sullivan, J., & Barner, D. (2010). Mapping number words to approximate magnitudes: Associative learning or structure mapping?. In *Proceedings of the 32nd Annual Conference of the Cognitive Science Society* Austin, TX: Cognitive Science Society.

Thomas, A. (1994). BUGS: A statistical modelling package. *RTA/BCS Modular Languages Newsletter, 2*, 36–38.

Whalen, J., Gallistel, C. R., & Gelman, R. (1999). Nonverbal counting in humans: The psychophysics of number representation. Psychological Science, *10*, 130–137.

Wood, J. N., & Spelke, E. S. (2005). Infants' enumeration of actions: numerical discrimination and its signature limits. *Developmental Science, 8*, 173–181. doi:10.1111/j.1467-7687.2005.00404.x.

Wynn, K. (1996). Infants' individuation and enumeration of actions. Developmental Science, 7, 164–169. doi:10.1111/j.1467-9280.1996.tb00350.x.

Wynn, K. (1990). Children's understanding of counting. *Cognition, 36*(2), 155–193.

Wynn, K. (1992a). Addition and subtraction in human infants. *Nature, 358*(6389), 749–750.

Wynn, K. (1992b). Children's acquisition of number words and the counting system. *Cognitive Psychology, 24*(2), 220–251.

Wynn, K. (1996). Infants' individuation and enumeration of actions. *Psychological Science, 7*, 164–169. doi:10.1111/j.1467-9280.1996.tb00350.x.

Xu, F. (2003). Numerosity discrimination in infants: Evidence for two systems of representations. *Cognition, 89*, B15–B25.

Xu, F., & Spelke, E. S. (2000). Large number discrimination in 6-month old infants. *Cognition, 74*(1), B1–B11.

Xu, F., Spelke, E. S., & Goddard, S. (2005). Number sense in human infants. *Developmental Science, 8*(1), 88–101.

CHAPTER TEN

# Finding New Facts; Thinking New Thoughts

## Laura Schulz

Department of Brain and Cognitive Sciences, Massachusetts Institute of Technology, Boston, Massachusetts
E-mail: lschulz@mit.edu

## Contents

## Abstract

The idea of the child as an active learner is one of Piaget's enduring legacies. In this chapter, I discuss the ways in which contemporary computational models of learning do, and do not, address learning as an active, child-driven process. In Part 1, I discuss the problem of search and exploration. In Part 2, I discuss the (harder and more interesting) problem of hypothesis generation. I conclude by proposing some possible new directions for research.

Constructivism is a clunky word. Arguably, however, only such a ponderous term could stand up to those venerable pillars of epistemology: nativism and empiricism. In contrast to both, Piaget insisted that learning was driven by interactions between the child's representations and her experience of the environment. Today, we can express this insight with mathematical precision; prior hypotheses constrain our interpretation of evidence and affect whether and how we revise our beliefs from evidence (see Tenenbaum, Kemp, Griffiths, & Goodman, 2011, for exposition and review). In adding

*Advances in Child Development and Behavior*, Volume 43
ISSN 0065-2407,
http://dx.doi.org/10.1016/B978-0-12-397919-3.00010-1

clarity and rigor to concepts like accommodation and assimilation, computational models introduced rational analyses to constructivism and motivated much of the enterprise to which this volume pays homage. A decade of empirical support speaks to the success of this approach (Gopnik & Wellman, 2012; Schulz, 2012). In this chapter, however, and mindful of the mandate to reflect critically on "needed theoretical, technological, and empirical advances," I will focus on an idea that is critical to the constructivist vision but largely missing from contemporary accounts of learning: the idea of the child as an active learner.

Consider this passage, written in 1937:

> Such construction is not the act of an a priori deduction, nor is it due to purely empirical gropings. The sequence ... testifies much more strongly to progressive comprehension than to haphazard achievements. If there is experimentation, the experiments are directed.
>
> **Piaget, The Construction of Reality in the Child.**

The excerpt refers to the development of the infants' object concept. Never mind the details (which are wrong; Baillargeon & Luo, 2002; Spelke, 1999; Spelke, Brinlinger, Macomber, & Jacobson, 1992). For my purposes, Piaget's central claim is not a less rigorous, less precise instantiation of the Bayesian idea that prior knowledge and evidence interact. The central claim is that the child actively seeks to understand the world.

What might *active learning* mean? It could mean what we sometimes mean by "hands-on learning": that children like to do things and that the things they do can sometimes generate evidence that supports new inferences. Such activities, however, presumably fall under the purview of "empirical gropings." Piaget's claim is stronger. He suggests that the child generates hypotheses about how the world works and that the child's actions—starting with literal manipulations of objects but ending in "cognitive acts" ranging from mental rotation to thought experiments—are systematic attempts to understand how the world works.

As someone who putatively works on exploration and active learning in early childhood, I find it hard to overstate the degree to which this vision of active learning is absent from current research on cognitive development (my own included). Even my writing betrays this; I find myself repeatedly opting for periphrastic locutions ("make inferences"; "distinguish hypotheses") over verbs that more clearly ascribe intentional activity to the child: "thought," "decided," "wondered," and "tried." To the degree that grammar is "the metaphysics of the people" (Nietzsche, 1882, 1974), I would seem to be an agnostic about active learning.

This grammatical timidity is due in part to the problematic nature of making claims about children's internal states. However, I think the phrasing also accurately reflects the current state of our theories of learning. It is one thing to talk about how learners draw rational inferences from data; it is another to suggest that children actively work to construct new knowledge. The latter commitment poses at least two problems that current accounts of cognitive development elide.

First, accounts of cognitive development have focused primarily on problems of inductive inference. Principles of induction have implications for but do not directly address problems equally critical to learning: problems of search, exploration, or decision making. Thus, our current accounts of constructivism tend to stop precisely where the active part of active learning begins.

The second and to my mind more fascinating problem (impatient readers should skip directly to Problem Two) is that, we routinely generate new ideas without having access to new data. With all due respect to the innovative proposals currently in play, we still do not understand how learners think of new ideas. The hard part of this problem goes beyond a search problem. I think a precise formal solution to this problem is a ways off but I will talk about what I think is missing from the current proposals and suggest possible new directions for research.

## 1. PROBLEM 1: EXPLORING

Why do we explore? Intuitively, we explore either when we encounter something surprising or when we encounter something (even a perfectly ordinary something) that we cannot explain. Bayes' law can illustrate the common principle underlying these two seemingly quite different motivational states.

Bayes' law states that the learner's belief in a hypothesis after observing evidence, the *posterior probability of the hypothesis*, $P(h|e)$, is proportional to both to its *likelihood*, $P(e|h)$, the probability that the hypothesis, if true, would have generated the observed evidence, and its *prior probability*, $P(h)$, the probability that the hypothesis is generated by the learner's background theories. Formally: $P(h|e) \propto P(e|h)P(h)$.

If the posterior probability (the probability of the hypothesis given the evidence) of two or more hypotheses is approximately equivalent ($P(h1|e) \approx P(h2|e)$), the learner will be uncertain which hypothesis is true. This can occur either if the prior probability favors one hypothesis and the likelihood another

(P(e|h1) < P(e|h2) and P(h1) > P(h2)) or if the prior probability and the likelihood of multiple hypothesis are equivalent (e.g. P(h1) ≈ P(h2) and P(e|h1) ≈ P(e|h2)). The first is a formalization of what it means for evidence to be surprising; the second is a formalization of what it means for evidence to be confounded. Thus Bayes' law provides an intuitive account of why exploration in the face of surprise and confounding derive from a common principle.

So far, so good, and numerous empirical studies attest to the fact that children selectively explore when confronted either with theory-violating evidence (Bonawitz, van Schijndel, Friel, & Schulz, 2012) or with evidence that is confounded (Schulz & Bonawitz, 2007). Patently, however, both children and adults can experience inductive uncertainty without engaging in exploration. Understanding when and why children do or do not engage in exploration will require understanding both how children decide when exploration is valuable and how children know what exploratory actions to take. These processes are not independent (e.g. the learner's assessment of the value of exploration depends on her assessment of the availability of potentially informative actions). However, progress has been made on each of these fronts across quite different disciplines, suggesting the possibility that an integrated approach to understanding exploration could predict and explain more of children's behavior.

## 1.1. Knowing When to Explore

When children explore, there are other things they are not doing. Children have to decide when the potential advantages of exploration exceed the costs. A number of fields, including machine learning (Gittens, 1979; Kaebling, 1993; Kaelbling, Littman, & Moore, 1996; Kaelbling, Littman, & Cassandra, 1998; Tong & Koller, 2001), decision making (Sutton & Barto, 1998), neuroscience (Daw, Niv, & Dayan, 2005; Daw, O'Doherty, Dayan, Seymour, & Dolan, 2006; McClure, Daw, & Read Montague, 2003), and ethology (Charnov, 1976, 2006; Krebs, Kacelnik, & Taylor, 1978; Stephens & Krebs, 1996), have proposed resolutions to such exploration/exploitation dilemmas. These accounts suggest search strategies that consider various reward functions and constraints on the organism and maximize the expected cost to benefit ratio of staying in a given state relative to transitioning to a new one (predicting, for instance, that organisms should stay longer at a food patch as the distance between patches increases; Charnov, 1976).

If applied to problems of learning in early childhood, comparable approaches might help predict and explain children's exploratory behavior beyond what can be explained by epistemic uncertainty alone. It seems intuitive, for instance, that children will be more likely to explore in contexts where there are just a few plausible hypotheses than when there are many. However, formalizing even such simple intuitions requires integrating problems of inductive inference with a consideration of the relative value of exploratory actions (e.g. if the same action can eliminate a single hypothesis from consideration across cases, the potential for information gain is greater when hypotheses are fewer).

Typically, however, solutions to exploration/exploitation dilemmas have been proposed, not for challenging learning problems but for cases where the epistemic component is relatively straightforward. In particular, optimal search processes have been developed to maximize rewards when the distribution of rewards is uncertain but arbitrary (e.g. rewards distributed among slot machines with different payoffs (Daw et al., 2006; Gittins, 1989; Strehl et al., 2006), decks of cards with different values (Bechara, Damasio, Tranel, & Damasio, 1997; Sang, Todd, & Goldstone, 2011), or food patches with different caloric and nutritional worth (Kacelnik & Bateson, 1996; Stephens & Krebs, 1986).[1] Although the organism's search may be affected by rational considerations of expected costs and benefits, such search processes nonetheless arguably remain closer to "empirical groping" than to constructivism. The search process is not random but neither is it guided by an abstract theory of the domain. Arbitrary distributions of rewards are unlikely to lend themselves to "progressive comprehension."

Recently, however, researchers in machine learning have begun to consider how search might proceed in domains that support more structured representations. Robots, for instance, may start with a map of the terrain and search for efficient routes to a goal within the terrain (Leonard & Durrant-Whyte, 1991). Researchers have also begun to address chicken-and-egg problems of exploration: designing robots that can simultaneously use a map to evaluate the expected utility of various state transitions and use the information gained during exploration to revise the map (Durrant-Whyte & Bailey, 2006; Thrun, Burgard, & Fox, 2005). Although these particular approaches only solve these problems for finite two-dimensional spaces, they offer a hint as to how we might begin to formalize the idea of theory-guided and theory-shaping exploration in higher dimensional spaces.

---

[1] Of course, the actual distribution of calories across patches is not arbitrary; in the case of food patches, it is more accurate to say that the foraging animal is presumably ignorant of the biological and ecological factors that affect the distribution of rewards.

Such approaches would seem to lend themselves well to an understanding of the exploratory aspect of constructivism. If we can consider the relative utility of competing courses of action in the context of hierarchical representations of the domain being explored, we might be able to better explain both when exploration is likely to occur and how the child's exploration is likely to transform the child's knowledge. A full analysis of the relative costs and benefits of different actions may be intractable, such an account would have to consider not only the value of non-exploratory behaviors—playing, eating, daydreaming—to the child but also the effect of the child's culture, temperament, upbringing, and individual interests on how she perceives the value of the information she might gain through exploration. Nonetheless, advancing our understanding of how children assess the relative value of information gain seems critical, given that competing utilities can have determinative effects on learning.

## 1.2. Knowing How to Explore

Understanding the expected utility of exploratory actions helps answer the question of *when* the child should engage in exploration. However, the child must know not only that there is information to be gained but also *how* precisely to gain it. Even the simplest forms of exploratory behavior raise questions about how humans (Adolph, Eppler, & Gibson, 1993; Berger, Adolph, & Lobo, 2005; Brown, 1990; Gibson, 1977; Lockman, 2000; Norman, 1988, 1999) and other animals (Brauer, Kaminski, Reidel, Call, & Tomasello, 2006; Emery & Clayton, 2004; Hood, Carey, & Prasada, 2000; Mendes, Hanus, & Call, 2007; Stulp, Emery, Verhulst, & Clayton, 2009) learn to recognize the possible actions that the environment affords. Nonetheless, in cases where there is a direct mapping between an action and information gain, the question of how to explore has a relatively straightforward answer: act on the entity with greatest uncertainty (e.g. by pulling a lever, putting a block on a machine, or lifting a card to learn its value; see Oaksford & Chater, 1994).

Sometimes, however, no single action available to the learner will support information gain. The learner may have to plan a complex series of actions in order to isolate variables or may have to resign herself to the fact that isolating the relevant variables is impractical or impossible. Effectively generating informative evidence requires combining an understanding of the probability of information gain together with an understanding of the affordances that might permit it.

In principle, children might both learn from informative evidence (see Gopnik & Wellman, 2012; Schulz, 2012, for review) and engage in exploration when they observe uninformative evidence (Schulz & Bona-witz, 2007) without understanding either what it is about evidence that makes it informative or how to generate such evidence. However, we now know that at least in very simple contexts, children have both of these abilities. Preschoolers, for instance, not only selectively explore when they are uncertain which of two connected beads activate a toy, they also separate the beads and test each one individually. Moreover, if the beads cannot be detached, children orient the connected bead so that only a single bead makes contact with the toy at a time (Cook, Goodman, & Schulz, 2011). Thus, preschoolers seem to understand not only when there is potential for information gain but also the probability that particular actions will generate data relevant to a particular hypothesis (see also Sodian, Zaitchik, & Carey, 1991).

Needless to say, the real world rarely makes it so easy. Part of what distinguishes science from cognition more broadly is the cultural accumulation of tools and knowledge that can support information gain in ways that go well beyond naive exploration. However, at least in simple contexts, researchers have made progress in analyzing and formalizing the cognitive processes involved in optimizing information gain (Cook et al., 2011; Klayman, 1988; Klayman & Ha, 1987; Oaksford & Chater, 1994; Sobel & Kushnir, 2006; Steyvers, Tenenbaum, Wagonmakers, & Blum, 2003). To the degree that we can show how these abilities manifest in infants and young children, we may come closer to understanding of what it means for children to actively construct knowledge.

## 2. PROBLEM 2: THINKING

Thus far I have focused on how children might construct new knowledge by gathering more data. Arguably, however, the distinguishing attribute of human cognition is that we can arrive at new ideas—some of which turn out to be true—merely by thinking of them. How is this possible?

As noted, hierarchical Bayesian inference models provide an elegant account of how learners integrate theories on different levels of abstraction with the interpretation of new evidence. They thus provide a way of thinking about some key points of comparison between scientific inference and cognition in early childhood (see Gopnik, in press; Gopnik, & Wellman, 2012; Schulz, 2012). In light of the ways that probabilistic inference models have revolutionized cognitive science (Tenenbaum et al., 2011), it might seem churlish to suggest that they do not really address the core issue at the heart of constructivism. However, these models explain how learners select among competing hypotheses; for the most part, they do not attempt to explain how learners construct hypotheses in the first place. They tell us how we might choose the best idea from the ideas we have but they do not tell us how we might think of something new.

Note that the problem of how we think of new ideas is not reducible to the (also interesting) problem of how to make Bayesian inference algorithmically tractable (Bonawitz chapter, this volume; Bonawitz & Griffiths, 2010; Sanborn, Griffiths, & Navarro, 2010; Shi, Feldman, & Griffiths, 2008).[2] As Bonawitz et al. note, in simple cases, all the relevant hypotheses may be available to the learner in principle if not at any given moment. Given, for instance, three colors of chips that activate a machine, the learner might believe the machine is activated only by red chips but can also entertain the possibility that it is activated only by blue chips, only by green chips, only by red and blue chips, etc. Monte Carlo (randomized, sampling-based) algorithms provide an efficient way to search among the hypotheses. The idea of inference by rationally randomized sampling (i.e. sampling from hypotheses with the highest posterior probability) also reconciles the empirical evidence of variability in children's learning with ideal Bayesian analysis; the learner can entertain only a single hypothesis at a time and nonetheless converge on the correct hypothesis. However, efficiently sampling hypotheses is not the same as constructing them.

## 3. THEORY-GUIDED STOCHASTIC SEARCH

A closer approximation to constructivist learning comes from a family of computational models, which suggest that learners have a "grammar" for generating potentially infinitely many hypotheses (Goodman, Ullman, &

---

[2] The problem of how we think of new ideas is also distinct from the so-called "old evidence" problem (Glymour, 1980). The supposed problem is that you can't learn anything from old evidence because once evidence is known, it has a prior probability of $1 (p(e) = 1)$, therefore also a likelihood of $1 (p(e|h) = 1)$ and a posterior probability of $1 (p(h|e) = 1)$. This would contradict our intuition that, for instance, well-known anomalies in Mercury's orbit provided evidential support for Einstein's theory of relativity. There are many responses to this (Eels, 1982; Garber, 1983; Howson, 1985), most of which dispute the grounds for assuming that $p(e)$ and $p(e|h) = 1$. However, the point here is simply that the old evidence problem is different from the problem of how we generate new hypotheses in the first place. Thanks to the editors for suggesting that I draw this distinction.

Tenenbaum, 2011; Tenenbaum, Griffiths, & Niyogi, 2007; Ullman, Goodman, & Tenenbaum, 2012). If the learner's initial theory fails to account for the data in some respect, she can engage in a sampling-based stochastic search process, proposing randomized changes to the hypothesis, constrained by the prior probability that the grammar will generate the new hypothesis. Efficient learning is further enabled by "templates": grammatical predicates that encode common logical, causal, or constitutive relations (e.g. transitive relationships among variables). Rather than only constructing new hypotheses piecemeal, the learner can sample from the space of existing templates. The stochastic search through the "outer loop" of the hypothesis space is then grounded out by a search through an "inner loop," testing how well the new candidate hypothesis applies to the learner's observations. If the new hypothesis predicts the data better than the previous hypothesis, the new hypothesis is likely to be accepted. In simulated experiments, this approach shows dynamic features commensurate with what we know about children's learning: individual learning curves are variable but learning on average is predictable, often following characteristic sequences of transitions and typically proceeding from simpler to more complex hypotheses.

This approach represents an exciting and welcome development. Rather than simply describing data-driven learning, the account of theory acquisition as stochastic search explains how structured representations can change in the absence of new evidence. In this, it seems to capture some of what we mean by "thinking." And may be search by means of random variation and selection is enough. Certainly, evolution testifies to the power of random variation, together with the re-use of components that have functioned well in the past. Perhaps, thought does not require any more intelligence in its design than life itself.

Perhaps. However, with only the minimal constraints of simplicity, grammaticality, and previously productive templates, changes to hypotheses generated by random variation seems at best inefficient. More importantly, our minds seem to have access to rich sources of information that could better constrain the process of hypothesis generation and that current approaches do not exploit. I will discuss these additional possible constraints on hypothesis generation in the hopes that they might inspire new directions for both computational and empirical research. As will be obvious, all the ideas to follow are shamelessly speculative. I am taking advantage of the genre of "chapter" rather than "journal paper" to advance ideas that are just at their inception. However, begging the reader's indulgence for the paucity of detail, I hope this attempt to think new thoughts about thinking new thoughts might at least spark conversation.

## 4. ABSTRACT ERROR MAPS AS CONSTRAINTS ON HYPOTHESIS GENERATION

The first kind of knowledge that could help guide a learner's search for new ideas is an abstract representation of the flaws in her current theory, what we might call an "error map." Here, I mean not a record of individual prediction errors but a more abstract inference drawn from them: a representation of the kind of errors being made and the relationship among those errors. That is, much as the learner can draw inferences from individual events to abstract categories and relationships, the learner might draw inductive inferences from specific prediction errors to general kinds of errors and the relations among them.

I will spell this idea out in the examples to follow. First, however, I want to stress that my use of the phrase "error map" is provisional. As I discuss below, the gaps that matter can occur not just between hypotheses and data but also between hypotheses and explanatory desiderata or between hypotheses and functional goals. Thus, the notion of error here refers to something less like a prediction error and more like the learner's subjective error signal and her abstract representation of why her current hypothesis is unsatisfactory. It might be better to think of these as "gap maps," "goodness-of-fit maps," or simply "maps of our discontents." Nonetheless, in many cases, these gaps present as prediction errors (including both events that the learner predicted wrongly and those she failed to predict at all), so for the time being I will stick with the notion of error maps.

In almost any conventional approach to learning (whether connectionist or Bayesian; McClelland, 1988; Munakata & McClelland, 2003; Ullman et al., 2012), prediction errors inform hypothesis selection. All else being equal, learners will retain new hypotheses that improve the fit to the data and reject those that do not. However, even in theory-guided stochastic search (Ullman et al., 2012), prediction errors are put to use only at the stage of hypothesis selection, *after* a new hypothesis has been generated. Suppose instead that learners could use a representation of the gaps between their current hypotheses and the evidence to constrain the process by which they generate new ideas in the first place. If so, many simple, grammatical changes to the current hypothesis that would be randomly generated only to be rejected will not even be attempted; the constraints imposed by such an abstract error map might mean that learners could recognize a priori that most of the new ideas she could generate are unlikely to solve her problem.

## 5. AN EXAMPLE: MAKING SENSE OF NOISE

Imagine, for instance, a child who knows many things about airplanes and many things about phones. However, nothing in her intuitive theory of airplanes or phones predicts that passengers will be asked to turn off their phones on take-off. She does not have the concept of radio interference and (like many of us, albeit for rather different reasons) she wants to understand why you have to turn off your phone on the airplane. Now imagine that the child's only option is to randomly add or delete simple, logical predicates that have a high probability given her prior beliefs about airplanes and phones. She could connect the two artifacts with infinitely many simple constitutive, causal, or other relational claims consistent with her prior beliefs and expressible in the grammar of her theories: perhaps airplanes, like phones, have push buttons; perhaps airplanes and phones are both manu-factured in Ohio; perhaps airplanes fly over the earth, and the earth has phones, so airplanes sometimes fly over phones. On any account, these hypotheses, once generated, will be swiftly rejected because none predicts that you should shut off your phone when flying. But the odds of converging on a valuable new idea through this kind of process seem, prima facie, low.

Suppose instead that the child can constrain the space in which she generates hypotheses by availing herself of an abstract representation of the problem: the unanticipated but evident incompatibility between planes and phones. She need not bother hypothesizing that planes and phones have infinitely many commensurable features. She can randomly generate only hypotheses in which some feature of planes is in conflict with some feature of phones. In this way, she might selectively generate hypotheses that are recognizably "good" hypotheses (in that, if true, they would solve the problem), even though they might not be "good" with respect to their truth value. Consider, for instance, the following (true) anecdote:

Adele (age 4): "Mommy, I know why they make you turn off your phone when the plane is taking off."

Me: "Oh really? Why?"

Adele: "Because when the plane takes off it's too noisy to talk on the phone."

## 6. GOOD WRONG IDEAS AND BAD ONES

This is of course wrong; it is wrong even about the direction of causality. At the same time, it is recognizably a good hypothesis. And it is a remarkable feature of human cognition that we can simultaneously recognize the "goodness" of an idea and its falsity. I suggest that we can do this is because we evaluate a new idea first on the extent to which it is consistent with the constraints of our abstract error map and only subsequently on its truth value or fit to the data.

The idea that a learner first generates and evaluates hypotheses through the constraints of an abstract error map (and only secondarily through an "inner-loop" checking the degree to which the hypothesis accounts for the data) predicts many features of human cognition that seem intuitively to be true. For instance, we seem to know that we are on the right (or wrong) track in thinking about a problem well before we know whether our ideas generate better fits to the data. Arguably this is because the ideas we generate may have (or lack) key features of the abstract form of the solution to a problem well before they are in fact solutions to the problem. Similarly, we seem to have an internal "stopping function" that lets us know we have arrived at a good idea (or lets us dismiss an idea out of hand) well before we have tested its predictions. Our "ah ha" moments (see Gopnik, 2000) can come months, even years, before we have any evidence that our great new breakthrough idea is true; indeed, even when our great new breakthrough turns out to be false, it might only slightly diminish our sense of its brilliance. This is reasonable if our criterion for the elegance of an idea is its congruence with an error map, rather than with the world. Finally, we seem to have an intuitive sense of how tractable problems are, even in cases where tractability does not reduce to technological or resource limitations. In such cases what it might mean for a problem to be tractable is that the representation of the problem—the abstract error map—sufficiently constrains the search space for new hypotheses. If this account is correct then learning might sometimes be facilitated not by changing our prior beliefs or the evidence but merely by changing how we represent the gap between them. As one outstanding generator of new hypotheses put it: "The formulation of the problem may be more important than the solution, which may simply be a matter of mathematical or experimental skill" (Einstein, in Chang, 2006, p. 179).

## 7. ABSTRACT ERROR MAPS AND VARIABILITY IN LEARNING

As researchers have noted (see Bonawitz chapter, this volume), sampling-based approaches to Bayesian inference can help account for individual differences in children's learning. It is interesting to consider how adding error maps as a top–down constraint on hypothesis generation might affect individual variability in learning.

Imagine, for instance, two children, Jane and Michael. Borrowing and extending the Ullman et al. (2012) example, suppose both children have an incorrect theory of magnetism. The children are playing with magnets, paperclips, and pennies but believe that they are playing with magnets and non-magnets; they have failed to consider the possibility that paperclips belong in a third category: ferrous non-magnets. Suppose further, that the children have mis-categorized the paperclips in different ways. Jane (who has noticed some magnetized paperclips sticking together) has classified the paperclips as magnets; Michael has classified them with the pennies, as non-magnets. The children's different subtheories generate slightly different prediction errors. Jane wrongly predicts that any paperclip will interact with any other paperclip. When she gets data to the contrary, she will have to explain how magnetism might sometimes disappear. Michael wrongly predicts that no paperclip will interact with any other paperclip; he will have to explain how magnetism could sometimes appear.

This asymmetry may lead the children to generate quite different abstract representations of the problem and different abstract criteria that constrain their search for new ideas. Jane is trying to generate new hypotheses that satisfy the (perceived) desiderata of including a variable whose value can diminish over time. Thus, Jane may come up, for instance, with the idea that magnetism is a kind of energetic force that (like the energy in batteries) sometimes runs out. Michael, by contrast, represents the problem as a problem of explaining the unexpected appearance of a rare property (rather than the less surprising problem of explaining its diminishment or disappearance). Michael may thus be faster to recognize that only objects made of specific materials can become magnetized and that they can be magnetized only immediately after the relatively rare event of contacting a magnet.

Each of these different error maps may lead to new hypotheses that get different things right and wrong. Jane may correctly think of magnetism as an energetic force but overlook the role of the particular materials; Michael may recognize that the property of magnetism can be transferred from some materials to others but fail to subsume magnetism into the more general category of a kind of energy. In short, because learners' theories constrain what they represent as errors or gaps in their understanding, learners with even subtly different theories may generate different abstract representations of the problems they are trying to solve. To the degree that these different abstract error maps constrain the generation of new hypotheses, differences in the ways that learners represent the problem they are solving could lead to quite different learning outcomes.

## 8. ABSTRACT ERROR MAPS, QUINIAN BOOTSTRAPPING, AND ANALOGICAL REASONING

The ideas behind theory grammars and stochastic search (Goodman et al., 2011; Ullman et al., 2012) were themselves partly motivated by another account of how learners might move beyond hypothesis selection: Quinian bootstrapping (Carey, 2009). Quinian bootstrapping is a proposal for how learners might generate genuinely new representational resources. Two key ideas are critical to the account. Quinian bootstrapping depends first on the learner having access to explicit symbols (e.g. through language or mathematics). These enable the learner to develop representations whose meaning is genuinely novel in that it inheres in the relationship among the symbols rather than only in earlier concepts (see also Block, 1986). The learner can then use these to construct "placeholder" representations that support inductive inferences about the specific role and meaning of the new concepts.[3] For instance, a child may notice the similarity between the order of words in the count list and words corresponding to larger analog magnitudes. The words then serve as a placeholder representation allowing the child to bootstrap an explicit representational system in which she infers the meaning of the number words.

---

[3] The computational proposals echo this insofar as variables get their meaning from their relationship to other terms in the theory grammar and serve as placeholder concepts (Goodman et al., 2011; Ullman et al., 2012).

This brief description in no way does justice to the work (see Carey, 2009, for exposition and review; see also Herme & Spelke, 1996 and Spelke, 2003). Here I merely want to note that the current proposal is both indebted to and compatible with these ideas. In the number example, for instance, neither the child's earliest understanding of the count list nor her representation of analog magnitudes predicts any similarity between the two. Insofar as the child is able to constrain the new ideas, she generates to just those that posit a commonality between the count list and analog magnitudes, one could think of that as a constraint on hypothesis generation imposed by an abstract error map.

Arguably, however, the current proposal is more general than the case of Quinian bootstrapping in two respects. First, learning need not depend on the learner's exposure to explicit linguistic or mathematical symbols nor the learner happening to notice analogical mappings between representations. To the degree that the learner can formulate an abstract representation of the gaps between her current hypotheses and the evidence (i.e. by categorizing the problem as one involving an unexpected conflict between two variables, a diminishing property, an appearing property), she might constrain the new hypotheses she generates to those that might fill the gap.

Second, real discontinuities in development (e.g. manifest in the development of the child's understanding of number or the development of the child's ability to differentiate weight and density; see Carey, 2009, for exposition and review) are compelling case studies in hypothesis generation. However, there are many more mundane instances of hypothesis generation (e.g. as manifest in Adele's explanation of airplane regulations) that do not involve radical conceptual change but are also not merely data driven. Even in such ordinary cases, there is a real puzzle about how learners think of new ideas. Nothing in the current account depends on the incommensurability of earlier and later ideas or requires the construction of altogether new mental symbols. Constraints imposed by abstract error maps might support the generation of new ideas quite broadly.

Finally, considering more narrowly just the role of analogical reasoning (Christie & Gentner, 2010; Gentner et al., 1997; Gentner, 2002; Gentner, Holyoak, & Kokinov, 2001; Gentner & Markman, 1997; Gentner & Namy, 1999; Gentner & Smith, 2012; Holyoak & Thagard, 1996), it seems clear that once we have an analogy—either because the relevant relationships are given to us pedagogically or because we ourselves notice a surprising coincidence in structural relations across events[4]—it constrains the hypotheses we generate (Christie & Gentner, 2010). What makes learning difficult, however, is that fruitful analogical relations are not always obvious; the critical question is how we know what kinds of events can be meaningfully compared. In principle, abstract error maps might serve as higher order constraints, constraining even the kinds of analogies we generate. If, for instance, you represent a problem as a problem involving dissipating properties, you can then consider other kinds of events that involve dissipating properties. In this way, you might arrive at an analogy, for instance, between paperclips losing their sticking power and batteries losing their charge.

Importantly, however, even when our abstract representation of a problem does *not* generate meaningful analogies, it can still effectively constrain hypothesis generation. If, for instance, we represent being asked to turn off our phone on the plane as a problem of an unexpected incompatibility between events, we can restrict our hypotheses to potential incompatibilities between phones and planes without analogical reasoning per se. Similarly, if we represent the problem of sticking paperclips as the problem of the unexpected appearance or transfer of a property, we can constrain our hypotheses to those involving specific materials or rare events without comparing these events to structurally similar ones. Thus, I suggest that analogical reasoning is an effective constraint on hypothesis generation insofar as it constrained by the more general ability to come up with an abstract representation of problems in the first place—and this representation can constrain hypothesis generation in ways that extend beyond analogical reasoning.

## 9. FUNCTIONAL ROLES AS CONSTRAINTS ON HYPOTHESIS GENERATION

So far I have discussed constraints on hypothesis generation that are, so to speak, epistemically respectable. Constraints imposed by abstract error maps

---

[4] I suggest that the learner starts with an abstract representation of a problem and this can constrain the kinds of analogies she generates. Sometimes, however, the learner may observe an unexpected structural alignment between events and register this alignment as a coincidence in need of explanation (Griffiths & Tenenbaum, 2007). If the learner happens to start with an analogy she is looking to explain (rather than starting with a problem and looking for analogies that might elucidate it), the analogy may itself support the construction of an abstract error map, constraining the learner's generation of new hypotheses to those that might explain the otherwise surprising relational alignment.

plausibly increase the probability that we will get at least some aspects of the world right. Intuitively, however, there are less truth-preserving, but arguably no less advantageous, considerations that seem to constrain the ideas we generate.

Specifically, we have goals for our ideas. We want our ideas to do things: to persuade, cajole, impress, explain, deceive, entertain, or instruct. We can readily distinguish "good" and "bad" ideas on prudential grounds independent of the extent to which they get the facts right. Given that we can evaluate ideas with respect to our goals, it seems plausible that we might also use our goals to constrain the ways we construct knowledge in the first place. To the degree that we propose randomized changes to our current hypotheses subject to the constraint of an abstract representation of what function we want our ideas to fulfill, we may not only be more likely to select but also to generate ideas that are in fact likely to do what we want them to do.

Indeed, the possibility that hypothesis generation is constrained by our goals may go a long way to explaining the diversity of ideas that human beings entertain. In science, for instance, it is a desiderata of our hypotheses that they be falsifiable. This is a functional constraint, not a normative one. It is in no way incumbent on the truth that it be falsifiable. However, if we specifically and selectively generate hypotheses that meet the goal of being falsifiable, we can substantially constrain the space of new ideas. In other disciplines, by contrast, the functional constraint on generating a hypothesis is that the idea be plausible within the social, political, and economic conditions of the day. Ideas are dismissed not for being unfalsifiable but for being "ahistorical." In the same vein, novelists may generate new ideas in proportion to the probability that they are "in character," engineers to the extent that the new idea is feasible, business executives to the degree that the new idea is profitable, and divinity students to the extent that the new idea might provide spiritual guidance or inspiration.

These of course are merely the functional desiderata of our professions. As human beings, we look for ideas to fill an even broader range of goals. Even supposing we were confronted with the same problem in all cases, we would generate different solutions depending on whether we wanted the new idea to impress a superior, entertain a crowd, teach a child, win an election, or woo a lover. Such constraints may or may not serve the function of getting the world right but they allow us to constrain the space in which we generate new ideas beyond merely the limit of whatever might be lawfully expressed in the grammar of our current theories.

If our goals are the top of our hierarchy of constraints on hypothesis generation, these goals may probabilistically generate a constraint one level lower: the criteria for fulfilling those goals. Suppose, for instance, you have the goal of wanting to get from point A to point B. Having the goal of navigation might generate a set of subordinate desiderata (e.g. to find variously, the shortest distance between two points, the fastest route between two points, the most scenic route between two points, or the route between two points most likely to run into a certain someone). These criteria might in turn be more likely to generate some hypotheses for abstract structural forms than others (e.g. two-dimensional maps may be more probable than tree structures; see Kemp & Tenenbaum, 2008).

By contrast, if our goal is explanation, then our constraints on hypothesis generation might include all the criteria that psychologists and philosophers have proposed for hypothesis selection (e.g. simplicity, non-circularity, the ability to subsume specific relations under an abstract kind of relation, an appeal to plausible causal, mechanistic relations; Bonawitz & Lombrozo, in press; Hempel & Oppenheim, 1948; Keil & Wilson, 2000; Keleman, 1999; Kitcher, 1989; Legare, Gelman, & Wellman, 2010; Lombrozo, 2006, 2007, 2012; Lombrozo & Carey, 2006; Salmon, 1984; Strevens, 2004; Woodward, 2009). Again, these criteria might be more likely to generate some hypotheses for abstract structural forms than others (e.g. in this case, tree structures may be more probable than two-dimensional maps; Kemp & Tenenbaum, 2008). It is a well-established, if somewhat mysterious, fact that explaining something to oneself can affect learning and discovery, even in the absence of new data (Amsterlaw & Wellman, 2006; Chi, Bassok, Lewis, Reimann, & Glaser, 1989; Chi, de Leeuw, Chiu, & LaVancher, 1994; Roscoe & Chi, 2007, 2008; Siegler, 2002; Williams & Lombrozo, 2009). If we do have abstract representations of what might count as good explanations with respect to a problem, and we could condition randomized changes to current hypotheses on these desiderata, we might avoid generating any number of hypotheses that are simple, plausible, grammatically lawful, and unsatisfying. One way in which explanatory desiderata may support learning is by constraining the generation of new ideas to those new ideas to those that have a chance of being, in fact, explanatory.

In pursuing the goals of navigation or explanation, we are arguably trying to get the world right. However, even when our goals are more venal or more frivolous, constraining our ideas by the extent to which they serve a functional goal need not *lessen* our sensitivity to the facts of the matter.

Once generated, any hypothesis can be subject to a "fact-checking" process that assesses the extent to which the new idea predicts observed data. Still, our willingness to accept a new hypothesis may be a function jointly of its fit to the criteria set by a desired functional role and its fit to the data. If a new hypothesis succeeds admirably at the former, it might be accepted despite substantial difficulties with the latter.

Our all-too-human ability to admire ideas for reasons other than their truth can provoke considerable and sometimes comedic, hand wringing about human irrationality. In the latter vein, Stephen Colbert coined the term "truthiness" to poke fun of what we might value in false, or at the very least unsubstantiated, ideas. However, if by truthiness we mean something like an idea's ability to fill explanatory (or other) criteria generated by a functional goal, our predilection for truthiness may be a feature, not a bug, of human cognition.

Indeed, in order to be the kind of organism who can think of new ideas at all, it may be critical that we are not overly wedded to the facts. The state of having no new ideas and no new data might be rather like gambling on a single-armed bandit machine or foraging in a landscape with a single berry patch; even if the existing payoff is low, there is little reason to explore. No idea that we do not have will, at the time of not yet having it, fit the data better than whatever we currently believe. Given the low odds that random gropings will improve our lot, if we were committed only to maximizing our best fit to the data, an idea in the hand might always be preferred to the two not yet even in the bush. If instead we have truth-independent criteria for hypothesis generation, we might be motivated to generate ideas that payoff in other ways, by being explanatory, entertaining, provocative, or useful. We can find out later if they are true.

Indeed, it is a curious feature of human cognition that the kinds of goals that lead us to pursue new ideas are often neither here nor there with respect to the significance of the ideas themselves. The colonialists did not profit any less from the Americas because Columbus discovered them in a misguided search for the West Indies. Similarly, whatever you think of the medieval monks' quest for incontrovertible proof of the existence of God, it did not diminish the magnitude of their contributions to analytic logic. It is not merely that the merit of our discoveries is independent of the merit of our motivations but that the merit of our motivations may be precisely in imposing critical constraints on our search processes and enabling discovery at all.

## 10. CONSTRUCTIVISM AND IMAGINATION

I'll end with a speculation about imagination. There are many ways in which human beings interact with the world that seem peculiarly divorced from reality. We confabulate explanations for our behavior, both in sickness (Gazzaniga, 1998; Phelps & Gazzaniga, 1992) and in health (Carruthers, 2009; Nichols & Stich, 2000). We develop elaborate, coherent autobiographical narratives that are false and misleading (Kopelman, 1987; Kopelman, Ng, & Van den Brooke, 1997). We fret over imagined events. We engage in pretend play as children and we daydream as adults. We report our actual dreams as stories. We create and enjoy cultural artifacts ranging from myths to movies.

These phenomena are united primarily in being puzzling. Given our considerable aptitude for exploring the real world, why is so much of human cognition devoted to the construction and contemplation of fictional ones? What advantage does unreality confer that we should find it so compelling? Researchers have long pointed to the value of being able to reason counterfactually for planning, for causal reasoning, and for novel interventions (Gopnik, 1990; Harris, 2000; Harris, German, & Mills, 1996; Weisberg & Bloom, 2009; Buchsbaum, Bridgers, Weisber, & Gopnik, 2012; Walker & Gopnik, under contract; Weisberg & Sobel, 2012). However, the demands of counterfactual reasoning would not seem to require the wanton disengagement with reality manifest across these diverse cognitive phenomena. As Jerry Fodor noted sardonically in response to Steven Pinker's suggestion that we appreciate fiction because it offers us insight into situations we might encounter in real life:

> ... what if it turns out that, having just used the ring that I got by kidnapping a dwarf to payoff the giants who built me my new castle, I should discover that it is the very ring that I need in order to continue to be immortal and rule the world? It is important to think out the options betimes, because a thing like that could happen to anyone and you can never have too much insurance (Fodor, 1998).

Here is a different proposal. What matters about our fictions is not that they tell us the content of possible worlds or that they exercise our ability to reason through the consequences of false premises. What matters is our ability to create the false premises in the first place. Being able to disengage from data may be requisite to being the kind of creature that can go beyond data-driven learning. Indeed, it may be that thinking of new ideas requires precisely the ability to impose a kind of cognitive firewall between the criteria for constructing an idea and the criteria for verifying it. This is not to say that there are not constraints, even on our fictions (Harris, 2000; Shtulman, 2009; Weisberg & Bloom, 2009; Weisberg & Goodstein, 2009; Weisberg & Sobel, 2012; Wyman, Rakoczy, & Tomasello, 2009). However, the constraints most important for learning may be "narrative" constraints. Good narratives do not have to be true, but they do have to do all of the following: provide an abstract representation of a problem and its solution, satisfy criteria consistent with the narrative goal (e.g. perhaps by fulfilling causal and subsumptive explanatory demands), and fulfill a functional role for entertainment, persuasion, illustration, provocation, explanation, soothing, or stimulation. In short, the constraints on a good narrative are plausibly the rational constraints for hypothesis generation generally.

On this account, we spend our time telling stories for the same reason that monkeys spend their time climbing trees, not because it usually solves a problem but because it is hard to know when a problem will appear. If we engage in the activity continually, then when a problem does come along, we may find ourselves making the right leap at the right time. In engaging, from early childhood onward, in acts of fictional narratives, in telling stories about what we experience even in our sleep, in retaining this ability even in the face of devastating insults to our bodies and brains, and in finding this engagement sufficiently pleasurable that we seek it out in our cinemas, theaters, novels, and fire circles, we may be manifesting the most distinctively human aspect of our ability to learn: the ability to step away from the real world in order to better see the world as it really is.

## ACKNOWLEDGMENTS

Thanks to Fei Xu and Tamar Kushnir for (respectively) talking me into starting and finishing this chapter and for many helpful ideas along the way. Thanks to Rebecca Saxe and the members of the MIT Imagination Reading Group—Eyal Dechter, Daniel Friel, Julian Jara-Ettinger, John McCoy, Max Siegel, Tomer Ullman, and Nathan Winkler-Rhoades—for hours of interesting conversation that helped constrain and generate these ideas. Finally, warm thanks to Susan Kaufman, Margot and Isaac Schulz, and Josh Tenenbaum for improving my fit to both the data and the grammar —and for helping me tell a better story.

## REFERENCES

Adolph, K. E., Eppler, M. A., & Gibson, E. J. (1993). Development of perception of affordances. *Advances in Infancy Research, 8,* 51–98.
Amsterlaw, J., & Wellman, H. (2006). Theories of mind in transition: a microgenetic study of the development of false belief understanding. *Journal of Cognition and Development, 7,* 139–172.

Baillargeon, R., & Luo, Y. (2002). Development of the object concept. In *Encyclopedia of cognitive science*, *3*, (pp 387–391). London: Nature Publishing Group.

Bechara, A., Damasio, H., Tranel, D., & Damasio, A. R. (1997). Deciding advantageously before knowing the advantageous strategy. *Science, 275*(5304), 1293–1295.

Bell, W. J. (1991). *Searching behaviour: The behavioural ecology of finding resources.* New York: Chapman/Hall.

Berger, S. E., Adolph, K. E., & Lobo, S. A. (2005). Out of the toolbox: toddlers differentiate wobbly and wooden handrails. *Child Development, 76*(6), 1294–1307.

Berry, D. A., & Fristedt, B. (1985). *Bandit problems: Sequential allocation of experiments.* London: Chapman and Hall.

Block, N. (1986). Advertisement for a semantics for psychology. In P. A. French, et al. (Eds.), *Midwest studies in philosophy*, Vol. X, (pp. 615–678). Minneapolis: University of Minnesota Press.

Bonawitz, E. B., & Griffiths, T. L. (2010). Deconfounding hypothesis generation and evaluation in Bayesian models. *Proceedings of the 32nd Annual Conference of the Cognitive Science Society.*

Bonawitz, E. B. & Lombrozo, T. (in press). Occam's rattle: children's use of simplicity and probability to constrain inference.

Bonawitz, E. B., van Schijndel, T. J. P., Friel, D., & Schulz, L. E. (2012). Children balance theories and evidence in exploration, explanation, and learning. *Cognitive Psychology, 64*(4), 215–234.

Botvinick, M. M., Niv, Y., & Barto, A. C. (2009). Hierarchically organized behavior and its neural foundations: a reinforcement learning perspective. *Cognition, 113*, 262–280.

Brauer, J., Kaminski, J., Riedel, J., Call, J., & Tomasello, M. (2006). Making inferences about the location of hidden food: social dog, causal ape. *Journal of Comparative Psychology, 120*(1), 38–47.

Brown, A. L. (1990). Domain-specific principles affect learning and transfer in children. *Cognitive Science, 14*(1), 107–133.

Buchsbaum, D., Bridgers, S., Weisberg, D., & Gopnik, A. (2012). The power of possibility: causal learning, counterfactual reasoning, and pretend play. *Philosophical Transactions, 367*(1599), 2202-2212.

Carey, S. (2009). *The origin of concepts.* Oxford University Press.

Carruthers, P. (2009). How we know our own minds: the relationship between mind-reading and metacognition. *Behavioral and Brain Sciences, 32*, 121–138.

Chang, L. (2006). *Wisdom for the soul: Five millennia of prescriptions for spiritual healing.* Washington: Snosophia.

Charnov, E. L. (1976). Optimal foraging: the marginal value theorem. *Theoretical Population Biology, 9*, 129–136.

Chi, M. T. H., Bassok, M., Lewis, M. W., Reimann, P., & Glaser, R. (1989). Self-explanations: how students study and use examples in learning to solve problems. *Cognitive Science, 13*(2), 145–182.

Chi, M. T. H., De Leeuw, N., Chiu, M., & Lavancher, C. (1994). Eliciting self-explanations improves understanding. *Cognitive Science, 18*(3), 439–477.

Christie, S., & Gentner, D. (2010). Where hypotheses come from: learning new relations by structural alignment. *Journal of Cognition and Development, 11*(3), 356–373.

Cook, C., Goodman, N., & Schulz, L. E. (2011). Where science starts: spontaneous experiments in preschoolers' exploratory play. *Cognition, 120*(3), 341–349.

Daw, N. D., Niv, Y., & Dayan, P. (2005). Uncertainty-based competition between prefrontal and dorsolateral striatal systems for behavioral control. *Nature Neuroscience, 8*, 1704–1711.

Daw, N. D., O'Doherty, J. P., Dayan, P., Seymour, B., & Dolan, R. J. (2006). Cortical substrates for exploratory decisions in humans. *Nature, 441*, 876–879.

Durrant-Whyte, H., & Bailey, T. (2006). Simultaneous localization and mapping (SLAM): part I the essential algorithms. *Robotics and Automation Magazine, 13*(2), 99–110.

Emery, N. J., & Clayton, N. S. (2004). The mentality of crows: convergent evolution of intelligence in corvids and apes. *Science, 306*(5703), 1903–1907.

Fodor, J. (1998). *In critical condition: Polemical essays on cognitive science and the philosophy of mind. Representation and mind.* Cambridge, Mass: MIT Press.

Gazzaniga, M. S. (1998). The split brain revisited. *Scientific American, 279*(1), 35–39.

Gentner, D., Brem, S., Ferguson, R. W., Wolff, P., Markman, A. B., & Forbus, K. D. (1997). Analogy and creativity in the works of Johannes Kepler. In T. B. Ward, S. M. Smith, & J. Vaid (Eds.), *Creative thought: An investigation of conceptual structures and processes* (pp. 403–459). Washington, DC: American Psychological Association.

Gentner, D. (2002). *Analogical reasoning, psychology of encyclopedia of cognitive science.* London: Nature Publishing Group.

Gentner, D., Holyoak, K. J., & Kokinov, B. (Eds.). (2001). *The analogical mind: Perspectives from cognitive science.* Cambridge, MA: MIT Press.

Gentner, D., & Markman, A. B. (1997). Structure mapping in analogy and similarity. *American Psychologist, 52*, 45–56.

Gentner, D., & Namy, L. (1999). Comparison in the development of categories. *Cognitive Development, 14*, 487–513.

Gentner, D., & Smith, L. (2012). Analogical reasoning. In V. S. Ramachandran (Ed.), *Encyclopedia of human behavior* (2nd ed.) (pp. 130–136). Oxford, UK: Elsevier.

Garber, D. (1983). Old evidence and logical omniscience in Bayesian confirmation theory. In J. Earman (Ed.), *Testing scientific theories, minnesota studies in the philosophy of science*, Vol. X. Minneapolis: University of Minnesota Press.

Gibson, J. J. (1977). The theory of affordances. In R. Shaw, & J. Bransford (Eds.), *Perceiving, acting, and knowing.* Hillsdale, NJ: Erlbaum.

Griffiths, T. L., & Tenenbuam, J. B. (2007). From mere coincidences to meaningful discoveries. *Cognition, 103*(2), 180–226.

Gittins, J. (1989). *Multi-armed bandit allocation indices.* Wiley.

Gittins, J. C., & Jones, D. M. (1979). A dynamic allocation index for the discounted multiarmed bandit problem. *Biometrika, 66*(3), 561–565.

Glymour, C. (1980). *Theory and evidence.* Princeton, NJ: Princeton University Press.

Goodman, N. D., Ullman, T. D., & Tenenbaum, J. B. (2011). Learning a theory of causality. *Psychological Review, 118*(1), 110–119.

Gopnik, A. (2000). Explanation as orgasm and the drive for causal understanding: the evolution, function and phenomenology of the theory-formation system. In F. Keil, & R. Wilson (Eds.), *Cognition and explanation.* Cambridge, Mass: MIT Press.

Gopnik, A. and Wellman, H. M. (2012). Reconstructing constructivism: causal models, Bayesian learning mechanisms and the theory. *Psychological Bulletin.* doi: 10.1037/a0028044.

Griffiths, T. L., & Tenenbaum, J. B. (2007). From mere coincidences to meaningful discoveries. *Cognition, 103*(2), 180–226.

Harris, P. L. (2000). *The work of the imagination.* Blackwell.

Harris, P. L., German, T., & Mills, P. (1996). Children's use of counterfactual thinking in causal reasoning. *Cognition, 61*(3), 233–259.

Hempel, C., & Oppenheim, P. (1948). Studies in the logic of explanation. *Philosophy of Science, 15*, 135–175.

Holyoak, K., & Thagard, P. (1996). *Analogy in creative thought.* Cambridge, MA: MIT Press.

Hood, B., Carey, S., & Prasada, S. (2000). Predicting the outcome of physical events: two-year-olds fail to reveal knowledge of solidity and support. *Child Development, 71*(6), 1540–1554.

Howson, C. (1985). Some recent objection to the Bayesian theory of support. *The British Journal for the Philosophy of Science, 36*, 305–309.

Kaelbling, L. P. (1993). *Learning in embedded systems*. Cambridge, Mass: MIT Press.

Kaelbling, L. P., Littman, M. L., & Moore, A. W. (1996). Reinforcement learning: a survey. *Journal of Artificial Intelligence Research, 4*, 237–285.

Kaelbling, L. P., Littman, M. L., & Cassandra, A. R. (1998). Planning and acting in partially observable stochastic domains. *Artificial Intelligence, 101*(1–2), 99–134.

Kahneman, D., & Tversky, A. (1979). Prospect theory: an analysis of decision under risk. *Econometrica, 47*(2), 263–292.

Keil, F. C., & Wilson, R. A. (2000). In *Explanation and cognition*. Cambridge, MA: MIT Press.

Kelemen, D. (1999). Functions, goals and intentions: children's teleological reasoning about objects. *Trends in Cognitive Sciences, 12*, 461–468.

Kemp, C., & Tenenbaum, J. B. (2008). The discovery of structural form. *Proceedings of the National Academy of Sciences, 105*(31), 10687–10692.

Kitcher, P. (1989). Explanatory unification and the causal structure of the world. In P. Kitcher, & W. Salmon (Eds.), *Scientific explanation*. University of Minnesota Press.

Klayman, J. (1988). On the how and why (not) of learning from outcomes. In B. Brehmer, & C. R. B. Joyce (Eds.), *Human judgment: the social judgment theory approach*. Amsterdam: North-Holland.

Klayman, J., & Ha, Y. (1987). Confirmation, disconfirmation, and information in hypothesis testing. *Psychological Review, 94*(2), 211–228.

Kopelman, M. D. (1987). Two types of confabulation. *Journal of Neurology, Neurosurgery, and Psychiatry, 50*, 1482–1487.

Kopelman, M. D., Ng, N., & Van den Brooke, O. (1997). Confabulation extending across episodic, personal and general semantic memory. *Cognitive Neuropsychology, 14*, 683–712.

Krebs, J. R., Kacelnik, A., & Taylor, P. (1978). Tests of optimal sampling by foraging great tits. *Nature, 275*, 27–31.

Legare, C. H., Gelman, S. A., & Wellman, H. M. (2010). Inconsistency with prior knowledge triggers children's causal explanatory reasoning. *Child Development, 81*(3), 929–944.

Leonard, J. J. & Durrant-whyte, H. F. (1991). Simultaneous map building and localization for an autonomous mobile robot. *Intelligent robots and systems' 91.'Intelligence for mechanical systems, proceedings IROS'91. IEEE/RSJ International Workshop*, 1442–1447.

Lockman, J. J. (2000). A perception-action perspective on tool use development. *Child Development, 71*(1), 137–144.

Lombrozo, T. (2006). The structure and function of explanations. *Trends in Cognitive Sciences, 10*(10), 464–470.

Lombrozo, T. (2007). Simplicity and probability in causal explanation. *Cognitive Psychology, 55*(3), 232–257.

Lombrozo, T., & Carey, S. (2006). Functional explanation and the function of explanation. *Cognition, 99*(2), 167–204.

Lombrozo, T., Williams, J., & McClelland, J. L. (1988). Connectionist models and psychological evidence. *Journal of Memory and Language, 27*(2), 107–123.

McClure, S. M., Daw, N. D., & Montague, P. R. (2003). A computational substrate for incentive salience. *Trends in Neurosciences, 26*(8), 423–428.

Mendes, N., Hanus, D., & Call, J. (2007). Raising the level: orangutans use water as tool. *Biology Letters, 3*(5), 453–455.

Munakata, Y., & McClelland, J. L. (2003). Connectionist models of development. *Developmental Science, 6*(4), 413–429.

Nietzsche, F. (1882). *The gay science (Walter Kaufmann, Trans.)*. New York: Vintage. (Original work published 1974).

Norman, D. A. (1988). *The psychology of everyday things*. Basic Books.

Norman, D. A. (1999). *The invisible computer*. MIT Press.

Oaksford, M., & Chater, N. (1994). A rational analysis of the selection task as optimal data selection. *Psychological Review, 101*(4), 608–631.

Phelps, E. A., & Gazzaniga, M. S. (1992). Hemispheric differences in mnemonic processing: the effects of left hemisphere interpretation. *Neuropsychologia, 30*, 293–297.

Piaget, J. (1937). *NonEnLa construction du reel chez l'enfant.* Oxford: Delachaux & Niestle.

Piantadosi, S. T., Tenenbaum, J. B., & Goodman, N. D. (2012). Bootstrapping in a language of thought: a formal model of numerical concept learning. *Cognition, 123*, 199–217.

Roscoe, R., & Chi, M. (2007). Understanding tutor learning: knowledge-building and knowledge-telling in peer tutors' explanations and questions. *Review of Educational Research, 77*(4), 534–574.

Roscoe, R. D., & Chi, M. T. H. (2008). Tutor learning: the role of explaining and responding to questions. *Instructional Science, 36*(4), 321–350.

Salmon, W. (1984). *Scientific explanation and the causal structure of the world.* Princeton University Press.

Sanborn, A. N., Griffiths, T. L., & Navarro, D. J. (2010). Rational approximations to rational models: alternative algorithms for category learning. *Psychological Review, 117*(4), 1144–1167.

Schulz, L. (2012). The origins of inquiry: Inductive inference and exploration in early childhood. *Trends in Cognitive Sciences, 16*(7), 382-389.

Schulz, L. E., & Bonawitz, E. B. (2007). Serious fun: preschoolers engage in more exploratory play when evidence is confounded. *Developmental Psychology, 43*(4), 1045–1050.

Shi, L., Feldman, N. H., & Griffiths, T. L. (2008). Performing Bayesian inference with exemplar models. *Proceedings of the 30th Annual Conference of the Cognitive Science Society.*

Siegler, R. S. (2002). Microgenetic studies of self-explanations. In N. Granott, & J. Parziale (Eds.), *Microdevelopment: Transition processes in development and learning* (pp. 31–58). New York: Cambridge University Press.

Shtulman, A. (2009). The development of possibility judgment within and across domains. *Cognitive Development, 24*, 293–309.

Sloman, S. (1994). When explanations compete: the role of explanation on judgements of likelihood. *Cognition, 51*(1), 1–21.

Sobel, D., & Kushnir, T. (2006). The importance of decision making in causal learning form interventions. *Memory & Cognition, 34*(2), 411–419.

Sodian, B., Zaitchik, D., & Carey, S. (1991). Young children's differentiation of hypothetical beliefs from evidence. *Child Development, 62*(4), 753–766.

Spelke, E. S., Brinlinger, K., Macomber, J., & Jacobson, K. (1992). Origins of knowledge. *Psychological Review, 99*, 605–632.

Spelke, E. S. (1999). Innateness, learning, and the development of object representation. *Developmental Science, 2*, 145–148.

Stephens, D. W., & Krebs, J. R. (1986). *Foraging theory.* Princeton, NJ: Princeton University Press.

Steyvers, M., Tenenbaum, J. B., Wagenmakers, E. J., & Blum, B. (2003). Inferring causal networks from observations and interventions. *Cognitive Science, 27*, 453–489.

Strehl, A., Mesterharm, C., Littman, M., & Hirsh, H. (2006). Experience-efficient learning in associative bandit problems. *Proceedings of the 23rd international conference on machine learning (ICML-06).*

Strevens, M. (2004). The causal and unification accounts of explanation unified – causally. *Nous, 38*, 154–179.

Stulp, G., Emery, N. J., Verhulst, S., & Clayton, N. S. (2009). Western scrub-jays conceal auditory information when competitors can hear but cannot see. *Biology Letters, 5*(5), 583–585.

Sutton, R. S., & Barto, A. G. (1998). *Reinforcement learning: an introduction.* Cambridge: MIT Press.

Tenenbaum, J. B., Griffiths, T. L., & Niyogi, S. (2007). Intuitive theories for grammar as causal inference. In A. Gopnik, & L. Schulz (Eds.), *Causal learning: psychology, philosophy, and computation*. Oxford University Press.

Tenenbaum, J. B., Kemp, C., Griffiths, T. L., & Goodman, N. D. (2011). *Science, 331*(6022), 1279–1285.

Thrun, S., Burgard, W., & Fox, D. (2005). *Probabilistic robotics*. Cambridge, Mass: MIT Press.

Tong, S., & Koller, D. (2001). Active learning for structure in Bayesian networks. *Seventeenth International Join Conference on Artificial Intelligence*. 863–869.

Ullman, T. D., Goodman, N. D., & Tenenbaum, J. B. (2012). Theory acquisition as stochastic search. *Cognitive Development*. http://dx.doi.org/10.1016/j.bbr.2011.03.031.

Walker, C., & Gopnik, A. (under contract). Causality and imagination. In M. Taylor (Ed.), *The development of imagination*. New York: Oxford University Press.

Weisberg, D. S., & Bloom, P. (2009). Young children separate multiple pretend worlds. *Developmental Science, 12*(5), 699–705.

Weisberg, D. S., & Goodstein, J. (2009). What belongs in a fictional world? *Journal of Cognition and Culture, 9*, 69–78.

Weisberg, D. S., & Sobel, D. M. (2012). Young children discriminate improbable from impossible events in fiction. *Cognitive Development, 27*, 90–98.

Williams, J. J., & Lombrozo, T. (2010). The role of explanation in discovery and generalization: evidence from category learning. *Cognitive Science, 34*, 776–806.

Woodward, J. (2003). *Making things happen: a theory of causal explanation*. Oxford University Press.

Woodward, J. (2009). Scientific explanation. Available at:. In E. N. Zalta (Ed.), *The Stanford encyclopedia of philosophy* (spring 2009 ed.). http://plato.stanford.edu/archives/spr2009/entries/scientific-explanation/.

Wyman, E., Rakoczy, H., & Tomasello, M. (2009). Normativity and context in young children's pretend play. *Cognitive Development, 24*(2), 146–155.

CHAPTER ELEVEN

# Unifying Pedagogical Reasoning and Epistemic Trust

## Baxter S. Eaves Jr.[1] and Patrick Shafto

Department of Psychological and Brain Sciences 317 Life Sciences Building, University of Louisville, Louisville, Ky 40292, USA
[1]Corresponding author: E-mail: b0eave01@louisville.edu

## Contents

## Abstract

Researchers have argued that other people provide not only great opportunities for facilitating children's learning but also great risks. Research on pedagogical reasoning has argued children come prepared to identify and capitalize on others' helpfulness to teach, and this pedagogical reasoning allows children to learn rapidly and robustly. In contrast, research on epistemic trust has focused on how the testimony of others is not constrained to be veridical, and therefore, children must be prepared to identify which informants to trust for information. Although these problems are clearly related, these two literatures have, thus far, existed relatively independently of each other. We present a formal analysis of learning from informants that unifies and fills gaps in each of these literatures. Our analysis explains why teaching—learning from a knowledgeable and helpful informant—supports more robust inferences. We show that our account predicts specific inferences supported in pedagogical situations better than a standard account of learning from teaching. Our analysis also suggests that epistemic trust

*Advances in Child Development and Behavior*, Volume 43
ISSN 0065-2407,
http://dx.doi.org/10.1016/B978-0-12-397919-3.00011-3

should depend on inferences about others' knowledge and helpfulness. We show that our knowledge and helpfulness account explains children's behavior in epistemic trust tasks better than the standard knowledge-only account. We conclude by discussing implications for development and outline important questions raised by viewing learning from testimony as joint inference over others' knowledge and helpfulness.

One of the most remarkable aspects of human learning is the ability of children to learn so much, so quickly. This ability defies the common wisdom from learning theory, where research has suggested that learning should be impossibly hard (e.g. Gold, 1967). Indeed, humans' ability to learn is so robust that we, but not other animals, are able to accumulate knowledge over generations (Tomasello, 1999). What underlies these remarkable abilities?

One proposed explanation for these impressive feats of learning is an intrinsic understanding of teaching, termed *natural pedagogy* (Csibra & Gergely, 2009). Csibra and Gergely (2009) proposed that people spontaneously engage in, and that children come prepared to identify and understand, acts of teaching. In short, they argue that pedagogy is indicated by ostensive cues—forming joint attention, speaking in child-directed tones, etc.—and in these situations, the information presented is understood to be purposefully communicated and generalizable.

In an effort to understand why pedagogical situations might afford more rapid learning, recent research has presented a formal analysis of pedagogical data selection and its implications for learning, instantiated in a computational model (Shafto & Goodman, 2008). Pedagogical reasoning is formalized as a two-part problem: from the teacher's perspective, which data should be chosen for the learner, and from the learner's perspective, which inferences are afforded by the teacher's choices. The teacher is assumed to be knowledgeable and helpful—she knows the correct hypothesis and chooses examples to increase the learner's belief in that hypothesis. The learner is assumed to know that the teacher is knowledgeable and helpful. The learner then updates her beliefs accordingly. Recent research has investigated the predictions of the model, suggesting that children make stronger inferences from pedagogically chosen data as predicted by the model (Bonawitz et al., 2011; Buchbaum, Griffiths, Gopnik, & Shafto, 2011).

Pedagogical reasoning assumes that informants are trustworthy, but children cannot simply trust everyone they encounter. Recent research on epistemic trust has investigated how children identify which informants to trust for information. Koenig and Harris (2005) showed that by 4 years of age children reliably preferred previously correct informants over incorrect informants in a word-learning task. Subsequent research has shown that children make inferences about informants based on relative accuracy (Fitneva & Dunfield, 2010; Pasquini, Corriveau, Koenig, & Harris, 2007), group consensus (Corriveau, Fusaro, & Harris, 2009), informant familiarity (Corriveau & Harris, 2009), expertise (Sobel & Corriveau, 2010), and more (Fusaro & Harris, 2008; Jaswal & Neely, 2006; Mascaro & Sperber, 2009; Kinzler, Corriveau, & Harris, 2011; Nurmsoo & Robinson, 2009; VanderBorght, 2009).

Children's success on epistemic trust tasks is generally interpreted as reflecting their ability to track informants' knowledge. However, there is reason to believe that knowledge is not the only factor at play. Intuitively, the simple fact that someone is knowledgeable does not preclude them from deceiving. Indeed, a parallel line of research has suggested that 4-year old children are also able to reason about informants' mal-intentions (Mascaro & Sperber, 2009). Specifically, children are able to use behavioral cues such as violence as well as information from other informants—e.g. *that guy is a liar*—to make judgments about informants' reliability. This raises the possibility that 4-year olds' performance in epistemic trust may not be simply attributable to inferences about knowledge alone.

We propose that pedagogical reasoning and epistemic trust are two sides of the same coin. We present a unified framework, within which pedagogical reasoning is a special case of a broader set of models which allow informants to be knowledgeable or not and helpful or not (Shafto, Eaves, Navarro, & Perfors, 2012). We will show how this model can account for learning in pedagogical settings and findings from the literature on epistemic trust, by focusing on specific examples from these literatures. We conclude by discussing implications for cognitive development, connections to related areas of research, and important future directions.

## 1. A UNIFIED FRAMEWORK OF EPISTEMIC TRUST AND PEDAGOGY

In pedagogical reasoning, informants are assumed to be knowledgeable and helpful; learners use this assumption to guide learning. In epistemic trust, informants may be knowledgeable or not or helpful or not; learners must simultaneously make inferences about the world and about their informants. Therefore, a unified framework must formalize the behavior of different kinds of informants and specify how learners leverage an informant's testimony when the informant's kind is known and when the informant's kind is unknown.

Recent work has formalized aspects of these problems. Shafto and Goodman (2008) proposed a model of pedagogical sampling. Their model formalizes teaching by a knowledgeable and helpful informant as choosing data that tend to maximize the learner's belief in the correct hypothesis and learning as updating one's beliefs assuming that the data have been chosen by a knowledgeable and helpful teacher. Shafto et al. (2012) proposed a model of epistemic trust, where learners simultaneously learn about the world and infer whether informants are knowledgeable or not and helpful or not. Our goal here is to sketch the general framework that unifies these models and to show how this provides a single account for children's behavior across these tasks.

We begin by sketching the modeling framework. We then consider two classes of behavioral tasks that can be captured by the model—pedagogical learning and epistemic trust—and contrast current theoretical accounts with the account offered by the model. By accounting for data across an array of recent work in pedagogy and trust, we unify learning in these scenarios under a common framework.

## 1.1. The Unified Framework

A model of learning from informants needs to capture two things: how informants select data and how learners learn from different kinds of informants. We adopt a standard probabilistic learning framework (Tenenbaum, Griffiths, & Kemp, 2006). In probabilistic learning, the learner's goal is to update their belief about a hypothesis given data. Bayes' rule dictates that these posterior beliefs are proportional to the product of two quantities: the prior probability of the hypothesis and the probability of observing the data given the hypothesis is true. Thus, given a generative model for the data—a model that specifies how hypotheses are selected and how data are sampled given hypotheses—Bayes' rule specifies how to invert the process—how to infer the hypothesis and the sampling model, given the data.

Generally, models of learning assume that data are *randomly sampled*, that is, data are sampled in proportion to their consistency with the hypothesis. In social learning, it seems that random sampling is rarely applicable. People *choose* data purposefully. Data are not sampled based on their consistency with the hypothesis, but based on the informant's helpfulness, given her knowledge. The key challenge here is to formalize how different kinds of informants produce data. To do this, we must specify how knowledgeability and helpfulness relate to the choices informants make.

Figure 11.1 presents two graphical models depicting how helpfulness and knowledgeability relate to informants' actions in causal and word learning. Graphical models are a powerful tool for defining causal relationships among variables (Pearl, 2009; Spirtes, Glymour, & Scheines, 1993). The fundamental components of graphical models are nodes and edges. A node represents a latent or observed variable; an edge represents a conditional dependency between nodes. Edges are directed and point from parents to children.

Here the goal is to specify how two latent variables corresponding to informants' knowledgeability, $k$, and helpfulness, $h$, affect their choice of action (see Fig. 11.1). Knowledgeability determines the relationship between the informant's beliefs, $b$, and the true state of the world $w'$. Helpfulness determines the types of actions, $a$, informants choose based on their beliefs. Actions in turn produce effects, $e$, based on the state of the world.

More specifically, knowledgeability, $k$, and helpfulness, $h$, are binary-valued variables corresponding to knowledgeable/naïve and helpful/unhelpful. Beliefs, $b$, model informants' beliefs about the world, $w$; $b$ belongs to $B$, the set of possible beliefs; $w$ belongs to $W$, the set of states of the world. In word learning, $B$ and $W$ are sets of labels, and in causal learning, they are sets of causal graphs. For example, in a game in which an informant points to one of two cups under which a ball is hidden, $B$ and $W$ would both be composed of the set of possible locations of the ball, $\{cup1, cup2\}$. This task

Causal learning                          Word learning

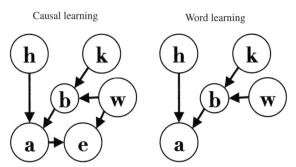

**Figure 11.1** Graphical representation of the model. On the left is the causal learning model. On the right is the word-learning model. In causal learning, an informant's action, $a$, is an intervention on the world, $w$, which elicits a response from the world: an effect, $e$. In word learning, actions are labels and do not affect the world; thus, the effect node is not present in the word learning model.

can be thought of as a labeling task because the informant labels a cup *as the one containing the ball.*

Knowledgeability specifies the relationship between the informant's beliefs and the world. If an informant is knowledgeable, then her beliefs, $b$, correspond to the true state of the world, $w'$; she would know which cup the ball is under. In contrast, if an informant is naive, then her beliefs are uniform over the set of possible beliefs; she would not know which cup the ball was under. More formally,

$$P_I(b = w'|k) = \begin{cases} 1 & \text{if knowledgeable} \\ 1/|W| & \text{if naïve} \end{cases}, \qquad (11.1)$$

where $|W|$ is number of possible hypotheses about the world.

Actions, $a$, are chosen based on the informant's helpfulness and beliefs. If an informant is helpful, she will act to maximize the learner's belief in the belief she holds; if she is not helpful, she will act to minimize the learner's belief in the belief she holds. Formally,

$$P_I(d|b_I) \propto P_L(b_L = b_I|d)^\alpha, \qquad (11.2)$$

where

$$\alpha = \begin{cases} 1 & \text{if helpful} \\ -1 & \text{if not helpful.} \end{cases} \qquad (11.3)$$

When $\alpha$ is 1, the informant chooses data that tend to lead the learner to her belief. When $\alpha$ is $-1$, the informant chooses data that tend to lead the learner away from her belief. In the cup game, a knowledgeable and helpful informant would point to the cup she believed the ball was hidden under; a knowledgeable but unhelpful informant would point to the cup opposite the one she believed the ball was hidden under. Because actions are based on informants' beliefs, and beliefs are based on informants' knowledgeability, naive informants, regardless of helpfulness, will appear to produce actions scattershot. In the cup game, a naive informant will point to the correct cup half of the time. The helpful naive informant points at the correct cup because she has guessed correctly and the unhelpful naive informant points at the correct cup because she believes the ball is under the wrong cup and attempts to lead the learner away from it.

In causal learning (see Fig. 11.1), there is an additional factor, the effects of actions. The effects of actions are determined by the action chosen and the true causal structure of the world. In word learning (see Fig. 11.1), the action is an utterance, and because an utterance does not affect the world, the effect node is removed.

This sampling model allows us to consider which actions are likely to be chosen by different kinds of informants and, given actions, allows learners to infer what kind of informant they are dealing with. In different social (and experimental) scenarios, informants' helpfulness and knowledgeability may implicitly take on certain values. When the informant claims to be knowledgeable and helpful or if certain social cues are present (Csibra & Gergely, 2009), learners may assume the informant is knowledgeable and helpful. Similarly, learners may be exposed to cues which lead them to believe an informant is knowledgeable and unhelpful (deceptive). Importantly, Bayesian inference allows us to learn who to trust and what to infer from informants' actions.

## 1.2. Modeling Pedagogical Learning

To illustrate how the model accounts for learning from pedagogically selected data, we consider two sets of results. The first is from Shafto and Goodman (2008), which examined pedagogical sampling and how it affects what is learned, and the second is from Bonawitz et al. (2011), which looked at how pedagogy affects future exploration. In both these cases, we contrast the model predictions with the strong sampling proposal offered by Xu and Tenenbaum (2007).

In Shafto and Goodman (2008), participants played a concept learning game in which they were to locate a hidden rectangle using pairs of points labeled as inside (positive) or outside the rectangle (negative). In the pedagogical sampling condition, participants both taught and learned. When teaching, participants observed the rectangle and chose points to mark. When learning, participants saw labeled points on a blank screen and then drew a rectangle which they believed was the actual rectangle the teacher intended. In the non-pedagogical sampling condition, participants searched for the rectangle themselves. They observed a blank screen and chose points to have labeled. Once the points were placed on the screen, the software labeled them as in or out of the rectangle.

The results showed that in the pedagogical conditions teachers chose to place pairs of positive examples at opposite corners and pairs of negative examples at opposite edges or corners. The intuition here is that teachers choose points to maximize a learner's belief in a single hypothesis and placing the positive examples at the opposite corners rules out all rectangles smaller than the actual rectangle (see also Rhodes, Gelman, & Brickman, 2010).

Learners' inferences in the pedagogical condition showed a distinct pattern. Rectangles were drawn with the two positive examples in the corners and with edges close to negative examples. In the nonpedagogical sampling condition, rectangles drawn by participants did not show any discernible pattern, suggesting that learners in the pedagogical condition inferred that teachers choose data purposefully—positive examples in the corners of the rectangle, and negative examples at the boundaries—while learners in the non-pedagogical condition did not.

Previous accounts of word learning have suggested that learners' inferences from teachers' demonstrations in word learning may be modeled by assuming strong sampling (Xu & Tenenbaum, 2007; see also Tenenbaum, 1999). In strong sampling, learners assume that examples are selected randomly *from the true concept*. Because this creates a natural preference for smaller concepts (that are consistent with the examples), given only positive examples, learners will rapidly converge to the correct concept. Strong sampling can, therefore, account for learning from positive examples. But because examples are assumed to be randomly sampled, it cannot explain teachers' preference for examples in the corners. Similarly, because strong sampling assumes that only positive examples are chosen, it cannot explain negative example selection or learning from negative examples.

Under our model, a teacher is someone who is knowledgeable, $k = 1$, and helpful, $h = 1$; they know about the world, and they want learners to as well. Teachers therefore choose data to increase learners' beliefs in the true state of the world (see Eqn 11.2). In this case, because the teacher is knowledgeable, her belief is assumed to match the true state of the world, $b_i = w'$, and because she is helpful, the exponent, $\alpha$, is 1. In the rectangle game, $W$ and $B$ are both the set of possible rectangles, where $b$ is a single rectangle, and $w'$ is the true rectangle. Possible data are the set of possible pairs of negative or positive examples. For positive examples, if a teacher chooses narrow data, positive examples closer to the center of the true rectangle, they rule out fewer incorrect rectangles than if they choose data in the corners, $P(w'|D = \text{narrow}) < P(w'|D = \text{corners})$, and therefore, $P(D = \text{narrow}|w') < P(D = \text{corners}|w')$.

Negative examples should be chosen to constrain the number of possible rectangles. Choosing negative examples at the sides rules out all rectangles larger than the boundaries of the points. As before, placing negative examples away from the rectangle boundaries (wide data) rules out fewer rectangles larger than the target and makes learning the target rectangle less likely, $P(w'|D = \text{wide}) < P(w'|D = \text{sides})$, and therefore, $P(D = \text{wide}|w') < P(D = \text{sides}|w')$. Because learners use their knowledge of how points are chosen, when points are chosen at random (nonpedagogical condition), the model cannot make assumptions about *why* specific points were chosen and therefore chooses randomly based on the examples present.

The model explains why faster learning is achieved in pedagogical learning. Using their knowledge of how teachers choose data, people are able to infer the correct rectangle with two points, rather than six perfectly placed points (four negative examples, one at each side to constrain the maximum size and two positive examples at opposite corners to constrain the minimum size). One implication of this increased confidence is that after observing pedagogically sampled data, one may be less curious than after observing the same data chosen in a nonpedagogical setting. Bonawitz et al. (2011) explored this possibility: would learners presented with pedagogically sampled data be less likely to search for additional data?

Children were presented with a novel, complex-looking toy. Unbeknownst to the children, the toy was built to have four nonobvious functions: a knob that caused squeaking, a key that made music, a button that turned on a light, and a tube with a mirror that reversed the child's face. The toy was designed to appear complex looking to lead children to believe that there could be many functions of the toy.

Children were randomly assigned to one of a number of conditions. We focus on two: the pedagogical condition and the accidental condition. These conditions were set up such that children observed the same data: pulling a knob causes squeaking. Across conditions, the social context was manipulated. In the pedagogical condition, the demonstrator was presented as knowledgeable (stating, "This is my toy") and helpful [via pedagogical cues such as establishing joint attention, repeating the child's name, etc. (Csibra & Gergely, 2009)]. In the accidental condition, the demonstrator was presented as naive (saying, "Look at this toy I found") and the demonstration was presented as accidental. As the demonstrator put the toy down, their hand hit the knob, causing a squeak. In both conditions, there were two demonstrations to ensure that the child saw the cause of the squeak. After the demonstration, the child was allowed to play with the toy. Experimenters

tracked various measures of how much exploration children engaged in as
well as the total number of built-in functions children discovered. The
results showed that children in the pedagogical condition explored less and
discovered fewer functions of the toy than did children in the accidental
condition.

Under strong sampling, data are selected randomly from the true
concept. However, strong sampling does not specify how much data to
select. Therefore, strong sampling offers no explanation as to why a specific
number of demonstrations are better than any other.

To explain these results under our model, we must specify the possible
beliefs/states of the world and data. Possible states of the world (and beliefs)
include different numbers of possible functions. $W$ includes the possibility
that the toy has no functions $w = 0$, one function $w = 1$, two functions
$w = 2$, etc. Possible actions include no demonstration $a = 0$, performing one
action $a = 1$, two actions $a = 2$, etc. In the experiment, the question is what
should a learner infer from the teacher's choice to *only* demonstrate that
pulling the knob leads to squeaking. Intuitively, given the teacher is
knowledgeable and helpful, if the toy had any other functions, we would
expect the teacher to have shown them to us. The model predicts that,
given a toy with $n$ functions, i.e. $w' = n$, we would expect $n$ demonstrations, $a = n$. Consider what would happen if the teacher demonstrated only
$n - 1$ functions. The learner could rule out all hypotheses in which there are
less than $n - 1$ functions. However, all hypotheses with $n$ or more functions
are still possible. By demonstrating one more function, the teacher
would eliminate one more possibility, increasing the learner's belief in $n$
functions, $P(w = n|a = n) > P(w = n|a = n - 1)$. Thus, the model
predicts that teachers demonstrate all functions, $P(a = n|w' = n) >
P(a = n - 1|w' = n)$, and given such a demonstration, learners infer
no more functions exist, $P(w = n|a = n) > P(w = n + 1|a = n)$.[1]
Because the chance that other functions exist is low, there is no need to
spend time looking for them.

On the other hand, when the demonstrator accidentally elicits a squeaks,
the data rule out the possibility that there are zero functions, but because the
action and effect were a result of a chance occurrence (random sampling),
one cannot assume there are not more functions. In this case, if one wishes to
learn about the toy, one must explore.

[1] This discussion assumes that all hypotheses are equally likely. The assumption is made for
expository simplicity, and the conclusions hold across a range of scenarios.

## 1.3. Modeling Epistemic Trust

The previous section focuses on situations in which the knowledge and intent of the informant are known (or can be reasonably assumed). Of course, that is not the problem that people typically face in the world. Informants may or may not be trustworthy, and research shows that children track who to trust. We present a standard account of children's reasoning—the knowledge heuristics account—and contrast it with our own. We begin by discussing three representative findings from epistemic trust literature. Finally, we will show how our model of learning from informants can account for all the results discussed and, thus, all corresponding heuristics.

The trust tasks examined in this section each follow a similar format. Learners are given some demonstrations, which they can use to make inferences about their informants. For example, in Pasquini et al. (2007), informants label four common objects with varying accuracy; in Corriveau, Fusaro, et al. (2009), several informants point to an object after hearing a label given by an experimenter. After the demonstration, learners must choose which informant to ask or which informant's information to endorse when faced with a novel object or label (novel trial). The key question is whether children show systematic preferences for different informants, and if so, what kinds of experience lead children to choose one informant over another?

In Pasquini et al. (2007), kids observed two informants label four common objects, such as a ball or a shoe, with varying accuracy: 100%, 75%, 25%, or 0%. After these familiar trials, children were presented a novel object. In *ask* trials, children asked one of the two informants for the label, and in *endorse* trials, both informants labeled the object with different labels, and the child was then asked which she thought the object was called. The results showed that children indeed form preferences for more accurate informants, meaning children prefer to ask, or endorse the label given by more accurate informants more often. Qualitatively, for both 3- and 4-year olds, the results showed that the preference for the more accurate informant decreased with the relative accuracy of the informants, e.g. children in the 75% versus 0% accurate condition showed a higher preference for the 75% accurate informant than did children in the 75% versus 25% accurate condition. However, whereas 3-year olds showed less and less differentiation across the 100% versus 0%, 100% versus 25%, 75% versus 0%, and 75% versus 25% conditions, 4-year olds at minimum show a sharp differentiation of the 75 versus 25 condition from the others and appear to have somewhat improved performance in the 100% versus 0% condition relative to the others.

To explain these differences, Pasquini et al. (2007) suggested that children's choices are guided by heuristic monitoring of the inaccuracy of the informant. That is, to begin both informants are categorized as trustworthy, but when an informant labels incorrectly, that informant is categorized as inaccurate. According to Pasquini et al. (2007), for 3-year olds, the strategy stops here. An informant is either accurate or inaccurate, and this binary explanation accounts for 3-year olds' poor performance when both informants have labeled one or more object inaccurately. To explain the differences between 3- and 4-year olds, Pasquini et al. (2007) propose that 4-year olds also use the frequency of informants' mislabelings and are thus better able to choose between inaccurate informants than 3-year olds.

Corriveau and Harris (2009) carried out an experiment nearly identical to Pasquini et al. (2007), with two differences: one of the informants was the child's preschool teacher, and rather than parametrically altering accuracy on familiar object trials, informants labeled 100% or 0% accurately. When the child first encountered the two informants, one novel and one familiar, the child was presented with a novel object and answered ask and endorse questions. Both 3- and 4-year-old children preferred the familiar informant. After the novel trials, children observed familiar object trials in which the familiar informant labeled 100% accurately and the novel informant labeled 0% accurately or the familiar informant labeled 0% accurately and the novel informant labeled 100% accurately. Four-year olds preferred the familiar informant after having seen her label correctly, more so than in novel trials. When the familiar informant labeled incorrectly, 4-year olds preferred the novel informant who had labeled correctly. Three-year olds still preferred the familiar informant even when she had labeled incorrectly.

According to the heuristic account proposed by Pasquini et al. (2007), all informants initially belong to the trustworthy category. If this were true, given a novel and a familiar informant, children should choose both informants equally because they are both trustworthy. Corriveau and Harris (2009) suggest that perhaps children have witnessed the familiar informant label accurately many times in the past and have some bias toward accurate information which would create the familiarity bias. Under this proposal, children must be tracking some kind of frequency of correct answers. Given that 3-year olds also show a preference for familiar informants, this creates a contradiction with the previous experiment, where their behavior was explained by not attending to the frequency information but by categorization. To explain the current results, it seems necessary to propose that familiarity is an additional heuristic that guides children's choices in the pretest.

For the posttest (once the informants have labeled familiar objects), a familiarity and accuracy account would have to specify how these two factors interact. When the familiar informant labeled accurately and the novel informant labeled inaccurately, 4-year olds' preference for the familiar informant increased compared to the pretest, but 3-year olds' preference remained the same. When the familiar informant labeled inaccurately and the novel informant labeled accurately, 4-year olds then preferred the novel informant, but 3-year olds continued to prefer the familiar informant. If children used the raw frequency of informant's truthful productions, we would expect to see preferences for the familiar informant to remain for both groups even when the familiar informant labeled inaccurately, as it would be reasonable to assume that a teacher has produced enough truthful information (likely hundreds of productions) to outweigh four mislabelings. Accordingly, Corriveau and Harris (2009) suggest that there is a bias for recent accuracy as well. This, however, does not explain 3-year olds' continued preference for the inaccurately labeling familiar informant or why their preference for the familiar informant does not increase when she labeled accurately. For this reason, the authors suggest that for 3-year olds, familiarity, and not the productions of information that comprise it, outweighs accuracy as a heuristic.

Corriveau, Fusaro, et al. (2009) looked at how children choose informants and data when learning about novel objects from a group of novel informants given only a set of novel labels. Four informants are presented with three novel objects. An experimenter asks, "Show me the modi" after which, each informant points to an object. Three informants agree and one dissents. This occurs for several trials. On each trial, the same informants agree, and the same informant dissents. After the informants have pointed, the child is asked which she believes is the modi. Here, learners have only labels from a few informants by which to make inferences and therefore cannot use an inaccuracy strategy. The results showed that children prefer the object indicated by the majority and that there were no differences in age groups. After group trials, children participated in novel object labeling trials in which one informant was from the majority and the other was the dissenter. Again, children preferred the informant from the majority, and there was no effect of age.

Corriveau, Fusaro, et al. (2009) argue that children prefer informants who are part of a broader consensus and that children may believe informants from a majority are more epistemically trustworthy or may otherwise form some kind of emotional attraction to non-dissenters. In other words, children exhibit a heuristic majority bias: when learners have only a set of novel object labels, they choose the one that is most agreed upon. Note that this bias cannot be derived from previous biases. The accuracy bias cannot be applied because there is only novel information, so learners cannot judge the accuracy of the information; the familiarity bias cannot be applied because all the informants are novel. Also note that in this study, no developmental differences were observed, and therefore, no developmental change in this ability was proposed.

These studies paint an interesting picture of children's abilities: they show remarkable subtlety in reasoning, with developmental differences in some cases, but not others. For each subtle variation in behavior, the heuristic account proposes more heuristics, leading to complex and often under-specified interactions given a specific scenario or a developmental stage. The accuracy bias works differently for 3- and 4-year olds. When at least one informant is familiar, it works differently still for 4-year olds and not at all for 3-year olds. When groups of informants are involved, 3- and 4-year olds do not differ, they use the same heuristic of choosing with the majority. Similarly, it is not clear how the existing heuristics apply in minimally different scenarios. If a dissenting informant were familiar, which heuristic would children use: majority or familiarity? Would this change with age? What is needed is an account that provides a more parsimonious explanation of existing phenomena and makes principled generalizations across scenarios.

We propose that behavior can be understood as joint inference about informants' knowledge and intent (Shafto et al., 2012). The model observes informants' actions and decides which kind of informant is most likely to have produced those actions, e.g. helpful/unhelpful, knowledgeable/naive. On novel trials, the model uses what it knows about how different types of informants choose data, along with the inferences it has made about its informants, to predict which informant is most likely to produce correct labels in the future.

The model both learns about informants and predicts their future behavior. In Pasquini et al. (2007) and Corriveau and Harris (2009), during familiar object labelings, the values of $w'$ and $a$ are fixed because the objects are familiar and the labels are observed. Learners leverage this information in order to infer $k$ and $h$, whether an informant is knowledgeable and helpful. Informants who label more accurately are more likely to be helpful. Informants who always label accurately are likely helpful and knowledgeable, and informants who never label correctly are likely knowledgeable, but unhelpful because naive informants, whether helpful or not, will occasionally produce the correct labels. Like in the account proposed by Pasquini et al. (2007), learners use accuracy/inaccuracy to choose informants. However, rather than an ad hoc approach based on tallying correct answers directly, we propose that children are actually inferring unobserved causal properties of informants—whether the informant is knowledgeable and whether the informant is helpful. Developmental differences are explained in our framework as changing assumptions about people. While 4-year olds' behavior is best explained by a model that infers knowledgeability and helpfulness, 3-year olds' behavior is best explained by a model that infers knowledgeability but assumes helpfulness. Based on knowledgeability alone, informants who have mislabeled one or more times become similar. Under the model, this accounts for 3-year olds' performance in choosing between inaccurate informants.

Inferences are made similarly when learning from familiar informants. In the case of Corriveau and Harris (2009), where the informant is a preschool teacher, familiarity is modeled as positive past experience. In contrast with Corriveau and Harris (2009), in our model, this experience manifests as strengthened prior beliefs on k and h (see Equation 11.5 and 11.7) rather than a heuristic assumption of a truth bias. In familiar object labeling trials, learners' preferences are not affected as much by the familiar informant's labels as they are by the novel informant's labels. Learners already have strong beliefs about the familiar informant. Stronger beliefs are more difficult to override; it takes more evidence to do so. Age differences are explained as earlier. Without the ability to account for the helpfulness of informants, the knowledge-only model does not differentiate as much between always and never accurate informants.

The models account for the result in both phases of Corriveau, Fusaro, et al. (2009), and both show similar predictions. Because there are only informants' labels from which to infer the correct label, actions are fixed, and the informants' knowledgeability and helpfulness as well as the correct object must be learned. Because the probability of naive, or not helpful informants converging on the same label is low, the model infers that the agreeing informants are likely knowledgeable and helpful and indicate the correct label. After the model has made inferences about informants' knowledgeability and helpfulness, it can use this information to decide which informants are more likely to label correctly in the future. The model chooses informants based on the probability they will label correctly in the future, accounting for the preference for non-dissenting informants.

Therefore, the majority bias proposed by Corriveau, Fusaro, et al. (2009) is a manifestation of the non-dissenting informant's past labelings, which in the group trials were inferred to be accurate.

Three findings from the epistemic trust literature—parametrically varying preference for accurate informants, variations in preference based of familiarity and accuracy, and preference for informants from groups over dissenters—illustrate differences between a standard heuristic-based account and our modeling framework. Whereas the heuristic account incurs a proliferation of explanations to account for variations depending on the task and children's location on a developmental trajectory, we propose an inference framework that explains variations in children's behavior across tasks in terms of reasoning about informants' knowledge and helpfulness. We showed that the model explains why these heuristics work, and as such, they need not be thought of as heuristics, but as similar inferences under a common mechanism. Children learn about informants underlying epistemic qualities and in turn use what they have learned to infer informants' future accuracy.

## 2. CONNECTIONS, IMPLICATIONS, AND FUTURE DIRECTIONS

Researchers almost universally agree that other people play a key role in explaining the power of human learning. Researchers also agree that learning from others leaves us potentially vulnerable to misinformation. These two lines of research—on pedagogical reasoning and epistemic trust—have advanced largely independently of each other. We have presented a unified approach in which pedagogical reasoning and epistemic trust are different facets of the same problem: reasoning about other people's knowledge and intent. We have illustrated how our framework predicts pedagogical data selection and its implications for learning and explains children's behavior when learning who to trust for information.

We have contrasted our approach with an account from each of these literatures: strong sampling for pedagogical learning and heuristic monitoring for epistemic trust. In each case, we argue that our model represents an improvement over these previous accounts. Unlike strong sampling, our approach to pedagogical reasoning explains teachers' choices of evidence, learning from negative evidence and learning from variable amounts of data. Unlike the heuristic account, our approach explains variation in children's behavior across situations and developmental stages in terms of a simple set of principles based on reasoning about informants' knowledge and helpfulness.

Together, these arguments illustrate how pedagogical learning and epistemic trust can be viewed as two sides of the same coin. In pedagogical learning, the informant is known to be knowledgeable and helpful, and the goal is to learn about the world. In epistemic trust, often the world is known, and the goal is to learn about the informant. In the former case, knowledge about the informant provides leverage for learning about the world. In the latter, knowledge about the world provides leverage for learning about the informant.

However, as demonstrated by Corriveau, Fusaro, et al. (2009), learning about the world and informants may also occur simultaneously, and our model captures this ability too. This highlights a remarkable ability of children—the ability to perform joint inference (or learning) over multiple variables. While in some ways this appears remarkably sophisticated, this ability is the crux of the explanation for how social learning affects learning about the world; arguably, the problem of childhood is one of learning about both the physical and social worlds.

In the remainder of the paper, we briefly consider connections to previous research, implications for other literatures, and outline potential future directions.

## 2.1. Connections

Our unified framework suggests that children reason about other people's knowledge and helpfulness. This proposal contrasts with standard work on theory of mind (ToM), where children have been shown to have difficulty reasoning about other people's knowledge (Baron-Cohen, Leslie, & Frith, 1985; Wimmer & Perner, 1983; Wellman, Cross, & Watson, 2001). In standard ToM tasks, children must reason about other people's behavior when the person's beliefs are false. In these tasks, results suggest that 3-year-old children have difficulty predicting people's behavior, while 4-year old children do not (but see Onishi & Baillargeon, 2005). The key element of these tasks is that the actor's beliefs are not in accord with the truth while the child's are.

In contrast, in the pedagogical reasoning tasks we considered, the learner does not know the true state of the world and tries to infer it based on the assumption the informant is knowledgeable and known to be helpful, as in pedagogy. Similarly, in epistemic trust tasks, the learner either knows the state of the world and assesses the informant's behavior against that or the learner does not know the true state of the world and assesses multiple informants against each other. In either case, children do not need to predict an informant's behavior based on that informant's false beliefs; informants either have true beliefs or are uncertain. Thus, there is no necessary reason why pedagogical or epistemic trust reasoning necessarily depends on false belief reasoning.

Our approach also differs from previous research modeling aspects of ToM. Butterfield, Jenkins, Sobel, and Schwertfeger (2009) formalized certain aspects of ToM using Markov random fields, providing qualitative arguments that the model can capture effects of uncertainty and reliability and gaze following abilities. Baker, Saxe, and Tenenbaum (2009) formalize action understanding as inverse planning and provide evidence based on adults' judgments about the goals of animated agents in sprite worlds. Unlike Butterfield et al. (2009), our approach has been to not only demonstrate capabilities of our models but to leverage models to provide explanations for developmental changes in performance. Unlike Baker et al. (2009), our focus is on learning about the world and others through intentional acts of communication, as opposed to simple observation.

## 2.2. Implications

The unified framework covers a wide variety of research and therefore potentially has broad implications. Here, we focus on the two literatures for which it has the most obvious implications: broader literature on epistemic trust and research on deception.

We have focused on the subset of epistemic trust literature which investigates what informant characteristics children track by manipulating the data informants produce. There is an extensive literature suggesting that these are not the only characteristics that children attend to. Children also attend to perceptual aspects of the stimuli (Corriveau, Harris, et al., 2009), informants' accents (Kinzler et al., 2011), and others' nonverbal cues such as bystander reactions (Fusaro & Harris, 2008). Each of these situations leverages additionally information that does not simply reduce to reasoning about the evidence that people provide. Consequently, to model these scenarios would require additional machinery. For instance, with a model of the relationship between perceptual similarity and categories (e.g. Anderson, 1991), the framework could be extended to generate predictions regarding how perceptual similarity of stimuli interacts with judgments about trust. With a model of the relationship between social groups and accents and a distinction between different groups of informants, the framework could be extended to explain the effects of accent on trust. These suggest interesting directions for future research.

There is also a vast body of work which examines children's ability understand and engage in deception. These works cover white lies (Lee & Talwar, 2002), concealing transgressions (Lewis, Stanger, & Sullivan, 1989; Talwar & Lee, 2002), deception games (Chandler, Fritz, & Hala, 1989; Hala, Chandler, & Fritz, 1991; Couillard & Woodward, 1999; Sodian & Frith, 1992), and deception for self-gain (Peskin, 1992). Our model formalizes two types of intentions that a communicative agent may have: helpfulness, and what we have called unhelpfulness. Note that we formalized unhelpfulness as minimizing the learners' belief in the correct hypothesis. This represents a weak case of what may be considered deception—the goal is to mislead the learner.

It is interesting to ask whether the modeling framework may be used to model development of reasoning about deception. A key issue would be identifying cases which have properties similar to the studies we focused on when modeling trust: a simple manipulation of helpfulness and knowledgeability. Couillard and Woodward (1999) designed an experiment in which the informant's helpfulness was left unknown, but could be learned from data, which is a similar design to the epistemic trust studies, where aspects of the informant must be inferred based on the data that they choose. Mascaro and Sperber (2009) follow a format similar to Couillard and Woodward (1999). Here children were told beforehand by the experimenter, in the liar condition, that the informant was a "big liar" and always told lies. Clearly, these are cases where our framework could be applied and used to generate predictions. In the former case, the model would reason about a knowledgeable informant and infer their intent based on the outcome of the trials. In the latter case, the model would make predictions about the outcomes of the trials given the informant's knowledge and intent (Shafto et al., 2012). These examples indicate that systematic investigation of predictions about the development of reasoning about deception is an important direction for future work.

## 2.3. Future Directions

The literatures on pedagogical reasoning and epistemic trust stand in contrast with each other. The literature on pedagogical reasoning seeks to explain how children could learn so much, so quickly. In order to explain these abilities,

Csibra and Gergely (2009) and colleagues (see also Tomasello, 1999; Tomasello, Carpenter, Call, Tanya, & Moll, 2005) have suggested that infants come prepared to identify and interpret acts of teaching. In contrast, the literature on epistemic trust notes that not all informants should be trusted and seeks to explain how children determine who is trustworthy. Thus, while the pedagogy literature emphasizes the need to assume that informants are knowledgeable and helpful, the epistemic trust literature emphasizes the need to assume that informants are *not* always knowledgeable and helpful.

Confounded with this difference in emphasis is a difference in the ages of the children studied. The literature on pedagogy seeks to study children as young as possible [often from 1 year of age and on through school ages (Gergely, Egyed, & Király, 2007; Topál, Gergely, Miklósi, Erdohegyi, & Csibra, 2008)], while the literature on epistemic trust tends to study children 3 years old and up. The differences between these literatures belie the common developmental questions: what assumptions/abilities are built in and what is the developmental trajectory of learning from informants.

There are two main possibilities for resolving these differences. First, it could be that children innately assume informants are knowledgeable and helpful, and this is gradually unlearned through experience with older siblings and tricky grandfathers. Or second, it could be that children begin with weak assumptions about the nature of informants, and their early pedagogical reasoning and later skepticism are both a consequence of their changing experiences with informants and beliefs about the world.

A key question for future research is to characterize and test the consequences of each position, a task that computational modeling is uniquely positioned to facilitate. Our recent research suggests that developmental changes between 3 and 4 years of age on epistemic trust tasks may be attributable to changes in expectations about informants (Shafto et al., 2012). Similarly, computational simulations can be used to ask to what degree can each hypothesis explain the speed of learning and what kinds of developmental trajectory could we expect from each hypothesis? These represent important directions for future research and ways in which computational models and empirical research may mutually inform each other.

## 3. CONCLUSION

We have presented a unified account of reasoning about learning from pedagogically sampled data and epistemic trust. We propose that these are instances of the broader problem of reasoning about informants' knowledgeability and intent. We illustrated the workings of our framework on representative problems from each literature and contrasted the account provided by our model with theoretical explanations specific to each domain. We suggest that our approach to modeling children's learning and development points to fruitful avenues for future research. There is much to be learned about how other people affect children's learning and development, but we are confident that continued integration of computational modeling and empirical methods points a way forward.

# APPENDIX: MODEL SPECIFICATION

Here we describe in detail how the individual components of the model function and interact. We then describe mathematically how the model chooses informants.

## Helpfulness and Knowledgeability

Learners' beliefs about helpfulness and knowledgeability can be broken down into three levels: beliefs about informants in general, beliefs about an individual informant, and beliefs about an informant on a given trial. Working from the bottom up, in the model, the informant is knowledgeable on a given trial with probability $\theta_k$ or $P(k) = \theta_k$. That is,

$$k \sim \text{Bernoulli}(\theta_k), \tag{11.4}$$

where $k$ describes an informant's knowledgeability on a particular trial and $\theta_k$ describes the tendencies of an individual informant.

These tendencies are derived from the learner's prior beliefs about informants in general, which follow a Beta distribution with two hyperparameters: uniformity, $\gamma_k \in (0, \infty)$, and bias, $\beta_k \in (0, 1)$. Uniformity corresponds to the beliefs that people are uniform in their knowledgeability (high uniformity, $\gamma_k \to \infty$) or that people tend to have different levels of knowledgeability (low value, $\gamma_k \to 0$). Bias corresponds to the belief that people are knowledgeable ($\beta_k \to 1$) or not ($\beta_k \to 0$). Putting these pieces together,

$$\theta_k \sim \text{Beta}(\gamma_k \beta_k, \gamma_k(1 - \beta_k)). \tag{11.5}$$

Helpfulness is defined similarly to knowledgeability,

$$h \sim \text{Bernoulli}(\theta_h) \tag{11.6}$$

$$\theta_h \sim \text{Beta}(\gamma_h \beta_h, \gamma_h(1 - \beta_h)). \tag{11.7}$$

## State of the World

The true state of the word is distributed uniform over possible states,

$$P(w') = \frac{1}{|W|}, \tag{11.8}$$

where $|W|$ is the number of possible states of the world.

## Beliefs

Informants' beliefs are determined by their knowledgeability and the true state of the world. Informants who are knowledgeable have beliefs corresponding to the true state of the world; naive informants have beliefs distributed uniformly over all possible states of the world. Formally,

$$P_I(b = w'|k) = \begin{cases} 1 & \text{if } k \\ 1/|W| & \text{if naïve.} \end{cases} \tag{11.9}$$

## Actions

The action performed by an informant is dependent on that informant's beliefs and helpfulness. Here we must specify the model for two types of actions: intervention on a causal device (e.g. Fig. 11.1, left) and labeling (e.g. Fig. 11.1, right). In the case of labeling, a helpful informant will utter the label corresponding to her beliefs; an unhelpful informant will choose any label other that the one corresponding to her beliefs. Formally,

$$P(l|b, h) = \begin{cases} 1 & \text{if } l = b \text{ and } h = 1 \\ 0 & \text{if } l \neq b \text{ and } h = 1 \\ 0 & \text{if } l = b \text{ and } h = 0 \\ 1/(|W| - 1) & \text{if } l \neq b \text{ and } h = 0 \end{cases}. \tag{11.10}$$

In the case of interventions on a causal device, actions are chosen according to Eqn 11.2. Effects are then determined by the intervention and the underlying causal structure of the world.

## Learning about and Choosing Informants

The studies in section require learners to choose informants for information (ask trials). As in the studies, we focus here on world learning. The model chooses informants with probability proportionate to how likely they are to produce correct labels in the future given their knowledgeability, helpfulness, and previous experience, $E$. To do this, the model must predict the probability of each informant labeling correctly for each possible true state of the world, $w' \in W$. For each informant,

$$P(l = w'|k, h, E) = \sum_{w' \in W} P(w') \int P(l = w'|w', \theta) P(\theta|\gamma, \beta, E) d\theta,$$

(11.11)

where, for purposes of brevity, $\theta = \theta_h, \theta_k, \gamma = \gamma_h, \gamma_k$, and $\beta = \beta_h, \beta_k$. The integral over $\theta$ is not analytically solvable. We therefore approximate using Monte Carlo methods (here, rejection sampling).

The probability in Eqn 11.11 is then normalized over informants. For example, given two informants $a$ and $b$, the model chooses to ask informant $a$ with probability equal to

$$P(a) = \frac{P_a(l = w'|k, h, d)}{P_a(l = w'|k, h, d) + P_b(l = w'|k, h, d)}.$$

(11.12)

Results for endorse trials can be similarly captured by taking inferences summed over informants and normalized over each true state over the world.

## REFERENCES

Anderson, J. (1991). The adaptive nature of human categorization. *Psychological Review, 98*(3), 409.

Baker, C. L., Saxe, R., & Tenenbaum, J. B. (2009). Action understanding as inverse planning. *Cognition, 113*, 329–349.

Baron-Cohen, S., Leslie, A. M., & Frith, U. (1985). Does the autistic child have a "theory of mind"? *Cognition, 21*(1), 37–46.

Bonawitz, E., Shafto, P., Gweon, H., Goodman, N. D., Spelke, E., & Schulz, L. (2011). The double-edged sword of pedagogy: instruction limits spontaneous exploration and discovery. *Cognition, 120*(3), 322–330.

Buchbaum, D., Griffiths, T., Gopnik, A., & Shafto, P. (2011). Children's imitation of causal action sequences is influenced by statistical and pedagogical evidence. *Cognition, 120,* 331–340.

Butterfield, J., Jenkins, O. C., Sobel, D. M., & Schwertfeger, J. (2009). Modeling aspects of theory of mind with Markov random fields. *International Journal of Social Robotics, 1,* 41–51.

Chandler, M., Fritz, A., & Hala, S. (1989). Small-scale deceit: deception as a marker of two-, three-, and four-year-olds' early theories of mind. *Child Development, 60*(6), 1263–1277.

Corriveau, K., & Harris, P. L. (2009). Choosing your informant: weighing familiarity and recent accuracy. *Developmental Science, 12*(3), 426–437.

Corriveau, K. H., Fusaro, M., & Harris, P. L. (2009). Going with the flow: preschoolers prefer nondissenters as informants. *Psychological Science, 20*(3), 372–377.

Corriveau, K. H., Harris, P. L., Meins, E., Fernyhough, C., Arnott, B., Elliott, L., et al. (2009). Young children's trust in their mother's claims: longitudinal links with attachment security in infancy. *Child Development, 80*(3), 750–761.

Couillard, N., & Woodward, A. (1999). Children's comprehension of deceptive points. *British Journal of Developmental Psychology, 17*(4), 515–521.

Csibra, G., & Gergely, G. (2009). Natural pedagogy. *Trends in Cognitive Sciences, 13*(4), 148–153.

Fitneva, S. A., & Dunfield, K. A. (2010). Selective information seeking after a single encounter. *Developmental Psychology, 46*(5), 1380–1384.

Fusaro, M., & Harris, P. L. (2008). Children assess informant reliability using bystanders' non-verbal cues. *Developmental Science, 11*(5), 771–777.

Gergely, G., Egyed, K., & Kiraly, I. (2007). On pedagogy. *Developmental Science, 10*(1), 139–146.

Gold, E. (1967). Language identification in the limit. *Information and Control, 10,* 447–474.

Hala, S., Chandler, M., & Fritz, A. S. (1991). Fledgling theories of mind: deception as a marker of three-year-olds' understanding of false belief. *Child Development, 62*(1), 83.

Jaswal, V. K., & Neely, L. A. (2006). Adults don't always know best: preschoolers use past reliability over age when learning new words. *Psychological Science, 17*(9), 757–758.

Kinzler, K. D., Corriveau, K. H., & Harris, P. L. (2011). Children's selective trust in native-accented speakers. *Developmental Science, 14*(1), 106–111.

Koenig, M. A., & Harris, P. L. (2005). Preschoolers mistrust ignorant and inaccurate speakers. *Child Development, 76*(6), 1261–1277.

Lee, K., & Talwar, V. (2002). Emergence of white-lie telling in children between 3 and 7 years of age. *Merrill-Palmer Quarterly, 48*(2), 160–181.

Lewis, M., Stanger, C., & Sullivan, M. W. (1989). Deception in 3-year-olds. *Developmental Psychology, 25*(3), 439–443.

Mascaro, O., & Sperber, D. (2009). The moral, epistemic, and mindreading components of children's vigilance towards deception. *Cognition, 112*(3), 367–380.

Nurmsoo, E., & Robinson, E. J. (2009). Identifying unreliable informants: do children excuse past inaccuracy? *Developmental Science, 12*(1), 41–47.

Onishi, K. H., & Baillargeon, R. (2005). Do 15-month-old infants understand false beliefs? *Science, 308*(5719), 255–258.

Pasquini, E. S., Corriveau, K. H., Koenig, M., & Harris, P. L. (2007). Preschoolers monitor the relative accuracy of informants. *Developmental Psychology, 43*(5), 1216–1226.

Pearl, J. (2009). *Causality: Models, Reasoning and Inference* (2nd ed.). New York: Cambridge University Press.

Peskin, J. (1992). Ruse and representations: on children's ability to conceal information. *Developmental Psychology, 28*(1), 84.

Rhodes, M., Gelman, S. A., & Brickman, D. (2010). Children's attention to sample composition in learning, teaching, and discovery. *Developmental Science, 13*(3), 421–429.

Shafto, P., Eaves, B., Navarro, D., & Perfors, A. (2012). Epistemic trust: modeling children's reasoning about others' knowledge and intent. *Developmental Science, 15*(3), 436–447.

Shafto, P., & Goodman, N. (2008). Teaching games: statistical sampling assumptions for learning in pedagogical situations. In *Proceedings of the Thirtieth Annual Conference of the Cognitive Science Society.*

Sobel, D. M., & Corriveau, K. H. (2010). Children monitor individuals' expertise for word learning. *Child Development, 81*(2), 669–679.

Sodian, B., & Frith, U. (1992). Deception and sabotage in autistic, retarded and normal children. *Journal of Child Psychology and Psychiatry, 33*(3), 591–605.

Spirtes, P., Glymour, C., & Scheines, R. (1993). *Causation, prediction, and search, volume 81 of lecture notes in statistics.* New York, NY: Springer.

Talwar, V., & Lee, K. (2002). Development of lying to conceal a transgression: children's control of expressive behaviour during verbal deception. *International Journal of Behavioral Development, 26*(5), 436–444.

Tenenbaum, J. B. (1999). Bayesian modeling of human concept learning. In M. Kearns, S. A. Soller, T. K. Leen, & K. R. Muller (Eds.), *Advances in neural processing systems 11* (pp. 59–65). Cambridge: MIT Press.

Tenenbaum, J. B., Griffiths, T. L., & Kemp, C. (2006). Theory-based Bayesian models of inductive learning and reasoning. *Trends in Cognitive Sciences, 10*(7), 309–318.

Tomasello, M. (1999). *The cultural origins of human cognition.* Cambridge: Harvard University Press.

Tomasello, M., Carpenter, M., Call, J., Tanya, B., & Moll, H. (2005). Understanding and sharing intentions: the origins of cultural cognition. *Behavioral and Brain Sciences, 28*, 675–735.

Topál, J., Gergely, G., Miklósi, A., Erdohegyi, A., & Csibra, G. (2008). Infants' perseverative search errors are induced by pragmatic misinterpretation. *Science, 321*(September), 1831.

VanderBorght, M. (2009). Who knows best? Preschoolers sometimes prefer child informants over adult informants. *Infant and Child Development, 71*(November 2008), 61–71.

Wellman, H. M., Cross, D., & Watson, J. (2001). Meta-analysis of theory-of-mind development: the truth about false belief. *Child Development, 72*(3), 655–684.

Wimmer, H., & Perner, J. (1983). Beliefs about beliefs: representation and constraining function of wrong beliefs in young children's understanding of deception. *Cognition, 13*(1), 103–128.

Xu, F., & Tenenbaum, J. B. (2007). Sensitivity to sampling in Bayesian word learning. *Developmental Science, 10*(3), 288–297.

# CHAPTER TWELVE

# The Influence of Social Information on Children's Statistical and Causal Inferences

## David M. Sobel*,[1] and Natasha Z. Kirkham**

*Department of Cognitive, Linguistic, and Psychological Sciences, Brown University, Providence, Rhode Island, USA
**Centre for Brain and Cognitive Development, Birkbeck College, University of London, London, England, UK
[1]Corresponding author: E-mail: david_sobel_1@brown.edu

## Contents

## Abstract

Constructivist accounts of learning posit that causal inference is a child-driven process. Recent interpretations of such accounts also suggest that the process children use for causal learning is rational: Children interpret and learn from new evidence in light of their existing beliefs. We argue that such mechanisms are also driven by informative social cues and suggest ways in which such information influences both preschoolers' and infants' inferences. In doing so, we argue that a rational constructivist account should not only focus on describing the child's internal cognitive mechanisms for learning but also on how social information affects the process of learning.

*Advances in Child Development and Behavior*, Volume 43
ISSN 0065-2407,
http://dx.doi.org/10.1016/B978-0-12-397919-3.00012-5

321

## 1. INTRODUCTION

Imagine if a child never encountered another sentient being. She would acquire some pieces of knowledge, mostly about what is directly observable in the physical world (e.g. concepts of object continuity, solidity, gravity, support, containment, even if she would have no language to describe these concepts). It is even possible that she would learn some pieces of biological knowledge (e.g. knowledge that inanimate objects, even natural kinds, don't eat, drink, or breathe, again even if she would have no language to describe these concepts). But clearly, what she would lack is any knowledge of convention or an understanding of structures that involve hidden or unobservable events. In general, children do not spontaneously form beliefs about Santa Claus, angels, germs, Scientology, vitamins, the meaning of words, and the rules of Chutes and Ladders without input from people. This is all information learned from others (e.g. Harris & Koenig, 2006).

There is now a long literature on "selective trust"—the hypothesis that children are not as overly credulous as was once thought (e.g. Coady, 1992; Reid, 1764/1970) but that they evaluate the reliability of an informant as a source of knowledge based on a variety of factors, including their existing knowledge of people in general (e.g. Jaswal & Neely, 2006; Kinzler, Corriveau & Harris, 2011) as well as that particular individual's history of generating accurate information (e.g. Koenig & Harris, 2005; Pasquini, Corriveau, Koenig & Harris, 2007). One way of thinking about this literature is that young children use whatever existing causal or conceptual knowledge they possess to evaluate whether individuals are reliable sources of knowledge (Koenig & Jaswal, 2011; Sobel & Corriveau, 2010). Indeed, computational descriptions of selective trust (e.g. Butterfield, Jenkins, Sobel & Schwertfuger, 2009; Eaves & Shafto, in this volume; Shafto, Eaves, Navarro & Perfors, 2012; Sobel, Buchanan, Butterfield & Jenkins, 2010) have emphasized that the way children learn from others' testimony is by rationally integrating their existing knowledge with the data they observe from others.

The goal of this chapter was to consider the opposite relation—how social knowledge affects reasoning and learning about statistical and causal knowledge, following the idea that most of our knowledge comes from social interaction (e.g. Bruner, 1990; Vygotsky, 1978). Elsewhere, we have suggested that infants' causal learning abilities emerge from their early-developing sensitivities to statistical relations among physical events (Sobel & Kirkham, 2007a, 2007b). Here, we will expand that theory and argue that infants' and young children's abilities to learn both statistical and causal information are moderated by social information inherent in the environment.

Our thesis is that there are various ways in which social information from the environment influences the interaction between the child's existing knowledge and the data they observe. In some cases, particularly early in development, these influences are attentional. Social information guides what data infants are more likely to pay attention to (e.g. Wu & Kirkham, 2010; Wu, Gopnik, Richarson & Kirkham, 2011). These cases are particularly important in infancy when children are faced with the problem of picking out the appropriate relations in the environment from which to learn. From a constructivist perspective, knowing what data to attend to in order to learn information might provide children with critical developmental insights. For example, 14-month-olds will register any kind of statistical regularity among object parts and their function, including that the shape of one object's part affects the function of another part. Eighteen-month-olds, in contrast, given the same exposure, will not register this same regularity (Madole & Cohen, 1995). Presumably, what the older children have learned is that this kind of regularity is not mechanistically plausible (even if they cannot express that concept linguistically), so it can be ignored. We suggest that social information provides the foundation for what is worth attending to and what is not crucial for making ontological commitments.

Later in development, the influence becomes more cognitive. Preschoolers are better able to focus their attention in a noisy environment, and thus, social information or presenting information in a social context allows these older children to interpret data in different ways than would occur in the absence of or in different contextual environment of that information. Moreover, such effects are not limited to a particular age group—rather, they are dependent on the nature of the task. For instance, effects of "pedagogy"—making inferences based on what others do and say, but also what they do not do and say—might be present (e.g. Bonawitz, Shafto, Gweon et al., 2011) or absent (Sobel & Sommerville, 2009) in a particular age group (e.g. 4-year-olds) or might be present in very young children (e.g. Gweon, Tenenbaum & Schulz, 2010), depending on the nature of the task. Collectively, as children come to understand how to focus attention in a complex environment, social cues can provide them with information beyond what they directly observe; this information can then be used for statistical and causal learning.

The plan of this chapter is as follows: We will first describe three lines of research. Line 1 describes statistical learning capacities in infants, which are potentially useful in learning pieces of physical knowledge (e.g. about the composition of objects from component features). Within this line, we will describe particular effects of social information on these learning mechanisms as well as the developmental trajectory of these effects. The goal here is to outline how social information initially focuses children's attention in a distraction-filled environment. Line 2 will then describe how various ways social information influences preschoolers' causal inferences. In this case, the focus will predominantly be on how social cues are not focusing attention, but rather providing children with additional information beyond the data presented. Line 3 will then examine a case in which children's ability to make rational inferences differs across the physical and social domain. Again, a critical point is that there is not a point in development in which rational inference emerges—rather, children are potentially capable of such inferences at very young ages but are potentially limited by information processing capacities or by what existing knowledge they possess at a given point in time. Finally, we will end with two discussion points—one about the nature of rationality and one about the relation between natural pedagogy (or social cues more generally) and children's causal inference.

## 2. SOCIAL INFLUENCES ON INFANTS' STATISTICAL LEARNING

Over the past two decades, it has become evident that infants and young children have access to a powerful domain-general learning device, which allows for quick learning of statistically defined (or probabilistic) patterns in both the auditory and visual domain (e.g. Fiser & Aslin, 2002; Kirkham, Slemmer & Johnson, 2002; Kirkham, Slemmer, Richardson & Johnson, 2007; Saffran, Aslin & Newport, 1996; Thiessen, 2011). For example, 9-month-old infants prefer to look at shapes that previously predictably co-occurred, rather than at shapes that did not co-occur in a predictable manner (Fiser & Aslin, 2002). Infants can then use statistical regularities inherent in the environment to identify what to learn and to make further inferences. Several developmental skills, such as object recognition (e.g. Biederman, 1987), categorization (e.g. Mareschal, Quinn & French, 2002; Rakison & Butterworth, 1998; Schyns & Rodet, 1997; Younger & Cohen, 1986), and word learning (e.g. Estes, Evans, Alibali & Saffran, 2007), benefit from learning the statistical regularities of visual and auditory features. For instance, during word learning, infants group co-occurring phonemes into words (Saffran et al., 1996) and then attach those newly segmented words to objects (Estes et al., 2007).

Even if infants can learn from the regularity with which events co-occur, the natural environment often presents infants with multiple simultaneous co-occurrences. How do infants know which regularities to attend to, learn from, and maintain for use in further tasks? Social cues are one of the ways in which infants may have their attention directed to the appropriate information.

Infants seem well prepared to be supported by such cues. By the first few months of life, infants engage in joint attention (Butterworth, 2004) elicited by eye gaze, infant-directed speech, initial eye contact, head turn, and gestures (Carpenter, Nagell & Tomasello, 1998; Senju & Csibra, 2008). Many investigators have suggested that this attentional bias helps infants develop their social cognition and competence (e.g. understanding beliefs, desires, goals, and communicative intent; see e.g. Carpenter et al., 1998; Csibra & Gergely, 2006; Kushnir, Xu & Wellman, 2010; Repacholi & Gopnik, 1997). However, these cues also can shape cognitive development by helping infants learn what to learn in a distraction-filled environment. The concept of "natural pedagogy" (cf. Csibra & Gergely, 2009) suggests that infants are prepared to accept social information by showing an early-developing sensitivity to ostensive signals and contexts. In other words, young infants might be capable of understanding that a social cue has a communicative intent and therefore is of immediate importance.

Along these lines, Wu and Kirkham (2010) found that 8-month-olds were better able to learn regularity among audiovisual events when those events were cued by social cues (i.e. a dynamic turning face that used direct eye contact, followed by a head turn and infant-directed speech) than nonsocial cues (i.e. flashing squares that shift attention to the target location). This deeper learning occurred, even though there was no difference in looking time during familiarization between the two conditions, which suggests that the social cue offered more than just a direction of attention but also an idea of intentional communication.

Social cues can also impact how infants use statistical regularity to make deeper cognitive inferences, such as object segmentation. Wu et al. (2011) familiarized 8-month-olds with a series of statistically defined objects, consisting of three parts: Two of the parts always co-occurred, while the third part changed in each presentation. During test trials, the objects would split apart, with one part drifting away, leaving two remaining together; the split was either consistent with the co-occurrences (i.e. the part that changed during presentations would split off) or inconsistent (i.e. the split would occur

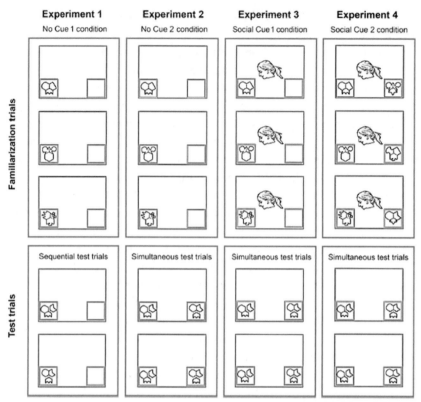

**Figure 12.1** Schematic representation of Wu et al. (2011) procedure.

between the parts that always stayed together; see Fig. 12.1). In other words, if the infants had been following the relations between the parts, they would learn that the changing part was more likely to split off. Importantly, these objects were not alone on the screen—during familiarization and during test, there were distracting objects that were equally as interesting, but which had completely different internal correlations. Therefore, in order to perform well on test trials that measured learning of the target correlations, the infant had to attend to the appropriate objects. A social cue (again a turning face, using infant-directed speech) focused infants' attention on the cued target pattern during familiarization, and infants were capable of learning the correlations and showed longer looking time to the inconsistent splits, a violation of expectation result. Without the social cue, even in absence of the competing event during familiarization, infants were not capable of learning the correct co-occurrences. Taken together, this suggests that social cues not only support direction of attention but also quality of learning.

Although this is only the beginning of work looking at the relation between social cueing and statistical learning, there is already some suggestion of a developmental trajectory. We know that the ability to detect gaze direction forms the backbone of joint attention and develops quickly over the first 4 months of life (e.g. Vecera & Johnson, 1995). Studies using an adapted Posner cueing paradigm have found facilitated target detection from gaze direction with a computerized face in 3-month-olds (Hood, Willen & Driver, 1998) and more recently in newborns (Farroni, Massaccesi, Pividori, Simion & Johnson, 2004). By 3–4 months of age, infants can follow a "looker" to a target and do so reliably by 5–6 months of age under simple ideal conditions (Butterworth, 2004; Flom & Pick, 2007; Poulin-Dubois, Demke & Olineck, 2007; Senju & Csibra, 2008; Striano & Reid, 2006). All these data suggest sensitivity to ostensive cueing early in infancy, but there has not been much work addressing when these cues begin to support learning in a way that is qualitatively different from less social cues. Interestingly, using the same social cueing paradigm, Wu and Kirkham (2010) found that 4-month-olds were capable of following the face cue to the correct audiovisual event but did not benefit from this cue. They showed identical performance to the 8-month-olds in the *nonsocial* cueing condition. In other words, 4-month-olds were successfully directed by the cue, but the quality of learning was not enhanced. These preliminary data suggest that infants might have to "learn to learn" from social cues, in the same way as they do with other ostensive cues (e.g. arrows; Kingstone, Smilek, Ristic, Friesen & Eastwood, 2003; Varga et al., 2009).

In sum, we would like to suggest that infants have an early-developing, robust capacity for picking up on the statistical structure within multimodal, complex events and that this capacity supports infants' representation of their world. Importantly, social cueing may provide a parameter within which infants can focus their attention on the appropriate structures.

## 3. A NOTE ABOUT THE RELATION BETWEEN STATISTICAL AND CAUSAL LEARNING

None of the ideas presented in the previous section, however, are specifically about children's ability to learn novel pieces of causal information or make causal inferences about novel systems. Describing how children engage in causal learning and inference brings up a particular problem. While some causal relations are directly perceivable (e.g. Michotte's billiard balls), most causal knowledge is not. Statistical regularity offers a good starting point. Knowing that a particular causal relation exists suggests that certain regularities will occur; if event X causes event Y, then the occurrence of X will make the occurrence of Y more likely (all other things being equal). Similarly, observing such regularity offers insight into causal structure. If Y is more likely in the presence of X than in its absence, we might believe that X causes Y. Indeed, some adult experiments on causal learning suggest that such probabilistic reasoning might be considered a normative model of causal inference (Allan, 1980; Shanks, 1995).

Statistical regularity does not always indicate causality. Any case in which the dependence relation between two events (X and Y) switches, given the presence or absence of a third (Z) suggests a causal structure in which a direct causal relation does not exist between them (e.g. $X \rightarrow Z \rightarrow Y$). To learn causal structures, children must have a mechanism for recognizing statistical regularities among events, but also parsing out conditional independence and dependence relations.

Several researchers have suggested that by the second half of the first year of life, infants make complex causal inferences in which they resolve their perception of ambiguous events in terms of mechanistic or intentional causality (e.g. Kosugi, Ishida & Fujita, 2003; Muentener & Carey, 2010; Saxe, Tenenbaum & Carey, 2005; Teglas et al., 2011). Similarly, 8-month-olds appear capable of intuitive statistical reasoning, relating the samples they observe to the population of objects from which those samples were taken (e.g. Xu & Garcia, 2008). These findings, however, tend to be mostly limited to infants in the second half of the first year of life. This leaves open the possibility that a more sophisticated system for causal inference emerges from statistical learning mechanisms. Cohen and colleagues (Cohen & Amsel, 1998; Cohen & Oakes, 1993; Oakes, 1994; Oakes & Cohen, 1990) have suggested that the perception of simple causal relations develops between approximately ages 5–10 months. More relevant to the present discussion, Sobel and Kirkham (2006, 2007a, 2007b) found that children's ability to recognize conditional independence and dependence in statistical regularity developed between the ages of 5 and 8 months. They hypothesized that a mechanism for causal learning emerged from children's statistical learning capacities. This would be consistent with infants' developing statistical reasoning capacities: Denison, Reed, and Xu (in press) found that 6-month-olds, but not 4.5-month-olds, registered the relation between the distribution of a sample and the population from which it came (similar to Xu & Garcia's findings on 8-month-olds). We take this finding as evidence in favor of a developing mechanism for causal inference that goes beyond registering mere statistical regularity among events (although other interpretations are possible).

In the rest of this chapter, we will focus on research on older children. We suggest, however, that this discussion leads to a particularly important open question that must be addressed: How does social information influences the emergence of a causal reasoning system in very young children? We think that there is little data to address this particularly important question, but one that should motivate future investigations.

## 4. INFLUENCES OF SOCIAL INFORMATION ON PRESCHOOLERS' CAUSAL INFERENCES

By the age of 4, children have the ability to make relatively sophisticated causal inferences (e.g. Bullock, Gelman & Baillargeon, 1982; Gopnik, Sobel, Schulz & Glymour, 2001; Schulz & Gopnik, 2004; Schulz & Sommerville, 2006; Sobel, Tenenbaum & Gopnik, 2004). That said, children's causal inference capacities have not developed completely. In some cases, what's still developing is appreciation of specific kinds of causal mechanisms, like those that act at a distance (e.g. Kushnir & Gopnik, 2007; Sobel & Buchanan, 2009; see also Shultz, 1982, Experiment 2). In other cases, what's developing is more domain-general, like the explicit role of probabilistic information in causal inferences or children's capacity to integrate a set of causal relations together to form a causal structure. In this section, we examine how social information might influence children's developing capacities to engage in these inferences.

### 4.1. Understanding Probabilistic Information

Many investigations of preschoolers' reasoning suggest that they have difficulty with explicit probabilistic concepts (e.g. Davies, 1965; Hoemann & Ross, 1982; Piaget & Inhelder, 1975; Schlottman, 2001). Piaget and Inhelder (1975), for example, showed that 3–7-year-olds' choices on various probabilistic tasks were arbitrary and that it was not until the concrete operational stage that children could differentiate between deterministic and probabilistic relations. They suggested that preoperational children only focused on surface associations, like magnitude estimations. Similarly, Hoemann and Ross (1971) presented 4- through 10-year-old children with spinners, divided into different areas of black and white. In their critical "probability" condition, they showed children a spinner and asked them to predict the color where the pointer would land. Children younger than 6 years chose colors randomly; older children demonstrated an emerging understanding of probability. Follow-up experiments led them to conclude that 3–5-year-olds do not have even "a glimmer of probability understanding" (Hoemann & Ross, 1982, p. 116).

However, other investigations have found that 4- and 5-year-olds have some understanding of probability (e.g. Beck, Robinson, Carroll & Apperly, 2006; Fischbein, 1975; Kushnir & Gopnik, 2005; Kuzmak & Gelman, 1986, Perner, 1979). For instance, Perner (1979) found that 4–5-year-olds could reason appropriately about probabilistic contrasts when they were quite large (where one event was likely 7/8th of the time and the other would occur 1/8th of the time). Furthermore, 4- and 5-year-olds' inferences overall improved over the course of his experiments, suggesting that this understanding was not completely impenetrable. Kushnir and Gopnik (2005) showed that 4-year-olds could make some explicit probability judgments from observational data, again when the contrasts were relatively high—for instance, when shown that one object always activated a machine and another object activated a machine one out of three times, children chose the first object as more likely to activate the machine.[1]

Sobel, Sommerville, Travers, Blumenthal, and Stoddard (2009) examined how children engaged in category-based induction of causal properties given probabilistic data. They introduced 3-, 4-, and 5-year-olds to a novel machine that lit up and played music when objects were put on it and showed children two sets of three identical objects. In their baseline experiment, on *deterministic* trials, all members of one set of objects activated the machine, while no member of the other set did so. Children then saw novel members of each set and were asked to pick which object was the best choice to make the machine go. Unsurprisingly, children in all age groups chose the object that was identical to the efficacious set. The more interesting case was when the data were *probabilistic*. On these trials, children observed that two members of one set of three activated the machine (while

---

[1] They also found in some (but not all) cases that 4-year-olds reliably chose an object that activated the machine two out of three times over one that activated the machine one out of three times. As shown in the paragraphs below, however, we could not replicate this finding using a slightly different method. Whether our failure to replicate resulted from our methodological difference or children's explicit probabilistic reasoning capacities is an open question.

the third did not) and one member of the other set of three activated the machine (while the other two did not). Children were asked the same test question—new members of each set were brought out and children were asked to pick the best one to make the machine go. Three- and 4-year-olds chose randomly; only the 5-year-olds picked the object from the set with two out of three efficacious members over the set with one out of three efficacious members reliably above chance.

Can social information help children's probabilistic inferences? Sobel et al. (2009) presented a new group of 3- and 4-year-olds with the same kinds of probabilistic data, but in addition to the information about each objects' efficacy, children observed the experimenter react to those data. For the set with two efficacious objects, the experimenter acted positively when the two objects made the machine go and exclaimed how strange it was that the one object that failed to activate the machine did so. For the set with only one efficacious object, the reactions were reversed; the experimenter thought the one object that activated the machine was strange while his reaction to the two that failed to activate the machine was approving. The hypothesis was that if children observed that the experimenter believed the data should have been deterministic, they would be more likely to treat it in that manner. This was not the case, and the overall choices that children made in this condition were no different from chance (i.e. exactly half of the time they chose the object from the set with two efficacious objects and half of the time they chose the object from the set with only one).

However, in order to appreciate the role of the experimenter's expectations, children must recognize that those expectations are in conflict with the actual observed data. That is, only children who recognize that the experimenter's beliefs about these data could possibly be inconsistent with the actual state of the world should be able to integrate those beliefs into a judgment of efficacy. As a simple measure for this possibility, all children were given a standard unexpected contents (based on Gopnik & Astington, 1988) false belief measure. When responses on the test question were considered as a function of performance on this measure, the children who showed a reliable understanding of others' false beliefs chose the novel object from the set with two efficacious objects ~70% of the time, reliable above chance and more than the children who did not show this understanding (who made this response only ~40% of the time).

The conclusion here is relatively simple—that children can go beyond the observed data and integrate another's expectations about what information is presented in order to make a causal inference. In this case, however, the social information necessary involves appreciating that what they actually observe is in conflict with those expectations. Hence, it is possible that an explicit understanding of another possessing a false belief might be necessary.

## 4.2. "Natural Pedagogy" Revisited

One could argue that in the previous example, the social information provided to children presented a test of their cognitive resources—they had to integrate the experimenter's expectations with the actual data and could only do so if they understood how to resolve the difference between those two pieces of information. Research on "natural pedagogy" (Csibra & Gergeley, 2009), in contrast, focuses on infants' and toddlers' capacities to learn from the intentional actions of others as they attempt to communicate or teach the child some piece of information (although it is also the case that toddlers appear capable of making inferences about statistical structure based on such pedagogical information, see Gweon et al., 2010; Yang, Bushnell, Buchanan & Sobel, 2012).

Assumptions about how others teach information are present in older children as well. Bonawitz, Shafto, Gweon et al. (2011) showed that 4–6-year-olds were sensitive to a teacher's intentions when demonstrating the function of a novel causal system. Children were introduced to an apparatus that afforded four nonobvious causal relations. In one condition, the teacher intentionally demonstrated one of the causal relations to the child. In the other conditions, the teacher engaged in a nonpedagogical demonstration, by (1) discovering that same function accidentally, (2) demonstrating that function, but then interrupting the demonstration session, or (3) doing nothing (a baseline condition). Children were more likely to replicate the demonstrated action in the first case but less likely to discover the other causal properties. In contrast, they were more likely to explore the apparatus and discover those properties in the latter cases but imitated the demonstrated function less frequently.

What's interesting about these effects is the ubiquitous nature of these pedagogical demonstrations. Unlike the previous example, where only children who could interpret the conflict between their mental state knowledge and the observe data used that social information, children in these experiments seem to evaluate *any* interaction between themselves and an agent in terms of the pedagogical cues (indeed Bonawitz, Shafto, Gweon et al., 2011 showed that children made these inferences even in indirect settings, where the demonstration was ostensibly to another child).

This stands somewhat in contrast to data from our laboratories. Sobel and Sommerville (2009) presented 4-year-olds with a lightbox (shown in Fig. 12.2). The box had four buttons on it, color coded to four lights (red, yellow, blue, and green). Children played a game with the experimenter where they were first introduced to the box as a puzzle box in which lights could activate each other deterministically. For instance, if red activated blue, then pressing the red button would activate the red and blue lights simultaneously, but pressing the blue button would just activate the blue light. Children observed the experimenter's steps and then through several of these puzzles (a button on the side of the box "changed" the puzzle. It was pressed in between each example).

At test, children observed the experimenter demonstrate ambiguous data to the child. The experimenter pressed the blue button, which made the blue (B), green (G), and yellow (Y) lights activate. He then pressed the yellow light, which made only the yellow light activate. At this point, he explained that he was confused about how the lights caused one another and that it could be that blue caused green and yellow directly (a common cause model in which $G \leftarrow B \rightarrow Y$) or that blue caused green and green caused yellow (a chain model in which $B \rightarrow G \rightarrow Y$). At this point, the experimenter presented a datum that disambiguated these models—he brought out a cover, which had previously been established to effectively remove a light's effects from the box and covered the green light while activating the blue button. This produced either only the blue light (indicating a chain model) or both the blue and yellow lights (indicating a common cause model). Right before he activated the blue button, the experimenter offered one of three rationales for his actions. He either said that he was performing these

**Figure 12.2** Lightbox used in Sobel and Sommerville (2009, 2010).

actions "so we can see what happens when we press the blue button without the green light" (the *appropriate rationale* condition) or "because I don't like the green light that much, and we can press the blue button because I think the blue light is pretty" (the *inappropriate rationale* condition) or offered no rationale for these actions (*baseline*). After this demonstration, children were shown pictorial representations of the appropriate chain and common cause models, and they were asked to point to the one they thought was how the lights were connected (i.e. the appropriate solution to the puzzle).

Consistent with the findings on children appreciating the pedagogical nature of demonstrated material, 4-year-olds accurately evaluated the data (i.e. they chose the correct causal model) in the appropriate rationale condition 70% of the time, significantly above chance and more than both the baseline and the inappropriate rationale condition, in which they only evaluated the data and selected the appropriate causal model 50% and 40% of the time, respectively. Critically, performance in this inappropriate rationale was not significantly different from the baseline condition, and both were not different from chance.

Performance in the baseline condition is critical here. If children are constantly evaluating the pedagogical nature of their interactions with others, then one might expect the difference between the appropriate and inappropriate rationale conditions, but that the baseline condition would be more like the appropriate rationale condition than the inappropriate one. Of course, there are critical differences between these results and the ones presented by Bonawitz, Shafto, Gweon et al. (2011). We did not offer children the opportunity to engage in exploratory play with the lightbox nor did we use a measure in which children had to imitate observed causal relations. Instead, our dependent measure was how well children could reconstruct a representation of the causal relations they observed. It is quite possible that there are fundamental differences between how children behave in a free play setting, given pedagogical information, and how they would respond to direct questions about the nature of the causal structure.

In particular, free play might afford children the opportunity to resolve ambiguous information. Indeed, Schulz and Bonawitz (2007) found that preschoolers play more with a toy when its causal efficacy is ambiguous than when they are shown unconfounded evidence about what the toy does. Similarly, Cook, Goodman, and Schulz (2011) showed that children explored novel objects more when their causal efficacy was known to be stochastic as opposed to deterministic. In stochastic cases, children do not know whether any particular objects are efficacious, which makes engaging in novel behaviors on the objects to discover potential hidden efficacy rational. Critically, children are doing this on their own (i.e. unprompted), and Cook et al. conclude that this proclivity for discovery might be part of a rational system for exploration.

## 4.3. Learning from Action versus Observation

We have tried to test out the importance of such discovery in causal learning for young children. In the adult literature, there is a large amount of evidence that we learn better from acting on a causal system than just observing it function (e.g. Lagnado & Sloman, 2004; Steyvers, Tenenbaum, Wagenmakers & Blum, 2003). But why might acting on the environment produce more accurate causal learning than merely observing data? Acting provides a learner with conditional probability information (e.g. in the lightbox example above, knowing whether blue activates yellow in the absence of green allows the child to discern between the common cause and chain models). Young children can recognize such conditional probability information from observing intervention data (e.g. Gopnik et al., 2001; Schulz & Gopnik, 2004; Sobel & Kirkham, 2006). Acting also provides anticipatory information: When you observe results based on your actions, those actions should be considered a cause of any subsequent or concurrent event. Lagnado and Sloman (2004) demonstrated that adults are sensitive to this anticipatory information (even over conditional probability information). Infants have little trouble anticipating events (e.g. Haith, 1993), and such anticipation can indicate their understanding of statistical regularities, including some that are critical to causal inference (e.g. Johnson, Amso & Slemmer, 2003; Sobel & Kirkham, 2006).

But critically, actions also allow children to be active in the learning process—they must decide what to do, and this decision process might influence how they act and how they learn from those actions. Adults and elementary school children learn causal structures more accurately from observing the results of their own actions than from observing another learner who generate the same data (e.g. Kuhn & Ho, 1980; Lagnado & Sloman, 2004; Sobel & Kushnir, 2006). Preschoolers show similar effects (e.g. Fireman, Kose & Solomon, 2003; Kushnir & Gopnik, 2005; Kushnir, Wellman & Gelman, 2008). Even infants, who clearly learn from imitation (e.g. Meltzoff, 1988), register the importance of their own actions when recognizing causal structure from the environment (e.g. Sommerville & Woodward, 2005; Sommerville, Woodward & Needham, 2005).

The trouble is, in free play settings that are dedicated to causal learning, that there is rarely much structure to children's actions. For instance, Schulz, Gopnik, and Glymour (2007) presented children with a gearbox toy that could afford one of four causal structures. In their critical experiment, 4–5-year-olds were allowed to play with the toy in order to learn the structure. They found that children who generated all of the relevant conditional probability information necessary to isolate the particular causal structure that governed how the gears worked were better able at reconstructing that causal structure, but, for instance, when the model was a chain, children only responded at 39% accuracy (above chance, but with much room to improve).

In this experiment, however, children were not simply given the toy to play with—they were introduced to it and its structure, and critically, observed the experimenter generating interventions on it, in order to demonstrate its efficacy and the problem at hand. This demonstration might have eliminated a potential critical piece of information inherent in the ability to act on an environment: discovery. In educational settings, Bruner (1961) emphasized that students who discover information for themselves were more motivated to achieve goals and more likely to remember information.

Sobel and Sommerville (2010) tried to translate that idea to a causal learning environment by again using the lightbox paradigm, which afforded many possible different learning puzzles. We introduced children to the basic workings of the box and then set the puzzle up differently for them each time. Critically, children were asked to learn these puzzles in one of three conditions: a *discovery* condition, in which they were allowed to press the buttons and activate the lights first, and then at the conclusion of their free play, watched the experimenter press each button and narrate the results; a *confirmation* condition, in which the order of this procedure was reversed—children watched the experimenter act first and then their actions merely produced the same results as the experimenter's; and a *baseline* condition, in which children only watched the experimenter and were not allowed to act on the box at all. Children were then asked a set of causal structure questions to see whether they had learned what model we presented.

The results are shown in Fig. 12.3. Across a variety of models (including a chain model, which children in Schulz et al.'s [2007] procedure found difficult), performance was above chance in all of the conditions. However, there was a clear advantage to children in the discovery condition over those in the confirmation or baseline conditions, which did not differ from one

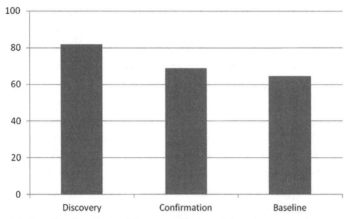

**Figure 12.3** Results of Sobel and Sommerville (2010) learning procedure contrasting discovery with confirmatory learning. For color version of this figure, the reader is referred to the online version of this book.

another. This latter finding again is relatively important: Children whose actions exploit what another does, as opposed to discovers efficacy on their own showed no benefit to acting on the causal system than children who simply observed another act. Actions that discover efficacy, in contrast, benefited the child's ability to learn the structure.

## 4.4. Interim Conclusions

We have presented three cases in which social information, in the form of others' expectations, rationales, and actions provide information that changes how young children are able to learn causal structures or make causal inferences. In the first case, children must be aware of the importance of the social information—the contrast between the experimenter's belief state and the actual data—to use that information for inference.

In the latter cases, however, we would suspect that the influence of the social information is more ubiquitous. Appropriate rationales benefit children learning because they potentially set the stage for children to appreciate the pedagogical information inherent in others' actions. Similarly, the child's own actions that discover information promote better learning than cases in which children only exploit the function of a causal system that they have already observed. One critical difference is that unlike other findings on children's learning from pedagogy (e.g. Bonawitz, Shafto, Gweon et al., 2011), our baseline condition did not afford the same learning. One explanation for this might be that children must first be put into a mindset to learn. For instance, in the baseline condition of Sobel and Sommerville (2009), the absence of any explanation for the experimenter's actions might lead children to believe that they are not being shown this information as a demonstration that would afford learning any novel information. After all, children are simply being shown lights activate on a box—there is not much at stake. In contrast, Bonawitz et al.'s display is much larger and holds the potential for many more discoveries. A critical open question is whether some overall mindset that the social interaction is in an environment specifically for learning must be present in order to see children use intentional or pedagogical information.[2] Younger children might potentially believe that all interactions afford such learning opportunities (which would be consistent with Csibra and Gergeley's "natural pedagogy" as well as findings on pedagogical inferences seen in infants, see e.g. Gweon et al., 2010; Yang, Bushnell, Buchanan & Sobel, submitted for publication). Older children might need these environmental cues. This is an important question for future investigations.

## 5. RATIONAL CAUSAL INFERENCES IN THE PHYSICAL AND SOCIAL DOMAINS

The final example we present more directly tests children's inferences as rational, by considering whether they integrate their existing knowledge with the data they observe to make inferences. Inspired by Bayesian models (Tenenbaum & Griffiths, 2003), Sobel et al. (2004) introduced 3- and 4-year-olds to a machine that lit up and played music when certain objects were placed on it. They instructed children that objects that activated the machine were called "blickets" objects that did not activate the machine were "not blickets." Their goal was to examine how manipulating the base rate of blickets affected how children reasoned about ambiguous evidence. Children observed a set of identical blocks and that of the first 12 blocks placed on the machine, either 2 or 10 activated it. Children next saw a test trial in which two new (but still perceptually identical) blocks (A and B) activated the machine together, followed by object A activating the machine by itself. Children were asked whether each was a blicket.

All children categorized object A as a blicket, but the causal status of B is uncertain. A Bayesian model predicts that the probability that B is a blicket is

---

[2] We are indebted to Kathy Hirsh-Pasek for pointing out this possibility.

equivalent to the base rate of blickets and critically that children should be more likely to categorize object B as a blicket in the common than the rare condition (see Griffiths, Sobel, Tenenbaum & Gopnik, 2011 for a detailed description of this model). This is how 4-year-olds responded: they categorized object B as a blicket ~80% of the time in the common condition and ~20% of the time in the rare condition. Three-year-olds, however, were unaffected by the base rate and categorized B as a blicket ~80% of the time in both conditions. Adults, incidentally, respond similarly to 4-year-olds, and 4-year-olds make other inferences about ambiguous evidence by appealing to base rate information (Griffiths et al., 2011).

It is tempting to conclude that rational causal inference develops during the preschool years, but it is equally possible that 3-year-olds are perfectly rational in this experiment. A strength of the blicket detector paradigm is that researchers can control the amount of prior knowledge children bring to the testing environment. The detector and label "blicket" are obviously novel; as a result, the familiarization should be an adequate reflection (to the child) of the base rate of blickets. However, the machine is physically instantiated and thus must conform to certain causal laws, such as temporal priority and spatial independence. Understanding these concepts, which appear to be in place by the time children are three (e.g. Bullock et al., 1982; Sophian & Huber, 1984) means that children should recognize that objects placed on the machine make it activate and that activation does not cause the experimenter to place an object on the machine. Similarly, children should recognize that one object being a blicket does not cause another object to be a blicket. While these facts might seem trivial, they constrain what hypotheses one considers as an explanation for the machine's activation.

Also critical is an understanding of the relation "blickets" have to hold with the blicket machine. The data children observe are only ambiguous if children believe that there is a deterministic relation between an object being a blicket and it activating the machine (what Tenenbaum & Griffiths, 2003, called the *activation law*). Without this, the test trial is more consistent with object B being a blicket than the base rate—even though object A is a blicket, it might have failed to be efficacious when A and B were presented together. Critically, this argument does not imply that 3-year-olds are indeterminists (in fact there is good evidence that they are not, see e.g. Kuzmak & Gelman, 1986). Rather, the argument is that 3- and 4-year-olds potentially have different mechanistic understanding about the relation between blickets and blicket machines. Indeed, 4-year-olds, but not 3-year-olds, recognize that an object that can activate the machine has a stable mechanism by which a blicket causes the detector to activate (Sobel, Yoachim, Gopnik, Meltzoff & Blumenthal, 2007). It is doubtful that 4-year-olds know what the nature of that mechanism is (indeed, it is doubtful that adults would know the nature of that mechanism, see Rozenblit & Keil, 2002), but it is likely that 3- and 4-year-olds bring different mechanistic knowledge to interpreting the blicket machine environment.

Is it possible that this different (and developing) knowledge allows children to recognize the inherent ambiguity in the rare common manipulation described above? That is, if 3-year-olds could be made aware of the relation between objects' causal properties and another stable nonobvious property, would they interpret the data they see as ambiguous and rely on the base rate information inherent in the procedure? Sobel and Munro (2009) presented 3-year-olds with Mr. Blicket (see Fig. 12.4): a blicket detector with cardboard eyes on top, which spontaneously activated contingent on the experimenter's voice (such that Mr. Blicket and the experimenter could converse, akin to a manipulation used by Johnson, Slaughter & Carey, 1998). After talking with Mr. Blicket, the experimenter told children that Mr. Blicket would tell them what objects he likes. Drawing from the theory of mind literature, by the age of 3, most children recognize that their own desires can be different from others' (Repacholi & Gopnik, 1997), that fulfilled and unfulfilled desires have causal consequences (Wellman & Woolley, 1990), and that shared preferences for objects relate to nonobvious properties of those objects (Fawcett & Markson, 2010; Kushnir et al., 2010). These data suggest that 3-year-olds might understand that Mr. Blicket's wants particular objects for some reason, which is stable in the context of the experiment.

**Figure 12.4** The *Mr. Blicket* stimulus used in Sobel and Munro (2009).

Using Mr. Blicket's desires, instead of a blicket machine, 3-year-olds showed the same kind of understanding of stable internal properties as in Sobel et al. (2007). Moreover, and more importantly, when we replicated the base rate experiment, in which Mr. Blicket was first shown to like either few or many things (2 or 10 of the first 12 identical blocks in a box, the *rare* and *common* conditions, respectively), and then that he liked objects A and B together and object A by itself, all children stated that he liked object A. Critically, 93% of 3-year-olds in the common condition stated he liked object B compared to the 44% who said so in the rare condition.

Three controls were critical. First, we wanted to ensure that children were not relying on the spontaneous activation of the detector, but rather understood that there was a difference between the causal relations indicated by Mr. Blicket's desire toward an object and an object making the blicket machine activate. Another group of 3-year-olds were introduced to a spontaneously activating blicket machine. These children categorized object B as having efficacy 72% of the time in the rare condition, significantly more often than children in the Mr. Blicket desire condition. This suggests that when the same data are presented as a machine activating, children respond associatively, and do not use the base rate information.

Second, we wanted to ensure that children did not simply find Mr. Blicket more interesting and thus brought more cognitive resources to the task. Another group of 3-year-olds were introduced to Mr. Blicket in the same manner and shown that activation was rare, except that they were told that Mr. Blicket's activation indicated that he was "thinking about" an object—a mental state 3-year-olds struggle to understand (e.g. Flavell, Green & Flavell, 1995; Wellman, Cross & Watson, 2001). Again, 72% of the children stated object B had efficacy, significantly more often than children in the desire condition.

Finally, we also wanted to ensure that 3-year-olds were not confused when asked to relate Mr. Blicket's activation with his thoughts as opposed to his preferences. Children might believe that desires are based on stable dispositions, while thoughts are more fleeting (e.g. Eisbach, 2004). Thus, another group of 3-year-olds were told that Mr. B (we didn't call him Mr. Blicket in this case to avoid confusion) knew which of the objects were "blickets" and his activation indicated that a blicket was on him (i.e. he acted like a blicket machine). Given 3-year-olds struggles understanding knowledge as a mental state (again, compared to desire, e.g. Gopnik & Slaughter, 1991), we predicted that children would not use the base rate information. They did not, categorizing object B as a blicket 80% of the time.

In each of these controls cases, we hypothesized that 3-year-olds would be less likely register the relation between a stable property of the objects and those objects' efficacy (i.e. whether they activated the spontaneously activating machine or Mr. Blicket/Mr. B agent). However, a critical prediction of this account is that small subset of 3-year-olds that do register these relations would be sensitive to the base rate manipulation. To examine this, we performed a posttest on children in the rare condition of the Mr. Blicket desires procedure, and the three of the control procedures just described. In this posttest, we measured how much children knew about the relation between the particular causal relation that was presented and whether it related to a stable property of the objects. Across the conditions, the higher the percentage of responses in which the child related the internal properties of the objects to their causal properties, the more likely children were to respond consistently with the base rate. What knowledge children brought to the environment about the particular pieces of social knowledge under consideration (desire, thought, knowledge, etc.) influenced how children resolved the ambiguous information. Critically, if they recognized that the particular social relation indicated a stable feature, they acted in accord with the rational (in this case, a Bayesian) model.

## 6. CONCLUDING THOUGHTS

### 6.1. Theory and Models

In thinking about describing children's causal inferences as rational, particularly in relation to social information, we had reason to be influenced by sociological ideas proposed by Weber (1962/1925). Weber made two points about the definition of rational behavior that we believe apply to a psychological description of rationality, and particularly to how children's causal inference can be thought of as rational.

The first is that social behavior comes in many forms and that much of it can be defined as rational, particularly given the fact that individuals have diverse desires and knowledge states. For Weber, the most important kind of social behavior was reciprocal (or "goal-directed"), in which individuals base their actions on the expected behavior of other people. Basing actions on the expectations of others' behavior is certainly part of contemporary theories of rational behavior (e.g. Csibra & Gergeley's, 2009 "Natural Pedagogy," as mentioned previously, and to be discussed further below). We take as a starting point that arguing that children's causal inferences are rational implies that they have a set of expectations about how people (but also objects and events) behave and makes inferences from those beliefs. This is hopefully uncontroversial.

The second point that Weber emphasized is that there are compelling reasons to compare individuals' behaviors (and the behaviors of societies, but we will not consider this issue here) to some kind of ideal model. Weber's emphasis is reflected in the set of computational models describing the process by which information gathered from others can affect children's inferences about causal, statistical, or linguistic information (e.g. Butterfield et al., 2009; Eaves & Shafto, in this volume, Shafto et al., 2012; Sobel et al., 2010). These models have particularly relied on Bayesian methods.

Some have argued that such models of rational inference are implausible as descriptions of human cognition (see e.g. Jones & Love, 2011; Holyoak & Cheng, 2011). Weber himself did emphasize that ideal models should be descriptive (as opposed to normative) and plausible given the data (as opposed to requiring implausible calculations). Bayesian models have been incredibly important to advancing our understanding of causal inference, in both children and adults, but they are also (usually) intended as computational-level (cf. Marr, 1982) descriptions of reasoning processes. What this means is that when we argue that children's reasoning at certain points is consistent with Bayesian models, this is not to imply that they are engaging in Bayesian calculations (either explicitly or implicitly); rather, that such models describe group behavior well given a particular set of assumptions. Our hope is that other researchers share this belief, even if they do not explicitly state it.

Furthermore, there are promising computational models that potentially reveal the ways children might be engaging in such inferences that approximate Bayesian calculations (e.g. Bonawitz, Denison, Chen, Gopnik & Griffiths, 2011). These models, however, are still very much under development. Whether plausible computational descriptions of the process by which children make inferences from others' information ultimately emerge from this kind of investigation, from algorithms that use completely different kinds of architecture (e.g. McClelland & Thompson, 2007), or from algorithms yet undescribed, is an open question.

## 6.2. Natural Pedagogy in Statistical and Causal Learning

The preceding sections have outlined how social information influences ideas about causal relations in the preschool years, but what is now clearly necessary is work looking at the beginning of social influence in infancy. We have argued that early in infancy, children are using social cues to attend to relevant information, helping them discern what regularities are important to their ontological commitments. Such a hypothesis seems quite consistent with Csibra and Gergeley's (2009) ideas about "natural pedagogy." If infants recognize that human communication and interaction provides them with the means to make inferences beyond the information they observe, then one such piece of information should involve where to focus their mechanism for constructing useful representations of the environment. But critically, if we accept this hypothesis, then "natural pedagogy" should also apply to how children learn causal structure. As such, we would hypothesize that rational learning about causal efficacy from others should occur very early in development.

Much of the data supporting this hypothesis come from imitation. Meltzoff demonstrated that 18-month-olds' imitative abilities were "goal-directed"—infants imitate goals and not actions themselves (see also Schwier et al., 2006, for some evidence that this ability is in place by the first birthday). Various researchers suggest that toddlers can imitate causally effective means to bring about a modeled action (e.g. Elsner & Aschersleben, 2003; Herbert, Gross & Hayne, 2006). Furthermore, toddlers ignore unnecessary actions unless there is a clear rationale for why those actions were generated (e.g. Brugger, LaRiviere, Mumme & Bushnell, 2007; Gergely, Bekkering & Kiraly, 2002; Nielsen, 2006), a behavior that emerges between 12 and 18 months. This understanding of "natural pedagogy" suggests that once infants understand that statistical regularity indicates causal structures, they should begin to make further inferences from the pedagogical information in others' actions.

There are at least two ways in which pedagogical information can influence infants' inferences. First, by the end of the first year, infants orient to the direction of gaze and pointing fingers (e.g. Gredebäck, Melinder & Daum, in press; Hood et al., 1998; Senju & Csibra, 2008). More importantly, they expect this information to communicate something in the indicated location (Gliga & Csibra, 2009; Tomasello, Carpenter & Liszkowski, 2007). These cues can shape cognitive development by helping infants learn what to learn in a distraction-filled environment (Wu & Kirkham, 2010; Wu et al., 2011). We propose that knowledge of causal structure can be reinforced and strengthened by similar social cues.

Second, between 6 and 11 months old, infants register information about the relation between a sample and a population and integrate intentional information, such as gaze following, into making such inferences (e.g. Denison et al., 2012; Xu & Denison, 2009; Xu & Garcia, 2008). At 15 months (and potentially earlier), infants' ability to make causal generalizations is influenced by contextual factors (i.e. by information they observe, but also by what they specifically did not observe; Gweon et al., 2010; Yang et al., submitted for publication). At 20 months, toddlers use others' intentional actions about samples as a basis for making causal inferences—infants infer that an individual who selects a sample nonrandomly has a preference for the contents of that sample, but one who constructs the same sample randomly potentially does not (Kushnir et al., 2010). While understanding the causal efficacy of preference develops between 14 and 18 months (e.g. Repacholi & Gopnik, 1997), it is quite possible that even younger infants are sensitive to this intentional information, particularly when learning from data obtained from imitation. More generally, understanding knowledge (causal or otherwise) from others—the basis of the "trust in testimony" research program—might be considered as a rational process as well (Butterfield et al., 2009; Eaves & Shafto, in this volume; Shafto et al., 2012). Describing how this process unfolds and develops are important open questions for subsequent research.

## REFERENCES

Allan, L. G. (1980). A note on measurement of contingency between two binary variables in judgment tasks. *Bulletin of the Psychonomic Society, 15*, 147–149.

Beck, S. R., Robinson, E. J., Carroll, D. J., & Apperly, I. A. (2006). Children's thinking about counterfactuals and future hypotheticals as possibilities. *Child Development, 77*, 413–426.

Biederman, I. (1987). Recognition-by-components: a theory of human image understanding. *Psychological Review, 94*, 115–147.

Bonawitz, E., Denison, S., Chen, A., Gopnik, G., & Griffiths, T. L. (2011). A simple sequential algorithm for approximating Bayesian inference. *Proceedings of the thirty-third cognitive science society*.

Bonawitz, E. B., Shafto, P., Gweon, H., Goodman, N. D., Spelke, E., & Schulz, L. E. (2011). The double-edged sword of pedagogy: teaching limits children's spontaneous exploration and discovery. *Cognition, 120*, 322–330.

Brugger, A., Lariviere, L. A., Mumme, D. L., & Bushnell, E. W. (2007). Doing the right thing: infants' selection of actions to imitate from observed event sequences. *Child Development, 78*, 806–824.

Bruner, J. S. (1961). The act of discovery. *Harvard Educational Review, 31*, 21–32.

Bruner, J. S. (1990). *Acts of meaning*. Cambridge, MA: Harvard University Press.

Bullock, M., Gelman, R., & Baillargeon, R. (1982). The development of causal reasoning. In W. J. Friedman (Ed.), *The developmental psychology of time* (pp. 209–254). New York: Academic Press.

Butterfield, J., Jenkins, O. C., Sobel, D. M., & , & Schwertfuger, J. (2009). Modeling aspects of theory of mind with Markov Random Fields. *International Journal of Social Robotics, 1*, 41–51.

Butterworth, G. (2004). Joint visual attention in infancy. In G. Bremner, & A. Slater (Eds.), *Theories of infant development* (pp. 317–354). Oxford: Wiley-Blackwell.

Carpenter, M., Nagell, K., & Tomasello, M. (1998). Social cognition, joint attention, and communicative competence from 9- to 15-months of age. *Monographs of the Society for Research in Child Development, 63*.

Coady, C. A. J. (1992). *Testimony: A philosophical study*. New York: Oxford University Press.

Cohen, L. B., & Amsel, G. (1998). Precursors to infants' perception of the causality of a simple event. *Infant Behavior and Development, 21*, 713–732.

Cohen, L. B., & Oakes, L. M. (1993). How infants perceive simple causality. *Developmental Psychology, 29*, 421–433.

Cook, C., Goodman, N., & Schulz, L. E. (2011). Where science starts: spontaneous experiments in preschoolers' exploratory play. *Cognition, 120*, 341–349.

Csibra, G., & Gergely, G. (2006). Social learning and social cogniton: the case for pedagogy. In Y. Munakata, & M. H. Johnson (Eds.), *Processes of change in brain and cognitive development. Attention and performance*, vol. XXI (pp. 249–274). Oxford: Oxford University Press.

Csibra, G., & Gergely, G. (2009). Natural pedagogy. *Trends in Cognitive Sciences, 13*, 148–153.

Davies, C. M. (1965). Development of the probability concept in children. *Child Development, 36*, 779–788.

Denison, S., Reed, C., &, Xu, F. (in press). The emergence of probabilistic reasoning in very young infants: evidence from 4.5- and 6-month-olds. *Developmental Psychology*.

Eaves, B., & Shafto, P. (2012). Unifying pedagogical reasoning and epistemic trust. In F. Xu, & T. Kushnir (Eds.), *Advances in Child Development and Behavior*.

Eisbach, A. O. (2004). Children's developing awareness of the diversity in people's trains of thought. *Child Development, 75*, 1694–1707.

Elsner, B., & Aschersleben, G. (2003). Do I get what you get? Learning about the effects of self-performed and observed actions in infancy. *Consciousness and Cognition, 12*, 732–751.

Estes, K. G., Evans, J. L., Alibali, M. W., & Saffran, J. R. (2007). Can infants map meaning to newly segmented words? Statistical segmentation and word learning. *Psychological Science, 18*, 254–260.

Farroni, T., Massaccesi, S., Pividori, D., Simion, F., & Johnson, M. H. (2004). Gaze-following in newborns. *Infancy, 5*, 39–60.

Fawcett, C., & Markson, L. (2010). Children reason about shared preferences. *Developmental Psychology, 46*, 299–309.

Fireman, G., Kose, G., & Solomon, M. J. (2003). Self-observation and learning: the effect of watching oneself on problem solving performance. *Cognitive Development, 18*, 339–354.

Fischbein, E. (1975). *The intuitive sources of probabilistic thinking in children*. Boston, MA: Reidel.

Fiser, J., & Aslin, R. N. (2002). Statistical learning of new visual feature combinations by infants. *Proceedings of the National Academy of Sciences of The United States of America, 99*, 15822–15826.

Flavell, J. H., Green, F. L., & Flavell, E. R. (1995). *Young children's knowledge about thinking*. In: *Monographs of the Society for Research in Child Development, 60*. (1, Series No. 243).

Flom, R., & Pick, A. D. (2007). Gaze-following: its development and significance. In R. Flom, K. Lee, & D. Muir (Eds.), *Gaze following: Its development and significance* (pp. 95–111). Mahwah, NJ: Lawrence Erlbaum Associates.

Gergely, G., Bekkering, H., & Kiraly, I. (2002). Rational imitation in preverbal infants. *Nature, 415*, 755–756.

Gliga, T., & Csibra, G. (2009). One-year-old infants appreciate the referential nature of deictic gestures and words. *Psychological Science, 20*, 347–353.

Gopnik, A., & Astington, J. W. (1988). Children's understanding of representational change and its relation to the understanding of false belief and the appearance-reality distinction. *Child Development, 59*, 26–37.

Gopnik, A., & Slaughter, V. (1991). Young children's understanding of changes in their mental states. *Child Development, 62*, 98–110.

Gopnik, A., Sobel, D. M., Schulz, L. E., & Glymour, C. (2001). Causal learning mechanisms in very young children: two, three, and four-year-olds infer causal relations from patterns of variation and covariation. *Developmental Psychology, 37*, 620–629.

Gredebäck, G., Melinder, A., & Daum, M. (in press). The development and neural basis of pointing comprehension. *Social Neuroscience*.

Griffiths, T. L., Sobel, D. M., Tenenbaum, J. B., & Gopnik, A. (2011). Bayes and blickets: effects of knowledge on causal induction in children and adults. *Cognitive Science, 35*, 1407–1455.

Gweon, H., Tenenbaum, J. B., & Schulz, L. E. (2010). Infants consider both the sample and the sampling process in inductive generalization. *Proceedings of the National Academy of Sciences of the United States of America, 107*, 9066–9071.

Haith, M. M. (1993). Future-oriented processes in infancy: the case of visual expectations. In C. Granrud (Ed.), *Visual perception and cognition in infancy* (pp. 235–264). Hillsdale, NJ: Erlbaum.

Harris, P. L., & Koenig, M. A. (2006). Trust in testimony: how children learn about science and religion. *Child Development, 77*, 505–524.

Herbert, J., Gross, J., & Hayne, H. (2006). Age-related changes in deferred imitation between 6 and 9 months of age. *Infant Behavior and Development, 29*, 136–139.

Hoemann, H. W., & Ross, B. M. (1971). Children's understanding of probability concepts. In W. W. Hartup (Ed.), *Review of child development research*, Vol. 6 (pp. 600–668). Chicago: University of Chicago Press.

Hoemann, H. W., & Ross, B. M. (1982). Children's concepts of chance and probability. In C. J. Brainerd (Ed.), *Children's logical and mathematical cognition* (pp. 93–121). New York: Springer.

Holyoak, K. J., & Cheng, P. W. (2011). Causal learning and inference as a rational process: the new synthesis. *Annual Review of Psychology, 62*, 135–163.

Hood, B. M., Willen, J. D., & Driver, J. (1998). Adult's eyes trigger shifts of visual attention in human infants. *Psychological Science, 9*, 131–134.

Jaswal, V. K., & Neely, L. A. (2006). Adults don't always know best: preschoolers use past reliability over age when learning new words. *Psychological Science, 17*, 757–758.

Johnson, S. C., Slaughter, V., & Carey, S. (1998). Whose gaze will infants follow? The elicitation of gaze-following in 12-month-olds. *Developmental Science, 1*, 233–238.

Johnson, S. P., Amso, D., & Slemmer, J. A. (2003). Development of object concepts in infancy: evidence for early learning in an eye tracking paradigm. *Proceedings of the National Academy of Sciences of The United States of America, 100*, 10568–10573.

Jones, M., & Love, B. C. (2011). Bayesian fundamentalism or enlightenment? On the explanatory status and theoretical contributions of Bayesian models of cognition. *Behavioral and Brain Sciences, 34*, 169–231.

Kingstone, A., Smilek, D., Ristic, J., Friesen, C. K., & Eastwood, J. D. (2003). Attention, researchers! It is time to take a look at the real world. *Current Directions in Psychological Science, 12*, 176–180.

Kinzler, K. D., Corriveau, K. H., & Harris, P. L. (2011). Children's selective trust in native accented speakers. *Developmental Science, 14*, 106–111.

Kirkham, N. Z., Slemmer, J. A., & Johnson, S. P. (2002). Visual statistical learning in infancy. *Cognition, 83*, B35–B42.

Kirkham, N. Z., Slemmer, J. A., Richardson, D. C., & Johnson, S. P. (2007). Location, location, location: development of spatiotemporal sequence learning in infancy. *Child Development, 78*, 1559–1571.

Koenig, M. A., & Harris, P. L. (2005). Preschoolers mistrust ignorant and inaccurate speakers. *Child Development, 76*, 1261–1277.

Koenig, M. A., & Jaswal, V. K. (2011). Characterizing children's expectations about expertise and incompetence: halo or pitchfork effects. *Child Development, 82*, 1634–1647.

Kosugi, D., Ishida, H., & Fujita, K. (2003). 10-month-old infants' inference of invisible agent: distinction in causality between object motion and human action. *Japanese Psychological Research, 45*, 15–24.

Kuhn, D., & Ho, V. (1980). Self-directed activity and cognitive development. *Journal of Applied Developmental Psychology, 1*, 119–133.

Kushnir, T., & Gopnik, A. (2005). Young children infer causal strength from probabilities and interventions. *Psychological Science, 16*, 678–683.

Kushnir, T., & Gopnik, A. (2007). Conditional probability versus spatial contiguity in causal learning: preschoolers use new contingency evidence to overcome prior spatial assumptions. *Developmental Psychology, 44*, 186–196.

Kushnir, T., Wellman, H. M., & Gelman, S. A (2008). The role of preschoolers' social understanding in evaluating the informativeness of causal interventions. *Cognition, 107*, 1084–1092.

Kushnir, T., Xu, F., & Wellman, H. M. (2010). Young children use statistical sampling to infer the preferences of other people. *Psychological Science, 21*, 1134–1140.

Kuzmak, S. D., & Gelman, R. (1986). Young children's understanding of random phenomena. *Child Development, 57*, 559–566.

Lagnado, D., & Sloman, S. A. (2004). The advantage of timely intervention. *Journal of Experimental Psychology Learning Memory and Cognition, 30*, 856–876.

Madole, K. L., & Cohen, L. B. (1995). The role of object parts in infants' attention to form-function correlations. *Developmental Psychology, 31*, 637–648.

Mareschal, D., Quinn, P. C., & French, R. M. (2002). Asymmetric interference in 3- to 4-month-olds' sequential category learning. *Cognitive Science, 26*, 377–389.

Marr, D. (1982). *Vision: A computational investigation into the human representation and processing of visual information.* San Francisco: W.H. Freeman.

McClelland, J. L., & Thompson, R. M. (2007). Using domain-general principles to explain children's causal reasoning abilities. *Developmental Science, 10*, 333–356.

Meltzoff, A. N. (1988). Infant imitation and memory: nine-month-olds in immediate and deferred tests. *Child Development, 59*, 217–225.

Muentener, P., & Carey, S. (2010). Infants' causal representations of state change events. *Cognitive Psychology, 61*, 63–86.

Nielsen, M. (2006). Copying actions and copying outcomes: social learning through the second year. *Developmental Psychology, 42*, 555–565.

Oakes, L. M. (1994). Development of infants' use of continuity cues in their perception of causality. *Developmental Psychology, 30*, 869–879.

Oakes, L. M., & Cohen, L. B. (1990). Infant perception of a causal event. *Cognitive Development, 5*, 193–207.

Pasquini, E. S., Corriveau, K., Koenig, M. A., & Harris, P. L. (2007). Preschoolers monitor the relative accuracy of informants. *Developmental Psychology, 43*, 1216–1222.

Perner, J. (1979). Discrepant results in experimental studies of young children's understanding of probability. *Child Development, 50*, 1121–1127.

Piaget, J., & Inhelder, B. (1975). *The origins of the idea of chance in children* (L. Leake, Jr., P. Burrell, & H. Fischbein, Trans.). New York: Norton. (Original work published in 1951).

Poulin-Dubois, D., Demke, T. L., & Olineck, K. M. (2007). The inquisitive eye: infants' implicit understanding that looking leads to knowing. In R. Flom, K. Lee, & D. Muir (Eds.), *Gaze-following: Its development and significance* (pp. 263–281). Mahwah, NJ: Lawrence Erlbaum Associates.

Rakison, D. H., & Butterworth, G. E. (1998). Infants' use of object parts in early categorization. *Developmental Psychology, 34*, 49–62.

Reid, T. (1764/1970). *An inquiry into the human mind.* Chicago: University of Chicago Press.

Repacholi, B. M., & Gopnik, A. (1997). Early reasoning about desires: evidence from 14- and 18-month-olds. *Developmental Psychology, 33*, 12–21.

Rozenblit, L. R., & Keil, F. C. (2002). The misunderstood limits of folk science: an illusion of explanatory depth. *Cognitive Science, 26*, 521–562.

Saffran, J. R., Aslin, R. N., & Newport, E. L. (1996). Statistical learning by 8-month-old infants. *Science, 274*, 1926–1928.

Saxe, R., Tenenbaum, J. B., & Carey, S. (2005). Secret agents: inferences about hidden causes by 10- and 12-month-old infants. *Psychological Science, 16*(12), 995–1001.

Senju, A., & Csibra, G. (2008). Gaze following in human infants depends on communicative signals. *Current Biology, 18*, 668–671.

Schlottman, A. (2001). Children's probability intuitions: understanding the expected value of complex gambles. *Child Development, 72*, 103–122.

Schulz, L. E., & Bonawitz, E. B. (2007). Serious fun: preschoolers play more when evidence is confounded. *Developmental Psychology, 43*, 1045–1050.

Schulz, L. E., & Gopnik, A. (2004). Causal learning across domains. *Developmental Psychology, 40*, 162–176.

Schulz, L. E., Gopnik, A., & Glymour, C. (2007). Preschool children learn causal structure from conditional independence. *Developmental Science, 10*, 322–332.

Schulz, L. E., & Sommerville, J. A. (2006). God does not play dice: causal determinism and preschoolers' causal inferences. *Child Development, 77*, 427–442.

Schwier, C., van Maanen, C., Carpenter, M., & Tomasello, M. (2006). Rational imitation in 12-month-old infants. *Infancy, 10*, 303–311.

Schyns, P. G., & Rodet, L. (1997). Categorization creates functional features. *Journal of Experimental Psychology Learning Memory and Cognition, 23*, 681–696.

Shafto, P., Eaves, B. S., Navarro, D. J., & Perfors, A. (2012). Epistemic trust: Modeling children's reasoning about others' knowledge and intent. *Developmental Science, 15*, 436–447.

Shanks, D. R. (1995). Is human learning rational? *Quarterly Journal of Experimental Psychology, 48A*, 257–279.

Shultz, T. R. (1982). Rules of causal attribution. *Monographs of the Society for Research in Child Development, 47*(1), 1–51.

Sobel, D. M., & Buchanan, D. W. (2009). Bridging the gap: causality at a distance in children's categorization and inferences about internal properties. *Cognitive Development, 24*, 274–283.

Sobel, D. M., Buchanan, D. W., Butterfield, J., & Jenkins, O. C. (2010). Interactions between causal models, theories, and social cognitive development. *Neural Networks, 8*(9), 1060–1071.

Sobel, D. M., & Corriveau, K. H. (2010). Children monitor individuals' expertise for word learning. *Child Development, 81*, 669–679.

Sobel, D. M., & Kirkham, N. Z. (2006). Blickets and babies: the development of causal reasoning in toddlers and infants. *Developmental Psychology, 42*, 1103–1115.

Sobel, D. M., & Kirkham, N. Z. (2007a). Bayes nets and blickets: infants' developing representations of causal knowledge. *Developmental Science, 10*, 298–306.

Sobel, D. M., & Kirkham, N. Z. (2007b). Interactions between causal and statistical learning. In A. Gopnik, & L. E. Schulz (Eds.), *Causal learning: Psychology, philosophy, and computation* (pp. 139–153). New York: Oxford University Press.

Sobel, D. M., & Kushnir, T. (2006). The importance of decision demands in causal learning from interventions. *Memory & Cognition, 34*, 411–419.

Sobel, D. M., & Munro, S. A. (2009). Domain generality and specificity in children's causal inferences about ambiguous data. *Developmental Psychology, 45*, 511–524.

Sobel, D. M., & Sommerville, J. A. (2009). Rationales in children's causal learning from others' actions. *Cognitive Development, 24*, 70–79.

Sobel, D. M., & Sommerville, J. A. (2010). The importance of discovery in children's causal learning from interventions. *Frontiers in Developmental Psychology, 1*, 176–183.

Sobel, D. M., Sommerville, J. A., Travers, L. V., Blumenthal, E. J., & Stoddard, E. (2009). Preschoolers' use of others' beliefs to make causal inferences from probabilistic data. *Journal of Cognition and Development, 10*, 262–284.

Sobel, D. M., Tenenbaum, J. B., & Gopnik, A. (2004). Children's causal inferences from indirect evidence: backwards blocking and Bayesian reasoning in preschoolers. *Cognitive Science, 28*, 303–333.

Sobel, D. M., Yoachim, C. M., Gopnik, A., Meltzoff, A. N., & Blumenthal, E. J. (2007). The blicket within: preschoolers' inferences about insides and causes. *Journal of Cognition and Development, 8*, 159–182.

Sommerville, J. A., & Woodward, A. L. (2005). Pulling out the intentional structure of action: the relation between action processing and action production in infancy. *Cognition, 95*, 1–30.

Sommerville, J. A., Woodward, A. L., & Needham, A. (2005). Action experience alters 3-month-old infants' perception of others' actions. *Cognition, 96*, B1–B11.

Sophian, C., & Huber, A. (1984). Early developments in children's causal judgments. *Child Development, 55*, 512–526.

Steyvers, M., Tenenbaum, J. B., Wagenmakers, E. J., & Blum, B. (2003). Inferring causal networks from observations and interventions. *Cognitive Science, 27*, 453–489.

Striano, T., & Reid, V. M. (2006). Social cognition in the first year. *Trends in Cognitive Science, 10*, 471–476.

Teglas, E., Vul, E., Girotto, V., Gonzalez, M., Tenenbaum, J. B., & Bonatti, L. L. (2011). Pure reasoning in 12-month-old infants as probabilistic inference. *Science, 332*, 1054–1059.

Tenenbaum, J. B., & Griffiths, T. L. (2003). Theory-based causal inference. *Proceedings of the 14th annual conference on the advances in neural information processing systems*, Vancouver, CA.

Thiessen, E. D. (2011). Domain general constraints on statistical learning. *Child Development, 82*, 462–470.

Tomasello, M., Carpenter, M., & Liszkowski, U. (2007). A new look at infant pointing. *Child Development, 78*, 705–722.

Varga, K., Frick, J.E., Stansky, L., Beck, H., Dengler, M.J., & Bright, M.A. (2009). *I saw the sign: the development of directional understanding*. In Poster presented at the meeting of the society for research in child development, Denver, CO.

Vecera, S. R., & Johnson, M. H. (1995). Gaze detection and the cortical processing of faces: evidence from infants and adults. *Visual Cognition, 2*, 59–87.

Vygotsky, L. S. (1978). *Mind in society: The development of higher psychological processes*. Cambridge, MA: Harvard University Press.

Weber, M. (1962/1925). *Basic concepts in sociology*. New York: Citadel Press.

Wellman, H. M., Cross, D., & Watson, J. K. (2001). A meta-analysis of theory of mind: the truth about false belief. *Child Development, 72*, 655–684.

Wellman, H. M., & Woolley, J. D. (1990). From simple desires to ordinary beliefs: the early development of everyday psychology. *Cognition, 35*, 245–275.

Wu, R., & Kirkham, N. Z. (2010). No two cues are alike: depth of learning during infancy is dependent on what orients attention. *Journal of Experimental Child Psychology, 107*, 118–136.

Wu, R., Gopnik, A., Richardson, D. C., & Kirkham, N. Z. (2011). Infants learn about objects from statistics and people. *Developmental Psychology, 47*, 1220–1229.

Xu, F., & Denison, S. (2009). Statistical inference and sensitivity to sampling in 11-month-old infants. *Cognition, 112*, 97–104.

Xu, F., & Garcia, V. (2008). Intuitive statistics by 8-month-old infants. *Proceedings of the National Academy of Sciences of the United States of America, 105*, 5012–5015.

Yang, D.J., Bushnell, E.W., Buchanan, D.W., & Sobel, D.M. *Infants' use of contextual cues in imitation and generalization of effective causal actions*. Manuscript submitted for publication, Brown University.

Younger, B. A., & Cohen, L. B. (1986). Developmental changes in infants' perception of correlations among attributes. *Child Development, 57*, 803–815.

CHAPTER THIRTEEN

# The Nature of Goal-Directed Action Representations in Infancy*

## Jessica A. Sommerville, Michaela B. Upshaw, and Jeff Loucks

Department of Psychology & Center for Child and Family Well-being, University of Washington, Campus Box 351525, Seattle, WA 98195
Corresponding author: E-mail: sommej@uw.edu

## Contents

## Abstract

A critical question for developmental psychologists concerns how representations in infancy are best characterized. Past and current research provides paradoxical evidence regarding the nature of early representations: in some ways, infants appear to build concrete and specific representations that guide their online perception and understanding of different events; in other ways, infants appear to possess abstract representations that support inferences regarding unseen event outcomes. Characterizing the nature of early representations across domains is a central charge for developmentalists because this task can provide important information regarding the underlying learning process or processes that drive development. Yet, little existing work has attempted to resolve this paradox by characterizing the ways in which infants' representations may have both abstract and concrete elements. The goal of this chapter is to take a close look at infants' early representations of goal-directed action in order to describe the nature of these representations. We first discuss the nature of representations of action that infants build through acting on the world and argue that these representations possess both concrete and abstract elements. On the one hand,

---

* To appear in *Rational Constructivism*

*Advances in Child Development and Behavior*, Volume 43
ISSN 0065-2407,
http://dx.doi.org/10.1016/B978-0-12-397919-3.00013-7

infants appear to build representations of action that stress goal-relevant features of actions in an action- or event-specific fashion, suggesting specificity or concreteness. On the other hand, these representations are sufficiently abstract to not only drive action but also support infants' perception of others actions and to support inferences regarding unseen action outcomes. We next discuss evidence to suggest that by the end of the first year of life, infants possess increasingly abstract representations of the actions of others and use contextual cues, including linguistic statements accompanying action, to flexibly specify the level of representational specificity. We further consider the possibility that language may play a role in infants' ability to build more abstract representations of goal-directed action.

## 1. THE NATURE OF EARLY LEARNING AND REPRESENTATIONS

A critical question for developmental psychologists concerns how representations in infancy are best characterized. Are infants largely sensorimotor learners that come to understand the world in a concrete, trial–and–error fashion, as Piaget (1952) would have suggested? Or can infants form abstract representations and engage in inferentially based learning? This central question dates back to Plato and Aristotle and permeates not only classic and contemporary debates regarding the nature of early learning but also impacts societal views of infants more broadly.

Historical views, and some contemporary perspectives, portray infants as primarily specific, concrete, and perceptual-motor learners (Cohen & Cashon, 2006; Haith, 1998; Haith & Benson, 1998; Piaget, 1952; Smith, 1999). In contrast, more recent perspectives have granted infants' abstract knowledge and inferential skills (Carey, 2009; Leslie, 1988; Spelke, 2000; Xu, 2007). Tension remains with respect to the nature of learning in early infancy, however, because in some ways, early learning does appear to produce specific and concrete representations, and whereas in other ways, learning appears to drive the acquisition of abstract representations that support inferences. Critically, then, to make progress in the field, the nature of early learning requires further consideration. The goal of this chapter is to examine early learning with respect to how infants construct representations of goal-directed action. Specifically, by selectively focusing on this topic, we seek to describe the ways in which infants' representations, in the arena of goal-directed action, can be best characterized.

In Sections 2 and 3 of this chapter, we discuss evidence to suggest that infants build representations of actions on an action-by-action basis, suggesting concreteness and specificity in infants' representations. These findings suggest that at first, infants' understanding of goals may be embedded within particular actions. However, these representations also possess elements of abstractness: the representations that infants form through acting on the world are also available to guide perception and to serve to support inferences regarding unseen action outcomes in infants' own and others' actions. In Section 4, we discuss new evidence to suggest that, by the end of the first year of life, infants may possess the ability to build representations of the actions of other that are increasingly abstract and that infants may use contextual cues, such as the linguistic statements accompanying action, to determine the appropriate level of representational specificity (e.g. does an object selection reflect a transient goal, or enduring preference, for the object?). We consider the possibility that language may play a driving force in the creation of increasingly abstract representations of action. We close by considering the implications of these claims for not only how infants produce action and understand the action of others but also for the nature of early learning more broadly.

## 2. LEARNING AND REPRESENTATIONS AS CONCRETE AND SPECIFIC VERSUS ABSTRACT AND INFERENTIAL

Research over the past several decades has demonstrated that infants make inferences about the world based on abstract knowledge. Work on infants' understanding of the physical world and infants' early categorization abilities has, in fact, used infants' ability to make inferences about novel events and exemplars as evidence of the *possession* of abstract knowledge. For example, research on infants' perception and understanding of the physical world has revealed that infants, from very young ages, make inferences about the outcomes of hidden events based on their knowledge of abstract physical principles that govern object motion (e.g. continuity, solidity, inertia, gravity, etc.; e.g. Baillargeon, 1987; Spelke, 1994). Research has also demonstrated that infants make inferences about the sorts of entities that engage in particular behaviors as a function of category membership versus mere perceptual similarity to a prior exemplar (McDonough & Mandler, 1998; Mandler & McDonough, 1998).

Other studies have directly investigated infants' ability to make inferences per se. In a landmark paper, Baldwin, Markman & Melartin (1993) took up the issue of whether infants, before the end of the first year of life, can make inferences about nonobvious object properties after seeing a single exemplar. Nine- and 16-month-old infants were shown two toys in succession: one that possessed an interesting nonobvious property (e.g. it made a noise when squeezed) and one that was perceptually similar but lacked the nonobvious property. Infants at both ages attempted to reproduce the property when playing with the second toy, suggesting that infants inferred that the second object would possess the same property as the first based on its similar appearance (in a follow-up study, infants did not expect a second dissimilar object to possess the unseen property).

Subsequent work by Xu and colleagues has revealed that infants possess quite impressive inferential abilities: by 8–12 months of age (Denison & Xu, 2010; Dewar & Xu, 2010; Xu & Garcia, 2008), and perhaps as early as 6 months of age (Denison, Reed & Xu, in press), infants make inferences from populations to samples and vice versa. Moreover, infants take into account a number of different pieces of information in forming inferences (e.g. number of objects of each type in the scene, their physical arrangement, etc.; Téglás et al., 2011). This work suggests that infants appear to possess abstract representations and that these representations drive inferences.

Yet, there is evidence to suggest that, at least in certain domains, what infants learn appears to be highly specific to the task at hand. In terms of motor development, Adolph and colleagues (Adolph, 2000; Kretch & Adolph, in press) have shown that infants learn in a posture-specific manner. For example, consider infants' ability to navigate a risky drop-off (Kretch & Adolph, in press). Twelve-month-old experienced crawlers refuse to climb down drop-offs that are too steep to navigate; in contrast, novice walkers of the same age step over the very same drop-off. Just 6 months later, as a function of walking experience, 18-month-old experienced walkers will not step down a risky drop-off but instead use alternate strategies to navigate the drop-off. These findings suggest that rather than learning a general fear of heights, infants learn which drop-offs can be descended one posture at a time.

Similarly, with respect to learning how to use tools, 12- to 18-month-old infants appear to learn about which part of a tool is meant to be held rather than learning about tool function (Barrett, Davis & Needham, 2007). After training with a tool, infants succeeded on novel tool use tasks that required similar grasp placement to that of the training tool but not a novel task that required a similar functional use of the training tool. These findings suggest that infants of this age may be learning the specifics of how to act on a tool through active experience, but not more abstract features of tool use events like a tool's function.

Memories in early infancy, too, appear to be characterized by a high degree of specificity. Between 2 and 6 months of age, infants trained to kick in order to move a mobile attached to their legs with ribbon must be tested with the original mobile in order for them to evince memory of the original event. With age, infants can retrieve memories across changes in the context. Similar results have been obtained using deferred imitation paradigms (see Rovee-Collier, 1999).

Finally, infants' ability to understand how properties of objects influence event outcomes appears to develop in an instance-by-instance fashion (Baillargeon, 2004; Baillargeon, Li, Gertner & Wu, 2011). Rather than learning how a given object property, such as object height, influences outcomes across a range of event outcomes, infants appear to learn in a category-specific fashion. For example, infants recognize how object height influences outcomes for occlusion events prior to when they learn how height influences outcomes in containment events (Hespos & Baillargeon, 2006).

Taken together, the above findings suggest that in some ways, infants' early representations are abstract, yet in other ways, infants' learning and representations appear to be quite concrete and specific to the task at hand. Our goal in the remainder of the chapter is to look closely at infants' representations of goal-directed action as a means to gain leverage on the question of whether and when infants build representations of human action that are more toward the concrete and specific end versus whether and when infants build representations of human action that are more toward the abstract end as well as to discuss the means by which infants acquire and construct these representations.

## 3. INFANTS' EARLY REPRESENTATIONS OF GOAL-DIRECTED ACTION

Goal-directed action provides a fertile starting ground for addressing questions regarding the nature of early representations for several reasons. Most critically, infants *learn* to produce and understand goal-directed action. Over the first two years of life, infants' production of action becomes increasingly sophisticated: infants progress from protoreaching, to reaching for objects, to producing means-end sequences, to using simple tools (Gibson, 1988; Rochat, 1989). Paralleling these developments, infants' ability to recognize the goal of others' actions becomes increasingly sophisticated over the first two years of life: infants start by identifying the goal of simple reach and grasp acts (Woodward, 1998), progress to understanding the nature of referential acts (Woodward & Guajardo, 2002), and subsequently come to recognize the goal of more complex action chains (Sommerville & Woodward, 2005a; Woodward & Sommerville, 2000). The fact that there is clear evidence for learning with respect to the construction of representations of goal-directed actions provides the opportunity for characterizing these representations and infants' means of acquiring them. And, specifying the nature of infants' representations of goal-directed action is a critical step to identifying the underlying learning process or processes supporting the construction of these representations. In the following sections, we examine infants' representations of goal-directed action by characterizing what aspects are concrete and specific versus what aspects are abstract and general, and how these representations are established.

## 3.1. Concrete and Specific Aspects

Infants appear to learn to produce goal-directed actions in a somewhat concrete and specific manner, one action at a time. Infants learn to reach (Bertenthal & Clifton, 1998; Rochat, 1989), before they learn to produce means-end sequences (Willatts, 1999) and before they can use tools (Piaget, 1952). Thus, it does not appear that infants are developing the ability to have goals or act toward goals rather they appear to be learning how to enact goals in action.

According to Piaget (1952), development in infancy consists of the elaboration, differentiation, and ultimately the combination of different sensorimotor schemas. For example, Piaget argued that the ability to produce means-end sequences (sequences in which direct access to a goal is blocked and infants have to act on an intermediary object to achieve the goal; e.g. pulling a cloth to retrieve an out-of-reach toy that the cloth supports) at stage 4 (about 8 to 12 months of age) came about because infants learn that (a) sensorimotor schemas can be combined and (b) one sensorimotor schema (in this case, the act of pulling) can be subjugated to another sensorimotor schema (in this case, the act of grasping the toy). That is, infants appear to be learning that one action can be a "means" to another action or outcome, the "end," implying that at some level, infants represent such sequences with respect to their underlying logical structure (e.g. get $X$ to achieve $Y$). For Piaget (1952), the production of means-end sequences was an important development, as it signaled the onset of truly intentional behavior on the part of infants (providing evidence that infants separate means from ends).

Yet, as Piaget (1952) noted, and as modern research has confirmed, décalage exists in infants' production of means-end sequences. To illustrate, consider two different means-end sequences: one in which infants must pull a cloth to retrieve an out-of-reach toy that is supported by the cloth and another in which infants must use a plastic cane to retrieve a toy that sits in the crook of the cane. Both sequences fit Piaget's criteria of means-end sequences, and both involve similar subgoal and goal actions (pulling on an intermediary object to retrieve a goal object). Yet the cloth-pulling problem is solved several months before the cane-pulling problem (Piaget, 1952; Schlesinger & Langer, 1999), suggesting that infants' performance on these tasks may be driven by separate event-specific representations. Put another way, infants may be learning how goals can be achieved in the context of different objects or situations based on the properties of such objects or situations rather than globally learning that one act or action can be used as a means to another act or action.

In a recent study, our lab evaluated whether infants represent means-end sequences based on their underlying structural similarity (Sommerville, 2007). To do so, we gave 10-month-old infants and 12-month-old infants the opportunity to solve four different types of means-end problems. Infants received trials in which they could pull a string attached to a toy in order to retrieve an out-of-reach toy, trials in which they could pull a cloth supporting an out-of-reach toy in order to retrieve the toy it supported, trials in which they could open a translucent box to retrieve a toy it contained, and trials in which they could pull a cane that surrounded a toy to obtain the toy. Infants received 4 trials of each type in a fixed order (in the order described in order to maximize the investigation of individual differences), based on the level of difficulty (easier to harder), as determined by pilot work.

We sought to compare rates of solving the different problem types and potential interrelations in performance across the tasks. Although past work had demonstrated décalage in performance across the means-end tasks, we reasoned that if common abstract representations of the underlying structure of such tasks drive, at least in part, infants' performance on the tasks, then infants' ability to solve the different problem types should be strongly interrelated. That is, independent of task difficulty, infants who are good at solving the cloth-pulling task (with respect to other infants), for example, should also be good at solving the cane-pulling task (with respect to other infants), for example.

Perhaps unsurprisingly, infants' performance varied as a function of task type (see Fig. 13.1). Figure 13.1 indicates the average number of planful solutions (solutions that appeared clearly directed toward retrieving the toy; see Sommerville & Woodward, 2005a for specific criteria) for each of the tasks. The string- and cloth-pulling problems were significantly easier for infants to solve than the box-opening and cane-pulling problems. Moreover, interrelations among different means-end problems were weak at best, as Table 13.1 indicates. Infants' performance on the string and cloth problems were weakly related, but performance on all other problems was independent of one another. Taken together, these findings suggest that it is unlikely that infants are representing these problems in terms of their underlying means-end structure; if they were, interrelations across the tasks would be expected. Instead, our results raised the possibility that infants' performance across the tasks differed either due to differences in the nature of the problem (e.g. support vs. surround), the extent of the spatial relation (e.g. weak contact vs. strong contact) between the intermediary and goal object, or in terms of the motor demands of the task.

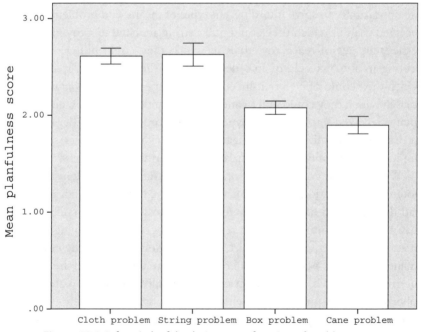

**Figure 13.1** Infants' planful solutions as a function of problem type.

**Table 13.1** Interrelations among different means-end problems

| | Cloth problem | String problem | Box problem | Cane problem |
|---|---|---|---|---|
| Cloth problem | — | $r(79) = 0.28$, $p = 0.01$ | $r(71) = -0.09$, $p = 0.48$ | $r(63) = -0.16$, $p = 0.21$ |
| String problem | — | — | $r(71) = 0.09$, $p = 0.44$ | $r(63) = 0.03$, $p = 0.81$ |
| Box problem | — | — | — | $r(63) = 0.20$, $p = 0.12$ |
| Cane problem | — | — | — | — |

We attempted to distinguish these possibilities in a subsequent study (Sommerville, 2007). We specifically focused on the cloth and cane problems because prior work has implied that the two problems may differ in difficulty due to differences in the involved spatial relations. For example, Schlesinger and Langer (1999) labeled the cloth-pulling problem as the support problem and the cane-pulling problem as the surround problem, implying that any task differences may be driven by differences in the abstract spatial relation between the intermediary object and goal object across the two problems. We tested this possibility by comparing infants' performance on the typical cane problem with their performance on a modified cane problem in which a support sat beneath the toy, attached to the crown of the cane. By placing a support under the crown of the cane, we effectively turned a surround problem into a support problem. We reasoned that if differences in understanding the abstract spatial relations involved in the task drove differences in performance across the cane and cloth problems, then turning a surround problem into a support problem would significantly improve infants' performance. This modification, however, did not significantly improve infants' ability to solve the task, suggesting that it was unlikely that the difference in the abstract spatial relations in the task accounted for differences in performance across the tasks. Instead, it may be differences in the motoric demands that account for infants' differential performance across the tasks or the relative familiarity of the objects involved in the problem. Although the cane and cloth problems involve similar subgoal actions, using the cane to retrieve an out-of-reach toy may be significantly more difficult due to the fact that the stalk must be grasped in order to pull the cane (infants can merely put their hand down on the cloth and pull to make the cloth move), and because the cane has more degrees of freedom than the cloth. Alternately, infants may have more experience interacting with cloths and strings than canes and boxes. In either case, the findings challenge the idea that infants represent these problems in terms of their underlying means-end structure per se.

Further support for the finding that infants may build action- or event-specific representations of particular means-end sequences comes from a study by Sommerville & Woodward (2005b). This study investigated infants' ability to take into account the causal constraints of support sequences in which a toy was placed, out-of-reach, on a supporting object: infants received trials on which a toy sat on a support versus trials in which a toy sat adjacent to the support and they were encouraged to get the out-of-reach toy. Whereas 10-month-old infants' tendency to pull the support in order to get the toy did not vary with respect to the toy's location when the toy was supported by a flat cloth, infants at the same age varied their cloth-pulling behavior systematically, pulling the support more frequently when it supported the toy than when it sat adjacent to the toy, when the support was a more substantial box. These findings suggest that although both events consisted of support problems, infants' performance varied significantly as a function of the identity of the support. Again, motoric differences between the tasks or the relative familiarity of cloths versus boxes may factor into differential task performance.

Taken together, the results of the above studies suggest that infants may build, via experience, specific representations of particular means-end sequences rather than learning about means-end sequences as a whole. That is, infants may learn to solve (and understand, see below) different action sequences not based on their underlying means-end structure or based on the particular spatial relations involved in the sequences, but rather based on their experience with and understanding of how different objects can be used (cf. Lockman, 2000).

The account above is similar to arguments that have been made with respect to infants' developing knowledge of the physical world. Baillargeon and colleagues (Baillargeon, 2004; Baillargeon et al., 2011) have argued that infants possess event categories, such as containment, occlusion, collision, and covering, and that learning about how event and object properties influence event outcomes happens within a given event category, one category at a time. For example, infants learn how the variable of object height influences event outcomes in occlusion prior to the time at which they learn how this same variable influences event outcomes in containment (Hespos & Baillargeon, 2006). Differences in learning across categories are assumed to reflect differences in the relative frequency of different events in the real world (e.g. occlusion is more frequent than containment), and thus infants' exposure to these events, and ability to learn from these events (Baillargeon et al., 2011). Similarly, we argue that infants learn how to perform different goal-directed actions in an "event-specific" fashion. What may differ across the two accounts, however, is the proposal of how infants define events. According to Baillargeon's theory (Baillargeon, 2004; Baillargeon et al., 2011) events are defined by the types of objects involved and the particular spatial relation between the involved objects. In contrast, our findings suggest that infants' ability to perform particular actions may depend on the motoric difficulty or demands of the task and/or the relatively familiarity of the objects involved. Indeed, our findings suggest that "events" of the very same type or category (e.g. surround events) can differ fairly dramatically in their difficulty for infants depending on the particular objects involved.

In other ways the picture that we paint is similar to affordance-based learning accounts (e.g. Gibson & Pick, 2000; Lockman, 2000). According to these accounts, infants learn about the possibilities for action that different objects offer that are based on both the properties of a given object and the infants' own capabilities. In the same vein, our findings suggest that infants are learning something object and action specific. However, affordance accounts stress the role of trial-and-error exploration on infants' learning (Gibson & Pick, 2000). As we suggest below, we argue that there are some instances in which direct experience with objects is not necessary for building representations of goal-directed actions. Below we discuss evidence that infants can infer action outcomes, both in their own and others' actions, in the absence of direct experience with these outcomes.

## 3.2. Abstract and Inferential Aspects

### 3.2.1. Representations of Goal-Directed Action also Subserve Perception

Over the first year of life, infants' perception and understanding of the goal-directed actions of other people undergo developments that parallel those seen in action. Infants first appear to selectively encode the actor-goal object relation in simple reach and grasp events (Woodward, 1998), prior to the point at which they can understand the goal-directed nature of referential acts, such as eye gaze (Woodward, 2003), and pointing (Woodward & Guajardo, 2002), and prior to when infants identity the goal object of more elaborate action and tool use sequences (Sommerville & Woodward, 2005a; Sommerville, Hildebrand & Crane, 2008; Woodward & Sommerville, 2000). Consequently, Woodward and colleagues (e.g. Brune & Woodward, 2007; Gerson & Woodward, 2010; Woodward, Sommerville & Guajardo, 2001) have argued that developments in infants' understanding of goals happen in a piecemeal fashion, one action at a time. In addition to findings suggesting that infants' ability to identify goals within particular goal-directed actions follow different developmental timetables, there are other results to suggest that infants first recognize goals as embedded within particular actions. First, Brune & Woodward (2007) demonstrated that infants' understanding of eye gaze and pointing as relational is only weakly related and that these two aspects of action knowledge likely stem from distinct aspects of social responsiveness. Second, 10-month-old infants are successful at perceiving violations to the causal intentional structure of sequences that involve using a box to retrieve an out-of-reach toy that the box supports, but infants of this same age do not perceive these causal violations when a flat cloth acts as the support (Sommerville & Woodward, 2005b). These findings suggest that infants' ability to perceive the causal intentional structure of actions appear to develop in an action- or event-specific fashion, as does their ability to produce particular actions or action sequences.

Beyond the developmental parallels that exist in infants' action perception and production, research has revealed that developments in infants' ability to perform goal-directed actions *drive* developments in infants' perception of others' actions. First, individual differences in infants' ability to perform particular actions predict their ability to identify the goal of these actions in other people's behavior: 10-month-old infants who can use a cloth as an intermediary to retrieve an out-of-reach toy supported by the cloth interpret another person's actions on a cloth as directed toward a toy it supports rather than the cloth itself (Sommerville & Woodward, 2005a; see also Woodward & Guajardo, 2002 for evidence regarding infants' pointing gestures). Second, intervening to improve infants' ability to perform goal-directed actions facilitates their ability to identify the goals of others performing these same actions: 3.5-month-old, prereaching infants, given an intervention designed to improve their ability to apprehend objects, subsequently identify the goal of another person's reach and grasp, whereas those infants lacking this intervention do not (Sommerville, Woodward & Needham, 2005). Third, it appears to be the case that the production of goal-directed action per se, as opposed to increased visual familiarity with a given action as a result of being able to produce that action, drives developments in infants' goal understanding: 10-month-old infants given active training using a novel tool to retrieve an out-of-reach toy subsequently recognized another person's actions on the tool as directed toward a goal object, whereas infants given equated visual experience did not (Sommerville et al., 2008; Sommerville, Blumenthal, Venema & Braun, 2011).

Representations of goal-directed actions established via acting on the world may also be the source of infants' attention to and understanding of the causally relevant features of different goal-directed acts. Ten-month-old infants' ability to appreciate the causal structure of the cloth-pulling sequence (that is to, appreciate that the toy must sit atop, not merely adjacent to, the support when the support is pulled in order to yield the toy) is predicted by their ability to produce goal-directed solutions to the cloth-pulling problem in their own actions (Sommerville & Woodward, 2005b).

Taken together, these findings suggest that through acting on the world, infants build representations that are sufficiently abstract to drive their own actions as well as form a basis for their perception and understanding of the behavior as others. Recent work provides direct evidence that sensori-motor representations are invoked during action observation, starting in infancy (e.g. Nystrom, Ljunghammar, Rosander & von Hofsten, 2011), and some authors have suggested that the development and elaboration of a neuro-cognitive system that subserves action production and perception likely accounts for early developments in infants' ability to perceive and identify the goal of others' actions (Gerson & Woodward, 2010; Sommerville et al., 2008).

At this point, evidence suggests that the representations that commonly drive the perception and production of goal-directed action, appear to be preferentially established via active experience, as opposed to equated mere observation of goal-directed actions (Sommerville et al., 2008). These findings raise the question of what infants may be gaining via active experience that they are either not gaining via mere observation (or perhaps not gaining as efficiently).

Acting on the world may have unique effects on the structure of infants' representations of the actions of others by providing structure and/or content to infants' representations of action. Infants' ability to produce goal-directed action appears to enable the construction of novel representations of action that highlight, or emphasize, the goal-relevant aspects of action (such as the relation between an actor and her goal object), over and above aspect of action that are less relevant or irrelevant to the goal of an action (such as the spatial trajectory of a reach; Gerson & Woodward, 2010; Sommerville & Woodward, 2005a, 2005b). For example, Sommerville & Woodward (2005a, 2005b) demonstrated that whereas 10-month-old infants who were skilled at solving the cloth-pulling problem in their own actions demonstrated enhanced attention to a change in the ultimate goal of the cloth-pulling sequence (the toy) as performed by another person, 10-month-old infants who were unskilled at solving the cloth-pulling problem in their own actions showed enhanced attention to a change in the means of the cloth-pulling sequence (the cloth used to obtain the toy) as performed by another person. Thus, through experience, infants appear to be constructing representations of particular actions or action sequences that more strongly weight the goal of the sequence, and goal-relevant properties, than other elements of the sequence (e.g. the means of achieving the goal). Active experience, then, appears to generate representations of action that stress the goal-relevant structure of action.

Acting on the world, versus mere observation, may have unique or preferential effects on this restructuring process because of the prospective demands of producing action. Consider learning to serve a tennis ball: in order to be successful, one's actions must become directed toward the end goal of landing the ball on one's opponent's side of the court. Producing action, then, has a "prospective push" that observing action does not: producing action is necessarily forward looking, whereas observing action need not be. From this perspective, it is the real-world demands of producing successful actions that lead to the creation of representations that preferentially weight goal-relevant information over goal-irrelevant information and subsequently drive changes in how infants represent the actions of others.

In addition, to the role of active experience in creating goal-structured representations of action, it is also possible that acting on the world allows infants' to attach novel content to representations of action. Acting on the world is accompanied by internal states (such as feelings of striving, yearning, etc.) and driven by mental states (intentions). Infants' ability to track and attend to their own internal and mental states while acting may provide a means for attaching these internal and mental states to the actions of others (see also Meltzoff, 2002). For example, as infants become skilled at solving the cloth-pulling problem, they may recognize that just as they have a goal of obtaining the toy in this context, so too does another person when solving the cloth-pulling problem (Sommerville & Woodward, 2005a, 2005b). Here, active experience would play a privileged role in providing internal and mental states information since such information is not directly observable and therefore not readily derived from direct observation. According to this proposal, infants must possess at least a basic ability to reflect on their own internal and mental states.

Although there is evidence to suggest that experience acting on the world may preferentially lend structure, and perhaps content, to infants' representations of action, we do not intend to suggest that observation plays no role changing in influencing infants' action representations. Indeed, an important, outstanding question is whether differences in acting versus observing yield qualitatively different effects, or quantitatively different effects, on infants' perception and understanding of the goal-directed nature of action. Moreover, it is possible that the relative contributions of active and observational experience to infants' action representations may vary according to a range of factors, including infants' age and relative degree of expertise with a given action. For example, infants' ability to benefit from observation may depend on how closely a given observed action is to an action already in an infants' motor repertoire. When infants are young, novel actions may be quite distinct from actions that infants can perform and therefore difficult to relate to existing action representations; with age, infants can produce an increasingly broad and varied array of goal-directed actions, so novel actions observed by others may be more readily mapped on to infants' existing repertoire. Thus, observation may become an increasingly important source of learning with age. Similarly, infants' ability to benefit from observation may also depend on their relative experience and expertise with a particular action. When infants are completely inexperienced with a given action, observation may yield little benefit; with increasing experience and skill, it is possible that observation may serve to consolidate or expand on what is established through acting on the world. One important direction for future work is to determine the range of contexts in which acting on the world appears to be a privileged learning source for changing representations of action.

### 3.2.2. Representations of Goal-Directed Action Support Inferences

The preceding section suggests that infants' ability to act on the world, perhaps uniquely, provides them with a means for building novel representations of specific actions. These representations are concrete in the sense that they are action specific: rather than acquiring a general concept of a goal through acting, infants appear to perceive or understanding the goals underlying particular actions.

In the proceeding sections, we discuss evidence to suggest that infants' representations of goal-directed action also have some abstract elements. Specifically, they support inferences, both with respect to the likely goals and outcomes of the actions of others, and with respect to outcomes in their own actions. Existing evidence suggests that infants' representations of goal-directed action guide online action analysis (Cannon & Woodward, 2012). In addition, as discussed below, infants go beyond the information given to make predictions about unseen action outcomes in novel contexts.

### 3.2.2.1. Inferences in the Production of Goal-Directed Action

Across two recent studies, we investigated whether infants could apply information gained from a recent motor act to a novel situation in order to come up with a motor plan or decision in the absence of direct experience. According to some accounts (Gibson & Pick, 2000), infants combine information from different motor acts initially in a largely trial-and-error fashion. For example, infants might learn which objects are sufficient to use as tools to bring a given toy within reach by first trying to use a range of different objects, only a subset of which yield success, and only later selectively choose tools based on whether they can be used to obtain out-of-reach toys.

In the first study, we (Upshaw & Sommerville, in preparation; Yau, Upshaw & Sommerville, 2011) investigated whether, after learning about the unseen property of an object (i.e. the object's weight), infants could use this information to plan their actions toward that object in a novel context. Twelve-month-old infants received training and experience with two plastic blocks that were the same size and shape but that differed in color (one was red and one was yellow) and weight (one was 70 g—the weight of a typical bath toy—and one was 470 g—surreptitiously weighted so that it was considerably heavier than a typical bath toy). During a training session, infants were encouraged to imitate simple direct actions on the block, such as placing the block on a platform or dropping it into a bucket to allow them to encode the respective weight properties of the blocks.

On test trials infants were presented with a problem-solving task in which a single block was placed out-of-reach on a cloth, such that the cloth could be pulled to bring the block within reach, and they were encouraged to get the block. Past studies suggest that infants readily solve this problem by 12 months of age (Piaget, 1952; Willatts, 1999). On alternate trials, we varied the block identity, such that for half of the test trials, the block on the end of the cloth was heavy and for half of infants, the block was light. The question was whether infants would use information about the block weight to plan their actions on the cloth. We predicted that if infants do take into account an object's weight, we would observe differences in how infants acted on the cloth as a function of the block's weight. Critically, we examined differences from the very first test trial forward to determine whether infants' actions on the cloth reflected an inference about the impact of block weight on the infants' approach to the cloth or whether it reflected trial-by-trial learning.

Infants were randomly assigned to one of the two conditions: a control condition and a trick condition. Training was identical for both conditions. Test trials differed in that for the control condition, the color–weight pairings of the blocks were identical to training, whereas for trick condition, the color–weight pairings were reversed (unbeknownst to the infant). To determine whether infants' actions on the cloth reflected previously acquired information about the block's weight, we compared infants' actions on the cloth when the block was heavy. Critically, the two conditions differed on these trials because whereas in the control condition infants believed the block to be heavy, in the trick condition infants believed it to be light. We coded infants' failed attempts on the cloth on these trials; a failed attempt was defined as a pull produced by the infant that did not move the block toward the infant, presumably because the infant was exerting insufficient force on the cloth. As Fig. 13.2 indicates, infants in the trick condition had significantly more failed attempts when retrieving the heavy block than infants in the control condition. Because the cloth-pulling task was identical for the two conditions, the difference must have stemmed from the manner in which infants mentally represented the block. Thus, these findings suggest that infants use prior information about an object, in this case, an object's weight, to infer how to act in a novel context.

In the second study (Sommerville & Feldman, 2008), we asked whether inferences could also guide infants' motor decisions; that is, their choice of which of two objects to act on. Specifically, we asked whether, after training with a tool to retrieve an out-of-reach toy, infants could select between potential novel tools based on their causal efficacy. Past work by Brown (1990) has demonstrated that infants, by ages 18 to 24 months of age, select tools based on causally efficacious properties—that is, whether the tool possessed the properties necessary to bring an out-of-reach toy within reach. Our question was whether younger infants could take information gleaned from a novel motor act—using a P.V.C. cane to retrieve an out-of-reach toy—and combine this information with knowledge of the properties of

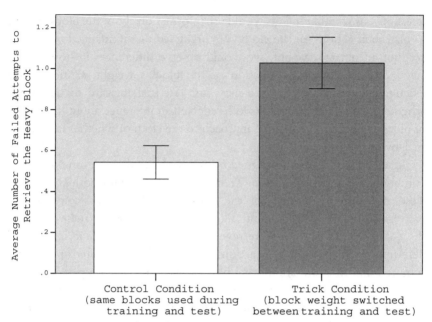

**Figure 13.2** Infants' failed attempts as a function of condition.

novel objects to decide which of these novel objects would be efficacious to use as a tool.

Ten-month-old infants received training with a yellow plastic cane until they became skilled at using the cane to retrieve an out-of-reach object (at the onset of training, infants rarely used the novel cane to retrieve an out-of-reach toy). Prior to test trials, infants were introduced to two novel objects. Each object was shaped like a shepherd's crook and differed from the training tool in size, shape, and material. One object was a piece of rope reinforced with silver duct tape, and the other object was a piece of lei, reinforced with wire. Infants were allowed to interact with only the end of the two novel objects in order to learn about their respective properties. Critically, although either novel potential tool could be used to retrieve the out-of-reach toy, only one (the duct taped rope) possessed the combination of object properties required to *efficiently* retrieve the toy.

On test trials, infants were allowed to select between the two novel objects. To ensure that infants', selections were not merely based on a baseline preference for either potential tool and to ensure that infants were selecting between the objects on the basis of their efficacy for retrieving the out-of-reach toy, infants received two types of test trials. During problem-solving trials, the potential tools surrounded identical out-of-reach toys, and infants could select a tool to retrieve the toy. During no-goal trials, administered as a measure of baseline preference, infants were presented with both potential tools but no toys were available to retrieve. If infants recognized that only one of the objects possessed the properties necessary for efficiently retrieving the toy, then they should preferentially select the rope on the problem-solving trials but not the no-goal trials.

Our question was whether infants could use representations gained from their tool use experience, in combination with information acquired about the properties of the potential tool, to guide their motor decisions. We found that, from the first trial onward, infants selected between the potential tools based on (a) whether they possessed the requisite properties to efficiently solve the problem and (b) whether or not a goal was present on the trial (see Fig. 13.3). On problem-solving trials, infants more frequently selected the rope than the lei; on no-goal trials they preferentially selected the lei. Thus, infants' choices varied systematically based on the task at hand and based on the properties of the objects. Infants showed this pattern of

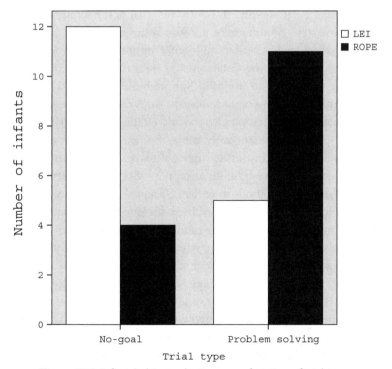

**Figure 13.3** Infants' object selections as a function of trial type.

performance from the very first test trial on. Critically, because infants never had the opportunity to use the novel objects as tools, and because these objects were entirely new to infants, infants needed to infer the impact of the felt properties of the two novel objects, based on a brief exposure, for the problem outcome. These findings suggest that at least in some cases, infants can additively and generatively combine information from different motor acts, without having to actively "try out" particular motor solutions, to come up with accurate motor decisions.

Taken together, these findings suggest that infants can sometimes combine information from different goal-directed actions in order to infer how to act and which objects to act on to produce a desired outcome.

### 3.2.2.2. Inferences in the Perception of Goal-Directed Action

To address the question of whether infants can infer outcomes of others' actions, we first investigated infants' inferences about the outcome of a tool use event, after only seeing the first step of the event. Past work has established that for 12-month-old infants, following habituation to a completed multi-step action sequence (pulling the cloth to get a toy it supported), infants can identify the toy as the goal of the sequence after only seeing the first step (Sommerville & Woodward, 2005a). In a subsequent study, we investigated whether, following training with a novel tool to retrieve an out-of-reach toy, infants could infer the actor's goal as the toy after only seeing her act on the tool (Sommerville et al., 2011).

Ten-month-old infants were trained to use a cane to retrieve an out-of-reach toy that sat in its crook. Past work established that 10-month-old infants were poor at spontaneously using the cane to obtain out-of-reach toys but could be trained to do so after a short session (Sommerville et al., 2008). Following an active training session, in which the experimenter used a number of different methods to enhance infants' ability to solve the cane-pulling problem, infants took part in a violation-of-expectancy (VOE) paradigm. Another group of 10-month-old infants were assigned to a matched observational session in which they watched an adult experimenter repeatedly solve the cane-pulling problem (infants in the observational condition were yoked to infants in the active training condition in terms of the number of trials they saw).

During the VOE, infants watched events in which an actor sat behind a stage supporting a cane that surrounded an out-of-reach toy. The actor reached for the stalk of the cane at which point an occluding screen was partially raised, obscuring the event outcome from view. To an adult observer, raising the screen at this point gave the impression that an ongoing event had been interrupted. Anecdotal evidence suggests that infants may have had the same impression, as they often tried to peek over the top of the screen when the screen was partially raised.

On test trials, the screen was lowered to reveal the actor holding the toy or holding the cane. We reasoned that if infants inferred that the toy was the actor's goal, after seeing her grasp the stalk of the cane, they would look longer to the cane outcome than the toy outcome, despite the fact that the cane event was more perceptually familiar than the toy event and that acting on the cane was the last thing they saw do. If so, this would be evidence that infants inferred that the actor's actions on the cane were directed toward the toy and not the cane itself.

Infants actively trained to use the cane demonstrated longer looking to the cane event than the toy event, whereas infants that received matched observational experience did not differentiate between the test events. These differential findings between conditions suggest that it was not mere prior visual exposure to the cane that drove the effects of the active training condition. Thus, infants appear to build representations of tool use events by acting on the world, and these representations support inferences about the goals behind others' actions. Research from other labs suggest that such inferences may also guide infants' ability to infer the goal of a goal-directed action after seeing only a failed attempt (Brandone & Wellman, 2009).

In two subsequent studies, we investigated whether infants cannot only infer the goal of an actor's goal-directed action but can also infer the *physical outcomes* of particular goal-directed actions. In one study (Loucks & Sommerville, 2011; Loucks & Sommerville, under review), we examined whether infants could infer the outcome of a goal-directed action that involved dropping an object into a container. In conditions in which individuals drop objects into containers, the outcome of the action (e.g. whether or not it lands in the container) is dependent on several factors, including the size of the container (success is more likely when a container is wide than narrow), the drop height (lower drops are more likely to be successful than higher drops), and the size of the object with respect to the container (if the object is small with respect to the container drops are more likely to be successful than if the object is large with respect to the container). We reasoned that if, when watching dropping actions, infants were inferring the outcome, then they would selectively attend to changes to dropping actions that influenced the likelihood of success (i.e. getting the object into the container).

Because we were investigating a previously unexplored aspect of action perception and understanding, we first carried out an experiment with adults. Adults participated in a perception task. During the perception task, adults watched videos of three different actors successfully dropping a small beanbag into both wide and narrow containers. Each of the actors dropped the beanbag from five different body-centered heights: hip height, middle torso height, shoulder height, forehead height, and overhead height. Importantly, the only difference between the wide and narrow container videos was the container itself. Still frames were taken from each of these videos for use in the perception task. Each still frame depicted an actor holding the beanbag over the container at one of the five heights.

During each trial of the perception task, adults watched a video of a dropping event and were then presented with a still frame image at which point they were asked to determine whether the frame was from the video or not. Still frames for half of the trials depicted the same height used in the video, whereas the other half depicted a different height. Half of the adults only viewed dropping into the wide container (wide condition), whereas the other half only viewed dropping into the narrow container (narrow condition). We hypothesized that adults would be especially accurate at detecting increases in height (upward changes) relative to decreases in height (downward changes) in the narrow condition since dropping from higher up increases the chance of a miss. We hypothesized that there would be no such differences in the wide condition.

In analyzing the results from the perception task, we focused only on trials in which the height changes were one step upward or downward (e.g. from shoulder to forehead and shoulder to torso). This was a measure of how finely sensitive adults were at detecting height changes. The analysis of the perception task confirmed the hypothesized pattern: adults were significantly more accurate at detecting one-step upward changes relative to one-step downward changes in the narrow condition but were equally accurate at detecting these same two height changes in the wide condition. Adults appear to be attempting to predict the outcome of the dropping action, as thus they key on information that will be relevant for this prediction. However, adults increase attention to this information only when it is directly relevant to predicting the outcome.

Adults also received a dropping task in which they attempted to drop the same beanbag from the same five body-centered heights into the same narrow container used in the videos. Each trial, after lifting the beanbag to a specified height, an experimenter positioned the container on the floor in front of the participant. Several floor positions were used in order to collect multiple trials for each height. The experimenter coded whether or not each drop was successful. The results of the dropping task revealed two key findings. First, as drop height increased, dropping accuracy decreased: This was reflected in a significant linear trend to the data. Thus, increasing drop height does indeed increase the variability in specifically targeting a drop location. To our knowledge, this is the first empirical evidence of this phenomenon. Second, there was a significant positive relation between overall performance on the perception task and overall performance on the dropping task. That is, adults who were more accurate at targeting their drops tended to be more accurate at detecting changes in drop height in another's dropping actions. Thus, adults' motor experience and expertise with the witnessed action may help them infer the outcome of the dropping action.

We next investigated whether infants also infer the outcome of dropping actions. We focused on infants at 10 months of age as it is by roughly this age that infants can engage in dropping behavior in their own actions (Ruff, 1984). We designed a habituation task that closely matched the perception task used with adults. The stimuli were six videos of precision dropping—a standard, higher height, and lower height video, involving both narrow and wide containers. Different groups of infants participated in each of the container conditions. For both conditions, infants were first habituated to the standard video in which the actor reached for and lifted an object (a purple elastic ball) over the transparent container and successfully dropped it in. Following habituation, infants were shown the higher height video, in which the object was dropped from higher than the standard, and the lower height video, in which the object was dropped from lower than the standard. Importantly, the height differences were matched between conditions, and the actor moved in sync with a metronome to equalize the duration of each movement. Thus, the only difference between conditions was the width of the container.

As predicted, we found an interaction between drop height and container width on infants' looking times. In the narrow container condition, infants looked significantly longer at the higher height over the lower height drop, but in the wide container condition, no significant preference was observed. These results indicate that by 10 months of age, infants infer the outcomes of dropping actions and selectively encode information that is relevant to the outcome. Infants likely inferred that an increase in drop height, when the container was narrow, might change the probability of whether or not the object would land in the container, and therefore selectively increased attention to an increase in drop height for the narrow container condition.

In another study (Loucks & Sommerville, 2012), we investigated whether 10-month-old infants could use information about the manner in which an actor grasped an object to make inferences about the event outcome. Specifically, we investigated infants' perception of events involving a precision grasp, and how their perception varied as a function of whether or not they, themselves, were capable of performing the precision grasp. We reasoned that infants might be able to use their motor experience to infer which actions could, or could not, be performed, using the precision grasp.

Infants in this experiment participated in a habituation task, designed to probe infants' understanding of the functional consequences of precision and whole-hand grasps, and a grasping task, designed to measure infants' ability to perform precision grasps in their own behavior. During the grasping task, infants were presented with five colorful "sticks" (stacked pieces of Lego) that were presented inside of one of the two transparent plastic containers: the wide container or the narrow container. Although both containers were approximately the same height as the sticks, the wide container was approximately twice the width of the sticks, and the narrow container was only slightly wider than the sticks. Critically, when the sticks were in the narrow container, a precision grip was the easiest and most efficient way to remove the toy from the container. Each trial, the infant was presented with one of the sticks inside one of the containers and was encouraged to retrieve the stick.

The grasp used to ultimately remove the stick from the narrow container was coded along two dimensions: (1) the type of grasp (i.e. precision or otherwise) and (2) the planfulness of the grasp (i.e. whether infants pre-configured their grasp). From this data, we categorized infants into groups of precision and nonprecision graspers. Precision graspers were those infants who produced at least one planful precision grasp, and nonprecision graspers were those infants who did not perform any planful precision grasps. Importantly, some nonprecision graspers may have produced some precision grasps, but they were never *planful* precision grasps.

During the habituation paradigm, infants were randomly assigned to one of the two conditions. In both conditions, infants watched the actor move a green bowl from one side of the stage to another. In the upright to inverted (UI) condition, the bowl began in the upright configuration, and infants were habituated to an actor using a two-finger, precision grasp to move the bowl across the table. In the Inverted to upright condition (IU), the bowl began in the inverted configuration, and infants were habituated to the actor using a whole-hand grasp to move the bowl across the table. Across both conditions, the bowl was decorated in such a way that it was easy to tell if the bowl was upright (with the concave surface pointing upward) or inverted. For this particular bowl, when it was upright, it was possible to grasp and move the bowl using a precision grip—with the index and middle fingers on the inside wall of the bowl and the thumb on the outside wall in line with the fingers—while a whole-hand grasp—with all the fingers and thumb reaching across the top—was not functional for moving the bowl. However, when the bowl was inverted, the functionality of these two grasps was reversed.

Following habituation, the bowl orientation was switched, such that infants in the UI condition saw the bowl oriented upside down, whereas those in the IU condition saw the bowl oriented right side up. Infants across both conditions saw two types of test events, one in which the actor grasped the bowl with a whole-hand grasp (whole-hand event), and one in which the actor grasped the bowl with a precision grasp (precision event). Importantly, the bowl was not moved across the table during test trials—the actor stopped her movement at the point of contact with the bowl.

Given the differential orientation of the bowl across the two conditions, the grasps featured in the test trials had different implications for event outcomes. For infants in UI condition (right side up bowl on habituation, upside down bowl on test), the precision grasp was no longer functional on test trials—that is, using the precision grasp would not be effective for moving the bowl, whereas the whole-hand grasp was effective for moving the bowl. In contrast for infants in the IU condition (upside down bowl on habituation, and right side up bowl on test), given the width of the bowl (the bowl was sufficiently wide so that a whole-hand grasp would not allow the actor to secure a firm enough purchase on the bowl to allow him or her to move it), a precision grasp would permit moving the bowl, but a whole-hand grasp would not allow the actor to move the bowl (the bowl was sufficiently wide so that a whole-hand grasp would not allow the actor to secure a firm enough purchase on the bowl to allow him or her to move it).

Our prediction was that infants' looking times to the test events would vary as a function of both the conditions they took part in and their ability to produce the precision grasp in their own behavior. Our predictions were born out in the findings. In both conditions, precision graspers recovered attention both when the actor used a different grasp than she had on habituation trials and when the grasp was the same as the habituation grasp but would no longer allow the actor to lift and move the bowl. Non-precision graspers behaved very differently: they only recovered to the perceptually novel grasp in each condition and not to the perceptually familiar grasps that now had different functional consequences.

Thus, infants who are relatively skilled at precision grasping presumably inferred the outcome of the test events using information about the actor's grasp type: infants recovered attention to events that would yield unsuccessful outcomes, even though these events featured perceptually familiar hand configurations. These findings suggest that infants' ability to produce the precision grasp provided them with a basis for generating outcomes for events involving the precision grasps of others.

An interesting and important question for future work concerns whether infants, in addition to combining information from different motor acts in their own actions to come up with novel actions and motor decisions, can combine information from other individuals' disparate motor acts to generate novel predictions about their behavior. Research to date suggests that this may be within infants' reach. Past work (Sommerville & Woodward, 2005a, 2005b) revealed that, as a group, infants do not identify the goal of a sequence in which an actor pulls a cloth supporting a toy in order to obtain the toy until roughly 12 months of age. Sommerville and Crane (2009) investigated whether 10-month-old infants could use information regarding an actor's prior goal in the context of a reach and grasp event to disambiguate a cloth-pulling sequence. Infants saw an actor reach for and grasp one of the two toys sitting side-by-side on a stage five times prior to taking part in a cloth-pulling habituation paradigm. During the cloth-pulling habituation paradigm, the actor pulled a cloth supporting an out-of-reach toy that supported her prior goal object. On test trials, the toy locations were reversed and infants saw the actor reach toward a new goal object by grasping the same cloth she had previously versus events in which the actor reached toward the same goal object she had previously by grasping a new cloth. The results revealed that infants used information from the actor's prior act (her pursuit of the toy when it was directly in front of her) to identify her goal in the cloth-pulling sequence, looking longer to the change in the actor's ultimate goal object than the change to the cloth she acted on. An interesting question is whether infants can go one step further to make an inference based on the actor's prior behavior: given evidence of an actor's goal in a direct reach and grasp event could infants use this information to identify the goal of an action sequence or tool use event after only seeing the first step of the sequence?

Taken together, the above studies suggest that infants are good at inferring the goals behind, and outcomes underlying, familiar actions, even when these actions occur in novel contexts. These results suggest that representations of goal-directed actions not only guide online in-the-moment action perception but also provide a basis for inferences about future actions and outcomes. Thus, even though infants build representations of goal-directed actions that appear to be fairly specific to particular motor acts, these representations are also sufficiently abstract to support inferences about outcomes in novel contexts.

## 4. INCREASING ABSTRACTEDNESS IN REPRESENTATIONS OF GOAL-DIRECTED ACTION

Taken together, the findings suggest that, by acting on the world, infants build action-specific representations that guide their perception and understanding of others' actions. A critical question then becomes how and when infants' representations of goal-directed action become more abstract. More mature representations of goal-directed action are more abstract in at least two senses. First, adults and older children can recognize goals as entirely divorced from action because they possess a general and broad concept of a goal. Second, adults and children recognize that instances of goal-directed action can be represented in various ways: goal-directed actions are not solely driven by transient desires for particular outcomes but can also be explained by enduring preferences for objects or as driven by societal conventions.

With respect to the first question, Woodward, Gerson and colleagues have suggested that infants may move toward more abstract representations of goals through an analogy-like process, based on their possession of a general cognitive mechanism that promotes structural mapping between their own familiar actions and novel actions that they witness (Gerson & Woodward, 2010). Infants may align familiar actions, for which they have already extracted the goal structure, with novel actions that share perceptual features with familiar actions. Such alignment in turn may support their extraction of high-level features of these novel events, such as the goals underlying these actions. New evidence from Gerson and Woodward (2012) provides support for this hypothesis: giving 7- and 10-month-old infants the opportunity to compare a familiar action with a novel, tool-use action produced by another person helps them to extract the goal of the tool-use action. This process may enable infants to begin to recognize goals as divorced from particular actions, allowing them to build a broader and more abstract concept of goals.

We addressed the second question concerning when infants can represent the same action at different levels, by looking at infants' expectations of an object selection event. Critically, such an event could be represented at a variety of different levels. The actor's object selection may indicate a transient action goal that is specific to a given time or place, or it could indicate a predisposition toward, or preference for a given object (among many other interpretations). Some accounts have suggested that infants, from an early age, necessarily represent events in which an actor reaches for one of the two objects as a preference (Luo & Baillargeon, 2007). However, because the mere selection of one object over another does not unambiguously imply a preference for one object over another object, we investigated whether infants might flexibly alter their interpretation of an object selection given information provided by the surrounding context.

To address this question, we (Sommerville, 2008; Sommerville, Crane & Yun, in preparation) habituated 10-month-old infants to an event in which an actor looked at and considered two toys sitting side-by-side on a table in front of her. She subsequently selected one of the two toys and picked it up, smiling at the toy. Infants were randomly assigned to one of the two conditions: in the dispositional statement condition, after the actor picked up the toy she indicated her liking of the toy (e.g. "I like frogs"), whereas in the general remark condition, she made a nonspecific remark directed toward the object (e.g. "Look. Wow"). Otherwise, the two conditions were identical.

Test trials took place in another room, just down the hall from the habituation room. During test trials, the toys appeared in reverse locations with respect to the actor. On the target trials, the actor reached for and grasped the same object she had during habituation trials. On the nontarget trials, the actor reached for and grasped the other object. There was no language accompanying the actor's object selection on test trials.

Our question of interest was whether, and under what circumstances, infants' interpretation or representation of the actor's object selection would generalize to the new room. We assumed that if infants represented the actor's original object selection in the first room as stemming from a transient goal, they would restrict their expectations regarding another person's object selection to the original context in which they witnessed the selection. In contrast, if they viewed the action as reflecting an enduring preference for the object, they would expect the actor to continue to choose their original object in a new room. If infants flexibly used contextual information to guide their interpretation of the actor's original object selection, we hypothesized that whereas infants who heard the general remark might represent the actor's object selection as a transient goal-directed act with no consequences for future actions, infants who heard the dispositional statement might build a more abstract representation of the object selection, representing it as stemming from an enduring preference for the selected object. If our hypothesis was correct, we expected that infants in the general remark condition would look equally to the test events because they construed her initial object selection as representing a transient goal, and therefore possessed no expectations regarding which of the toy objects the actor would pursue in a new room. In contrast, infants in the dispositional statement condition were predicted to represent the object selection as an enduring disposition or preference that persisted across space and time and thus demonstrate longer looking to test events in which the actor pursued the nontarget toy.

Our predictions were born out: infants in the dispositional statement demonstrated longer looking to the nontarget toy event over the target toy event, whereas infants in the general remark condition demonstrated equal looking to both test events. Critically, follow-up analyses confirmed that the effects of the dispositional statement did not merely make the habituation event more memorable, leading to greater generalization across the context: rates of habituation and looking times during habituation trials were identical across conditions. Infants' preference for the nontarget toy event in the dispositional statement condition was correlated with parental reports of infants' receptive vocabulary, raising the possibility that infants' understanding of the phrase or some part of it altered their interpretation of the habituation event. Moreover, additional conditions in which the actor produced nonsense language, matched in intonation and prosody to the dispositional statement, produced null findings, providing evidence that it was something about the meaning of the phrase, or particular words in the phrase, that influenced infants' inferences.

In a subsequent condition, we investigated whether infants could also use statements that indicated a dislike for an object to guide their inferences about another person's object selection in a new context. Ten-month-old infants were habituated to an actor reaching behind one of two opaque occluders to retrieve a toy. She subsequently picked up the toy and indicated her dislike with a facial expression and a dispositional statement (e.g. "I hate frogs"). The occluders were used to create an ecologically valid context in which an actor would repeatedly reach to a single location despite finding something she 'did not like there. As in the prior two conditions, test trials occurred in a separate room in reverse locations with respect to the actor.

In this condition, we found that infants 10 months of age and older expected the actor to pursue a novel object in the new room: infants demonstrated longer looking times to events in which the actor pursued the target toy than the nontarget toy. Thus, given repeated evidence that an actor dislikes a toy, infants appeared to expect that the actor would pursue a different object in a new room. Infants' preference for the target toy event was marginally related to parental reports of comprehensive vocabulary, suggesting that infants' comprehension of the dislike phrase, or some parts of the phrase, may have assisted them in making a dispositional attribution.

Taken together, our results indicated that infants, by 10 months of age, at least under certain conditions, possess the ability to recognize actions as stemming from preferences for particular objects, or dispositional attitudes toward objects (see also Luo & Baillargeon, 2007). Our results also indicate that infants are not beholden to representing a particular action in a partic- ular way: rather, depending on the surrounding context, infants can represent the same action as either reflecting a transient goal or an enduring preference. Thus, these findings suggest that infants may not possess a "default mode" for representing human action in a particular way (Csibra & Gergely, 2009; Gergely, Egyed & Király, 2007), and instead, toggle back and forth flexibly between different representational levels of human action depending on the context.

A critical question concerns the role of language in infants' under- standing of the actions of others. Our findings suggest that certain linguistic information accompanying human action, along with infants' burgeoning language comprehension, guides infants' expectations about another person's likely future actions. In our study, the accompanying linguistic phrase may have impacted how infants represented the actor's object selection (as a transient goal or as an enduring preference) and thus the expectations they drew from that representation (whether or not she would choose the object in another room).

In terms of the role of language in infants' understanding of action, more broadly our results are consistent with two possibilities. First, it is possible that infants' understanding of goal-directed action as stemming from enduring preferences results from another source (e.g. something other than language) and that the linguistic context accompanying action is just one of many cues that infants might use to specify whether a given goal-directed act specifies an enduring preference or a transient goal. Infants could potentially draw on other sources of information, such as pursuit of the object across multiple contexts to decide whether the object selection is an indication of an enduring preference or a transient goal. Second, it is possible that language plays a more profound role in infants' elaborating infants' understanding of the actions of others. Below, we consider some possible ways in which language might impact infants' action understanding.

Research by Waxman and colleagues (see Waxman & Leddon, 2011; Waxman, 2004 for reviews) has systematically demonstrated that the presence of labels accompanying the presentation of objects influences how or whether infants categorize these objects. Nine- to thirteen-month-old infants represent objects with respect to their category membership when objects are accompanied by a labeling phrase, but not a nonlabeling phrase, or a tone (Balaban & Waxman, 1997; Fulkerson & Haaf, 1998, 2003; Waxman & Markow, 1995). One possibility, then, is that language provides infants with a new means for categorizing actions that cut across or subsume the more specific representations that infants build through their own actions on the world, resulting in higher-level representations of the actions of others. We call this the "categorization" hypothesis. According to this hypothesis, adults may frequently produce utterances that contain language labels during the production of goal-directed action. The use of consistent labels accompanying action may have an effect on how infants categorize disparate actions. Specifically, a common label that accompanies disparate actions may lead infants to recognize commonalities among actions that have the same goal or outcome, thus, leading infants to establish a higher-order representation.

To play the categorization hypothesis out concretely, imagine an adult standing in the kitchen who reaches into a cookie box, retrieves a cookie and then says, "I love cookies." Twenty minutes later, the same adult, now sitting on the couch in the living room, pulls a newspaper supporting a plate of cookies toward her and reaches for a cookie, while saying, "I really love cookies." The presence of a common label across these different instances of goal-directed action may lead infants to form a new category that emphasizes the common goal of both instances that subsequently drives predictions across a wider range of circumstances.

Another, not necessarily mutually exclusive possibility, is what we will call the "bootstrapping" hypothesis. This hypothesis starts out the same way: in the course of every day life adults produce language labels that accompany goal-directed action. However, language exerts its influence on infants' representations not via categorization, but by leading infants to apply expectations that they hold regarding labels to the actions that accompany those labels. Very recent evidence suggests that infants as young as 6–9 months of age may have begun to appreciate defining features of labels (Bergelson & Swingley, 2012): infants of this age appear to recognize that labels refer to classes of objects, not individual exemplars, and are consistent across contexts. When labels accompany action, infants may transfer expectations that they hold about labels to actions: specifically, that actions are directed toward classes of objects, not individual exemplars, and that actions are not context specific. Under this hypothesis, infants possess certain expectations regarding labels, and when action and labels co–occur, action comes along for the ride.

At this point, both these accounts are merely speculative, and there may, of course, be other stories that fit the data equally well. Critically, however, these accounts yield predictions that could be empirically tested in future studies. First, central to both accounts is the suggestion that labels accompany the production of action in everyday contexts. Thus, this claim could be empirically evaluated by examining the production of labels accompanying action in naturalistic situations. Second, both accounts stress the role of labels, as opposed to nonlabels or nonlinguistic stimuli, in particular, in the birth of more abstract representations of action.

The categorization hypothesis could be tested using methods that are similar to those used by Waxman and colleagues (Balaban & Waxman, 1997; Fulkerson & Haaf, 1998, 2003; Waxman & Markow, 1995). For example, studies could contrast the effect of labels versus tones in habituation paradigms in which infants are habituated to different exemplars of goal-directed action with common goals (e.g. opening a box to get a toy car; pulling a cloth to get a toy car, etc.), and tested with events that feature a contrast between novel actions with the same goal (e.g. using a cane to get a toy car) and familiar actions with a novel goal (pulling a cloth to get a toy frog). The prediction here would be that labels accompanying action (vs. tones, or other nonlabels, accompanying action) would produce (a) faster habituation rates during habituation trials (because they assisted infants in recognizing the common goal across different actions) and (b) selective recovery of attention to new goal events and not as the categorization hypothesis new action events (because only the new goal event crosses the category boundary).

Similarly, the bootstrapping hypothesis could be tested by systematically manipulating the presence versus absence of a label in the language that accompanies action and testing infants' tendency to generalize the actor's object selection across the context (although Sommerville et al., in preparation, compared the dispositional statement—"I like frogs"—to a general remark—"Look. Wow"—it could be argued that it was not the absence vs. presence of a label per se that led to the differences across the conditions). For example, comparisons could be made between conditions in which a dispositional statement containing a label ("I like frogs") versus conditions in which the dispositional statement does not contain a label ("I like this"). According to the bootstrapping hypothesis, the prediction is that although the dispositional statements accompanying the action are nearly identical, save the presence or absence of a label, only infants in the dispositional statement with label condition would generalize the actor's object selection.

Taken together, these recent findings suggest that a promising new direction for research on action understanding concerns the role that language may play in the process of building more abstract representations.

## 5. CONCLUSIONS AND IMPLICATIONS FOR EARLY LEARNING MORE BROADLY

In this chapter, we discussed both the nature of infants' representations of goal-directed action as well as how these representations are constructed. In the first part of the chapter, we suggested that infants' developing ability to produce goal-directed action leads to the development of goal-centered representations of human action that guides their perception and understanding of others' actions. These representations possess a delicate blend of both abstract and concrete elements. They are concrete in so far as they are formed on an action-by-action basis. They are abstract in that they underlie both the production and perception of action and support inferences regarding upcoming actions and action outcomes both regarding infants' own actions and with respect to the actions of others.

These findings have important implications for early learning. First, they suggest that infants' early representations, more broadly, are likely characterized by both concrete and abstract elements. This recognition takes the emphasis away from categorizing representations as *either* abstract or concrete, describing the ways in which early representations may possess both elements. Second, they suggest that active and observational experience may play differential roles in the construction of early representations. Specifically, our findings suggest that active experience plays a privileged and/or preferential role in infants' ability to create goal-centered representations of others' actions. A critical question for future research is whether such differential effects of active versus observational experience extend to other domains, and the full range of conditions under which observational and active experience may exert differential or similar influences on early learning.

In the second half of the chapter, we reviewed evidence to suggest that by at least the end of the first year of life, infants may possess the ability to represent the very same action at different levels of representational specificity depending on the surrounding context. With respect to early learning more broadly, these findings suggest that contextual factors may heavily influence the level at which infants represent different objects or events, and, thus, serious attention should be given to the role of context in early learning. More specifically, our findings raise the possibility that the linguistic context accompanying action, or language more broadly, may facilitate infants' construction of more abstract interpretations of goal-directed action. We suggest novel ways in which labels may affect infants' developing understanding of action and perhaps the nature of infants' representations more broadly. Future work can help to determine whether language plays a causal role in the development of increasingly abstract representations of infants' own and others' actions.

## REFERENCES

Adolph, K. E. (2000). Specificity of learning: why infants fall over a veritable cliff. *Psychological Science, 11*, 290–295.

Balaban, M. T., & Waxman, S. R. (1997). Do words facilitate object categorization in 9-month-old infants? *Journal of Experimental Child Psychology, 64*, 3–26.

Baldwin, D. A., Markman, E. M., & Melartin, R. L. (1993). Infants' ability to draw inferences about nonobvious object properties: evidence from exploratory play. *Child Development, 64*(3), 711–728.

Baillargeon, R. (1987). Young infants' reasoning about the physical and spatial properties of a hidden object. *Cognitive Development, 2*, 179–200.

Baillargeon, R. (2004). Infants' reasoning about hidden objects: evidence for event-general and event-specific expectations. *Developmental Science, 7*, 391–424.

Baillargeon, R., Li, J., Gertner, Y., & Wu, D. (2011). How do infants reason about physical events? In U. Goswami (Ed.), *The Wiley-Blackwell handbook of childhood cognitive development* (2nd ed.). (pp. 11–48) Oxford: Blackwell.

Barrett, T., Davis, E. F., & Needham, A. (2007). Learning to use a tool in infancy. *Developmental Psychology, 43*, 352–368.

Bergelson, E., & Swingley, D. (2012). At 6 to 9 months, human infants know the meanings of many common nouns. *Proceedings of the National Academy of Sciences of the USA, 109*, 3253–3258.

Bertenthal, B., & Clifton, R. K. (1998). Perception and action. In W. Damon, D. Kuhn, & R. Siegler (Eds.), *Cognition, perception and language. Handbook of child psychology*, Vol. 2 (pp. 51–102). New York: Wiley.

Brandone, A., & Wellman, H. M. (2009). You can't always get what you want: Infants understand failed goal-directed actions. *Psychological Science, 20*, 85–91.

Brown, A. L. (1990). Domain-specific principles affect learning and transfer in children. *Cognitive Science, 14*, 107–133.

Brune, C. W., & Woodward, A. L. (2007). Social cognition and social responsiveness in 10-month-old infants. *Journal of Cognition and Development, 8*, 133–158.

Cannon, E., & Woodward, A. L. (2012). Infants generate goal-based action predictions. *Developmental Science, 15*, 292–298.

Carey, S. (2009). *The origin of concepts*. New York: Oxford University Press.

Cohen, L. B., & Cashon, C. H. (2006). Infant cognition. In W. Damon, R. M. Lerner, D. Kuhn, & R. S. Siegler (Eds.), *Cognition, perception, and language* (6th ed.).*Handbook of child psychology*, Vol. 2 (pp. 214–251). New York: Wiley, Series.

Csibra, G., & Gergely, G. (2009). Natural pedagogy. *Trends in Cognitive Sciences, 13*, 148–153.

Denison, S., & Xu, F. (2010). Twelve- to 14-month-old infants can predict single-event probability with large set sizes. *Developmental Science, 13*, 798–803.

Denison, S., Reed, C. & Xu, F. (in press). The emergence of probabilistic reasoning in very young infants: evidence from 4.5- and 6-month-old infants. *Developmental Psychology*.

Dewar, K., & Xu, F. (2010). Induction, overhypothesis, and the origin of abstract knowledge: evidence from 9-month-old infants. *Psychological Science, 21*, 1871–1877.

Fulkerson, A.L., & Haaf, R.A. (1998). *New words for new things: the relationship between novel labels and 12-month-olds' categorization of novel objects*. Poster session presented at the International Conference on Infant Studies, Atlanta, GA.

Fulkerson, A. L., & Haaf, R. A. (2003). The influence of labels, non-labeling sounds, and source of auditory input on 9- and 15-month-olds' object categorization. *Infancy, 4*, 349–369.

Gerson, S., & Woodward, A. L. (2010). Building intentional action knowledge with one's hands. In S. P. Johnson (Ed.), *Neo-constructivism*. Oxford University Press.

Gerson, S., & Woodward, A. (2012). A claw is like my hand: comparison supports goal analysis in infants. *Cognition, 122*, 181–192.

Gergely, G., Egyed, K., & Király, I. (2007). On pedagogy. *Developmental Science, 10*, 139–146.

Gibson, E. J. (1988). Exploratory behavior in the development of perceiving, acting, and the acquiring of knowledge. *Annual Review of Psychology, 39*, 1–41.

Gibson, E. J., & Pick, A. D. (2000). *An ecological approach to perceptual learning and development*. New York, NY US: Oxford University Press.

Haith, M. M. (1998). Who put the cog in infant cognition: is rich interpretation too costly? *Infant Behavior and Development, 21*, 167–179.

Haith, M. M., & Benson, J. B. (1998). Infant cognition. In R. Siegler, D. Kuhn, & W. Damon (Eds.), *Cognition, perception, & language* (5th ed.). *Handbook of child psychology* (pp. 199–254). NY: Wiley.

Hespos, S. J., & Baillargeon, R. (2006). Décalage in infants' knowledge about occlusion and containment events: converging evidence from action tasks. *Cognition, 99*, B31–B41.

Kretch, K.S. & Adolph, K.E. (in press). Cliff or step? Posture-specific learning at the edge of a drop-off. *Child Development*.

Leslie, A. M. (1988). The necessity of illusion: perception and thought in infancy. In L. Weiskrantz (Ed.), *Thought without language* (pp. 185–210). Oxford: Clarendon Press/ Oxford University Press.

Lockman, J. (2000). A perception–action perspective on tool use development. *Child Development, 71*, 137–144.

Loucks, J., & Sommerville, J. A. (2011, October). *Adult and infant attention during action perception is context dependent.* Poster presented at the biennial meeting of the Cognitive Development Society, Philadelphia, PA.

Loucks, J., & Sommerville, J. A. (2012). The role of motor experience in understanding action function: the case of the precision grasp. *Child Development, 83*, 801–809.

Loucks, J., & Sommerville, J.A. (under review). Prediction of action outcomes modulates attention during action observation in adults and young infants. *Child Development.*

Luo, Y., & Baillargeon, R. (2007). Do 12.5-month-old infants consider what objects others can see when interpreting their actions? *Cognition, 105*, 489–512.

McDonough, L., & Mandler, J. M. (1998). Inductive generalization in 9-and 11-month-olds. *Developmental Science, 1*(2), 227–232.

Mandler, J. M., & McDonough, L. (1998). Studies in inductive inference in infancy. *Cognitive Psychology, 37*, 60–96.

Meltzoff, A. N. (2002). Elements of a developmental theory of imitation. In A. N. Meltzoff, & W. Prinz (Eds.), *The imitative mind: Development, evolution, and brain bases* (pp. 19–41). Cambridge: Cambridge University Press.

Nystrom, P., Ljunghammar, T., Rosander, K., & von Hofsten, C. (2011). Using murhythm desynchronization to measure mirror neuron activity in infants. *Developmental Science, 14*, 327–335.

Piaget, J. P. (1952). *The origins of intelligence in children.* New York: W.W. Norton & Company, Inc.

Rochat, P. (1989). Object manipulation and exploration in 2- to 5-month-old infants. *Developmental Psychology, 25*, 844–871.

Rovee-Collier, C. (1999). The development of infant memory. *Current Directions in Psychological Science, 8*, 80–85.

Ruff, H. A. (1984). Infants' manipulative exploration of objects: effects of age and object characteristics. *Developmental Psychology, 20*, 9–20.

Schlesinger, M., & Langer, J. (1999). Infants' developing expectations of possible and impossible tool-use events between ages 8 and 12 months. *Developmental Science, 2*, 195–205.

Smith, L. B. (1999). Do infants possess innate knowledge structures? The con side. *Developmental Science, 2*(2), 133–144.

Sommerville, J. A. (2007). *From ends to means: infants' developing tool use representations.* Invited talk at Department of Psychology colloquium series, Duke University, Raleigh-Durham, NC.

Sommerville, J. A. (2008). *Infants' developing understanding of goal-directed action: Evidence for a two-step process.* Invited talk at the meeting of the Self and Other in Social Neuroscience and Philosophy of Mind. Alghero, Sardinia, Italy.

Sommerville, J. A., & Crane, C. C. (2009). Ten-month-old infants use prior information to identify an actor's goal. *Developmental science, 12*(2), 314–325.

Sommerville, J. A. & Feldman, E. N. (2008, April). *Tool use in the first year of infancy: infants select appropriate tool use actions based on tool and goal object properties.* Paper to be presented at the biennial meeting of the international society for infant studies, Vancouver, BC.

Sommerville, J. A., & Woodward, A. L. (2005a). Pulling out the intentional structure of action: the relation between action processing and action production in infancy. *Cognition, 50*, 431–445.

Sommerville, J. A., & Woodward, A. L. (2005b). Infants' sensitivity to the causal features of means-end support relations in action and perception. *Infancy, 8*, 119–145.

Sommerville, J. A., Woodward, A. L., & Needham, A. (2005). Action experience alters 3-month-old infants' perception of others' actions. *Cognition, 96*, B1–B11.

Sommerville, J. A., Hildebrand, E. A., & Crane, C. C. (2008). Experience matters: the impact of doing versus watching on infants' subsequent perception of tool use events. *Developmental Psychology, 44,* 1249–1256.

Sommerville, J. A., Blumenthal, E. J., Venema, K., & Braun, K. (2011). The body in action: the impact of self-produced action on infants' action perception and understanding. In V. Slaughter, & C. Brownwell (Eds.), *Early development of body representations* (pp. 247–266). Cambridge: Cambridge University Press.

Sommerville, J. A., Crane, C. C. & Yun, J.-E. (in preparation). Once a frog-lover, always a frog-lover? Ten-month-old infants use appropriate evidence to identify others' preferences

Spelke, E. S. (1994). Initial knowledge: Six suggestions. *Cognition, 50,* 431–445.

Spelke, E. S. (2000). Core knowledge. *American Psychologist, 55,* 1233–1243.

Téglás, E., Vul, E., Girotto, V., Gonzalez, M., Tennenbaum, J., & Bonatti, L. L. (2011). Pure reasoning in 12-month-old infants as probabilistic inference. *Science, 332,* 1054–1059.

Upshaw, K. & Sommerville, J. A. (in preparation). Object weight guides 12 month olds' actions in a novel problem-solving task.

Waxman, S. R. (2004). Everything had a name, and each name gave birth to a new thought: links between early word-learning and conceptual organization. In D. G. Hall, & S. R. Waxman (Eds.), *From many strands: Weaving a lexicon.* Cambridge: MIT Press.

Waxman, S. R., & Leddon, E. M. (2011). Early word learning and conceptual development: everything had a name, and each name gave birth to new thought. In U. Goswami (Ed.), *The Wiley-Blackwell handbook of childhood cognitive development* (pp. 180–208). Malden, MA: Wiley-Blackwell.

Waxman, S. R., & Markow, D. B. (1995). Words as invitations to form categories: evidence from 12- to 13-month-old infants. *Cognitive Psychology, 29,* 257–302.

Willatts, P. (1999). Development of means-ends behavior in young infants: pulling a support to retrieve a distant object. *Developmental Psychology, 35,* 651–667.

Woodward, A. L. (1998). Infants selectively encode the goal object of an actor's reach. *Cognition, 69,* 1–34.

Woodward, A. L. (2003). Infants' developing understanding of the link between looker and object. *Developmental Science, 6,* 297–311.

Woodward, A. L., & Guajardo, J. J. (2002). Infants' understanding of the point gesture as an object-directed action. *Cognitive Development, 17,* 1061–1084.

Woodward, A. L., & Sommerville, J. A. (2000). Twelve-month-old infants interpret action in context. *Psychological Science, 11,* 73–76.

Woodward, A. L., Sommerville, J. A., & Guajardo, J. J. (2001). How infants make sense of intentional action. In B. Malle, L. Moses, & D. Baldwin (Eds.), *Intentions and intentionality: foundations of social cognition* (pp. 149–169). Cambridge, MA: MIT Press.

Xu, F. (2007). Rational statistical inference and cognitive development. To appear in P. Carruthers, S. Laurence, and S. Stich (Eds.), *The innate mind: foundations and the future,* Vol. 3. Oxford University Press.

Xu, F., & Garcia, V. (2008). Intuitive statistics by 8-month-old infants. *Proceedings of the National Academy of Sciences of the United States of America, 105,* 5012–5015.

Yau, K., Upshaw, M. B., & Sommerville, J. A. (2011). *Twelve-month old infants anticipate object weight in a novel context.* Poster presented at the conference for the society for research in child development, Montreal, QC.

# SUBJECT INDEX

Page numbers with "f" denote figures; "t" tables.

# AUTHOR INDEX

## A

Aarts, H., 195–196
Abbot, S., 245
Abbott, S., 51–52
Abbot-Smith, K., 100
Acredolo, C., 31–32
Adelson, E. H., 165
Adolph, K. E., 274, 354
Aguado-Orea, J., 97
Akhtar, N., 197–198
Alibali, M. W., 132, 324–325
Allan, L. G., 327–328
Alvarez, G. A., 43
Alvarez, J. M., 148
Amati, D., 2
Amsel, G., 328–329
Amso, D., 335
Amsterlaw, J., 286
Anderson, J., 312–313
Anderson, N. H., 31–32
Andersson, A., 132
Andrews, J. M., 31–32
Angelaki, D.E., 188
Antell, S. E., 247–248
Apperly, I. A., 330
Archer, S. L., 108–109, 120
Aschersleben, G., 64, 71–72, 344
Aslin, R. N., 2–3, 8, 35, 46–47, 105–106,
    132, 203–204, 324–325
Asmuth, J., 255, 262
Astington, J. W., 331
Atran, S., 82, 220–221, 223–224,
    229

## B

Baer, L., 229–230
Bailey, T., 273
Baillargeon, R., 7, 36–37, 40, 63–67,
    197–198, 270, 311, 329, 353, 355,
    360–361, 378, 380
Baker, C. L., 312
Balaban, M. T., 381–382
Baldwin, D., 132–134, 353–354
Banaji, M. R., 128

Banks, L., 31–32
Banks, M. S., 133, 135
Barner, D., 246–247
Baron, A. S., 128
Baron-Cohen, S., 311
Barrett, T., 354
Barth, H., 256
Bartlett, E., 99t, 114–115
Barto, A. C., 274
Barto, A. G., 272
Bartsch, K., 211
Bassok, M., 286
Bates, E., 69
Baumeister, R. F., 195
Bechara, A., 273
Beck, J. M., 188
Beck, S. R., 330
Behne, T., 71, 197–198
Bekkering, H., 71–72, 136–137, 197,
    201, 344
Bell, W. J., 274
Benson, J. B., 352
Bergelson, E., 382
Berger, S. E., 274
Berndt, T. J., 229–230
Berry, D. A., 282
Bertenthal, B., 356
Biederman, I., 324–325
Bihua, C., 224
Bijeljac-Babic, R., 107–108
Birch, S. A. J., 127–128
Bíró, S., 7, 63–65, 197
Blakemore, S., 193–196
Blanc-Goldhammer, D., 256
Block, N., 282
Bloom, P., 127–128, 147, 197–198,
    288–289
Bloomfield, A., 255, 262
Blum, B., 275, 335
Blumenthal, E. J., 128, 330–331,
    339–340, 362–363
Bois, J., 133
Bolger, N., 148
Bollt, A., 97–98, 99t, 109–112

# CONTENTS OF PREVIOUS VOLUMES

413